Studying The 613 Mitzvot

By

David Yehuda Block

Table of Contents

Acknowledgments and Dedication

I owe a debt of gratitude to Rabbi Dan Wolpe, Rabbi Gary Charlestein, and my Partner in Torah, Mr. Moshe Orlian who gave me invaluable feedback after they read an earlier draft.

I owe a huge debt of thanks to Rabbi Robert Alpert who shared his great knowledge of Torah. His invaluable assistance enhanced this book.

I also owe a debt of gratitude to Gail McCown and Marian Leahy who proofread early versions of this manuscript. Because I am legally blind, they were my eyes for this project.

I want to thank Michael Trudgeon, CEO of Reliable Copy Service INC. and his staff for supporting this project.

I also appreciate that my loyal friend Joseph Bernstein, a student of Rabbi David Aaron, provided me with emotional support while I struggled to complete this work.

While writing this book, my family encouraged me to see this project through to fruition.

This book is not a conversation between my partner and me. It is a manifestation of what we learned and studied together for two wonderful years. For that reason, I dedicate this book to my Partner in Torah, Mr. Moshe Orlian.

Any mistakes found in this manuscript are entirely my fault. None of the people who helped me with this book are at fault–just me.

August 13, 2021

Introduction

why I wrote the book

When I was a student at Aish HaTorah Yeshiva, in the Old City of Jerusalem from December 1990 through January 1991, I took a class that covered the 613 Mitzvot. Due to my partial blindness and difficulty of learning new things quickly, I had trouble keeping up.

For the next 18 years, I never gave that problem a second thought, until my Partner in Torah, Moshe Orlian, and I studied all 613 Mitzvot over the phone from 2008 to 2010. Moshe read the Hebrew text to me in English, and he patiently waited while I typed them up.

This helped me understand the Mitzvot better than when I first studied them 18 years ago. If I had had these notes while taking the class, I might have done better. Maybe I would not have felt embarrassed every time I set foot in that classroom for struggling.

When I took the class, the instructor understandably did not have the time to slowly go over the Mitzvot with me, because that would have been unfair to my classmates. By the time I began taking notes on what he said about one Mitzvah, he had already moved ahead to a different one.

I wrote this book as a service to people with disabilities who want to learn Torah, but who need extra assistance.

My intended audience

My audience will be Jews and non-Jews who want a simple text that provides explanations of the 613 Mitzvot. My audience will also be people with disabilities who want to learn the Mitzvot, but who might have a hard time understanding them.

Explanations of the Mitzvot

In accordance with the Talmudic principle encouraging us to understand Mitzvot to the extent humanly possible, the author of Sefer HaHinnuch provides a rationale for each Mitzvah. However, Moshe told me that we cannot presume to understand Hashem's reasons for giving us specific commandments. (Hashem means The Name in Hebrew, and that is the term that I use throughout the text.) As a result of this apparent contradiction, we must accept that although this book provides explanations for the Mitzvot, that does not mean these explanations are definitive and exhaustive. Nobody, not even great Torah scholars today nor from past centuries could understand every nuance of Hashem's Torah. This raises the question: Why should we study this material?

Learning about the Mitzvot and providing plausible explanations helps provide a context and a rationale for their existence, thereby leading to more meaningful observance. We are encouraged to study the Mitzvot in depth and try to understand them in a rational way as much as is possible from the human perspective. Doing so gives us a greater level of understanding, which makes these Mitzvot more meaningful and attractive. However, we can never assume that any specific explanation, no matter how seemingly logical, is exactly what Hashem had in mind. Regardless of any Mitzvah explanation, we cannot conclusively assume that these are the true reasons for any of them. There is a fine line between analyzing Mitzvot to try and attain a depth of understanding in order to get closer to Hashem, versus being presumptuous and assuming that we can know Hashem's reason for a particular Mitzvah.

Why learn the Mitzvot now when many of them are not Applicable?

My Partner in Torah and I talked about the importance of studying the Mitzvot. A complete observance of the Torah includes the 613 Mitzvot, but we know that certain Mitzvot cannot be performed outside the Land of Israel nor when the Temple is in a state of destruction like it is today. The Talmud says that when one studies the content and rules of the Mitzvot, this is the equivalent to performing them. Therefore, it is possible to fulfill the entire Torah formula of 613 Mitzvot by the study of Torah.

This is discussed further in The 613 Mitzvahs and Torah Study Gate of Reincarnations, Chapter Eleven, Section 10
By Rabbi Yitzchak Luria as recorded by Rabbi Chaim Vital; translation from Sha'ar Hagilgulim by Yitzchok bar Chaim; commentary by Shabtai Teicher

The Book's Layout

My book's layout will be the Mitzvah typed in bold capital letters. The Torah verse will be underneath and it will be italicized. sometimes three or four Mitzvot used the same Bible verse. To avoid confusion, I underlined the part in each verse that is the source for each one of the Mitzvot

Why there are 613 Mitzvot

613 is NOT an arbitrary number. The Gematria of Moshe Rabbenu (Moses our teacher) add up to 613.

Sources Used

The key book I used was Sefer HaHinnuch because that is the book that Moshe and I studied from. While writing the book, I also consulted works, such as Ethics of the Fathers, The Mishnah,The Talmud, Book of Our Heritage by Eliyahu Kitov, and The Five Books of Moses. (I used additional material, which I cite in the text.)

According to the link, https://en.wikipedia.org/wiki/Gematria the English translation of Gematria is the "Greek system of alphanumeric code or cipher later adopted into Jewish culture that assigns numerical value to a word, name, or phrase in the belief that words or phrases with identical numerical values bear some relation to each other or bear some relation to the number itself as it may apply to nature, a person's age, the calendar year, or the like. A single word can yield multiple values depending on the system used."

Each Hebrew letter has a number. The numbers of the name Moshe Rabbenu add up to 613. That represents the entire Torah, which was given from the Mouth of G-d to the Hands of Moshe.

To give my book authenticity, I typed up the actual wording of each Mitzvah as it appeared in Sefer HaHinnuch, and then underneath each one, I wrote the Torah passage from where it derived. Underneath the Torah passages, are my explanations and comments about that specific Mitzvah.

Various books about the 613 Mitzvot number them differently. The numbering system that I used in my book corresponds with the English translation of Sefer HaHinnuch because my Partner in Torah used that text when he explained the Mitzvot to me. Choosing this approach was my way of honoring the time that My Partner I spent learning them.

Mitzvot from Genesis

1. BE FRUITFUL AND MULTIPLY

And God blessed them; and God said unto them: 'Be fruitful, and multiply, and replenish the earth, and subdue it; and have dominion over the fish of the sea, and over the fowl of the air, and over every living thing that creepeth upon the earth.' (Genesis 1:28)

Mitzvah 1 commands men to be fruitful and to multiply. When Hashem created the world, He wanted the world to be populated. Hashem did not create an empty barren world. He created a world for civilization.

This Mitzvah is applicable in all generations. A man must begin fulfilling this Mitzvah when he turns 18.

Women do not have to fulfill this Mitzvah because they are not planters. They cannot produce sperm. However, a wife who gives birth shares in her husband's Mitzvah because he cannot fulfill it without her.

My Partner in Torah told me that in Tractate Yevamot, Chapter 6, Mishnah 6 records a dispute between The House of Shammai and The House of Hillel. The House of Shammai argues that a man fulfills this Mitzvah with two sons, and The House of Hillel contends that this Mitzvah is fulfilled with one son and one daughter. Traditionally Jews accept Hillel's opinion.

To access the link to the English translation of Tractate Yevamot, Chapter 6, Mishnah 6, log onto http://www.emishnah.com/Nashim_Vol_1/Yev6.pdf

Rabbi Gary Charlestein added:

"this is only the minimum; that our tradition values children and encourages us to each have more than the minimum; hence the often very large religious families."

2. THE PRECEPT OF CIRCUMCISION

This is My covenant, which ye shall keep, between Me and you and thy seed after thee: every male among you shall be circumcised. And ye shall be circumcised in the flesh of your foreskin; and it shall be a token of a covenant betwixt Me and you. And he that is eight days old shall be circumcised among you, every male throughout your generations, he that is born in the house, or bought with money of any foreigner, that is not of thy seed. He that is born in thy house, and he that is bought with thy money, must needs be circumcised; and My covenant shall be in your flesh for an everlasting covenant. And the uncircumcised male who is not circumcised in the flesh of his foreskin, that soul shall be cut off from his people; he hath broken My covenant.' (Genesis 17:10-14)

Mitzvah 2 requires Jewish baby boys to be circumcised eight days after birth. (In Hebrew, the circumcision of the Jewish baby boy is called Brit Milah.) The Brit Milah can occur even if the eighth day falls on Shabbat, or on Yom Kippur, or if Yom Kippur falls on Shabbat, which is called the Sabbath of Sabbaths. The Eighth Day after a Jewish boy's birth is the only day that takes precedence over Shabbat, Yom Kippur, the Sabbaths of Sabbaths, and all other holidays.

One argument why the Mitzvah of Circumcision takes precedence over the Mitzvah of sanctifying Shabbat is that the former involves creating life, while the latter focuses on making Shabbat holy. Nothing is more important than life. True, the baby was born eight days earlier, but I have heard certain Rabbis say that there is still a final procedure to make him part of the Jewish nation. For the first eight days of his life, he breathes, cries, laughs, eats, and sleeps. The final act of circumcision is needed to make the procedure of life complete.

Not all Rabbis agree with this entire description. Rabbi Gary Charlestein shared his view with me:

"Circumcision does not, at best as I understand it, complete the young boy's membership in our nation. A child born of a Jewish mother is a member of our nation. The Brit Milah, however, is a most critical Mitzvah, which a father is obligated to have performed for his son. If a young man is not circumcised, then he should make sure this is done when he is under his own power at the age of 13."

There are instances when the circumcision cannot occur on Shabbat: If the eighth day does not fall on Shabbat or Yom Kippur, then he cannot be circumcised on any following Shabbat or Yom Kippur. If the eighth day falls on Shabbat, and the ceremony is postponed and does not occur that day, then it may not take place on a different Shabbat. The family can postpone the ceremony, but then having it on a future Shabbat is no longer an option. The reason that other Shabbatot are prohibited is that we cannot draw blood on the seventh day. Drawing blood can lead to slaughter and death. As mentioned, the exception is made on the eighth day of a baby boy's life, because Hashem commanded it. Even though the Brit Milah on the eighth day overrides everything, the Mohel (the Jew who performs the Brit Milah) must bring his equipment to where he will perform the ceremony before Shabbat begins. If the Brit Milah were to take place in the baby's home or at a synagogue, the Mohel makes sure that his tools are there beforehand so he does not violate the proscription about carrying items on Shabbat.

(The plural for Shabbat is Shabbatot.)

The Brit Milah is postponed when medically necessary. Sometimes the circumciser, the Mohel, is unavailable, due to questions of distance or of an intervening **Yom Tov or** Shabbat.

Rabbi Charlestein said:

"the circumcision may be postponed to the first immediate available non-holiday day if the Mohel is not comfortable with the arrangements to be made for a Shabbat circumcision."

3. NOT TO EAT THE SINEW OF THE THIGH VEIN

Therefore the children of Israel eat not the sinew of the thigh-vein which is upon the hollow of the thigh, unto this day; because he touched the hollow of Jacob's thigh, even in the sinew of the thigh-vein. (Genesis 32:33).

Mitzvah 3 forbids us to eat the sinew of the thigh-vein because when Jacob wrestled the angel, the angel put Jacob's hip out of joint.

The Sages stated that Jacob's assailant was Esau's guardian angel. Jacob won the fight, but the angel put Jacob's hip out of joint. This was a sign that the Jewish people would endure hardships at the hands of the other nations, yet in the end, the

Jews would triumph. Not eating the sinew helps remind us to be optimistic about the future.

Rabbi Abraham Isaac Kook argued that Esau and his guardian angel believed that one could not be dedicated to Hashem and have a normal family life. He stated that the angel dislocated Jacob's thigh, with the belief that "if you want to dedicate yourself to Hashem, you must divorce yourself from family and all other aspects of a normal life. Your thigh, from where your children issue, must be detached from you."

(Visit the link http://www.ravkookTorah.org/VAYISH64.htm for a more detailed discussion.)

Jacob did not share this view. He saw that one could dedicate himself to Hashem and have a normal family life. This leads back to the first Mitzvah. More than anything, Hashem wants us to be fruitful and to multiply.

Mitzvot from Exodus

4. THE PRECEPT OF ESTABLISHING THE MONTHS

And the LORD spoke unto Moses and Aaron in the land of Egypt, saying: 'This month shall be unto you the beginning of months; it shall be the first month of the year to you. (Exodus 12:1-2)

Mitzvah 4 pertains to sanctifying the New Moon. This Mitzvah has great significance because it is the first one given to the entire Jewish nation. At the time, the Jews were still in Egypt.

The solar year and the lunar year

Before clocks and calendars were invented, people marked the passage of time, (told time) by using the sun or the moon. They are two different cycles independent of each other.

The earth orbits around the sun, and one orbit of the earth around the sun is called a solar year. The sun and the earth rotating around the sun do not affect the moon.

The moon orbits around the earth, and one orbit of the moon around the earth is called a lunar month. The moon and the moon rotating around the earth do not affect the sun.

Therefore, the sun has no bearing on the moon and no bearing on when the lunar month starts or ends. In addition, the moon has no bearing on the sun and no bearing on when the solar year starts or ends. They are two separate ways of telling time that do not interact with each other.

Because of its location, the moon appears as partial slices. As it rotates around the earth, we see more of it. It appears to grow bigger from one quarter, to one half, to three quarters, to full moon. Then it appears to shrink and disappear as it completes its orbit around the earth.

In the Jewish calendar, the moon's orbit around the earth is the basis for delineating months. The beginning of the month is when the New Moon appears. When Jews first see the New Moon, it marks a new month–a new lunar month.

The other nations of the world use the Gregorian calendar to count the passage of time. The earth's orbit around the sun is the basis for one solar year (actually 365 days and a quarter). The Gregorian calendar divides one solar year into 12 segments. Each segment is called a month–a solar month. New solar months of the Gregorian calendar begin at a specific time each year, regardless of the moon's position.

These two calendars are not concomitant. The lunar month is less than a 12th of the solar year. The lunar cycle (the lunar month) is 29 days, 12 hours, 44 minutes, and 3 and one third seconds. If you multiply that by 12, the lunar months total 354 days, 8 hours, 48 minutes and 40 seconds. So, in a lunar year there are twelve lunar months totaling up to about 355 solar days. Twelve lunar months (one lunar year) are 10 days and 21 hours less than one solar year.

Because the lunar year is slightly over 354 days, Jews state that our years have 355 days. We have an allusion to this because the Hebrew word for year is Shanah, and the numeric value of Shanah, adds up to 355.

The solar calendar and the lunar calendar

Hashem commands us to celebrate Passover in the spring:

"And this day shall be unto you for a memorial, and ye shall keep it a feast to the LORD; throughout your generations ye shall keep it a feast by an ordinance forever. Seven days shall ye eat unleavened bread; howbeit the first day ye shall put away leaven out of your houses; for whosoever eateth leavened bread from the first day until the seventh day, that soul shall be cut off from Israel." (Exodus 12:13-14).

The Gregorian calendar / solar calendar year is 365 days plus one quarter day. Everyone is familiar with the Gregorian calendar / solar calendar's concept of a "leap year." One leap day or extra day is added every four years to accommodate that extra quarter day. That leap day keeps the seasons, holidays, etcetera in a regulated pattern so they occur at nearly the same point in every solar year.

The lunar calendar also needs some adjustments to keep Passover in the spring, to accommodate the extra 10 days and 21 hours in the solar year, and to make the lunar calendar line up more closely with the solar calendar. The Jewish calendar adds a **leap month** 7 times every 19 years. These leap years comprise a 19-year cycle.

The 19-year cycle is divided so that twelve years of the cycle have twelve months and seven years of the cycle have thirteen months. In this repeated, regulated pattern, leap years fall on the third, sixth, eighth, eleventh, fourteenth, seventeenth and nineteenth year. That leap month keeps the seasons, holidays, etcetera in a regulated pattern so they occur at nearly the same point in every lunar year.

Hashem explained to Moses how to calculate the Jewish calendar, and Moses passed that information on to Joshua, who then passed it onto a select group of Sages.

In each generation, only a select group of people (usually Sages or members of the Sanhedrin) knew the calculations.

The Muslims also rely on the lunar calendar, but their holidays never take place at the same time each year because they do not add leap years to their lunar calendar.

The Jewish calendar has the following months:

Month	Length	Gregorian Equivalent
Nisan	30 days	March-April
Iyar	29 days	April-May
Sivan	30 days	May-June
Tammuz	29 days	June-July
Av	30 days	July-August
Elul	29 days	August-September
Tishri	30 days	September-October
Heshvan	29 or 30 days	October-November
Kislev	30 or 29 days	November-December
Tevet	29 days	December-January
Shevat	30 days	January-February
Adar I (Adar Alef)–the leap month	30 days	February-March
Adar II (Adar Bet)	29 days	March-April

(Cited from the website: http://www.jewishvirtuallibrary.org/jsource/Judaism/calendar.html#Years)

In the Jewish calendar the extra month added to leap years is Adar I or Adar Alef. This leap month occurs 7 times in every

19-year cycle. This extra month is placed in the Jewish calendar **before** Adar II or Adar Bet to keep Passover in the spring as Hashem commanded us.

Hashem commanded us to celebrate Passover in the spring, so we celebrate Passover in the month of Nisan. Purim takes place 30 days before Passover, so Purim is celebrated in the month of Adar Bet.

The New Moon

In the Jewish calendar, the moon's orbit around the earth is the basis for delineating

months. The beginning of the month is when the New Moon appears. When Jews first see the New Moon, it marks a new month–a new lunar month.

Hashem explained to Moses how to calculate the Jewish calendar based on the rotation of the moon. Moses passed that information on to Joshua, who then passed it onto a select group of Sages.

In each succeeding generation, only a select group of people (usually Sages or members of the Sanhedrin) knew the calculations for the Jewish calendar.

Because the Jewish calendar affected the entire Jewish nation, the Mitzvah required two impartial witnesses to verify the New Moon as checks and balances to the system. This process started when two witnesses announced to the Sages (or to members of the Sanhedrin) that they had seen the New Moon. A panel of three judges, composed of Sages and / or members of the Sanhedrin who knew the calculations for the Jewish calendar, would question each witness separately to verify what they had seen. When the judges were satisfied that everything was correct, Jews celebrated Rosh Chodesh (the Beginning of the Month).

My Partner in Torah explained to me that, in order to fulfill the fourth Mitzvah, two honest observers, who were not Sages, had to witness and announce to the Sages that they saw the New Moon.

According to Rabbi Gary Charlestein:

"The two witnesses can be Sages, but they could not be the two Sages who come as witnesses and also act as judges in the very same case." Sages can be witnesses, but they cannot be BOTH witnesses and judges for the same case.

"The cross examination of each witness was done separately by a three judge-panel to make sure that they concurred on the facts of their sighting of the New Moon."

According to the Chabad.org's website:

While the Sanhedrin (Rabbinical Supreme Court) presided in Jerusalem, there was no set Jewish calendar. They would evaluate every year to determine whether it should be declared a leap year.

When my Partner in Torah and I studied from Book of Our Heritage by Eliyahu Kitov, we learned how the great Sage, Hillel II, wrote down the calculations for the lunar year and the Jewish calendar so everyone would know, thus eliminating the need for the two witnesses' monthly testimony.

In the fourth century CE, Hillel II instituted the perpetual calendar in anticipation of the disbandment of the Sanhedrin. He also incorporated leap years into the calendar.

Hillel II knew, that because there was a smaller pool of educated Jews, there were fewer people worthy of the responsibility of calculating the lunar calendar. Another factor was the Diaspora–not all Jews were living in Israel. Therefore, to preserve the knowledge of the Jewish lunar calendar, he wrote down the calculations, so that every Jew would know when to celebrate the holidays and Rosh Chodesh.

Cited at http://www.chabad.org/library/article_cdo/aid/526875/jewish/The-Jewish-Year.htm

Rosh Chodesh was exceedingly important in ancient times when there was no form of mass communication, and the average Jew had no clock and no calendar. The Beginning of the Month told the Jewish nation what calendar month they were in and what religious holidays to celebrate.

The Syrian-Greeks understood the importance of Rosh Chodesh. Therefore, they outlawed it when they tried to abolish the Jewish religion. (They also outlawed Shabbat and circumcision. The absence of these three rituals meant the inevitable extinction of the Jewish religion.)

Rabbi Charlestein added:

"When a month has 30 days, the 30th day is the first day of Rosh Chodesh for the next month, the liturgical celebration of the New Moon which calls for additional prayers. The first day of the next month is then also Rosh Chodesh—the Second day of Rosh Chodesh similarly with additional prayers. Prayers for Rosh Chodesh are added and recited even if the day co-insides with the Sabbath as well".

here are many other significant points about Rosh Chodesh, but to cover them would stray from this book. For more information about Rosh Chodesh see: http://www.jewfaq.org/chodesh.htm

5. THE RITUAL SLAYING OF THE PASSOVER OFFERING

and ye shall keep it unto the fourteenth day of the same month; and the whole assembly of the congregation of Israel shall kill it at dusk (Exodus 12:6)

Mitzvah 5 commands us to ritually slaughter a male sheep without blemish, in its first year, in the afternoon on the 14th of Nisan. A male goat in its first year without blemish can serve as a substitute. Fulfilling this Mitzvah reminds us of the great miracles that Hashem performed on our behalf when we were slaves in Egypt. Fulfilling this Mitzvah along with others that pertain to Passover, gives us a taste of what our ancestors experienced during their exodus. By saying, "we were slaves" instead of "our ancestors were slaves" bonds us to our ancestors.

Anyone who deliberately disobeys this Mitzvah suffers divine severance of existence. Rabbi Charlestein interpreted the punishment not as a literal death, but being completely excluded from the community of Israel.

RASHI implies that by offering this sacrifice in such a public manner, we defy our Egyptian overlords. Our defiance shows that we do not view these animals as gods, but as animals that we sacrifice to Hashem as a way of serving Him. We are free to follow His words. (RASHI is the Hebrew acronym for Rabbi Shlomo Yitzhaqi, a French Torah scholar, whom according to the Encyclopedia Britannica lived from 1040–1105 CE. Cited at https://www.britannica.com/biography/Rashi)

6. EATING THE PASSOVER OFFERING

And they shall eat the flesh in that night, roast with fire, and unleavened bread; with bitter herbs they shall eat it. (Exodus 12:8)

Mitzvah 6 commands us to eat the sacrificed lamb that we slaughtered for Passover on the 15th of Nisan, which is the First Night of Passover. It also commands us to eat the sacrificed lamb with bitter herbs and matzah.

7. NOT TO EAT THE PASSOVER OFFERING SLIGHTLY ROASTED OR COOKED

Eat not of it raw, nor sodden at all with water, but roast with fire; its head with its legs and with the inwards thereof. (Exodus 12:9)

Mitzvah 7 tells us that the meat we eat on Passover has to be roasted and well-done. It cannot be cooked any other way. Cooking it rare or medium is prohibited. It cannot be placed in liquid and boiled. (Roasting is the quickest way to cook. Eating a roasted dish is like eating a dish cooked for royalty.)

Traditionally, common people and slaves did not roast meat. Roasting was reserved for people of royalty and high ranking officers. On Passover, we eat roasted meat to show that we are no longer slaves, but regal like kings.

Today, we still eat roasted meat at the Seder. However, we place a roasted shank bone on the Seder plate, because we do not want to confuse what we do today with what the sacrifice was. The shank bone represents the memory of slaughtering the lamb.

8. TO LEAVE OVER NO FLESH OF THE PASSOVER OFFERING

And ye shall let nothing of it remain until the morning; but that which remaineth of it until the morning ye shall burn with fire. (Exodus 12:10)

Mitzvah 8 commands us to eat the sacrificed lamb the First Night of Passover. We cannot leave leftover food for the next day. We are like kings on Passover. Kings never left food over to be eaten the next day, so we follow that principle. Rabbi Alpert pointed out to me that slaves save their food, in case there is no food for them the next day. But free people do not because they are confident that there will be food the next day(which is similar to the Mitzvah of Manna).

9. THE PRECEPT OF HAMETZ

Seven days shall ye eat unleavened bread; howbeit the first day ye shall put away leaven out of your houses; for whosoever eateth leavened bread from the first day until the seventh day, that soul shall be cut off from Israel. (Exodus 12:15)

Mitzvah 9 is a positive commandment of getting rid of all our Leavened Food before Passover. We can only eat unleavened bread like Matzah.

“Leavening” is the ingredient added to bread and cakes to make the dough rise so the bread or cake is soft and fluffy to chew. Yeast is the most often used leavening, dating back to ancient times. After mixing together all the ingredients of your bread recipe, you must set the dough aside for one to two hours so that the dough will rise and double in size. Then you work on it some more before shaping it and baking it for an hour (or longer). The whole process can take 3 to 4 hours.

Unleavened bread has no yeast in it (other forms of leavening may be used). This means it does not rise as high or get as soft and fluffy as leavened bread or cakes. It also means there is no "resting time" or waiting time required for the dough. As soon as the dough is mixed together, it can be shaped and baked. Baking time is 15 to 30 minutes. This whole process usually takes about one hour.

Hametz are foods we are forbidden to eat on Passover. They use yeast as an ingredient when preparing the food.

Hametz means to ferment or sour. Yeast is activated by liquid (water or milk). It is a "good bacteria" that ferments and multiplies, giving off the gas / vapor that makes dough rise and creates the alcohol in beer.

Hametz also means to procrastinate in Hebrew. Our forefathers in Egypt had no time to procrastinate because they had to leave Egypt hastily.

10. THE PRECEPT OF EATING MATZAH ON PASSOVER

In the first month, on the fourteenth day of the month at even, ye shall eat unleavened bread, until the one and twentieth day of the month at even. (Exodus 12:18)

Mitzvah 10 commands us to eat Matzah on Passover. Observing this Mitzvah reminds us that because our ancestors left

Egypt in great haste, they prepared unleavened bread. Eating Matzah as they did, allows us to bond with them.

According to Rabbi Gary Charlestein, the Rabbis interpreted this Mitzvah to mean that we are obligated to eat Matzah on the First Day of Passover in Israel, and outside of Israel, on the First Two days of the Holiday. On the other Days of Passover, we cannot eat Hametz, but we are not mandated to eat Matzah.

11. TO HAVE NO HAMETZ IN OUR POSSESSION DURING PASSOVER

Seven days shall there be no leaven found in your houses; for whosoever eateth that which is leavened, that soul shall be cut off from the congregation of Israel, whether he be a sojourner, or one that is born in the land. (Exodus 12:19)

Mitzvah 11 states that we cannot have Hametz in our possession during the Days of Passover.

Before Passover, if you had Hametz in your possession that you did not own, you cannot have it in your possession during Passover.

If you owned Hametz before Passover, but it wasn't in your possession, then at the start of Passover, you cannot own the Hametz anymore.

Many people go through their cupboards and search their homes to remove all Hametz before Passover. Hametz includes bread, beer, pasta, and most whiskeys. There are four things we do with our Hametz before Passover:

1. We search for our Hametz.
2. We nullify our Hametz.

3. We burn our Hametz.
4. We sell our Hametz to non-Jews.

The person guilty of violating this Mitzvah faces Karet–a Divine Severance of Existence. Jews know that they are not to eat certain foods at any time of the year such as pork. Jews can eat leavened bread any time of the year except Passover. During Passover, eating leavened bread is forbidden. The repercussions for violating this Mitzvah are severe in order to help remove the temptation of eating leavened bread.

12. TO EAT NOTHING CONTAINING HAMETZ DURING PASSOVER

Ye shall eat nothing leavened; in all your habitations shall ye eat unleavened bread. (Exodus 12:20)

Mitzvah 12 states that we cannot eat food items that contain leavening. Leavened bread and cakes are easily recognized as forbidden during Passover. But Hametz also includes less obvious items that contain yeast or other forms of Hametz in their composition.

These forbidden mixtures include mustard, ketchup, items made with vinegar, and items made from Hametz. (No ketchup on your French fries.)

Rabbi Charlestein said the foods are allowed when they are made with permitted ingredients and contain a reliable symbol of Kashrut compliance. (The Hebrew term Kashrut means the body of dietary laws prescribed for Jews. Cited at https://www.dictionary.com/browse/kashrut)

There are five main species of grain: wheat, barley, oats, spelt and rye. Grinding the grain creates the flour used for bread, cakes, Matzah and many other foods.

To make your bread dough rise, you add yeast–a common leavening agent. Dry yeast is activated by letting it soak in a small amount of warm water for a short time. This starts the fermentation process. When the yeast and water mixture produces bubbles, it is added to the bread dough and mixed in.

Rabbis have determined that it takes 18 minutes to ferment from the time the yeast and water mixture is added to the dough.

From the Torah perspective, if you used fruit juice or eggs instead of water, then it wouldn't be considered Hametz. The accepted practice is not to use eggs or juice. The prohibition against Hametz is eating and deriving benefit from it.

Egg-Matzah is made from flour with eggs and Kosher for Passover apple juice, and is eaten only by the infirm, the elderly, and young children.

According to Sefer HaHinnuch, violating this Mitzvah subjects the guilty party to a flogging. At the same time, the culprit is spared from Karet, which is a Divine Severance of Existence because the Hametz was mixed into a greater part of the food.

The punishment for eating Hametz can be as severe as the punishment for eating food that is never kosher. All year long, Jews know that they are not to eat specific foods such as pork. However, when it is not Passover, Jews can eat bread. Then on Passover, the bread suddenly becomes forbidden.

Egg-Matzah can be consumed on the 14th of Nisan as it is not considered the Lehem Oni–The Bread of Affliction as it is called Matzah Ashirah, which means rich bread.

13. TO GIVE AN APOSTATE NO PART OF A PASSOVER OFFERING TO EAT

And the LORD said unto Moses and Aaron: 'This is the ordinance of the passover: there shall no alien eat thereof; (Exodus 12:43)

(The word apostate means someone who has left Judaism. I still placed the term above in order to copy verbatim the wording of the English translation of the Mitzvot from Sefer Ha-Hinnuch.)

Mitzvah 13 forbids us to allow a non-Jew to eat from the Passover Lamb. In days of old, the non-Jew did not believe in Hashem, and that was the reason for this Mitzvah.

Today, a non-Jew still may not eat any portion of the Passover sacrifice, that is if Passover sacrifices were still performed. Today, a non-Jew can attend our Seders. Seder attendance is not equivalent to participating in the Passover sacrifices. Non-Jews may participate, sit at, and join in the Seder meal.

14. TO GIVE NO PART OF A PASSOVER OFFERING TO A PARTIAL PROSELYTE AND RESIDENT

A sojourner and a hired servant shall not eat thereof. (Exodus 12:45)

(In Hebrew these people are called Ger Toshav–resident alien.)

(A resident is a member of the other nations, who renounced idol worship, but still eats non-kosher food. A hired servant is a partial convert to Judaism. He had been circumcised but had not experienced ritual immersion.)

Mitzvah 14 forbids non-Jewish immigrants in your community to eat the Passover Lamb. Even if they swear their allegiance to Hashem, they still cannot eat that food.

According to Rabbi Charlestein, they can eat that food after they convert to Judaism.

15. TO CARRY NO FLESH OF THE PASSOVER OFFERING OUTSIDE THE HOME

In one house shall it be eaten; thou shalt not carry forth aught of the flesh abroad out of the house; neither shall ye break a bone thereof. (Exodus 12:46)

Mitzvah 15 states that we cannot remove any of the food from the designated Seder to be eaten another time. For example, if a Seder dish is the lamb, the entire lamb needs to be eaten in the designated place, which is the Seder. We are supposed to treat ourselves like kings. The normal practice for guests attending a banquet given by a king or high ranking officer is to eat the meal there and not take any portion of it away to eat later. They don't need to hoard the food because they have enough money to buy more food. Poor people on the other hand, eat only a portion of their meal and save some for another time. On Passover, we are to eat as if we are kings.

Flesh of the Passover offering should not be confused with food taken from today's Seder because Pascal sacrifices are not performed while the Temple is not extant.

16. NOT TO BREAK ANY BONE OF THE PASSOVER OFFERING

In one house shall it be eaten; thou shalt not carry forth aught of the flesh abroad out of the house; neither shall ye break a bone thereof. (Exodus 12:46)

Mitzvah 16 commands us not to break bones from the sacrificed lamb. Only starving people would break bones to eat the marrow inside. Dogs do the same. Because we as Jews are to eat as if we are kings at the Seder, we do not need to break bones. A person's mind and behavior are linked together. Not only are we not to break bones, we are not to even entertain the idea of doing that. If we are doing Mitzvot, it would be shaped by our actions. The actions affect our hearts. If a person does not have Mitzvot to do, he has nothing to focus on. He is like an animal, just going through the motions of day to day life. By giving us this set of rules and by us performing them, it is a way to earn Hashem's favor. Having the Mitzvot is a way to focus on the things that Hashem wants.

Rabbi Alpert told me that another reason for this prohibition is that breaking the bone is connected to the Egyptian ritual of death. Passover, on the other hand, celebrates life.

17. NO UNCIRCUMCISED PERSON SHOULD EAT OF THE PASSOVER OFFERING

And when a stranger shall sojourn with thee, and will keep the passover to the LORD, let all his males be circumcised, and then let him come near and keep it; and he shall be as one that is born in the land; but no uncircumcised person shall eat thereof. (Exodus 12:48)

Mitzvah 17 forbids an uncircumcised person from eating the Passover Lamb. If he has older brothers who died due to circumcision, then he is exempt from this holy ritual. However, he still cannot eat from the Passover lamb.

18. SANCTIFYING THE FIRST BORN AND FIRSTLINGS IN THE LAND OF ISRAEL

'Sanctify unto Me all the first-born, whatsoever openeth the womb among the children of Israel, both of man and of beast, it is Mine.' (Exodus 13:2)

(In Sefer HaHinnuch, it states that this Mitzvah is to be carried out in the Land of Israel, but in truth, it can be performed anywhere in the world.)

Mitzvah 18 pertains to giving the First Born Son and a kosher animal's male firstling to the Kohanim.

The Kohanim must eat the kosher animal in Jerusalem.

My Partner in Torah told me that a first born male donkey is never given to the Kohamim because it is not kosher. It is either exchanged for a sheep, which is given to a Kohen, or the donkey is killed. (The donkey is mentioned here because some people only possessed that animal and not kosher ones.)

The Kohanim do not keep the First Born Son. The Kohanim conduct the ritual of Pidyon Ha-Ben (Redemption of the First Born Son).

As stated in Exodus 13:15:

and it came to pass, when Pharaoh would hardly let us go that the LORD slew all the first born in the land of Egypt, both

the first-born of man, and the first-born of beast; therefore I sacrifice to the LORD all that openeth the womb, being males; but all the first-born of my sons I redeem.

The family generally gives the Kohanim five silver dollars in exchange for their First Born Son. The Kohen says a blessing, and then gives the baby back to them.

Honors bestowed on the First Born Son include a double portion of inheritance, and a holier level of status than his siblings.

There are instances when the First Born Son is not given to the Kohanim: If his father is a Kohen or a Levi, or if his mother is a daughter of a Kohen or Levi. This practice applies when both his parents are Yisrael. (A Yisrael is a Jew who is neither a Kohen nor a descendant of the Tribe of Levi.)

Today, even though it is impossible to conclusively prove one's lineage as a Kohen or Levi, we accept a person's traditional status as inherited from his father.

Only the First Born male who opens his mother's womb for the first time has the special First Born status. If her first child is a girl, then none of her male sons would have the honor. If she first gives birth to a stillborn, and then she has a son who lived, he would not have the First Born status because it was the stillborn baby who first opened her womb. If her womb opened and then she was to remarry, none of her sons from the second marriage would have the special First Born status. The discussion of the First Born having special status is cited in Deutronomy 21:17

but he shall acknowledge the first-born, the son of the hated, by giving him a double portion of all that he hath; for he is the first-fruits of his strength, the right of the first-born is his.

One reason we perform this Mitzvah is to remember Hashem's mercy for us when He inflicted Egypt with the 10th plague; Slaying of the First Born. This Mitzvah is applicable in all locations, not just in the Land of Israel.

On the day before Passover, the 14th of Nisan, the oldest Jewish sibling, male or female, should fast to remember Hashem's compassion for our ancestors. If the 14th of Nisan falls on Shabbat or on Friday, the fast takes place on Thursday. Many First Born Jews observe this fast today.

People can be exempted from this fast if they participate in a Siyyum, on that day, which is the completion of a Rabbinic treatise during the morning services.

19. TO EAT NO HAMETZ ON PASSOVER

And Moses said unto the people: 'Remember this day, in which ye came out from Egypt, out of the house of bondage; for by strength of hand the LORD brought you out from this place; there shall no leavened bread be eaten." (Exodus 13:3)

Mitzvah 19 forbids us to eat leavened bread on Passover. This extends to cereal grains.

As mentioned, refraining from bread allows us to experience a small taste of what our ancestors who left Egypt experienced.

20. NO HAMETZ IS TO BE SEEN WITH US DURING PASSOVER

Unleavened bread shall be eaten throughout the seven days; and there shall no leavened bread be seen with thee, neither shall there be leaven seen with thee, in all thy borders. (Exodus 13:7)

Mitzvah 20 forbids us to possess leavened food on Passover. Mitzvah 11 commands that leavened food even if not ours, must not be found in our possession.

That is the difference between these two Mitzvot. Hence, we sell leavened food to a non-Jew so that it is not ours and it is not in our possession.

21. THE PRECEPT OF RECOUNTING THE EXODUS FROM EGYPT

And thou shalt tell thy son in that day, saying: It is because of that which the LORD did for me when I came forth out of Egypt. (Exodus 13:8)

Mitzvah 21 commands that the story of the Exodus from Egypt be told on the First Night of Passover. We practice this today.

22. THE PRECEPT OF REDEEMING A FIRST BORN DONKEY

And every firstling of an ass thou shalt redeem with a lamb; and if thou wilt not redeem it, then thou shalt break its neck; and all the first-born of man among thy sons shalt thou redeem. (Exodus 13:13) And the firstling of an ass thou shalt redeem with a lamb; and if thou wilt not redeem it, then thou shalt break its neck. All the first-born of thy sons thou shalt redeem. And none shall appear before Me empty. (Exodus 34:20)

Mitzvah 22 commands us to redeem (reclaim) our first born male donkey by giving a lamb to the Kohanim in exchange for the donkey. Hashem claimed the first born male donkey as His. A donkey is not kosher, and is therefore not an acceptable sacrifice to Hashem. Because it is not an acceptable sacrifice to

Hashem, the Kohanim must not eat it. Instead, we give a lamb to the Kohanim, which is an acceptable sacrifice to Hashem that the Kohanim can eat.

If the donkey's firstling is female, then her subsequent male babies would not have that special status. If a Jew owns the donkey in partnership with a Non-Jew, then this Mitzvah would not be applicable.

Even though the donkey is not kosher, we redeem it to remind ourselves of how we escaped from Pharaoh.

and it came to pass, when Pharaoh would hardly let us go that the LORD slew all the first born in the land of Egypt, both the first-born of man, and the first-born of beast; therefore I sacrifice to the LORD all that openeth the womb, being males; but all the first-born of my sons I redeem. (Exodus 13:15)

Ezekiel likened the Egyptians' flesh to that of donkeys.

23. TO BREAK THE NECK OF AN UNREDEEMED FIRST BORN DONKEY

And every firstling of an ass thou shalt redeem with a lamb; and if thou wilt not redeem it, then thou shalt break its neck; and all the first-born of man among thy sons shalt thou redeem. (Exodus 13:13)

Mitzvah 23 states that if a person refuses to redeem his donkey, the animal's neck must be broken, to prevent anyone from benefiting from it. A donkey is non-kosher, so it cannot be eaten. Consult Mitzvah 22 for the explanation of the donkey's special status.

24. NOT TO GO BEYOND PERMITTED LIMITS ON THE SABBATH

See that the LORD hath given you the sabbath; therefore He giveth you on the sixth day the bread of two days; abide ye every man in his place, let no man go out of his place on the seventh day. (Exodus 16:29)

Mitzvah 24 prohibits us to go beyond permitted limits on Shabbat.

How do we figure out the maximum length that we can walk on Shabbat?

Go to the last house in the town. Perhaps it is 2000 Amot. (Amot is the plural for Ammah, which means cubits. In this context, Ammah means a unit of length equal to about 48 centimeters, or 19.2 **inches, or one cubit–the length from the tip of the middle finger to elbow.**)

Walk a little further, but less than a mile past the last house. From this point, we make a circle or circumference around the town. That circle marks the maximum distance that we can walk on Shabbat.

It reminds us that Hashem rested on the Seventh Day. We also rest on the Seventh Day. It is not a day for traveling or any kind of work. The Manna story is applicable here because it teaches us the laws of neither cooking, nor baking nor preparing any food in any manner on Shabbat. All food is prepared on the Sixth Day.

Rabbi Charlestein added:

"While Shabbat is part of the works of creation (Genesis 2:1-3), the first command to observe Shabbat is found at the time of the giving of Manna in the wilderness.

25. TO BELIEVE IN THE EXISTENCE OF GOD

I am the LORD thy God, who brought thee out of the land of Egypt, out of the house of bondage. ***Thou shalt have no other gods before Me. (Exodus 20:2)***

Mitzvah 25 commands us to believe in one God–Hashem! Hashem is our one and only God. Hashem created the heaven and the earth. Hashem created the world and all its creatures. Hashem created us. Hashem is all loving and powerful. He is our father. He is our king. He is our divine ruler. He is Hashem!

According to Rabbi Charlestein, Hashem is the God of History since we say in the Ten Commandments: He brought us out of the house of bondage, that He is our liberator and watches us throughout time.

26. TO BELIEVE IN NO DIVINITY BUT GOD

I am the LORD thy God, who brought thee out of the land of Egypt, out of the house of bondage. ***Thou shalt have no other gods before Me.*** ***(Exodus 20:2)***

Mitzvah 26 forbids us to believe in any other God. This Mitzvah comes from the heart, a prohibition of belief. It would extend to worship as well. Worshipping another god is a capital crime. No value in life should supersede our belief in Hashem or take precedence over the all-encompassing devotion to Him.

27. NOT TO MAKE A GRAVEN IMAGE

Thou shalt not make unto thee a graven image, nor any manner of likeness, of any thing that is in heaven above, or that is in the earth beneath, or that is in the water under the earth; Exodus 20:3)

Mitzvah 27 prohibits us from making idols or graven images so we can worship the images as gods.

The Sages extended this Mitzvah: we are forbidden to make a physical representation of Hashem. It is forbidden to worship the work created by a person's hands.

28. NOT TO PROSTRATE ONESELF IN IDOL-WORSHIP

Thou shalt not bow down unto them, nor serve them; for I the LORD thy God am a jealous God, visiting the iniquity of the fathers upon the children unto the third and fourth generation of them that hate Me; (Exodus 20:4)

Mitzvah 28 forbids us to bow down to or perform any worship rituals to false gods. Idol-worshippers often prostrated themselves (laid on the ground) in front of their graven image as part of their worship or service to the false god.

The definition of false gods: Any God that is not Hashem is a false God.

Hashem does not have helpers; He does not need them because He is Hashem.

The angels in the Bible strictly perform tasks to fulfill Hashem's will.

29. NOT TO WORSHIP AN IDOL IN ITS USUAL WAY OF VENERATION

Thou shalt not bow down unto them, nor serve them; for I the LORD thy God am a jealous God, visiting the iniquity of the fathers upon the children unto the third and fourth generation of them that hate Me; (Exodus 20:4)

Mitzvah 29 forbids us to worship another god. We cannot worship a false god in any manner or in any method whatsoever. Jews cannot mimic the idol-worshipers' actions in any way or for any reason, not even to mock or show contempt to the idol.

My Partner in Torah wrote me that we cannot worship a false god through a universal method, or any other method that is "normal" for that false god. If one worships through a method that is non-universal or not normal for that false god, then one is not Biblically in violation, whether it be a universal method or not.

If two witnesses see a Jew Biblically in violation of this Mitzvah, and the culprit refuses to heed their warnings to stop, that violator would be put to death. (A lesser punishment would subject the guilty party to ex-communication.)

Throughout the Torah, Hashem stated that the punishment for committing certain crimes is being put to death. However, execution does not happen automatically. First, two witnesses must see the perpetrator committing the crime and then warn that person to stop in order to avoid being put to death. If their pleas go unheeded, then the judges would decide the individual's fate.

Although the laws of capital punishment were put in place during the time of the Sanhedrin, it did not mean that it was often practiced. The Torah places greater priority on preserving life than putting one to death. I cover this topic in greater detail in Mitzvah 76.

30. NOT TO SWEAR IN VAIN

Thou shalt not take the name of the LORD thy God in vain; for the LORD will not hold him guiltless that taketh His name in vain. (Exodus 20:6)

Mitzvah 30 relates to commandment number three of the 10 commandments: Do not take Hashem's name in vain.

We can't swear to tell the truth in court and then lie. For example, if you swear that a table is a table, that's so obvious it takes Hashem's name in vain, because you are unnecessarily swearing to something. To swear something against the Torah is a false swearing. The next aspect is to swear to do something that is impossible. Don't even say expressions like "I swear to Hashem or As Hashem as my witness, Good G-d! G-d All-Mighty!" Don't say expressions like 'Oh my G-d!"

Violating these Mitzvot subjects the guilty party to receiving lashes of the whip.

31. TO HALLOW THE SABBATH IN WORDS

Remember the sabbath day, to keep it holy. (Exodus 20:7)

Mitzvah 31 commands us to remember Shabbat, the Seventh Day and to keep it holy. We must remember that Shabbat is a special day and must be separated from the rest of the week. The Kiddush and Motzi are part of this Mitzvah. The Motzi represents the double portion of the Manna. We could still say the Kiddush without wine, if none is available.

We say those blessings to sanctify Shabbat and to remember the greatness of the day. We remember that Hashem created the world in six days, and rested on the seventh.

32. NOT TO DO ANY WORK ON THE SABBATH

but the seventh day is a sabbath unto the LORD thy God, in it thou shalt not do any manner of work, thou, nor thy son, nor thy daughter, nor thy man-servant, nor thy maid-servant, nor thy cattle, nor thy stranger that is within thy gates; (Exodus 20:9)

Mitzvah 32 is the prohibition from doing any work on Shabbat. This Mitzvah applies to every household member, including servants and one's animals. Renting out animals to work on Shabbat is forbidden. Doing that subjects the guilty party to capital punishment.

Tractate Shabbat, Chapter 7, Mishnah 2 identifies 39 areas of work. These are identical to the ones used at the time when the Children of Israel were in the wilderness for 40 years and used the Mishkan (Tent of Meeting). The Mishkan had the same level of holiness as the Holy Temple in Jerusalem would later have. These are identical to the tasks performed when the Children of Israel built the Mishkan in the wilderness.

Some of the levels of work include making bread for use in the Temple, ploughing, grinding, shearing, or weaving garments. We cannot cook. We cannot slaughter animals. Rabbi Gary Charlestein added, "exceptions (in sacrificing) were made for animals slaughtered as part of the public sacrifices offered on a daily, weekly, and holiday basis in the Temple."

On Shabbat, we cannot move an object from one domain to another if it is not to be used on Shabbat. For example, because driving on Shabbat is forbidden, a car owner cannot move his or her car keys from one spot to another.

Not working is a way to remember that Hashem created the world in six days and rested on the seventh. In addition, resting on Shabbat reminds us that Hashem liberated us from Egypt and that we are no longer slaves.

33. THE PRECEPT OF HONORING FATHER AND MOTHER

Honour thy father and thy mother, that thy days may be long upon the land which the LORD thy God giveth thee. (Exodus 20:11)

Mitzvah 33 commands us to honor our parents. We must show them gratitude for bringing us into the world. At the same time, we have to recognize Hashem for playing a part in this fabulous miracle. A parent provides for every need of a child. Hashem provides us with air to breath. Hashem allows us to interact with the world–that distinguishes us from animals. The Talmud says that there are three Partners in creation of a person (IE one's mother, one's father, and Hashem).

(The Partnership between Hashem and parents in creating life can be found at Kiddushin 30b Sefaria. Cited at https://www.sefaria.org/Kiddushin.30b).

It is commonly taught that the first five of the 10 commandments deal with Hashem and man, while commandments 6, 7, 8, 9 and 10 deal with men's relationships with other men. The way to honor our parents is a way to honor Hashem.

The reason the commandment to honor our parents, which on the surface seems like a Mitzvah between humans, is included among the first five commandments is that by honoring our parents, we also demonstrate our gratitude toward Hashem for the role that He played in our creation.

There are five things that constitute honoring our parents:

1. Giving our parents food and drink.
2. providing them with clothes.
3. Providing shelter
4. Bring them into a room.
5. Take them out of a room.

If our parents are weak and/or poor, then it is our obligation to support them.

Can our parents forgo the honor? If parents violate the Torah, we cannot tell them directly that they are wrong. We can hint at it. We have to honor and revere our parents whether they are still living or not.

In the observant Jewish community, our parents, and grandparents are revered because their generations are closer to Moses. Each generation has a tendency to lose its holiness because they are further removed from Moses.

In secular society, parents and grandparents are often treated with disrespect.

Whether they are still living

34. NOT TO PUT AN INNOCENT MAN TO DEATH

Thou shalt not murder. (Exodus 20:12)

Mitzvah 34 forbids us to kill an innocent person–an innocent person is made in G-d's image. (Criminals are also made in His image.) This is also the sixth commandment. The idea behind this Mitzvah is that it is cruel to kill another person. We view the Mitzvot through the eyes of Hashem.

If you kill another person, you are denying Hashem's intentions of fulfilling His wish. It does not preclude the concept of capital punishment. This Mitzvah pertains to innocent people, not those who are guilty of murder. A murderer is innocent when defending himself/herself from a person who is trying to kill him/her. The Israeli soldier has a similar responsibility. If one is trying to destroy Israel and Her people, the Israeli soldier be obligated to kill that individual.

35. NOT TO BE IMMORAL WITH ANOTHER'S WIFE

Thou shalt not commit adultery. (Exodus 20:12)

Mitzvah 35 runs parallel to the Seventh Commandment, which forbids a man to have sexual relations with another man's wife. One explanation is that it upsets the natural order of the world. The wife belongs to her husband. She is there so that her husband can fulfill the First Mitzvah, to be fruitful and multiply. The wife belongs to her husband and must be faithful.

36. NOT TO KIDNAP ANY JEWISH PERSON

Thou shalt not steal. (Exodus 20:12)

Mitzvah 36 corresponds with the commandment, 'thou shall not steal.' Not only are we forbidden to steal other peoples' possessions, we cannot kidnap a Jewish person either. Kidnapping and then selling the stolen person, even if he/she is a slave, is a capital offense.

37. NOT TO BEAR FALSE WITNESS

Thou shalt not bear false witness against thy neighbour. (Exodus 20:12)

Mitzvah 37 is the prohibition against bearing false testimony. In other words, don't lie! You can't lie under oath. This Mitzvah is in place because people can be swayed to testify on someone's behalf even if it means lying. Doing that demonstrates that the person can be bribed.

Professional gamblers cannot testify in court.

38. NOT TO COVET WHAT BELONGS TO ANOTHER

Thou shalt not covet thy neighbour's house; (Exodus 20:13)

Mitzvah 38 is the prohibition against coveting our neighbor's property. Although jealousy is frowned upon, and certain Mitzvot forbid us to be jealous, being jealous would not violate this particular Mitzvah. The only violation here is the act of coveting. In this Mitzvah, pestering our neighbors for his property, putting pressure on him to let us have it is coveting. Coveting can lead to stealing. Coveting can also cause mental anguish. If one is happy with his/her own lot, then that can reduce jealousy.

39. TO MAKE NO SCULPTURED HUMAN IMAGES, EVEN FOR ORNAMENTATION

Ye shall not make with Me—gods of silver, or gods of gold, ye shall not make unto you. (Exodus 20:19)

Mitzvah 39 forbids us to make an exact image of a person. Hashem commanded us not to make anything that resembles a human figure. Because we are created in Hashem's image, Making a sculpture of someone would be like creating an image of a false god.

If someone makes a physical representation of a person, that creates the potential to worship it. This Mitzvah focuses on not making a statue of a person because it could lead to worship of the statue.

40. NOT TO BUILD AN ALTAR OF HEWN STONES

And if thou make Me an altar of stone, thou shalt not build it of hewn stones; for if thou lift up thy tool upon it, thou hast profaned it. (Exodus 20:21)

Mitzvah 40 states that we cannot use metal tools to cut and shape the stones used to build an altar.

The concept behind this is that man is to instill peace in himself. Metal is used for destruction. Spears and swords, which are instruments of death, are made from metals. We keep the altar-stones holy because it brings us closer to Hashem. It helps lead to peace and calmness. Metal represents the opposite force.

41. NOT TO STRIDE BY STEPS TO THE ALTAR

Neither shalt thou go up by steps unto Mine altar, that thy nakedness be not uncovered thereon. (Exodus 20:22)

Mitzvah 41 explains that when the Holy Temple's altar was built, there was a ramp to go to the top instead of steps. Because of the way that the clothing was made during the time of the Temple, people wore robes that overlapped in front. Walking up steps could cause the robe to open accidentally, which exposed thighs and other body parts. When we walk up steps, we have to spread our legs more than if we were to walk up ramps. Walking up a ramp keeps the robe closed in front and is more modest because skin is not exposed.

Walking up steps displays a lack of modesty. In the Days of the Temple, people had to take small steps to the altar in order to maintain modesty. As a result, it internalized the Holiness of the Temple.

AUTHOR'S NOTE:

Because the topic of Jews owning slaves is mentioned in Mitzvot 42 through 46, I must address it.

Why did Jews have slaves? Hashem freed our ancestors from Pharaoh. Why would the Jews have slaves and why would Hashem allow it?

The link, http://www.faqs.org/faqs/judaism/FAQ/05-Worship/section-55.html explains that Jews never kidnapped people and forced them to become slaves. That link states that, "the non-Jewish slaves were purchased from themselves; i.e., they were offered a sum of money, or guaranteed shelter and food, in exchange for becoming slaves."

"Jewish slaves" were for the most part indentured servants for a period of seven years. Jews who were unable to pay their debts to another Jew, could work off that debt by becoming indentured servants for the Jew they owed. A Jewish thief could be sold as a slave for his/her theft if the thief could not provide restitution.

Jewish slaves would also be freed in the 50th year–the jubilee year.

These Jewish slaves must be set free after the seventh year of service. Jewish slaves were also freed during the Jubilee Year.

Jewish masters had to treat their Jewish and non-Jewish slaves humanely. The Jewish master was obligated to make sure that his slaves had all the necessary comforts. For example, if the master did not have enough pillows and blankets for both himself and his slaves, he had to give them to his slaves rather than take them himself and leave the slaves without.

Slaves could not be assigned useless work just for the sake of working them. If a master ever treated any of his slaves inhumanely, he had to free them at once. (My Partner in Torah explained this to me and then I heard certain Rabbis discuss this further.)

Sometimes, after six years of service, a Jewish slave preferred to remain with his Jewish master rather than go free:

But if the servant shall plainly say: I love my master, my wife, and my children; I will not go out free; then his master shall bring him unto God, and shall bring him to the door, or unto the door-post; and his master shall bore his ear through with an awl; and he shall serve him forever. (Exodus 21:5-6)

42. THE LAW OF THE HEBREW BONDSERVANT

If thou buy a Hebrew servant, six years he shall serve; and in the seventh he shall go out free for nothing. (Exodus 21:2)

Mitzvah 42 commands masters to treat their Jewish slaves humanely.

Before and during the time of the First and Second Temples, a Jew could become another Jew's slave (indentured servant) if that person was unable to pay a debt. The Jewish slave was usually set free in the seventh year of servitude.

One reason that masters had to treat their slaves kindly was that it forced them to practice the important art of being merciful. Another reason was that we were slaves in Egypt, and during that time were frequently mistreated.

We need to treat other people as we wish to be treated. This courtesy extends to fellow Jews who are unable to pay their debts and who end up as slaves.

43. MARITAL DESIGNATION OF THE HEBREW MAIDSERVANT

If she please not her master, <u>who hath espoused her to himself</u>, then shall he let her be redeemed; to sell her unto a foreign people he shall have no power, seeing he hath dealt deceitfully with her. (Exodus 21:8)

Mitzvah 43 allows the master of the house or his son to marry his Jewish servants. The servants would not be the men's only wives. The marriage is a way of developing the attribute of mercy. Simultaneously, the woman servant becomes the lady of the house. That act is a way of helping people and raising their stations in life. It helps equalize the classes.

The person who bought the Jewish woman slave cannot sell her to anyone else. If the master doesn't marry her, she has to go free in the seventh year. He has a choice whether or not to marry her. Even though it's a Mitzvah to marry her, he is not obligated to. With this said, the actual Mitzvah is, if you perform the act, it's a good deed, if you don't, it won't be punishable.

44. THE REDEMPTION OF THE HEBREW MAIDSERVANT

If she please not her master, who hath espoused her to himself, <u>then shall he let her be redeemed</u>; to sell her unto a foreign people he shall have no power, seeing he hath dealt deceitfully with her. (Exodus 21:8)

Mitzvah 44 pertains to assisting a Jewish maidservant who is serving a seven-year term as an indentured servant in your household. This Mitzvah obligates the head of the house to assist the maidservant to redeem herself. She can redeem herself mid-way through her sentence, so she would not have to work for seven years as a slave. The master who bought her should allow her to be redeemed mid-way through her sentence.

Should the master decide to free the maidservant before her seven-year period terminates, he needs to calculate how much money he paid for her, and how much time she has left to serve her sentence to determine her redemption price. He can show charity by reducing her redemption price to zero. Or he can show mercy and take her saved up money as long as it totals less than her purchase price.

45. THE BUYER OF A HEBREW MAIDSERVANT MAY NOT SELL HER

If she please not her master, who hath espoused her to himself, then shall he let her be redeemed; <u>to sell her unto a foreign people he shall have no power, seeing he hath dealt deceitfully with her</u>. (Exodus 21:8)

Mitzvah 45 forbids the master from selling his slaves to another party. The master shows compassion to his slaves by sparing them the embarrassment of being sold twice.

46. NOT TO WITHHOLD FROM ONE'S WIFE HER RIGHTFUL DUE

If he take him another wife, her food, her raiment, and her conjugal rights, shall he not diminish. (Exodus 21:10)

Mitzvah 46 states that if the master marries his slave, he is obligated to provide her with food, clothes, and sex. He may NOT withhold those things.

By extension, a husband is also required to fulfill these obligations for his free-born Jewish wife.

After he marries his former maid servant/slave, he must be extra certain that she is also provided with these benefits to further cement her higher station/status as second wife.

47. THE COURT IS TO EXECUTE BY STRANGULATION ANYONE WHO DESERVES IT

He that smiteth a man, so that he dieth, shall surely be put to death. (Exodus 21:12)

Mitzvah 47 commands the Jewish court to perform capital punishment if the party is guilty. Example: If you kill someone by striking him, then you will be put to death via strangulation.

The four forms of capital punishment in Jewish law are stoning, swallowing molten liquid, beheading, and hanging (strangulation).

If the law says for the guilty party to be hung, then he is to be hung.

If the guilty party commits homicide, the capital punishment would be death by hanging–death by strangulation. Hanging is viewed as the least painful because the guilty party dies faster that way than by the other three methods. Hanging the guilty party is an act of mercy.

For more information, consult Tractate Sanhedrin, Chapter 7, Mishnah 1.

48. NOT TO STRIKE ONE'S FATHER OR MOTHER

And he that smiteth his father, or his mother, shall be surely put to death. (Exodus 21:15)

Mitzvah 48 says: "Do not strike or wound your parent. Do not smite a parent. Do not draw their blood." Violating this Mitzvah results in capital punishment. We must always show gratitude toward our parents, so committing these heinous acts is a serious violation.

49. THE LAWS OF FINES–PENALTIES

if he rise again, and walk abroad upon his staff, then shall he that smote him be quit; only he shall pay for the loss of his time, and shall cause him to be thoroughly healed. (Exodus 21:19)

Mitzvah 49 is the obligation to provide compensation to the person(s) that you injured. If a person hurts another, the culprit must compensate his victim. This extends to paying medical bills and lost wages. The guilty party is required to pay for punitive costs and pay for what he had ruined.

These include:

1. Damages
2. Pain
3. Medical expenses
4. Being out of work
5. Disfigurement.

See Tractate, Bava Kamma, Chapter 8, Mishnah 1.

(In a capital punishment case, there must be at least 23 judges on hand to try the case, but for monetary lawsuits, only three judges preside.)

50. THE COURT SHOULD EXECUTE BY DECAPITATION ANYONE WHO DESERVES IT

And if a man smite his bondman, or his bondwoman, with a rod, and he die under his hand, he shall surely be punished. (Exodus 21:20)

Mitzvah 50 refers to Hashem's command that Jews who violate certain precepts of the Torah be put to death by the sword–beheading / decapitation.

Decapitation is the second most humane way to kill the culprit. Hanging (strangulation) is the most humane way.

If a man becomes so enraged that he kills his bondservant, (smites / beats to death) or kills his slave, or kills any person living in his home, the attacker is sentenced to death by decapitation.

Even if that bondservant or slave was a former heathen, the attackerstill faces decapitation.

51. THAT THE COURT SHOULD JUDGE DAMAGES BY DOMESTIC ANIMALS

***If an ox injures a man or damages his property, the ox would be tried by the court.* And if an ox gore a man or a woman, that they die, the ox shall be surely stoned, and its flesh shall not be eaten; but the owner of the ox shall be quit. (Exodus 21:28)**

Mitzvah 51 requires the Jewish court to judge cases that involve property damage and decide how much money is owed for those damages.

Animals are property. For example, if your ox gored mine, then you owe me for damages. The Torah discusses the case of oxen because oxen are more dangerous than other farm animals and need to be watched.

This Mitzvah also applies to other animals that have caused damage to people or property. There are other animals more dangerous than the oxen, such as the bear and the snake, but it is less likely for people to own them.

52. NOT TO EAT ANY OX SENTENCED TO DEATH BY STONING

And if an ox gore a man or a woman, that they die, the ox shall be surely stoned, and its flesh shall not be eaten; but the owner of the ox shall be quit. (Exodus 21:28)

Mitzvah 52 states that if an animal kills a person (personal injury), then that animal is put to death. Stoning the animal is the only way that we can kill it because that way we don't eat it. We cannot eat an animal that kills a human being because we cannot derive benefit from that bad animal. That animal's actions suggest that there is something morally wrong with that animal, so we should not even consider eating it.

This Mitzvah requires a court of 23 judges to try the animal because the case involves the death of a human being (personal injury).

(See Tractate Sanhedrin Chapter 1, Mishnayot 1, and 4. Mishnayot is the plural for Mishnah.)

53. THE OBLIGATION OF THE COURT TO JUDGE DAMAGES BY A PIT

And if a man shall open a pit, or if a man shall dig a pit and not cover it, and an ox or an ass fall therein, the owner of the pit shall make it good; he shall give money unto the owner of them, and the dead beast shall be his. (Exodus 21:33–34)

Mitzvah 53 requires the Bet Din, the Jewish court, to assess damages. If someone created a public hazard and a person or animal is injured by that hazard, the Bet Din determines the outcome. The court assesses how extreme the hazard is, and the extent of the damage it caused, to determine how much the negligent person has to pay.

Examples of a "public hazard" can include leaving lots of broken glass on the ground,

leaving an open pit or hole uncovered, failing to clear ice and snow off your sidewalk.

54. THAT THE COURT SHOULD IMPOSE PROPER PAYMENT ON A THIEF, OR HE MAY INCUR DEATH

If a man steal an ox, or a sheep, and kill it, or sell it, he shall pay five oxen for an ox, and four sheep for a sheep. (Exodus 21:37)

Mitzvah 54 states that if a thief steals an ox and then kills it or sells it, the thief must repay the owner with five oxen. If the thief steals a sheep and then kills or sells it, the thief must repay the owner with four sheep.

Mitzvah 54 also requires that all cases which involve stealing be judged by the court according to the circumstances.

If a person steals property, he has to pay back double the amount he had stolen. One reason the thief must repay the victim a double sum is that the theft caused two violations: A violation against the individual's right to own property and a violation against the general idea of respecting one's right to own property. The thief has to pay the value of the theft as restitution to the owner; and an equal sum for his contempt of the principle of general honesty against which he has offended. (For a more detailed discussion about theft being a double crime, log onto http://vbm-Torah.org/archive/salt-shemot/18-13mishpatim.htm)

Mitzvah 54 has been extended to include: a thief faces capital punishment for selling a person into slavery. (Consult Sefer HaHinnuch for more details.)

55. THE OBLIGATION OF THE COURT TO JUDGE DAMAGES BY A DOMESTIC ANIMAL'S GRAZING OR TRAMPLING

If a man cause a field or vineyard to be eaten, and shall let his beast loose, and it feed in another man's field; of the best of his own field, and of the best of his own vineyard, shall he make restitution. (Exodus 22:4)

Mitzvah 55 focuses on the property / things damaged by a person's animals or possessions.

If a person's ox caused damage by eating or trampling another man's crop, field, or vineyard, the court must determine the extent of the damage and the amount that the ox's owner must compensate the victim.

For example, if a man lets his goat wander into someone else's field and the goat eats that other person's flowers, the owner of the goat must compensate the victim.

The difference between Mitzvah 51 and 55:

Mitzvah 51 focuses on animals' damages toother people (personal injury).

Mitzvah 55 focuses on animals' damages to other people's property (property damage).

56. THE OBLIGATION OF THE COURT TO JUDGE DAMAGE BY FIRE

If fire break out, and catch in thorns, so that the shocks of corn, or the standing corn, or the field are consumed; he that kindled the fire shall surely make restitution. (Exodus 22:5)

Mitzvah 56 pertains to damages caused by fire. If the person lights a fire and it gets out of control, he is liable to pay for any damages that the fire caused.

When any person lights a fire or puts a fire out, that person is obligated to prevent damages from occurring.

57. THAT THE COURT SHOULD JUDGE CASES INVOLVING AN UNPAID CUSTODIAN

If a man deliver unto his neighbour money or goods to keep, and it be stolen out of the man's house; if the thief be found, he shall pay double. (Exodus 22:6)

Mitzvah 57 covers multiple scenarios:

a) if a man (or woman) agrees to watch his neighbor's property for no pay, he is obligated to keep his word. (The watchman is legally an "unpaid bailee.")

b) If the neighbor's property is damaged by the watchman's negligence, he must compensate the neighbor/owner.

c) If the neighbor's property is stolen out of the watchman's house, and the watchman is NOT negligent, he is not obligated to compensate the owner. (An unpaid bailee is only liable for his own negligence.)

d) If the thief who stole the neighbor's property out of the watchman's house is found, the thief must pay the neighbor/owner double the value of the stolen property.

The Bet Din rules on the extent of the damages and whether the watchman was negligent. If damages happen beyond the watchman's control, he is not obligated to pay the owner.

There are four bailees (watchmen). (For more information consult Mishnah Bava Metzia Chapter 7, Mishnah 8, and Tractate Shevuot, Chapter 8, Mishnah 1.)

58. THE COURT'S OBLIGATION TO JUDGE THE CASE OF A PLAINTIFF AND A DEFENDANT

For every matter of trespass, whether it be for ox, for ass, for sheep, for raiment, or for any manner of lost thing, whereof one saith: 'This is it,' the cause of both parties shall come before God; he whom God shall condemn shall pay double unto his neighbour. (Exodus 22:8)

Mitzvah 58 requires the Bet Din to judge cases involving disputes of any kind between two people. The Bet Din determines which person was at fault, determines which person was the victim, determines the extent of the damages, and determines the consequences to the person at fault. The consequences can range from paying money to physical punishment.

Example: If B borrows money from A, then refuses to repay the debt, plaintiff A files a claim against defendant B.The Bet Din hears the case and determines the consequences.

The Bet Din must also judge the counter claim: If B swears in court that he said to A, "I never borrowed the money," "I paid you back, partially," or "I already paid you back," coupled with the fact that there was no external proof that a loan was made, B would not be obligated to compensate A.

However, if defendant B says that he doesn't remember there being a debt to plaintiff A, then he would be obligated to repay it.

Women cannot be judges, but they can be plaintiffs or defendants.

59. THE COURT'S OBLIGATION TO JUDGE CASES INVOLVING A PAID CUSTODIAN OR A HIRER

If a man deliver unto his neighbour an ass, or an ox, or a sheep, or any beast, to keep, and it die, or be hurt, or driven away, no man seeing it; the oath of the LORD shall be between them both, to see whether he have not put his hand unto his neighbour's goods; and the owner thereof shall accept it, and he shall not make restitution. (Exodus 22:9-10)

Mitzvah 59 states that if a person is paid to watch his neighbor's property/goods, the watchman has a higher level of culpability if the neighbor's goods get damaged or stolen. The Bet Din will judge any dispute between these two people due to this scenario.

The key difference between Mitzvah 57 and 59 lies in the level of responsibility and holiness. Mitzvah 57 pertains to unpaid bailees who are only liable for their own negligence. Mitzvah 59 pertains to paid bailees who have a greater responsibility / duty to keep the neighbor's property safe because the watchman is being paid to do so.

60. THE COURT'S OBLIGATION TO JUDGE CASES INVOLVING A MAN WHO BORROWS AN OBJECT FOR USE

And if a man borrow aught of his neighbour, and it be hurt, or die, the owner thereof not being with it, he shall surely make restitution. (Exodus 22:13)

Mitzvah 60 states that if a man (or woman) borrows something from his neighbor, he has the highest level of responsibility to take care of it, especially if he uses that item when the owner is not present. If you borrow something and that item is damaged, whether it is your fault or not, you have to compensate the owner. Borrowing something gives the borrower benefit, while the lender gets nothing. That's why the borrower has a higher level of responsibility to uphold it than the owner.

The borrower is responsible for damages to the owner's item, if "***the owner thereof not being with it***"–only if the owner is not present during the task.

If a man (or woman) borrows an item from his neighbor, and they perform that specific task together, and the neighbor's item gets damaged, the borrower is not liable.

Example: I borrow a knife to carve meat from my neighbor, and my neighbor watches me or helps me carve the meat, but his knife breaks during the task. I am not liable for paying my neighbor for his knife because he was present when I used it and was able to instruct me on how to use it properly so it would not break.

61. THE DUTY OF THE COURT TO PASS JUDGMENT ON A SEDUCER

And if a man entice a virgin that is not betrothed, and lie with her, he shall surely pay a dowry for her to be his wife. If her father utterly refuse to give her unto him, he shall pay money according to the dowry of virgins. (Exodus 22:15-16)

Mitzvah 61 applies to cases of consensual sex, not rape. It includes the following parts:

a) if a man seduces an unmarried woman he must pay a dowry for her and marry her. (If he marries her, then he does not have to pay the fine or pay her father.)

b) if a man seduces an unmarried woman and doesn't marry her, he has to pay a fine and pay her father the fixed amount of money dictated by the dowry of virgins.

c) It is up to the girl and her father to decide if she will marry the seducer. The seducer/future husband must still pay a dowry for her.

d) If the girl's father is not alive, and the seducer does not want to marry her, then the seducer is not obligated to marry the girl or pay the fine or pay the dowry.

62. NOT TO ALLOW A SORCERER TO LIVE

Thou shalt not suffer a sorceress to live. (Exodus 22:17)

Mitzvah 62 commands us to put to death any person practicing sorcery or witchcraft. (Scripture speaks of what is usual–women are sorcerers to a greater extent than men.)

People in ancient times believed that certain individuals who had supernatural powers and who used them for evil purposes lived alongside the Chosen People whom the Torah chronicled. One of the practices of sorcery is to change the natural order of things, which is an absolute affront to Hashem because He created the natural order of things. No time in history, neither today nor in the future, can anyone practice this deed. However, witches are spared from persecution if they use their powers to heal people.

63. NOT TO VERBALLY OPPRESS A CONVERT TO JUDAISM

And a stranger shalt thou not wrong, neither shalt thou oppress him; for ye were strangers in the land of Egypt. (Exodus 22:20)

Mitzvah 63 forbids us to disparage and embarrass converts to Judaism. When we are angry at them or wish to hurt them we can't remind them that they are "just a convert to Judaism." Jews must not give the convert a negative depiction of the Jewish religion and the Jewish people.The Torah commands us to control our emotions and inclinations.

(See Mishnah Bava Metzia, Chapter 4, Mishnah 10, which deals with defrauding by words)

One famous example involved Rabbi Shimon ben Lakish (also known as Reish Lakish). He was a robber until Rabbi Yochanan compelled him to dedicate his life to Torah. They eventually became learning Partners and also brothers-in-law. Many years later, long after Reish Lakish had become a righteous and learned Sage, he and Rabbi Yochanan argued about how to use a knife. The latter became so enraged that he did the unthinkable. (I am paraphrasing.) He said: "Of course you would have expertise with the knife. You used one all the time when you robbed people." No upper cut to the jaw, no kick to the groin could have hurt him half as much. The insult reminded him of his terrible past, which he had put behind him.

My Partner in Torah and I discussed passages from Book of our Heritage by Eliyahu Kitov, in which Kitov stressed that speaking wickedly, telling lies and gossiping is a worse sin than committing a physical sin or crime. Like animals, we have the ability to kill, but unlike animals, Hashem gave us the ability to speak. Speaking elevates us above us from animals and places us closer to Hashem. Having the ability to speak is Hashem's gift to us. To use our tongues wickedly is a vulgar display of disrespect of Hashem's wonderful gift.

This Mitzvah reminds us that those who were born Jewish are not superior to converts. Ruth converted to Judaism and became one of the greatest individuals in our history. She also was King David's great-grandmother.

64. NOT TO WRONG A CONVERT IN MATTERS OF PROPERTY

And a stranger shalt thou not wrong, neither shalt thou oppress him; for ye were strangers in the land of Egypt. (Exodus 22:20)

Mitzvah 64 forbids us to mercilessly charge someone. We cannot cheat people. We cannot cheat our fellow Jews who were born into the religion. Cheating a person who converts to Judaism, violates two prohibitions:

(1) We cannot cheat a Jew.

(2) We cannot cheat a Jewish convert.

This prohibition extends to not cheating anyone, whether the person is a Jew or not. Cheating anyone would give us a bad name.

65. NOT TO AFFLICT ANY ORPHAN OR WIDOW

Ye shall not afflict any widow, or fatherless child. If thou afflict them in any wise—for if they cry at all unto Me, I will surely hear their cry— My wrath shall wax hot, and I will

kill you with the sword; and your wives shall be widows, and your children fatherless. (Exodus 22:21-22:23)

Mitzvah 65 prohibits us from oppressing widows and orphans because they are defenseless. No husband or parents are alive to protect them, so they can become an oppressor's easy target. We must make an extra effort to show them compassion because they are assumed to be weaker and assumed to be at a disadvantage because there is no one to look out for them. We don't make distinctions on whether the widow or orphan is rich or poor because this Mitzvah prevents us from cheating or embarrassing any of them.

For cases tried in court, the court would appoint someone to represent them because their husband or parents are dead.

66. THE MITZVAH OF LENDING TO THE POOR

If thou lend money to any of My people, even to the poor with thee, thou shalt not be to him as a creditor; neither shall ye lay upon him interest. (Exodus 22:24)

Mitzvah 66 commands us to lend money to the poor. The author of Sefer HaHinnuch states that this is more important than giving charity to the poor. A poor person in need of charity often suffers the ignominy of just being in that predicament. The loan can prevent him from becoming destitute. He can maintain his dignity.

The reason for this Mitzvah is for us to practice compassion and to remind us that we are to love fellow Jews. This Mitzvah is applicable today.

67. NOT TO DUN A POOR MAN UNABLE TO PAY HIS DEBT

If thou lend money to any of My people, even to the poor with thee, <u>thou shalt not be to him as a creditor; neither shall ye lay upon him interest.</u> (Exodus 22:24)

Mitzvah 67 forbids us from demanding that a poor person repay his debt to us if he does not have the funds. We cannot follow that person and harass him until he pays his debt. The poor borrower is already in an ignominious state for being unable to honor his debt. There is no need to make him feel worse. The root of this Mitzvah lies with having compassion for fellow Jews.

68. NOT TO HELP A BORROWER OR A LENDER TRANSACT A LOAN AT INTEREST

If thou lend money to any of My people, even to the poor with thee, thou shalt not be to him as a creditor; <u>neither shall ye lay upon him interest</u>. (Exodus 22:24)

Mitzvah 68 prohibits us from taking part in the process of lending money if interest is charged. We cannot even be a third person witness. Charging interest to a fellow Jew is odious because it can put him in a state of poverty. This can also make the lender miserly. Charging interest can cause friction among fellow Jews, because Hashem commanded us to love one another.

69. TO UTTER NO CURSE AGAINST A JUDGE

Thou shalt not revile God, nor curse a ruler of thy people. (Exodus 22:27)

Mitzvah 69 forbids us to curse the judge. The word G-d is used in the Scriptures to refer to (to mean) judges. The judges are carrying out the word of Hashem. Hashem's power rests in the hands of the judges. Cursing Hashem is a capital punishment.

The rationale of the 69th Mitzvah is to help the judge. It is to remove the fear. You cannot have a situation in which people hate the judges. It reduces respect for the station, and the judge's important position of authority.

70. THE PROHIBITION AGAINST CURSING THE NAME OF THE ETERNAL LORD

***Thou shalt not revile God**, nor curse a ruler of thy people. (Exodus 22:27)*

Mitzvah 70 is the prohibition against cursing Hashem. Behind this Mitzvah lies something fundamental: The power of speech. In the Book of Genesis, Hashem created man. When Hashem breathed a soul into man,it means He breathed the spirit of speech into man. Hashem gives us the ability to speak, which distinguishes us from the animals. Cursing Hashem would make us no better than the animals who do not have the power of speech.

71. TO UTTER NO CURSE AGAINST A SOVEREIGN LEADER

*Thou shalt not revile God, **nor curse a ruler of thy people**. (Exodus 22:27)*

Mitzvah 71 is the prohibition against cursing a prince or other sovereign leader. Each of the tribes had primary representatives who were like presidents, meaning a "prince." Case in point: Judah the Prince (135-217 CE), the Chief Redactor and

Editor of the Mishnah, was in actuality Judah the President. In Hebrew, Judah the Prince is called Yehuda haNasi.

The reason for the prohibition is to prevent strife within the tribes. Constant rebelling against leaders causes chaos and it has the potential to make the prince unable to perform his responsibility of being Israel's representative when dealing with other nations.

72. NOT TO SEPARATE THE DUES FROM PRODUCE IN IMPROPER ORDER

Thou shalt not delay to offer of the fulness of thy harvest, and of the outflow of thy presses. The first-born of thy sons shalt thou give unto Me. (Exodus 22:28)

Mitzvah 72 states that the owner of a farm or a vineyard is obligated to give a portion of his harvest as an offering or tithe (like a tax). These payments were made in a specific order to prevent confusion about who gets what and when they receive it.

The First Offering is called T'rumah and is given to a Kohen. The size of this offering is not stated in the Bible. Rabbis say it is two percent of the total harvest.

The Second Offering consists of 2 tithes:

The First Tithe is given to a Levite. It is the First 10th of the remaining 98 percent of the harvest.

The Second Tithe is given to the owner, who must eat it in Jerusalem as Hashem commanded. This tithe takes place in years 1, 2, 4, and 5 of the 7-year cycle of crop rotation. (Crop rotation is a program where 2 or 3 different crops are planted in the same field in alternating years, and the 7th year the field lies fallow–nothing is planted in it.)

We cannot combine food harvested last year with food harvested this year to make the offering or pay the tithe. Rosh Hashanah, when the new year begins, is used as the dividing line between last year's harvest and this year's harvest.

If we pick vegetables before Rosh Hashanah, we must separate them from the vegetables that we pick after Rosh Hashanah. The vegetables picked before Rosh Hashanah are counted in last year's harvest and apply to last year's tithe. The vegetables picked after Rosh Hashanah are counted in this year's harvest and apply to this year's tithe.

73. NOT TO EAT THE FLESH OF AN ANIMAL TORN BY BEASTS

And ye shall be holy men unto Me; therefore ye shall not eat any flesh that is torn of beasts in the field; ye shall cast it to the dogs. (Exodus 22:30)

Mitzvah 73 tells us to keep our bodies holy and healthy for Hashem through the practice of eating only kosher food. We are forbidden to eat animals that have been attacked by beasts or animals that have diseases.

The Torah tells us that if an animal has been attacked by another animal or a beast, it is no longer kosher.

The Mitzvah extends this prohibition to include sick kosher animals. If an animal becomes sick or has an internal ailment, we cannot eat it.

After any animal is slaughtered, the slaughterer checks the animal's insides to make sure that it is healthy. If it is not healthy, then it is T'refah (non-kosher).

The reason for this Mitzvah is that our bodies are vessels for our souls. Tainted foods make our bodies sick or may kill us. We must make sure that our bodies are at the peak level of health to serve Hashem properly.

The Torah does not explain why eating certain animals will cause harm. It would be inappropriate to explain why. Once a reason is given for not being allowed to eat something, rationalists will find loopholes.

74. NOT TO HEAR A LITIGANT IN COURT IN HIS OPPONENT'S ABSENCE

Thou shalt not utter a false report; put not thy hand with the wicked to be an unrighteous witness. (Exodus 23:1).

Mitzvah 74 forbids judges from hearing a claim of one of the litigants, if the second party is not there. If he were given such liberties, he could attempt to stretch the truth or speak Lashon HaRah (evil tongue) against the absent litigant.

If the other party were present, it would be harder to stretch the truth because the other person's presence serves as a deterrent.

This Mitzvah urges us to tell the truth at all times and avoid falsehood.

Emet is truth and Sheker is falsehood. Falsehood is the antithesis of truth and of what Hashem represents. Hashem's whole being is one of truth. Torah emanated from Hashem. Being truthful is a way of emulating Hashem.

75. THAT A SINNER SHOULD NOT GIVE TESTIMONY

Thou shalt not utter a false report; put not thy hand with the wicked to be an unrighteous witness. (Exodus 23:1).

Mitzvah 75 commands that we not assist those who do an 'Avera,' a sin. Such individuals cannot testify. Thieves are in that category because they proved that they cannot be trusted.

Today in the U.S. convictions take place because of plea bargaining. Plea bargaining counters this Mitzvah, because wicked people are allowed to testify even though they had transgressed.

76. NOT TO FOLLOW A MAJORITY OF ONE AMONG JUDGES IN A CAPITAL CASE

Thou shalt not follow a multitude to do evil; neither shalt thou bear witness in a cause to turn aside after a multitude to pervert justice; (Exodus 23:2)

Mitzvah 76 tells us not to follow a crowd of people doing evil (sinning or breaking the law). It also tells us not to give false testimony just to "go along with the gang" or side with the majority if it will pervert justice.

This Mitzvah also encompasses capital punishment trials by the Sanhedrin.

In capital punishment cases, 23 Sanhedrin judges hear the arguments and they render their verdicts. The odd number of judges prevents a tied verdict–an even number of judges for and an even number of judges against. (See Tractate Sanhedrin, Chapter 1, Mishnah 6.)

Capital punishment cases must last at least two days to give the Sanhedrin more time to weigh the evidence and to judge without haste. The Sanhedrin tries to acquit the person on trial in order to follow Hashem's commandment to preserve human life.

In these cases, if the person is found guilty, even if it is by a majority of just one vote, he goes free. For example: 12 judges vote guilty and 11 judges vote innocent, the accused goes free. If 13 judges vote guilty and 10 judges vote innocent, then the accused would be put to death.

If all 23 judges vote to put the defendant to death, then the defendant goes free because it meant that no judge tried to preserve the life of the accused person. Based on Hashem's teachings, every life is worth saving.

More details about how the unanimous death verdict spares the defendant will be covered in Mitzvah 261. Tractate Makkot, Chapter 1, Mishnah 10 deals with capital punishment: "R. Eliezer b. Azariah says: "A Sanhedrin that effects a capital punishment once in 70 years is branded a destructive tribunal."

Rabbi Shaul Rosenblatt, who taught at Aish HaTorah Yeshiva in the Old City of Jerusalem when I studied there from December 1990 through January 1991, offered his feedback about capital punishment. He wrote:

"One might add that the Gemara says a Bet Din that puts one person to death in seven years is considered a cruel Bet Din and another opinion says once in 70 years. The death penalty was much more so an expression of the magnitude of the mistake as opposed to an enforceable consequence."

To learn more about the Sanhedrin, consult the article, Bet Din, by Jacqueline Shields at the link: http://www.jewishvirtuallibrary.org/jsource/Judaism/BetDin.html

This Mitzvah is not enforced today because the Sanhedrin dissolved in 358 CE. Consult the article, "The Disbanding of the Sanhedrin, 358 CE," at http://www.alsadiqin.org/en/index.php?title=The_Disbanding_of_the_Sanhedrin,_358_CE. Also see Mishnah Sanhedrin, Chapter 1, Mishnah 6.

77. A JUDGE WHO ARGUES FOR INNOCENCE IN A CAPITAL CASE SHOULD NOT ARGUE FOR GUILTY AFTERWARD

Thou shalt not follow a multitude to do evil; neither shalt thou bear witness in a cause to turn aside after a multitude to pervert justice; (Exodus 23:2)

Mitzvah 77 forbids judges to change their deliberations when they try capital cases. They can change their minds when they cast their final vote of innocent or guilty. If a judge is arguing that the defendant is innocent, he cannot suddenly argue that that person is guilty and vice versa. Again, he can change his mind when it comes time to cast the final vote, but not during the phase of deliberation.

78. THE PRECEPT OF FOLLOWING THE MAJORITY IN LEGAL DECISIONS

Thou shalt not follow a multitude to do evil; neither shalt thou bear witness in a cause to turn aside after a multitude to pervert justice; (Exodus 23:2)

Mitzvah 78 states that in regular voting cases, the majority wins.

There are exceptions to this rule. The author of Sefer HaHinnuch points out that a large number of ignoramuses cannot overrule a few Torah scholars. (Consult Tractate Horayot, Chapter 3, Mishnah 8 where a Mamzer, who is a Sage, precedes a High Priest who is an ignoramus.)

Here is a noteworthy Talmudic passage where this Mitzvah rendered a controversial decision. All the evidence pointed one way, but the majority ruled in the opposite direction.

From the Babylonian Talmud, Bava Metzia 59A-B:

[An oven] that was cut into parts and sand was placed between the parts, Rabbi Eliezer maintained that it is pure (i.e., not susceptible to ritual impurity). The other Sages said that it is susceptible to ritual impurity ...

On that day Rabbi Eliezer brought them all sorts of proofs, but they were rejected. Said he to them: "If the law is as I say, may the carob tree prove it." The carob tree was uprooted from its place a distance of 100 cubits. Others say, 400 cubits. Said they to him: "One cannot prove anything from a carob tree."

Said [Rabbi Eliezer] to them: "If the law is as I say, may the aqueduct prove it." The water in the aqueduct began to flow backwards. Said they to him: "One cannot prove anything from an aqueduct."

Said he to them: "If the law is as I say, may walls of the house of study prove it." The walls of the house of study began to fall in. Rabbi Joshua rebuked them, "If Torah scholars are debating a point of Jewish law, what are your qualifications to intervene?" The walls did not fall, in deference to Rabbi Joshua, nor did they straighten up, in deference to Rabbi Eliezer. They still stand there at a slant.

Said he said to them: “If the law is as I say, may it be proven from heaven!” There then issued a heavenly voice which proclaimed: “What do you want of Rabbi Eliezer—the law is as he says...”

Rabbi Joshua stood on his feet and said: “The Torah is not in heaven!” ... We take no notice of heavenly voices, since You, G-d, have already, at Sinai, written in the Torah to “follow the majority” (Exodus 23:2).

Rabbi Nathan subsequently met Elijah the prophet and asked him: “What did G-d do at that moment?” [Elijah] replied: “He smiled and said: ‘My children have triumphed over Me,’”

79. NOT TO TAKE PITY ON A POOR MAN IN JUDGMENT

neither shalt thou favour a poor man in his cause. (Exodus 23:3)

Mitzvah 79 commands judges not to have extra mercy on a poor person. The judgment must be presided fairly.

This Mitzvah is about taking responsibility. No one may favor a rich person over a poor person and vice versa. There is no favoritism–period.

80. THE MITZVAH OF UNLOADING ANOTHER PERSON’S BURDEN

If thou meet thine enemy’s ox or his ass going astray, thou shalt surely bring it back to him again. If thou see the ass of him that hateth thee lying under its burden, thou shalt forbear to pass by him; thou shalt surely release it with him. (Exodus 23:4-5)

Mitzvah 80 states that if we find another man's animal that is lost or straying, we should return that animal to its owner, even if that owner is our enemy.

The Mitzvah also states that when we see an animal burdened under an excessively heavy load, it is our obligation to help the animal by unloading it. Even if it is our enemy's animal, we are still obligated to help unload the innocent animal to keep it from harm.

This Mitzvah is applicable today because it forces us to help individuals, whom we would prefer to have nothing to do with. Fulfilling this Mitzvah strengthens our realization that we cannot just think about ourselves and our petty grievances with other people. Helping our enemies and helping animals reminds us that Hashem is concerned with the welfare of the entire universe. Our enemies and the animals would not exist if Hashem did not have plans for them.

81. NOT TO PERVERT JUSTICE FOR A SINNER ON ACCOUNT OF HIS WICKEDNESS

You shall not pervert the justice due your poor in his contention. (Exodus 23:6)

Mitzvah 81 commands judges to judge fairly, no matter who the litigantsare.

This Mitzvah states that if someone comes before a judge as a litigant and has a bad reputation, the judge cannot take their reputation into account while presiding over the case. He cannot look at the litigant's past and just assume that he is guilty based only on the litigant's past.

This Mitzvah applies in every place, in every time, and for every person acting as a judge.

82. NOT TO DECIDE A CAPITAL CASE ON PROBABILITY

Keep thee far from a false matter; and the innocent and righteous slay thou not; for I will not justify the wicked. (Exodus 23:7)

Mitzvah 82 tells us to stay away from lies, deception and sin; tells us not to kill or harm the innocent and the righteous; because Hashem will not tolerate sinners.

It also implies that the verdict in capital punishment cases cannot be based on circumstantial evidence alone. There must be at least two specific witnesses who saw the event with their own eyes. Presumption is not allowed. In capital punishment cases, the testimony of the two witnesses must be identical.

83. A JUDGE IS NOT TO TAKE ANY BRIBE

And thou shalt take no gift; for a gift blindeth them that have sight, and perverteth the words of the righteous. (Exodus 23:8)

Mitzvah 83 commands judges NOT to accept bribes because it is their responsibility to judge cases fairly. It is forbidden for a judge to receive any benefit at all from the litigants in cases before him. (Even flattering words about the judge are forbidden.)

84. THE PRECEPT OF SH'MITTAH TO LEAVE THE LAND FALLOW IN THE SEVENTH YEAR

And six years thou shalt sow thy land, and gather in the increase thereof; but the seventh year thou shalt let it rest and lie fallow, that the poor of thy people may eat; and what they leave, the beast of the field shall eat. In like manner thou shalt deal with thy vineyard, and with thy oliveyard. (Exodus 23:10-11)

Mitzvah 84 commands the farmer, the vineyard owner, and the olive grower to plant, harvest and properly care for their land for six consecutive years. In the seventh consecutive year, owners are not only to let the land lie fallow (not plant anything), they are to let any food left after the harvest remain above ground, on the vines and on the trees, so that the poor people may eat it. Anything left uneaten by the poor may be eaten by animals.

This Mitzvah tells us Hashem commands us to leave the Land of Israel fallow in the Sh'mittah Year (seventh year) of the seven-year crop rotation cycle. During that year, no one is permitted to plant, harvest, fertilize, plough, or prune. (Pruning means to cut branches off things that are growing.) Fruits that grow without humans' assistance in the seventh year can be eaten, but they cannot be used for commercial purposes. The fruit on trees, even on someone's lawn, becomes public property in the Sh'mittah Year.

The idea behind this Mitzvah is to trust that Hashem will provide for us. Hashem will take care of the land in the Sh'mittah Year, because He promised that He would. We must have faith that Hashem will provide for us and we must refrain from taking what is not designated for us.

The Sh'mittah Year begins on the First Day of Tishri, the First Day of the Seventh Month–Rosh Hashanah. The Jubilee Year also begins on the First of Tishri.

According to Avot, Chapter Five, Mishnah 12, at four periods of the seven-year crop rotation cycle, pestilence increases: The fourth year, the seventh year, the year following the seventh year, and each year at the conclusion of Sukkot.

Pestilence increases in the fourth year as a result of neglecting to give poor people the tithes due to them in the third year.

Pestilence increases in the seventh year as a result of neglecting to give to the poor the required tithes of the sixth year.

Immediately following the sabbatical year, pestilence increases for violating the laws of the sabbatical produce.

The fourth time pestilence increases is at the end of Sukkot for neglecting to provide for the poor.

Observing the Sh'mittah Year is the ultimate test of having faith in Hashem. Not only are the farmers required to leave their fields and orchards fallow for a year, but also those people who do not earn their living by working the land. They are dependent on the produce of the land, and their faith is also tested by having to leave the land alone.

Failure to observe the Sh'mittah Year indicates a lack of faith and trust in Hashem. Observing the Sh'mittah Year indicates faith in Hashem.

85. THE MITZVAH OF RESTING ON THE SABBATH

Six days thou shalt do thy work, but on the seventh day thou shalt rest; that thine ox and thine ass may have rest, and the son of thy handmaid, and the stranger, may be refreshed. (Exodus 23:12)

Mitzvah 85 commands us to rest on Shabbat. Our servants and our animals must also rest on Shabbat.

86. NOT TO SWEAR BY ANY IDOL

And in all things that I have said unto you take ye heed; and make no mention of the name of other gods, neither let it be heard out of thy mouth. (Exodus 23:13)

Mitzvah 86 states that we are not to swear in the name of idols. Non-Jews are also prohibited from believing in false gods.

The names of false gods are not to be mentioned in passing (i.e. "Wait for me by xxxx statue" is forbidden to say.) The Torah contains 44 different warnings about swearing to and worshipping false gods.

87. NOT TO LEAD ISRAELITES ASTRAY INTO IDOLATRY

And in all things that I have said unto you take ye heed; and make no mention of the name of other gods, neither let it be heard out of thy mouth. (Exodus 23:13)

Mitzvah 87 is the prohibition against trying to get other Jews to worship false gods.

It prohibits a Jew, a Jew who converted to another religion, or a non-Jew from calling other Jews to idol-worship, or trying to convert other Jews to idol-worship, or make other Jews lose faith in Hashem and stray from Hashem's path.

This mitzvah is in force in every place, at every time, for both men and women.

88. THE PRECEPT OF CELEBRATION ON THE PILGRIMAGE FESTIVALS

Three times thou shalt keep a feast unto Me in the year. (Exodus 23:14)

Mitzvah 88 requires us to make pilgrimages to Jerusalem on Sukkot, Passover, and Shavuot. One can make the pilgrimage to Jerusalem for these three Hagim (holidays), either on foot or by using transportation. However, the person must enter the Temple Mount on foot.

This Mitzvah concentrates on the journeys. Just appearing in Jerusalem on these three holidays is part of the act of fulfilling Mitzvah 88, but you must bring an offering in order to complete the Mitzvah.

We are required to show Simcha (happiness and joy) as we fulfill this Mitzvah because we are honoring Hashem. Bringing the offerings is a way for us to establish a strong relationship with Hashem. Going into Jerusalem and being in the Temple is the closest we can come to Hashem on earth. Blind people are exempt from fulfilling this Mitzvah.

Rabbi Alpert explained to me that although this Mitzvah is not applicable today because of the absence of the Temple, we are reminded of it, and our ancestors' pilgrimages to Jerusalem, by putting an egg on our Seder plates, which refers to the special sacrifices of the Hagim.

For more information, consult the Mishnah tractate, Hagigah.

89. NOT TO RITUALLY SLAY THE PASSOVER OFFERING ON THE EVE OF PASSOVER WHILE THERE IS YET HAMETZ IN OUR POSSESSION

The feast of unleavened bread shalt thou keep; seven days thou shalt eat unleavened bread, as I commanded thee, at the time appointed in the month Abib—for in it thou camest out from Egypt; and none shall appear before Me empty; (Exodus 23:15)

Mitzvah 89 prohibits us from slaughtering the Passover sacrifice while we still have Hametz in our possession.

Six hours before Passover (at midday), Hametz must be gone. Five hours before Passover is when we can slaughter animals for the holiday. We wait one hour in order for us to experience the transition. It's vital that the Hametz and Passover offering do not co-mingle.

90. NOT TO LET THE 'EMURIM OF THE PASSOVER OFFERING REMAIN OVERNIGHT AND THUS BECOME IMPERMISSIBLE

('Emurim are the sacrificial portions.)

Thou shalt not offer the blood of My sacrifice with leavened bread; neither shall the fat of My feast remain all night until the morning. (Exodus 23:18)

Mitzvah 90 states that no parts of the Passover sacrifice shall (be leftover) remain overnight to be burned the next day. Jews burn the remainder of the food that was a sacrificed animal if you don't eat it all the day it was sacrificed.

Jews are forbidden to start a new fire. Jews are forbidden from striking a match to light a new fire. However, you can transfer a flame from an existing fire to the wood, sticks and kindling you had set up the day before strictly for the purpose of burning the remains of the sacrificed animal.

91. THE PRECEPT OF BRINGING FIRST-FRUITS TO THE HOLY TEMPLE

The choicest first-fruits of thy land thou shalt bring into the house of the LORD thy God. Thou shalt not seethe a kid in its mother's milk. (Exodus 23:19)

Mitzvah 91 commands us to bring our Bikkurim (first fruits) to Jerusalem, and give them to the priests at the Temple.

Seven fruits grow in Israel that can be used to fulfill this Mitzvah. The seven fruits are wheat, barley, grapes, figs, pomegranates, olives and dates. Because Hashem blessed Israel with these seven fruits, giving the first ripe fruit of the season to the priests is one way of thanking Hashem.

We recognize that our crops and everything else comes from Hashem. This Mitzvah tells us to be happy as we offer our first fruits to the priests because we are serving Hashem.

The Children of Israel performed this Mitzvah on Shavuot, which is the Sixth Day of Sivan, and that can be either in May or June. At the time of the First and Second Temples, the Children of Israel were required to make a pilgrimage to Jerusalem on Shavuot to offer their first fruits to the priests.

When the time came to bring the first fruits to Jerusalem, the people from one area would gather in a set location and travel together as one group. The rich people would bring their fruits in fancy and expensive baskets. The poor people used more modest ones. An ox led the way. The ox's horns were decorated with gold and a special wreath was placed on its head. They would have a musical accompaniment. As the group neared Jerusalem, they would send word ahead and important people from Jerusalem would come out to greet them. The travelers then formed a procession to the Temple. When they arrived at the Temple, each person would take their basket of fruit, bring it inside, and recite the special passages that the Torah required. When the ceremony was completed, the people would give their baskets of fruit to the priests. (See Chapter 3, Tractate Bikkurim.)

The Torah gives a detailed description of the duties, actions and prayers the Jews were to perform:

And it shall be, when thou art come in unto the land which the LORD thy God giveth thee for an inheritance, and dost possess it, and dwell therein; that thou shalt take of the first of all the fruit of the ground, which thou shalt bring in from thy land that the LORD thy God giveth thee; and thou shalt put it in a basket and shalt go unto the place which the LORD thy God shall choose to cause His name to dwell there. And thou shalt come unto the priest that shall be in those days, and say unto him: 'I profess this day unto the LORD thy God, that I am come unto the land which the LORD swore unto our fathers to give us.' And the priest shall take the basket out of thy hand, and set it down before the altar of the LORD

thy God. And thou shalt speak and say before the LORD thy God: 'A wandering Aramean was my father, and he went down into Egypt, and sojourned there, few in number; and he became there a nation, great, mighty, and populous. And the Egyptians dealt ill with us, and afflicted us, and laid upon us hard bondage. And we cried unto the LORD, the God of our fathers, and the LORD heard our voice, and saw our affliction, and our toil, and our oppression. And the LORD brought us forth out of Egypt with a mighty hand, and with an outstretched arm, and with great terribleness, and with signs, and with wonders. And He hath brought us into this place, and hath given us this land, a land flowing with milk and honey. And now, behold, I have brought the first of the fruit of the land, which Thou, O LORD, hast given me.' And thou shalt set it down before the LORD thy God, and worship before the LORD thy God. And thou shalt rejoice in all the good which the LORD thy God hath given unto thee, and unto thy house, thou, and the Levite, and the stranger that is in the midst of thee. (Deuteronomy 26:1-11)

92. NOT TO COOK MEAT IN MILK

The choicest first-fruits of thy land thou shalt bring into the house of the LORD thy God. Thou shalt not seethe a kid in its mother's milk. (Exodus 23:19)

(The prohibition against cooking a kid in its mother's milk appear two other times in the Torah: Exodus 34:26 and Deuteronomy 14:21. This is also discussed in Tractate: Chapter 8, Mishnah 1.)

Mitzvah 92 prohibits us from cooking meat products and milk products together. A standard explanation for separating these two food groups is that we are not to boil a lamb in the milk of its mother. This also applies to cooking any other type of animal in the milk of its mother.

My Partner in Torah told me that on a metaphysical level, we separate milk and meat because they have opposite representations. Milk represents life. For a baby animal or for a human baby to survive, they drink milk. Meat represents death. The meat we eat used to be a living animal. Life and death are opposite forces and are kept apart.

The Rabbis extended this Mitzvah to include not drinking milk with chicken. Why? Chickens do not give milk, so there is no risk of boiling a chicken in its mother's milk. One answer is that well-intentioned Jews could confuse chicken with other types of white meat, and could accidentally break the milk-meat law by mistakenly thinking they were eating chicken, when they were eating the flesh of an animal that gave milk (like pork). To avoid making this mistake, Jews refrain from mixing chicken with milk. (See Mishnah Hullin, Tracate: Chapter 8, Mishnah 4.)

Why can we eat fish and milk together? First and foremost, we would be unlikely to confuse fish with the other animals mentioned above. Fish do not drink milk from their mothers. In addition, fish are not sacrificed to Hashem. Milk is not the life force for fish as it is for animals that we slaughter and then eat.

93. TO MAKE NO TREATY WITH THE SEVEN NATIONS TO BE EXTIRPATED, OR WITH ANY IDOL WORSHIPPER

For Mine angel shall go before thee, and bring thee in unto the Amorite, and the Hittite, and the Perizzite, and the Canaanite, the Hivite, and the Jebusite; and I will cut them

off. Thou shalt not bow down to their gods, nor serve them, nor do after their doings; but thou shalt utterly overthrow them, and break in pieces their pillars. (Exodus 23:23-24)

Mitzvah 93 forbade the Children of Israel to enter peace treaties with seven specific nations that occupied the Land of Canaan because they worshipped idols. These idol worshipping nations were the Hittites, the Girgashites, the Amorites, the Canaanites, the Perizzites, the Hivites, and the Jebusites who occupied the Land of Canaan before the Israelites got there.

The idol-worshipping people of those seven nations, and all of their temples and idols, had to be destroyed to ensure that no idol worship took place in the Land of Israel.

If one of these nations gave up idol worship, then the Children of Israel were to leave that specific nation in peace.

94. NOT TO SETTLE ANY IDOL-WORSHIPPER IN OUR LAND

They shall not dwell in thy land—lest they make thee sin against Me, for thou wilt serve their gods—for they will be a snare unto thee. (Exodus 23:33)

Mitzvah 94 prohibits idol-worshippers from living in the Land of Israel. No homes or land can be sold or rented to idol-worshippers at any time.

The Children of Israel must not learn from the idol-worshippers' heresy.

95. THE PRECEPT OF BUILDING THE HOLY TEMPLE

And let them make Me a sanctuary, that I may dwell among them. (Exodus 25:8)

Mitzvah 95 commands Jews to build the Holy Temple and all the vessels and objects needed for the Divine services. The Temple was a special structure, where Hashem made His presence felt. Our ancestors built the Temple in order to bring Hashem sacrifices and as a holy place to worship him.

Even though the Third Temple is not under construction, we are not violating this Mitzvah because it can only be fulfilled when the majority of the Jewish people live in Israel. According to Rabbi Alpert, we are reaching a point where most Jews do live in Israel.

96. NOT TO REMOVE THE STAVES OF THE ARK FROM IT

The staves shall be in the rings of the ark; they shall not be taken from it. (Exodus 25:15)

Mitzvah 96 tells us not to remove the two poles from the rings on the Ark of the Covenant because they are carried on the shoulders and used to transport the Ark. See Numbers, Chapter 7, Verse 9. (The ark possibly disappeared after the destruction of the First Temple.) The ark represents holiness because the two tablets of the Torah were kept inside it. Having the poles with the ark indicates that we are ready to move the ark again, on short notice, if we have to do so.

97. THE PRECEPT OF ARRANGING THE SHEWBREAD AND THE FRANKINCENSE

And thou shalt set upon the table shewbread before Me always. (Exodus 25:30)

Mitzvah 97 commands us to have shewbread in the Temple at all times. One vessel in the Temple was a table, where bread was always placed.

The shewbread brings about the blessings for the nation of Israel.

The Talmud states that the priest receives a quarter size piece of bread. One small bite could satiate anyone.

98. THE PRECEPT OF KINDLING THE MENORAH IN THE SANCTUARY

In the tent of meeting, without the veil which is before the testimony, Aaron and his sons shall set it in order, to burn from evening to morning before the LORD; it shall be a statute for ever throughout their generations on the behalf of the children of Israel. (Exodus 27:21)

Mitzvah 98 commands that the Menorah inside the Temple remain lit at all times. The purpose is to magnify the glory and splendor of Hashem's Temple. The lighted Menorah infuses one's heart with reverence and awe for Hashem.

The first people to perform this Mitzvah were Aaron and his sons. Hashem instructed them to arrange the lamps/candles in the Tent of Meeting. The perpetual light was to be in front of the ark, hanging down. Aaron and his sons took out the burnt up oil, then replaced it with new oil to be lighted. It was an ongoing process.

For more information, see Numbers 8:1-3.

99. THE PRECEPT THAT THE KOHANIM SHOULD WEAR THEIR SPECIAL GARMENTS

And these are the garments which they shall make: a breastplate, and an ephod, and a robe, and a tunic of chequer work, a mitre, and a girdle; and they shall make holy garments for Aaron thy brother, and his sons, that he may minister unto Me in the priest's office. (Exodus 28:4)

Mitzvah 99 commands the priests to wear special garments in the Temple: special pants, a special tunic (long shirt), a special belt, and a special hat. The clothing was made from linen, and the belt was made out of wool. These garments were used for the Temple. No one could wear them if they were not serving in the Temple. They could go home wearing the garments, but they had to take the belt off.

The High Priest wore an apron that looked backwards. It had different colors. The front of the straps hung down in the front, with the breastplate attached. The straps held the breastplate in the front. The breastplate had an array of 12 stones on it, representing each tribe of Israel. The High Priest had a strap he wore over his hat containing a golden bar, which had Hashem's name on it.

Aaron was the High Priest and the direct sons of Aaron were the priests. Upon Aaron's death, his son Elazar became the High Priest. If the priests conducted a component of the service without wearing the required clothing, the service would automatically be invalidated.

Although it is forbidden to wear wool and linen together, the priests can while performing their duties inside the Temple; but outside the Temple, they cannot wear the two together. The positive commandment of wearing the priestly garments (during the service) overrides the negative commandment of wearing wool and linen together. The positive Mitzvot take precedence over the negative ones.

I discuss Shatnez (the prohibition of mixing wool with linen) in greater detail in Mitzvah 551.

100. THE BREASTPLATE SHOULD NOT COME LOOSE FROM THE EPHOD WORN BY THE KOHEN GADOL

And they shall bind the breastplate by the rings thereof unto the rings of the ephod with a thread of blue, that it may be upon the skillfully woven band of the ephod, and that the breastplate be not loosed from the ephod. (Exodus 28:28)

(The Ephod was like a backward apron that had straps that came from the wearer's back over his shoulders to the front. The ends of those straps were attached to the top of the breastplate.) (Kohen Gadol means High Priest.)

Mitzvah 100 commands that the breastplate not be removed from the apron. The ribbons and straps went through rings, which kept them attached and prevented them from bouncing around. Hashem designed these garments. Refusing to wear them shows a lack of completeness.

101. NOT TO TEAR THE ME'IL OF THE KOHANIM

(This means that no one is to tear the priests' robes.)

And it shall have a hole for the head in the midst thereof; it shall have a binding of woven work round about the hole of it, as it were the hole of a coat of mail that it be not rent. (Exodus 28:32)

Mitzvah 101 states that the priests' over cloaks cannot be torn, ripped or cut. The punishment for these infractions is a whipping.

102. THE PRECEPT TO EAT THE FLESH OF THE HATTATH AND THE ASHAM

(Hattath is the sin-offering and Asham is the guilt-offering.)

And they shall eat those things wherewith atonement was made, to consecrate and to sanctify them; but a stranger shall not eat thereof, because they are holy. (Exodus 29:33)

Mitzvah 102 requires the priests to eat a portion of the sacrificed animal used for the guilt-offering and the sin-offering to consecrate it and make it holy.

Eating a portion of the sacrifice displays honor. This food is for the priests to eat inside the Temple because it is holy. Nobody can give this food away, nor can one sell it at the market or wrap it up to take home.

The difference between the sin-offering and the guilt-offering is as follows:

A sin-offering is when someone violates a Mitzvah by mistake. The culprit knows what he did and is making atonement.

A guilt-offering is performed when the guilty party is not sure if he or she violated a Mitzvah by mistake or not. The guilt-offering presents a level of doubt because the culprit is uncertain whether the Mitzvah was violated.

103. THE PRECEPT OF BURNING INCENSE

And Aaron shall burn thereon incense of sweet spices; every morning, when he dresseth the lamps, he shall burn it. (Exodus 30:7)

Mitzvah 103 commanded Aaron, his four sons, and future priests to perform the service of burning incense. The incense was a mixture of herbs and spices. The priests brought this mixture and placed it on the small Golden Altar, not the larger one because that one had the sacrifices. The spice mixture was placed on coals resulting in a plume of an aromatic smell. By creating this pervasive aroma, it attracted Jews to the Temple.

The batch of incense would last the whole year. Every morning, the High Priest would take out the proper amount needed for the day and split it into two parts. The priest used part of it for the morning service and the remainder for the late afternoon service.

104. NOT TO BURN OR OFFER UP ANYTHING ON THE GOLDEN ALTAR

Ye shall offer no strange incense thereon, nor burnt-offering, nor meal-offering; and ye shall pour no drink-offering thereon. (Exodus 30:9)

Mitzvah 104 is a prohibition against bringing sacrifices to the Golden Altar because that is where the incense is placed. Sprinkling of the Yom Kippur sacrifices is allowed on the Altar, but NOT the sacrificed animal. This Mitzvah is applicable when the Temple exists.

105. THE PRECEPT OF GIVING HALF A SHEKEL EACH YEAR

In Exodus 30:11-12 below Hashem instructs Moses to take a census of all the Jews.

And the LORD spoke unto Moses, saying: 'When thou takest the sum of the children of Israel, according to their number, then shall they give every man a ransom for his soul unto the LORD, when thou numberest them; that there be no plague among them, when thou numberest them. (Exodus 30:11-12)

Mitzvah 105 uses the information derived from that census as follows:

This they shall give, every one that passeth among them that are numbered, half a shekel after the shekel of the sanctuary—the shekel is twenty gerahs—half a shekel for an offering to the LORD. Every one that passeth among them that are numbered, from twenty years old and upward, shall give the offering of the LORD. The rich shall not give more, and the poor shall not give less, than the half shekel, when they give the offering of the LORD, to make atonement for your souls. And thou shalt take the atonement money from the children of Israel, and shalt appoint it for the service of the tent of meeting, that it may be a memorial for the children of Israel before the LORD, to make atonement for your souls. (Exodus 30:13-16)

Mitzvah 105 requires every male Jew, age 20 and up, to give half a shekel each year to the Temple. This money pays for sacrifices, wine, oil, wood for the Altar and shewbread. Everyone is equal before Hashem. When it comes to matters of the Temple, everyone's share must be equal. Therefore, a wealthy man is prohibited from giving more than half a shekel and a poor man is prohibited from donating less than half a shekel. This means each person contributes equally to all the sacrifices performed.

All men must bring a half shekel for the current year, beginning the First Day of Adar, but it is not required to be brought that day. My Partner in Torah told me that they have from the First of Adar to the First of Nisan to fulfill this Mitzvah. My Partner in Torah told me that collected half shekels were used to purchase animals that would be sacrificed. We found this information in the Second Book of the Talmudic Encyclopedia.

This is an important Mitzvah because it is part of the Torah Parsha, Ki Tissa, (for thou shalt lift up), and we read Exodus Chapter 30 verses 11-16, (cited above) either on the Shabbat before the First of Adar, or on the First of Adar if it falls on Shabbat. It is read as the Maftir portion. (The Maftir is when the person reads the final portion of the Torah for that Shabbat service. Quite often, the "Maftir" reader will then read the Haftarah.)

It is no coincidence that this Parsha (Torah portion) falls near the time when all the male Jews, 20 and older, had to donate half a shekel. Neither is it a coincidence that the next week we read about how Amalek attacked us in the wilderness. Fulfilling the Mitzvah of contributing half a shekel pleased Hashem enough for Him to help us defeat Amalek's evil descendant, Haman. In Esther, Chapter 3 verse 9, Haman offered ten thousand talents of silver for the extermination of the Jews.

The merit the Jews gained in having performed this Mitzvah, which Hashem gave them in advance of Haman's attempt, helped them to foil Haman's evil intentions.

(For more information about the "Parsha" of Amalek following on the heels of the Mitzvah of the half shekel, consult Book of Our Heritage by Eliyahu Kitov.)

We read portions of "Parsha," "Ki Tissa," on fast days because one of the themes of this Torah section is atonement.

Fast days remind us to show compassion for poor people. Ta'anit means fast in Hebrew. If you switch around the Hebrew letters that spell it, you get the Hebrew word, Tat ani, which means give to a poor person. On all fast days except Yom Kippur, we should give food and/or money to poor people. We give to the poor the day before Yom Kippur because on the Day of Atonement, no transference of ownership takes place.

When my Partner in Torah and I studied this Mitzvah, we discussed why a half shekel was required instead of a full shekel:

According to the Jerusalem Talmud, the actual duration of the sin of the Golden Calf lasted half a day, from afternoon to evening. Therefore, half a shekel is required instead of a full one.

In Book of Our Heritage, Eliyahu Kitov explains that the half shekel signifies that our service to Hashem is never complete. We must always strive to increase our level of observance to Hashem. We can always improve our relationship with Him. In spiritual matters, there is no such idea of standing still. The Tractate Shekalim, Chapter 1, Mishnah 1, deals with the importance of this Mitzvah; to prepare the roads and Mikvaot, and to point out the location of cemeteries in preparation for Passover.

The Torah Parsha, Ki Tissa, also describes the sin of the Golden Calf. Women are exempt from this Mitzvah because it is their reward for refusing to participate in the sin of the Golden

Calf. Another reward is that Rosh Chodesh is a special day for them. For more information, go to http://www.jewishvirtuallibrary.org/jsource/Judaism/Rosh_Chodesh.html

This Mitzvah is enforced when the Temple exists.

Rabbi Yehdua Shurpin explained that a custom used today is based on this Mitzvah: "Since the Second Temple's destruction, through today, there is no biblical obligation to give a half shekel. However, there is a widespread custom that in commemoration of the half shekel, we give on the Fast of Esther a half of the standard currency of that particular country." For more info, consult: MachatzitHaShekelhttp://www.chabad.org/library/article_cdo/aid/260799/

106. THE PRECEPT OF RINSING HANDS AND FEET WHEN MINISTERING AT THE SANCTURARY

And Aaron and his sons shall wash their hands and their feet thereat; when they go into the tent of meeting, they shall wash with water, that they die not; or when they come near to the altar to minister, to cause an offering made by fire to smoke unto the LORD; (Exodus 30:19-20)

Mitzvah 106 commanded the priests to wash their hands and feet before entering the Temple because it was a way to honor its holiness and purity. Washing the dirt and dust off feet and hands showed humility and respect for the Lord's presence in the Temple.

107. THE PRECEPT OF ANOINTING OIL FOR EACH KOHEN GADOL AND KING

And thou shalt make it a holy anointing oil, a perfume compounded after the art of the perfumer; it shall be a holy anointing oil. (Exodus 30:25)

Mitzvah 107 commands us to anoint the High Priest and the Kings of Israel with holy oil. This oil was used from the time that the Tabernacle was built. (My Partner in Torah told me that this particular oil contained cinnamon.)

108. THAT AN OUTSIDER SHOULD NOT HAVE ANOINTING OIL APPLIED TO HIMSELF

Upon the flesh of man shall it not be poured, neither shall ye make any like it, according to the composition thereof;it is holy, and it shall be holy unto you.Whosoever compoundeth any like it, orwhosoever putteth any of it upon a stranger, he shall be cut off from his people.' (Exodus 30:32-33)

Mitzvah 108 is a prohibition for anyone, other than the High Priests and Kings of Israel, to use that special holy anointing oil. That oil was reserved exclusively for the High Priests and Kings of Israel. Violators of this Mitzvah received a spiritual death by being cut off from the Children of Israel.

109. NOT TO MAKE ANOINTING OIL ACCORDING TO THE SCRIPTURAL FORMULA

Upon the flesh of man shall it not be poured, neither shall ye make any like it, according to the composition thereof; it is holy, and it shall be holy unto you. Whosoever compoundeth any like it, or whosoever putteth any of it upon a stranger, he shall be cut off from his people.' (Exodus 30:32 Exodus 30:33)

Mitzvah 109 is the prohibition against creating any more of that special holy oil that was reserved for the High Priests and Kings of Israel. Moses created the original mixture, and that was supposed to last throughout the ages.

110. THE PROHIBITION AGAINST MAKING INCENSE ACCORDING TO THE TORAH'S FORMULA

And the incense which thou shalt make, according to the composition thereof ye shall not make for yourselves; it shall be unto thee holy for the LORD. Whosoever shall make like unto that, to smell thereof, he shall be cut off from his people.' (Exodus 30:3-38)

Mitzvah 110 is the prohibition against making a duplicate of the incense used in the Temple. Violators of this Mitzvah received a spiritual death. They were cut off from the Children of Israel.

111. THE BAN ON EATING OR DRINKING ANYTHING FROM AN OFFERING TO AN IDOL

Take heed to thyself, lest thou make a covenant with the inhabitants of the land whither thou goest, lest they be for a snare in the midst of thee. But ye shall break down their altars, and dash in pieces their pillars, and ye shall cut down their Asherim. For thou shalt bow down to no other god; for the LORD, whose name is Jealous, is a jealous God; lest thou make a covenant with the inhabitants of the land, and they go astray after their gods, and do sacrifice unto their gods, and they call thee, <u>and thou eat of their sacrifice</u>; (Exodus 34:12 Exodus 34:13 Exodus 34:14-15)

Mitzvah 111 forbids us to partake in eating or drinking of anything that was used in idol worship. These boundaries help prevent us from worshipping idols.

For example, if a non-Jew touches wine, we are not to drink from it because that person has great potential to worship idols. We need to distance ourselves from idol worshippers and fulfilling this Mitzvah helps us achieve that.

112. THE PRECEPT OF LETTING THE LAND LIE FALLOW IN THE YEAR OF THE SH'MITTAH

...in plowing time and in harvest thou shalt rest. (Exodus 34:21)

Mitzvah 112 commands us not to work the Land of Israel in the 7th year. I discussed this in my write-up of Mitzvah 84.

113. THE PROHIBITION ON MEAT WITH MILK

Thou shalt not seethe a kid in its mother's milk. (Exodus 23:19)

Mitzvah 113 prohibits us from deriving benefit of eating meat and milk together. Consult my write-up of Mitzvah 92 for more information.

114. THAT THE COURT SHOULD NOT CARRY OUT ANY EXECUTION ON THE SABBATH

Ye shall kindle no fire throughout your habitations upon the sabbath day. (Exodus 35:3)

Mitzvah 114 forbids the Rabbinical Court from carrying out death sentences on Shabbat.

If someone were sentenced to death by being forced to drink molten liquid, the sentence cannot be carried out on Shabbat because we are forbidden to light a spark or kindle a fire to heat the liquid.

The courts never had to deal with this problem because killing on Shabbat was and is still forbidden.

Traditionally, the seventh day of Sukkot, Hoshanah Rabbah (the Final Day of Hashem's Divine Judgment for the new year) was the day that court-ordered executions were carried out.

Complex scheduling is required to place Shabbat on the Jewish calendar so that it does not fall on Hoshanah Rabbah and does not negatively affect the other religious holidays.

The perpetual Jewish calendar was set up so that the seventh day of Sukkot, Hoshanah Rabbah (the Final Day of Hashem's Divine Judgment for the new year) would never fall on Shabbat.

To keep that from happening, Rosh Hashanah can only have the two-day combinations of Monday/Tuesday, Tuesday/Wednesday, Thursday/Friday, and Saturday/Sunday. This practice is called Lo Adu Rosh, meaning that Rosh Hashanah cannot begin on a Sunday, Wednesday, or Friday.

The custom of Lo B'du Pesach means that the First Day of Passover cannot begin on Monday, Wednesday, or Friday because it changes which day of the week Rosh Hashanah falls on.

If Hoshanah Rabbah would fall on a Saturday, the performance of that day's customs such as use of the Lulav and Etrog, and the processions would be prohibited.

If Rosh Hashanah were to start on a Wednesday or a Friday, Yom Kippur would fall on Friday or Sunday, adjacent to Shabbat. This is unacceptable because we would be prohibited from preparing food for 48 consecutive hours. Cooking is allowed on Rosh Hashanah and the other major holidays, but not on Yom Kippur.

According to Rabbi Alpert, we do have situations where the dead cannot be buried for 48 hours.

Mitzvot from Leviticus

115. THE PRECEPT OF THE SACRIFICE OF THE OLAH

(Olah means burnt offering.)

If his offering be a burnt-offering of the herd, he shall offer it a male without blemish; he shall bring it to the door of the tent of meeting, that he may be accepted before the LORD. (Leviticus 1:3)

Mitzvah 115 instructs a Jewish man to pick a male sheep or ox without any blemishes for his burnt-offering to Hashem and bring it to the Door of the Temple.

By extension, Mitzvah 115 details the process of how the priests were to sacrifice the animal for the burnt offering at the Tent of Meeting (later at the Holy Temple).

This mitzvah is performed when the Temple exists.

116. THE PRECEPT OF THE MINHAH OFFERING

(A Minhah is an offering from the species of flour.)

And when any one bringeth a meal-offering unto the LORD, his offering shall be of fine flour; and he shall pour oil

upon it, and put frankincense thereon. And he shall bring it to Aaron's sons the priests; and he shall take thereout his handful of the fine flour thereof, and of the oil thereof, together with all the frankincense thereof; and the priest shall make the memorial-part thereof smoke upon the altar, an offering made by fire, of a sweet savour unto the LORD. (Leviticus 2:1-2)

(Aaron's four sons were Nadav, Avihu, Ela'azar & Itamar. Nadav and Avihu were killed because they drew near before Hashem and by offering Him a foreign fire that they were not commanded to bring. See Leviticus, Chapter 10, Verse 1, and following for more details.)

Mitzvah 116 pertains to the flour offering.

There are a number of instances when an individual brings flour to be used as an offering. (The priests' action of burning the flour is part of the process of fulfilling this obligation.) An animal is supposed to be used for a sin-offering, but if the person does not own an animal, then he brings flour to be used for the sin-offering. One case in point: When a wife is having an extramarital affair and her husband suspects, she is brought before the priests, and she must provide flour for the sin-offering.

The brand new priest uses flour as an offering on his first day of working in the Temple. He is required to provide this offering his first day on the job. A High Priest must bring flour every day to be used for offerings.

117. THE PROHIBITION AGAINST OFFERING UP LEAVEN OR HONEY

No meal-offering, which ye shall bring unto the LORD, shall be made with leaven; for ye shall make no leaven, nor any

honey, smoke as an offering made by fire unto the LORD. (Leviticus 2:11)

Mitzvah 117 forbids honey and leavening agents to be placed on the Altar for sacrifice. The Torah uses the term honey, but literally it's a generic term for fruit juice. My Partner in Torah explained to me that one of the concepts behind the sacrifices is that we should envision them being the substitute for ourselves. We should imagine ourselves being brought before Hashem. By prohibiting the sacrifice of leavened foods, it creates efficiency. When our ancestors left Egypt, they did not procrastinate. That was why they used unleavened bread. As stated earlier in this text, leavened bread on Passover is Hametz, and Hametz is the Hebrew word for procrastination.

Mitzvah 117 teaches us not to go after what our tongues and stomachs desire, such as sweet foods. This can lead to us making that task more important than it deserves to be. It can lead to impulsiveness. If we only try to get sweet tasting foods, we can become too much the epicure. Prohibiting sweet stuff on the Altar teaches us not to gorge. It also encourages us to eat healthy foods. Doing this allows us to better serve Hashem.

118. NOT TO OFFER UP ANY SACRIFICE WITHOUT SALT

And every meal-offering of thine shalt thou season with salt; neither shalt thou suffer the salt of the covenant of thy God to be lacking from thy meal-offering; with all thy offerings thou shalt offer salt. (Leviticus 2:13)

Mitzvah 118 states that we cannot provide any offerings to Hashem without salt.

Salt prevents foods from rotting. Salt also enhances the taste of food. The salt represents completeness.

119. THE PRECEPT OF SALTING ALL OFFERINGS

And every meal-offering of thine shalt thou season with salt; neither shalt thou suffer the salt of the covenant of thy God to be lacking from thy meal-offering; with all thy offerings thou shalt offer salt. (Leviticus 2:13)

Mitzvah 119 states that offerings to Hashem must be salted. As stated in Mitzvah 118, salt provides taste, and for that reason salt is required on offerings that are presented to Hashem. The salt prevents food from becoming moldy. Just like salt protects whatever you put it on, salting the food that we sacrifice to Hashem, would in turn, strengthen Hashem's resolve to protect us. We salt bread before a meal for the same reason.

The home is (the Mikdash M'at) the small sanctuary.

120. THE OFFERING OF THE HIGH COURT IF IT ERRED IN A RULING

And if the whole congregation of Israel shall err, the thing being hid from the eyes of the assembly, and do any of the things which the LORD hath commanded not to be done, and are guilty: when the sin wherein they have sinned is known, then the assembly shall offer a young bullock for a sin-offering, and bring it before the tent of meeting. (Leviticus 4:13-14)

Mitzvah 120 states that if the Sanhedrin makes an error in ruling a case which leads to people acting incorrectly as a result, then the Sanhedrin must provide a sacrifice in order to be forgiven. This Mitzvah illustrates that even members of the

Sanhedrin can make grave errors, and like everyone else, they must rectify their wrong doings.

Sometimes today's leaders forget that they are not above the law. Mitzvah 120 reminds us that no one is.

(Consult Tractate Horayot, Chapter 1 for more information.)

121. THE PRECEPT OF A HATTATH FOR CERTAIN UNINTENTIONAL SINNERS

(Hattath means a sin-offering.)

And if any one of the common people sin through error, in doing any of the things which the LORD hath commanded not to be done, and be guilty: if his sin, which he hath sinned, be known to him, then he shall bring for his offering a goat, a female without blemish, for his sin which he hath sinned. And he shall lay his hand upon the head of the sin-offering, and kill the sin-offering in the place of burnt-offering. (Leviticus 4:27-29)

Mitzvah 121 states that when an individual makes an error where the punishment would be spiritual death, he must provide a sin offering as his way of atoning.

122. THE OBLIGATION TO BEAR WITNESS IN COURT

And if any one sin, in that he heareth the voice of adjuration, he being a witness, whether he hath seen or known, if he do not utter it, then he shall bear his iniquity; (Leviticus 5:1)

Mitzvah 122 commands us to provide testimony if we are called to do so. It is our obligation to state what we know about a case. Regarding regular court cases, such as those that involve money, we are not obligated to testify, unless we are subpoenaed. However, if it is a murder case, we have to testify, even if no one knows that we have knowledge of the matter. Whether it is a murder case or not, Testimony must be first-hand, it cannot be circumstantial.

123. THE PRECEPT OF THE OFFERING OF GREATER OR LESSER VALUE

And if any one sin, in that he heareth the voice of adjuration, he being a witness, whether he hath seen or known, if he do not utter it, then he shall bear his iniquity; (Leviticus 5:1)

Mitzvah 123 states that what the person brings to be sacrificed depends on how much money he has.

Common reasons for sin-offerings included actions such as: he had been impure and went into the Temple, or he ate from the wrong meat. When he was impure, he could not eat sacrificial meat. To atone for his sin, a person brought a sacrifice.

If the sinner was a wealthy man, he provided an animal to be sacrificed. A sinner who was a poor man provided a bird as a sin-offering. And if he no money to provide a bird offering, he brought flour instead.

If a person's status changed, and he went from poor to wealthy, he would need to bring an animal instead of flour.

124. NOT TO SEPARATE THE HEAD OF A BIRD BROUGHT AS A HATTATH

And if his means suffice not for a lamb, then he shall bring his forfeit for that wherein he hath sinned, two turtle-doves,

or two young pigeons, unto the LORD: one for a sin-offering, and the other for a burnt-offering. And he shall bring them unto the priest, who shall offer that which is for the sin-offering first, and pinch off its head close by its neck, but shall not divide it asunder. (Leviticus 5:7-8)

Mitzvah 124 commands that the priests who use a bird as sin-offerings cannot separate its head from the rest of its body. When a bird offering is brought, the priest does not slaughter it, he just snaps its neck. Because poor people were the only individuals who brought birds to be sacrificed, the priests were required to show compassion. Doing ritual slaughter was time consuming. For example, the priests had to make sure that the knives that they used were clean. Not using a knife to kill the birds, not performing the ritual slaughter, allowed the poor person more time to continue to either work or to find work. The poor individual did not have to remain at the Temple as long as a rich person who provided the priest with animals to sacrifice. This also spared the poor person embarrassment. People knew that only poor persons offered birds. By reducing the time that the poor person needed to be present spared him humiliation because fewer people would see that he was poor and unable to offer an animal.

Another reason the bird's head was not removed was to spare the poor person additional trouble and embarrassment. Decapitating the bird was an ugly sight, so by merely snapping its neck kept the poor person from having to see something gruesome.

Mitzvah 124 is about showing compassion for poor people. For more information, consult the write-up of Mitzvah 124 in Sefer HaHinnuch.

125. NOT TO PUT OLIVE OIL IN AN UNINTENTIONAL SINNER'S MEAL-OFFERING

But if his means suffice not for two turtledoves, or two young pigeons, then he shall bring his offering for that wherein he hath sinned, the tenth part of an ephah of fine flour for a sin-offering; he shall put no oil upon it, neither shall he put any frankincense thereon; for it is a sin-offering. (Leviticus 5:11)

Mitzvah 125 states that when a poor person provides flour to be used as a sin-offering, the priest is not to add oil to it. Should the priest add oil, he would receive lashes. Wealthy people provided the priests with animals to be sacrificed. Individuals with modest means offered birds, but the impoverished people offered flour, which would be used as meal offerings. Oil was a sign of richness, completeness and greatness. One reason that the priests were forbidden to add oil to the poor person's flour was that it spared the impoverished sinner the hardship of buying oil. Not everyone could afford oil. Everyone, even the poor people, could afford flour.

Mitzvah 125 teaches us to show compassion for individuals with pecuniary means.

126. TO PUT NO FRANKINCENSE IN AN UNINTENTIONAL SINNER'S MEAL-OFFERING

But if his means suffice not for two turtledoves, or two young pigeons, then he shall bring his offering for that wherein he hath sinned, the tenth part of an ephah of fine flour for a sin-offering; he shall put no oil upon it, neither shall he put any frankincense thereon; for it is a sin-offering. (Leviticus 5:11)

Mitzvah 126 prohibits the priests from adding spices to poor sinners' flour offerings. The spices are luxury items that impoverished individuals do not possess. The prohibition in Mitzvah 126, as in Mitzvah 125, comes down to showing compassion for poor people.

127. TO ADD A FIFTH OF THE VALUE IN PAYING FOR HALLOWED FOOD THAT WAS EATEN

If any one commit a trespass, and sin through error, in the holy things of the LORD, then he shall bring his forfeit unto the LORD, a ram without blemish out of the flock, according to thy valuation in silver by shekels, after the shekel of the sanctuary, for a guilt-offering. And he shall make restitution for that which he hath done amiss in the holy thing, and shall add the fifth part thereto, and give it unto the priest; and the priest shall make atonement for him with the ram of the guilt-offering, and he shall be forgiven. (Leviticus 5:15-16)

Mitzvah 127 commands individuals who take items from the Temple, items which they had no right to claim, to not only pay back what they took, but to also pay an additional 1/5 interest. At the time of the Temple, this was enforced when people committed the infraction inadvertently.

128. THE PRECEPT OF ASHAM TALUY, AN OFFERING FOR DOUBTFUL GUILT

(Asham Taluy means a suspended guilt offering. In layman's terms, the individual is uncertain whether or not he committed the offense.)

And if any one sin, and do any of the things which the LORD hath commanded not to be done, though he know it not, yet is he guilty, and shall bear his iniquity. And he shall bring a ram without blemish out of the flock, according to thy valuation, for a guilt-offering, unto the priest; and the priest

shall make atonement for him concerning the error which he committed, though he knew it not, and he shall be forgiven. (Leviticus 5:17-18)

Mitzvah 128 pertains to doubt about committing an offense. Sometimes people were uncertain whether or not they ate forbidden fats from an animal. If the person thought that he might have eaten prohibited fat, he had to bring a suspended guilt offering. The objective was to make people pay attention to their actions. The old saying, 'ignorance of the law is no excuse' was applicable under these circumstances. From the time of Moses, through the Days of the Temple, no one could say that they didn't know any better and then expect to be pardoned without punishment. Not sparing these individuals prevented other people from being careless and then claim that they were unaware of the laws.

129. THE PRECEPT OF ASHAM VADDAI, AN OFFERING FOR DEFINITE GUILT

(Asham Vaddai means a guilt offering of certainty.)

If any one sin, and commit a trespass against the LORD, and deal falsely with his neighbour in a matter of deposit, or of pledge, or of robbery, or have oppressed his neighbour; or have found that which was lost, and deal falsely therein, and swear to a lie; in any of all these that a man doeth, sinning therein; then it shall be, if he hath sinned, and is guilty, that he shall restore that which he took by robbery, or the thing which he hath gotten by oppression, or the deposit which was deposited with him, or the lost thing which he found, or any thing about which he hath sworn falsely, he shall even restore it in full, and shall add the fifth part more thereto; unto him to whom it appertaineth shall he give it, in the day

of his being guilty. And he shall bring his forfeit unto the LORD, a ram without blemish out of the flock, according to thy valuation, for a guilt-offering, unto the priest. (Leviticus 5:21-25)

Mitzvah 129 pertains to definite guilt offerings.

There are four general sins for which someone would bring guilt offerings:

1. If someone gave an individual something to watch, and the Bailee claims it was stolen or that he never received the item to watch. In such a case, the bailee has to swear that he has nothing to pay back. If he ever admitted that he swore falsely, and then he decided to tell the truth, in addition to paying back the item, he must also perform a guilt offering.

2. If someone derives benefit from an item that had belonged to the Temple, he must provide a guilt offering.

3. When a Nazir finishes his period of being a Nazir, he must bring a guilt offering. (A Nazir cannot cut his hair, drink alcohol, or vinegar from alcohol, and he cannot come in contact with corpses.)

4. When a leper recovers, he has to provide a guilt offering.

For cases involving maidservants: The Jewish maidservants have a certain status, while their Gentile counterparts do not. If the latter is half free and half servant, her value as a servant would be worth a thousand dollars. If a Jewish man had sexual relations with her, he must perform a guilt offering as if she had had the status of being partially free and a partial servant.

130. THE PRECEPT OF RETURNING PROPERTY SEIZED IN ROBBERY

then it shall be, if he hath sinned, and is guilty, that he shall restore that which he took by robbery, or the thing which he hath gotten by oppression, or the deposit which was deposited with him, or the lost thing which he found, (Leviticus 5:23)

Mitzvah 130 commands that stolen items be returned to their rightful owner. If a thief stole something, and it is in his possession, he must return the item in its original state. If he stole firewood and used it, he must pay back the money that the firewood was worth. If he stole wool worth ten dollars, then made a sweater worth twenty dollars from the stolen wool, he would have to return ten dollars, not the sweater. This deals with returning the minimum value of the stolen item. See Tractate Gittin, Chapter 5, Mishnah 5 for a parallel about this.

Even though the Torah commands that stolen items be returned, it is easier to have the thief return something rather than nothing at all. If the thief made the sweater out of the stolen wool, he'd be less likely to return anything if he had to return the sweater. Returning the lesser value prompts him to return something rather than nothing at all.

131. THE PRECEPT OF LIFTING OFF THE ASH FROM THE ALTAR

And the priest shall put on his linen garment, and his linen breeches shall he put upon his flesh; and he shall take up the ashes whereto the fire hath consumed the burnt-offering on the altar, and he shall put them beside the altar. (Leviticus 6:3)

Mitzvah 131 commands the priests to remove the ashes from the Altar in the Temple every day. It was a huge honor to clean the Altar.

The Altar was very high, and the ramp was not as wide as the Altar. Ashes were piled up at the corner of the ramp. The multitude of ashes signified honor because it showed that people made many sacrifices to Hashem.

On a personal note, when I attended Aish HaTorah Yeshiva in the Old City of Jerusalem, I overheard a fellow student convince a classmate to help him clean the Yeshiva library. At first, the classmate was reluctant, until the other reminded him that it was an honor to clean it. They talked about an Arab who worked at the Yeshiva and said that there was no way that they would allow the Arab to perform that honor. After studying Mitzvah 131, I now understand the Aish HaTorah students' point of view.

132. THE PRECEPT OF KINDLING FIRE ON THE ALTER

Fire shall be kept burning upon the altar continually; it shall not go out. (Leviticus 6:6)

Mitzvah 132 commands the priests to light a fire on the Altar every day. My Partner in Torah told me that special logs were used on Shabbat. That special wood was used SOLELY to light the fires on the Altar.

The lesson from this Mitzvah is that even though Hashem has the power to create the fires and miracles, we have to make our attempt, and cover up the miracle. We cannot rely on Hashem to do everything for us. There is an ongoing Partnership between Hashem and us.

133. NOT TO PUT OUT ANY FIRE ON THE ALTAR

Fire shall be kept burning upon the altar continually; it shall not go out. (Leviticus 6:6)

Mitzvah 133 states that the fire on the Altar cannot be extinguished. Anyone who allows even an ember to be extinguished would receive lashes.

134. THE PRECEPT OF EATING THE REMAINDERS OF MEAL-OFFERINGS

And that which is left thereof shall Aaron and his sons eat; it shall be eaten without leaven in a holy place; in the court of the tent of meeting they shall eat it. (Leviticus 6:9)

Mitzvah 134 commands the priests to eat the remainder of the flour offerings not burnt on the Altar. Poor people presented flour offerings. In order to show gratitude to poor people, the priests had to eat the left over portions not used for the sacrificial offerings. This shows that poor people can make worthy contributions and that they are not inferior to affluent individuals.

135. NOT TO MAKE THE REMAINDERS OF MEAL-OFFERINGS BECOME LEAVENED

It shall not be baked with leaven. I have given it as their portion of My offerings made by fire; it is most holy, as the sin-offering, and as the guilt-offering. Every male among the children of Aaron may eat of it, as a due for ever throughout your generations, from the offerings of the LORD made by fire; whatsoever toucheth them shall be holy. (Leviticus 6:10-11)

Mitzvah 135 states that the remnants of the flour offerings cannot be turned into

Hametz. The flour offering has to remain as presented.

136. THE PRECEPT OF THE KOHEN GADOL'S DAILY MEAL-OFFERING

(Kohen Gadol means the Priest with a higher status than his fellow priests.)

This is the offering of Aaron and of his sons, which they shall offer unto the LORD in the day when he is anointed: the tenth part of an ephah of fine flour for a meal-offering perpetually, half of it in the morning, and half thereof in the evening. (Leviticus 6:13)

Mitzvah 136 commands the High Priest to provide flour offerings every day. The priests represented the Children of Israel when they made offerings to Hashem. Because communal offerings were made to Hashem twice a day, the priests also made two of their own offerings as well. Like the communal offerings, the priests performed their flour offerings in the morning and evening.

137. THAT THE MEAL-OFFERING OF A KOHEN SHOULD NOT BE EATEN

And every meal-offering of the priest shall be wholly made to smoke; it shall not be eaten. (Leviticus 6:16)

Mitzvah 137 forbids priests to eat the portions of the flour that they bring for meal-offerings that were not burnt on the Altar.

Mitzvah 134 commands the priests to eat the remnants of the meal-offerings that poor people presented.

Mitzvah 137 prohibits the priests from eating even a mouthful of the flour they themselves brought to be sacrificed. No priest can eat the remnants of any meal-offerings made by any other priest. This prohibition made the priests focus on their sacrificial duties and their spiritual relationship with Hashem rather than on what might be the next meal-offering to fill their bellies.

138. THE PRECEPT OF THE SACRIFICE OF THE HATTATH

Speak unto Aaron and to his sons, saying: This is the law of the sin-offering: in the place where the burnt-offering is killed shall the sin-offering be killed before the LORD; it is most holy. The priest that offereth it for sin shall eat it; in a holy place shall it be eaten, in the court of the tent of meeting. (Leviticus 6:18-19)

Mitzvah 138 states that the animal used for the sin-offering shall be killed in the same location as animals used for burnt offerings. A sin-offering can either be a sheep, goat, or bird. It is communal. Some sin offerings are burnt outside the Temple, while others are burnt on the Altar.

139. NOT TO EAT OF ANY HATTATH WHOSE BLOOD IS SPRINKLED WITHIN

And no sin-offering, whereof any of the blood is brought into the tent of meeting to make atonement in the holy place, shall be eaten; it shall be burnt with fire. (Leviticus 6:23)

Mitzvah 139 states that if blood from the animals that were used for sin-offerings were sprinkled on the inner Altar, no one could eat that animal. That animal must be burned with fire.

However, if the sin-offerings were performed on the outer Altar, and no blood was sprinkled on the inner Alter, those sacrificed animals could be eaten.

Blood from the animals that were used for communal sin-offerings had to be sprinkled on the inner Altar, because they represented the entire nation of Israel.

Most individual sin-offerings were performed on the outer Altar of the Temple. After the animal was killed, its blood would drain into a bowl. The priest would dip his fingers in the blood in the bowl, and then sprinkle the blood on the corners of the outer Altar.

140. THE PRECEPT OF THE SACRIFICE OF THE ASHAM

And this is the law of the guilt-offering: it is most holy. In the place where they kill the burnt-offering shall they kill the guilt-offering: and the blood thereof shall be dashed against the altar round about. And he shall offer of it all the fat thereof: the fat tail, and the fat that covereth the inwards, and the two kidneys, and the fat that is on them, which is by the loins, and the lobe above the liver, which he shall take away by the kidneys. And the priest shall make them smoke upon the altar for an offering made by fire unto the LORD; it is a guilt-offering. Every male among the priests may eat thereof; it shall be eaten in a holy place; it is most holy. (Leviticus 7:1-6)

Mitzvah 140 spells out how the priests were required to perform the guilt-offerings. This ranged from sacrificing and slaughtering the animal, to the location where the slaughtering would take place, and the manner in which its blood was to be sprinkled.

This Mitzvah shows how the priests limited the suffering of the sacrificed animals while showing them compassion and respect.

141. THE PRECEPT OF THE SACRIFICE OF THE SH'LAMIM

(Sh'lamim means peace-offerings.)

And he shall present of the sacrifice of peace-offerings an offering made by fire unto the LORD: the fat that covereth the inwards, and all the fat that is upon the inwards, and the two kidneys, and the fat that is on them, which is by the loins, and the lobe above the liver, which he shall take away hard by the kidneys. And Aaron's sons shall make it smoke on the altar upon the burnt-offering, which is upon the wood that is on the fire; it is an offering made by fire, of a sweet savour unto the LORD. (Leviticus 3:3-5)

Mitzvah 141 pertains to peace-offerings. These offerings were brought as donations. At the time of the First and Second Temple, the Children of Israel were only obligated to bring these offerings on holidays. On Shavuot, communal peace-offerings were performed.

An Individual peace-offering was performed when a person ended his period of being a Nazirite. (For more information about the Nazir, consult Mitzvah 129.)

142. NOT TO LET THE FLESH OF A TODAH BE LEFT OVER

(A Todah means a thanksgiving offering.)

And the flesh of the sacrifice of his peace-offerings for thanksgiving shall be eaten on the day of his offering; he shall not leave any of it until the morning. (Leviticus 7:15)

Mitzvah 142 deals with thanksgiving offerings. The thanksgiving offering must be eaten the night that the people are celebrating. No remnants can be eaten after that.

Certain situations required people to present offerings of thanksgiving: being released from jail, recovering from a deadly illness, or crossing the ocean or desert. The person presenting the thanksgiving offering was required to say a blessing.

143. THE PRECEPT OF BURNING LEFTOVER REMNANTS OF SACRED OFFERINGS

But that which remaineth of the flesh of the sacrifice on the third day shall be burnt with fire. (Leviticus 7:17)

Mitzvah 143 states that if meat of a sacrifice is left over for 3 days, it must be burned.

Sacrifices were holy and you could eat the meat of a sacrificed animal. But after a certain amount of time had elapsed, that meat would spoil and rot. Burning the holy remains was a way to dispose of them respectfully.

This Mitzvah tells us that Hashem would provide for us in the future, therefore, there was no need to store the food interminably.

144. THE PROHIBITION AGAINST PIGGUL, "VILE MEAT"

(Piggul means that when the priest performed a sacrifice, he entertained negative thoughts.)

And if any of the flesh of the sacrifice of his peace-offerings be at all eaten on the third day, it shall not be accepted, neither shall it be imputed unto him that offereth it; it shall be an abhorred thing, and the soul that eateth of it shall bear his iniquity. (Leviticus 7:18)

Mitzvah 144 states that if the priest slaughtered the sacrificed animal and planned to do it improperly, nobody can eat it. The priest was prohibited from thinking such thoughts while performing the sacrifice.

If the priest sacrificed the animal properly, but thought about eating it on the Third Day, **after** the time-period to eat the animal expired, then no one could eat the animal at any time, not even the priest. Not only did the priest have to perform the sacrifice perfectly, his thoughts and heart had to match his actions.

The need to fulfill this Mitzvah materialized if the priest admitted that he had improper thoughts while performing the sacrifice.

145. THAT THE FLESH OF THE HOLY OFFERINGS IS NOT TO BE EATEN

And the flesh that toucheth any unclean thing shall not be eaten; it shall be burnt with fire. And as for the flesh, every one that is clean may eat thereof. (Leviticus 7:19)

Mitzvah 145 prohibits eating meat from a sacrifice that becomes impure. If the person became impure, he would then be forbidden to eat it. If the meat had become impure, no one may eat it.

146. THE PRECEPT OF BURNING HALLOWED FLESH THAT BECAME DEFILED

And the flesh that toucheth any unclean thing shall not be eaten; it shall be burnt with fire. And as for the flesh, every one that is clean may eat thereof. (Leviticus 7:19)

Mitzvah 146 states that if the meat that derived from an animal sacrifice becomes impure or defiled, it had to be burnt. No one could eat it.

147. NOT TO EAT HELEV, FORBIDDEN ANIMAL FAT

(Helev means fat from animals that we cannot eat.)

Speak unto the children of Israel, saying: Ye shall eat no fat, of ox, or sheep, or goat. (Leviticus 7:23)

Mitzvah 147 forbids us to eat fat from the ox, sheep, and goat because, according to the author of Sefer HaHinnuch, the fat from those animals is unhealthy. The author elaborated that we can eat fat from other kosher animals because eating their fat is like eating their meat. Eating forbidden fats leads to poor health and makes us unable to serve Hashem.

148. THAT WE SHOULD NOT EAT THE BLOOD OF ANY BEAST OR FOWL

And ye shall eat no manner of blood, whether it be of fowl or of beast, in any of your dwellings. Whosoever it be that

eateth any blood, that soul shall be cut off from his people. (Leviticus 7:26-27)

Mitzvah 148 forbids us from eating and drinking blood from any animals, whether or not they are slaughtered for sacrifice.

Blood is the life force. Eating and drinking blood is a vulgar display of disrespect for the animals slated for sacrifice to Hashem.

Although human blood is not included in the prohibition, the Sages added it because human blood looks similar to animal blood. The Sages said that if your mouth bleeds, you can suck or swallow the blood. However, should human blood spill onto bread or other foods, the human blood must be removed before eating.

Eating blood from kosher fish and blood from kosher insects is permitted, because they are not slaughtered for sacrifice.

We cannot eat the blood if it is visible on the outside of the dead creature. We can never drink blood because a bystander might think that we are devouring the blood of an animal slaughtered for sacrifice. For more information, see Tractate Kritut 21b or read the discussion of Mitzvah 148 in Sefer HaHinnuch.

Refraining from eating and drinking blood from humans, fish, and insects, in order to keep a bystander from thinking that one is eating and drinking blood from a ritually slaughtered animal, falls under the category of Marit Ayin (the appearance to the eye).

In Avot, Chapter 1, Mishnah 16, Rabbi Gamliel states, "Remove yourself from uncertainty." My Partner in Torah gave examples of things we should avoid today to remove ourselves from uncertainty. If someone needs to use the telephone, that person should not walk into a non-kosher restaurant to ask to use the phone because it might look as though that person were going to eat there. If someone steps in a puddle on Shabbat, he or she should be careful not to hang up his or her socks to dry because a bystander might think that that person is doing laundry on Shabbat.

On a personal note, while I was studying this Mitzvah, several learned people told me that they doubted that insects had blood. I consulted several Internet sources and found verification that insects do in fact have blood.

When I went to the link, http://www2.scholastic.com/browse/article.jsp?id=4628, I read the following explanation: From the link "Insects have blood, but it's not like our blood. Our blood is red because it has hemoglobin, which is used to carry oxygen to where it is needed in the body. Insects get oxygen from a complex system of air tubes that connect to the outside through openings called spiracles. So instead of carrying oxygen, their blood carries nutrients from one part of the body to another. They do bleed when they are hurt, and their blood can clot so they can recover from minor wounds." (Visit that link for more information about insects.)

149. THE KOHANIM MAY NOT ENTER THE HOLY TEMPLE WITH HAIR GROWN LONG

And Moses said unto Aaron, and unto Eleazar and unto Ithamar, his sons: 'Let not the hair of your heads go loose, neither rend your clothes, that ye die not, and that He be not wroth with all the congregation; but let your brethren, the whole house of Israel, bewail the burning which the LORD hath kindled. (Leviticus 10:6)

Mitzvah 149 forbids the priests to serve in the Temple with long, overgrown hair.

Mourners keep their hair long and unkempt. The priests have to cut their hair every 30 days to avoid looking like mourners. When the priests serve in the Temple, they must be happy and look happy. Having long and overgrown hair indicates that they are not elated about serving Hashem.

150. THE KOHANIM ARE NOT TO ENTER THE HOLY TEMPLE IN TORN CLOTHING

And Moses said unto Aaron, and unto Eleazar and unto Ithamar, his sons: 'Let not the hair of your heads go loose, neither rend your clothes, that ye die not, and that He be not wroth with all the congregation; but let your brethren, the whole house of Israel, bewail the burning which the LORD hath kindled. (Leviticus 10:6)

Mitzvah 150 prohibits priests from entering the Temple wearing torn clothing. Mourners tear their clothing to express grief and sorrow. When priests serve in the Temple, they cannot dress as mourners because they are commanded to be happy and to look happy.

151. THE KOHANIM ARE NOT TO LEAVE THE TEMPLE DURING THEIR SACRED SERVICE

And ye shall not go out from the door of the tent of meeting, lest ye die; for the anointing oil of the LORD is upon you.' And they did according to the word of Moses. (Leviticus 10:7)

neither shall he go out of the sanctuary, nor profane the sanctuary of his God; for the consecration of the anointing oil of his God is upon him: I am the LORD. (Leviticus 21:12)

Mitzvah 151 forbids the priests from leaving the Temple while serving there. Even if a priest lost a loved one, he must still remain in the Temple if he is required to be there. If he were on duty and heard that his close relative died, he cannot leave immediately. If an ordinary Kohan (priest) lost a loved one, he would not be permitted to serve in the Temple until the deceased was buried. However, the Kohen Gadol (High Priest) must serve in the Temple even before his loved one's interment. His immense responsibility of serving Hashem takes priority over everything, even his family.

Today, Jews in mourning need to remember that Hashem is the ultimate judge. When a loved one dies, the Jewish mourner tears his or her clothes and says the blessing:

"Baruch Atah Hashem, Eloheinu Melekh Ha-Olam Dayan Ha-Emet." **(Blessed are thou, Lord our G-d, King of the Universe, the True Judge.)**

In Avot, Chapter 3, Mishnah 16, Rabbi Yishmael says, "Be yielding to a superior, be pleasant to the young, and receive every person cheerfully."

An interpretation my Partner in Torah gave me was that we must respect judges' decisions. This reminds us to remain in awe of Hashem, even when we are mourning the loss of close relatives. Being pleasant to the young and receiving everyone cheerfully helps prevent us from acting superior to people. No one is to be treated as if they are inferior because everyone–the high and mighty–the rulers–the wealthiest people–are inferior to Hashem, the true and ultimate judge.

152. AFTER DRINKING WINE A KOHEN SHOULD NOT ENTER THE SANCTUARY, AND NO ONE IS TO GIVE A RULING

'Drink no wine nor strong drink, thou, nor thy sons with thee, when ye go into the tent of meeting, that ye die not; it shall be a statute forever throughout your generations. And that ye may put difference between the holy and the common, and between the unclean and the clean; and that ye may teach the children of Israel all the statutes which the LORD hath spoken unto them by the hand of Moses.' (Leviticus 10:9-11)

Mitzvah 152 forbids everyone, including the priests, the High Priest, and women from entering the Temple intoxicated.

If the priest came into the Temple drunk and he conducted his service, he would be subject to death at the Hands of Hashem. If he were under the influence of strong drink, which meant unmixed wine, he would be subject to lashes, but not death. The unmixed wine was weaker than wine. Strong drinks such as vodka, whiskey, and other such alcoholic beverages were unknown to the Children of Israel when the Holy Temple stood.

The priests can never render decisions while under the influence of alcohol. Like everyone else, priests have the potential to make bad decisions while drunk.

153. TO EXAMINE THE SIGNS OF ANIMALS WHICH DETERMINE IF THEY ARE KOSHER

Speak unto the children of Israel, saying: These are the living things which ye may eat among all the beasts that are on the earth. Whatsoever parteth the hoof, and is wholly cloven-footed, and cheweth the cud, among the beasts, that may ye eat. (Leviticus 11:2-3)

Mitzvah 153 commands us to check to see if an animal is kosher before eating it. In order for the animal to be kosher, it must chew its cud and possess split hooves. It must have BOTH to be kosher.

154. THE PROHIBITION AGAINST EATING ANY NON-KOSHER ANIMAL

Nevertheless these shall ye not eat of them that only chew the cud, or of them that only part the hoof: the camel, because he cheweth the cud but parteth not the hoof, he is unclean unto you. And the rock-badger, because he cheweth the cud but parteth not the hoof, he is unclean unto you. And the hare, because she cheweth the cud but parteth not the hoof, she is unclean unto you. And the swine, because he parteth the hoof, and is cloven-footed, but cheweth not the cud, he is unclean unto you. Of their flesh ye shall not eat, and their carcasses ye shall not touch; they are unclean unto you. (Leviticus 11:4-8)

Mitzvah 154 is the prohibition against eating non-kosher animals. The Torah forbids the eating of pigs, camels, and rabbits. The pig has split hooves but does not chew its cud. The camel chews its cud, but does not have split hooves.

These non-kosher animals are unclean in the eyes of Hashem. In order to serve Hashem, we are not to put anything unclean into our bodies.

155. THE PRECEPT OF EXAMINING THE SIGNS OF FISH TO SEE IF THEY ARE KOSHER

These may ye eat of all that are in the waters: whatsoever hath fins and scales in the waters, in the seas, and in the rivers, them may ye eat. (Leviticus 11:9)

Mitzvah 155 states that before we eat fish, we must make sure that it possesses the two kosher signs: fins and scales. Not having fins and scales makes them non-kosher.

Scales are the overlapping skin on the fish, while fins are the appendages that stick out from the sides of the fish. Fish use their fins to move through the water.

If you can see the fish's scales, they usually have fins. But having fins, does not automatically mean they have scales. If they have scales in the water, but if the scales fall off when taken out of the water, they remain kosher.

156. THE PROHIBITION AGAINST EATING NON-KOSHER SPECIES OF FISH

And all that have not fins and scales in the seas, and in the rivers, of all that swarm in the waters, and of all the living creatures that are in the waters, they are a detestable thing unto you, and they shall be a detestable thing unto you; ye shall not eat of their flesh, and their carcasses ye shall have in detestation. Whatsoever hath no fins nor scales in the waters, that is a detestable thing unto you. (Leviticus 11:10-12)

Mitzvah 156 is the prohibition against eating non-kosher fish. Like other non-kosher foods, non-kosher fish possess harmful elements, and Hashem deemed them detestable.

157. THE PROHIBITION AGAINST EATING NON-KOSHER SPECIES OF FOWL

And these ye shall have in detestation among the fowls; they shall not be eaten, they are a detestable thing: the great vulture, and the bearded vulture, and the ospray; and the kite, and the falcon after its kinds; every raven after its kinds; and

the ostrich, and the night-hawk, and the sea-mew, and the hawk after its kinds; and the little owl, and the cormorant, and the great owl; and the horned owl, and the pelican, and the carrion-vulture; and the stork, and the heron after its kinds, and the hoopoe, and the bat. (Leviticus 11:13-19)

Mitzvah 157 forbids us to eat non-kosher birds.

The Torah lists non-kosher birds, and whatever is not listed as non-kosher can be eaten.

Kosher birds have four signs:

1. They cannot be predatory.
2. They have one large extra appendage.
3. They have a crop, a compartment of muscle tissue that birds use to store and soften their food before it moves on to be processed by the gizzard.
4. They have a gizzard that can be peeled.

There needs to be a tradition of eating the specific bird.

158. THE PRECEPT OF EXAMINING THE SIGNS OF LOCUSTS, IF THEY ARE KOSHER

Yet these may ye eat of all winged swarming things that go upon all fours, which have jointed legs above their feet, wherewith to leap upon the earth; even these of them ye may eat: the locust after its kinds, and the bald locust after its kinds, and the cricket after its kinds, and the grasshopper after its kinds. But all winged swarming things, which have four feet, are a detestable thing unto you. (Leviticus 11:21-23)

Mitzvah 158 commands us to examine the signs of kosher insects. Kosher insects have three signs: First, the insect must have two sets of wings and when it folds its wings, it covers most of its body. Second, the kosher insect must have four main legs. Third, the insect must have two additional jointed upper legs, which it uses for jumping.

Sefer HaHinnuch lists eight kosher insects:
The Chagav (grasshopper),
the D'vanith (hammer-locust),
the Chargol (the cricket),
the Utzravya (a species of cricket),
the Arbeh (locust),
"the bird of the vineyards" (a species of locust),
The Sol'am (the bald locust),
and the Jerusalem Yohana (a species of bald locust).

If one cannot recognize the type of insect, he can at least look for the kosher signs.

Insects are not considered meat; like fish they are Parve.

159. THE RITUAL UNCLEANNESS OF EIGHT LOW CRAWLING CREATURES

And these are they which are unclean unto you among the swarming things that swarm upon the earth: the weasel, and the mouse, and the great lizard after its kinds, and the gecko, and the land-crocodile, and the lizard, and the sand-lizard, and the chameleon. These are they which are unclean to you among all that swarm; whosoever doth touch them, when they are dead, shall be unclean until the even. And upon whatsoever any of them, when they are dead, doth fall, it shall be unclean; whether it be any vessel of wood, or raiment, or skin, or sack, whatsoever vessel it be, wherewith any work is

done, it must be put into water, and it shall be unclean until the even; then shall it be clean. (Leviticus 11:29-33)

Mitzvah 159 states that should someone touch one of those eight dead rodents he or she becomes unclean. If an object touches one of those eight dead rodents, the object becomes unclean. Immersion in the Mikveh, a ritual purification bath, makes one spiritually pure after touching the dead rodent.

160. THE PRECEPT OF THE RITUAL UNCLEANNESS OF FOOD

All food therein which may be eaten, that on which water cometh, shall be unclean; and all drink in every such vessel that may be drunk shall be unclean. And every thing whereupon any part of their carcass falleth shall be unclean; whether oven, or range for pots, it shall be broken in pieces; they are unclean, and shall be unclean unto you. Nevertheless a fountain or a cistern wherein is a gathering of water shall be clean; but he who toucheth their carcass shall be unclean. (Leviticus 11:34-36)

Mitzvah 160 commands us to be wary of impure food.

Food becomes impure if water falls on it. Pure clean water comes from fountains and cisterns. Water from other sources could be polluted.

If an impure person touches a utensil, it becomes impure and if that utensil touches the food, then the food becomes impure.

Ways that a person becomes impure include coming in contact with a dead person, a dead reptile, or a dead animal.

161. THE PRECEPT OF THE RITUAL UNCLEANNESS OF ANIMAL CARCASSES

And if any beast, of which ye may eat, die, he that toucheth the carcass thereof shall be unclean until the even. And he that eateth of the carcass of it shall wash his clothes, and be unclean until the even; he also that beareth the carcass of it shall wash his clothes, and be unclean until the even. (Leviticus 11:39-40)

Mitzvah 161 states that a person would be unclean if he or she touches or eats the carcass of a dead animal if the animal died by means other than sacrifice.

162. THE PROHIBITION AGAINST EATING CREATURES THAT SWARM ON THE EARTH

And every swarming thing that swarmeth upon the earth is a detestable thing; it shall not be eaten. (Leviticus 11:41)

Mitzvah 162 forbids us from eating creatures that swarm and crawl on the ground. Such creatures include the serpent, the scorpion, and the centipede. The snake is a legless lizard, detestable and venomous. Anyone with even a grain of common sense would not touch it, whether it is alive or dead. More details about the snake will be covered in Mitzvah 545.

163. THE PROHIBITION AGAINST EATING MINUTE INSECTS ENGENDERED IN GRAINS AND FRUITS

Whatsoever goeth upon the belly, and whatsoever goeth upon all fours, or whatsoever hath many feet, even all swarming things that swarm upon the earth, them ye shall not eat; for they are a detestable thing. (Leviticus 11:42)

Mitzvah 163 states that if an insect or worm were born inside grain or fruit, then went onto the ground, those creatures would be forever detestable and not fit to eat.

The author of Sefer HaHinnuch states that eating those permissible creatures would be a modicum of abhorrence for the soul.

In sum, it seems advisable to refrain from eating any creature that emerges from fruit or grain, whether it had been on the ground or not.

164. THE PROHIBITION AGAINST EATING CREATURES THAT SWARM IN THE WATER

Ye shall not make yourselves detestable with any swarming thing that swarmeth, neither shall ye make yourselves unclean with them, that ye should be defiled thereby. (Leviticus 11:43)

Mitzvah 164 forbids us to eat creatures that swarm in the water. There are other creatures, besides fish, that swarm in the water. The only living things that we can eat from the water are fish that have both fins and scales. Everything else is non-kosher.

165. THE PROHIBITION AGAINST EATING SWARMING CREATURES ENGENDERED IN DECAY

For I am the LORD your God; sanctify yourselves therefore, and be ye holy; for I am holy; neither shall ye defile yourselves with any manner of swarming thing that moveth upon the earth. (Leviticus 11:44)

Mitzvah 165 prohibits us from eating swarming creatures that cause or feed on decay, rot, and garbage.

166. THE PRECEPT ABOUT THE RITUAL UNCLEANNESS OF A WOMAN AFTER CHILDBEARING

Speak unto the children of Israel, saying: If a woman be delivered, and bear a man-child, then she shall be unclean seven days; as in the days of the impurity of her sickness shall she be unclean. And in the eighth day the flesh of his foreskin shall be circumcised And she shall continue in the blood of purification three and thirty days; she shall touch no hallowed thing, nor come into the sanctuary, until the days of her purification be fulfilled. But if she bear a maid-child, then she shall be unclean two weeks, as in her impurity; and she shall continue in the blood of purification threescore and six days. And when the days of her purification are fulfilled, for a son, or for a daughter, she shall bring a lamb of the first year for a burnt-offering, and a young pigeon, or a turtle-dove, for a sin-offering, unto the door of the tent of meeting, unto the priest. And he shall offer it before the LORD, and make atonement for her; and she shall be cleansed from the fountain of her blood. This is the law for her that beareth, whether a male or a female. And if her means suffice not for a lamb, then she shall take two turtle-doves, or two young pigeons: the one for a burnt-offering, and the other for a sin-offering; and the priest shall make atonement for her, and she shall be clean. (Leviticus 12:2-8)

Mitzvah 166 states that when a woman gives birth to a boy, she is unclean for seven days and is not to have marital relations with her husband. If she conceived a girl, then that state lasts 14 days. Although she can resume sexual activity because her state of impurity ended, she cannot enter the Temple for the designated period listed above because she is still recovering from childbirth.

Not having marital relations immediately after childbirth is for the mother's benefit. She bleeds after giving birth. It is impossible for her womb to open without bleeding. She needs time to heal.

When a woman has her period, or after she gives birth, she is to abstain from sex for a specific duration because her body is expelling bodily fluids. It is not the time to have bodily fluids inserted into her.

For a boy, she would need a week to recover and for a girl, two weeks. If she gives birth to identical twin boys, triplets, etc., it is still a seven-day recovery period. Giving birth to twin girls, triplets, or more would still be 14 days. If she gave birth to fraternal twins (two children who are not identical twins), then the recovery period is 14 days.

Conceiving a son requires less time recovering than conceiving a daughter because the former indicates warmth in the mother; while the latter indicates coldness in the mother's physical nature.

Nahmanides (known as Rabbi Moshe ben Nachman 1194-1270 C.E. and by his acronym, RAMBAN) stated: "Because the physical nature of the woman was cold and moist, and the white humor in the mother's womb was of large amount and cold, she therefore bore a female. Hence she needs great cleansing, on account of the accretion of humors and the foul blood in them, and on account of their coldness. It is known that cold illnesses require for their cleansing a greater length of time than those with heat."

Rabbi Chaim ibn Attar (1669-1743) provided a spiritual explanation as to why the mother needs to abstain from sex after giving birth. He stated that a pregnant woman is similar to Hashem because she creates life. After her child is born, she returns to being a regular human being. The sudden absence of her creative potential creates a void.

Rabbi Chaim Ibn Attar argued: "When a woman is pregnant with a girl, an emerging creator, her degree of sanctity is at an all-time high. The void, or **Tumah**, created when she is no longer pregnant is thus proportionally larger than the vacuum created following the birth of a boy."

(Cited at http://www.chabad.org/library/article_cdo/aid/112384/jewish/Rabbi-Chaim-ibn-Attar.htm)

To learn more about Rabbi Chaim ibn Attar, go to https://www.chabad.org/library/article_cdo/aid/112384/jewish/Rabbi-Chaim-ibn-Attar.htm

167. A RITUALLY UNCLEAN PERSON IS NOT TO EAT MEAT OF HOLY SACRIFICES

And she shall continue in the blood of purification three and thirty days; she shall touch no hallowed thing, nor come into the sanctuary, until the days of her purification be fulfilled. (Leviticus 12:4)

Mitzvah 167 states that an impure person cannot eat sacrificed animals. Sacrificed animals are Holy, therefore only ritually pure individuals can derive benefit from them.

After fulfilling the requirements to regain purity, the person must still wait until the next day before he or she are pure again.

Some things that make a person impure include coming in contact with a dead person, a dead animal, or a dead rodent. A woman is impure during menstruation and immediately after giving birth.

168. THE PRECEPT OF A WOMAN'S OFFERING AFTER GIVING BIRTH

And when the days of her purification are fulfilled, for a son, or for a daughter, she shall bring a lamb of the first year for a burnt-offering, and a young pigeon, or a turtle-dove, for a sin-offering, unto the door of the tent of meeting, unto the priest. And he shall offer it before the LORD, and make atonement for her; and she shall be cleansed from the fountain of her blood. This is the law for her that beareth, whether a male or a female. And if her means suffice not for a lamb, then she shall take two turtle-doves, or two young pigeons: the one for a burnt-offering, and the other for a sin-offering; and the priest shall make atonement for her, and she shall be clean. (Leviticus 12:6-8)

Mitzvah 168 commands women who give birth to provide a burnt offering and a sin offering 41 days after bearing a boy and 81 days after bearing a girl. Some women who give birth experience such excruciating pain that they vow never again to have another child. Their offering absolves them of that oath. Another reason for presenting these offerings is to thank Hashem for rescuing them from their birth pains. Many women die while giving birth, therefore, those who survive need to show their gratitude to Hashem for allowing them to continue to live and for allowing them to keep experiencing the joy of raising children.

Why must the mother atone after completing her state of purification?

The argument is that she is in such excruciating pain while giving birth that she might say anything. She could easily vow never to become pregnant again. She might wish for something terrible.

After completing her state of purification, she is recovered and sometimes ready and enthusiastic about giving birth again.

Performing the offering absolves her of the vow that she might have said or quietly promised to fulfill, while giving birth.

Rabbeinu Bachya explained that the sin she requires atonement for is not one that she herself committed, but rather, a sin that Mother Eve committed. Prior to eating from the Tree of Knowledge, children were conceived and born without temptation or difficulty, just as trees produced fruit without struggle or any form of passionate engagement. After Eve sinned, the need for temptation arose and women were smitten with the difficulties and dangers of childbirth. The sin of the Tree of Knowledge entailed both thought and deed, and therefore, a new mother must bring two offerings: The Burnt-Offering to atone for the sinful thoughts, and the Sin-Offering to atone for Eve's sinful actions.

For more information, see Babylonian Talmud, Tractate Niddah 31b and go to the link, https://www.Partnersintorah.org/parsha-Partner/tazria-metzora-5770.

169. THE PRECEPT REGARDING THE RITUAL UNCLEANNESS OF A M'TZORA

(M'tzora means a disfiguring condition.)

When a man shall have in the skin of his flesh a rising, or a scab, or a bright spot, and it becomes in the skin of his flesh

the plague of leprosy, then he shall be brought unto Aaron the priest, or unto one of his sons the priests. And the priest shall look upon the plague in the skin of the flesh; and if the hair in the plague be turned white, and the appearance of the plague be deeper than the skin of his flesh, it is the plague of leprosy; and the priest shall look on him, and pronounce him unclean. And if the bright spot be white in the skin of his flesh, and the appearance thereof be not deeper than the skin, and the hair thereof be not turned white, then the priest shall shut up him that hath the plague seven days. And the priest shall look on him the seventh day; and, behold, if the plague stay in its appearance, and the plague be not spread in the skin, then the priest shall shut him up seven days more. And the priest shall look on him again the seventh day; and, behold, if the plague be dim, and the plague be not spread in the skin, then the priest shall pronounce him clean: it is a scab; and he shall wash his clothes, and be clean. (Leviticus 13:2-6)

Mitzvah 169 commands that when a person develops a skin problem, discoloration, or rash, he or she must show it to the priest. The priest determines if that person has leprosy–a highly contagious disease that had no cure before and during the Temple's existence. If he or she had leprosy, the priest quarantined that person for seven days. Even when the priest was unsure what the skin condition was, the priest quarantined the person. In that case, the person was in a state of limbo.

Leprosy is a spiritual sickness with a physical manifestation. People developed it for doing wrongful deeds or for Lashon HaRah (saying negative comments, whether true or false). People did not develop leprosy by chance.

Leprosy can be a blessing because the leper can think about his or her actions, repent, and become a more compassionate person.

170. THE PROHIBITION AGAINST SHAVING THE AREA OF A NETHEK

(Nethek means lesion.)

then he shall be shaven, but the scall shall he not shave; and the priest shall shut up him that hath the scall seven days more. And in the seventh day the priest shall look on the scall; and, behold, if the scall be not spread in the skin, and the appearance thereof be not deeper than the skin, then the priest shall pronounce him clean; and he shall wash his clothes, and be clean. (Leviticus 13:33-34)

Mitzvah 170 states that if we have a discoloration of the skin in a spot covered with hair, we cannot shave the hair off that spot. The hair must remain in order for the priests to discern the signs of defilement in the hair. We can shave around the spot, but not the spot itself. This allows the priest to see if the spot or discoloration spreads to other parts of the head or body. The spot spreading is a definitive sign of leprosy.

171. THAT ONE WITH A TZARA'AT CONDITION, ET AL SHOULD REND HIS CLOTHES

(TZARA'AT means leprosy.)

And the leper in whom the plague is, his clothes shall be rent, and the hair of his head shall go loose, and he shall cover his upper lip, and shall cry: 'Unclean, unclean.' All the days wherein the plague is in him he shall be unclean; he is unclean; he shall dwell alone; without the camp shall his dwelling be. (Leviticus 13:45-46)

Mitzvah 171 commands the leper to keep his or her hair long and to rend his or her clothing. The leper separates himself or herself from the community to think about his or her wrongful deeds and to repent.

172. THE PRECEPT ON TZARA'AT IN CLOTH

And when the plague of leprosy is in a garment, whether it be a woolen garment, or a linen garment; or in the warp, or in the woof, whether they be of linen, or of wool; or in a skin, or in any thing made of skin. If the plague be greenish or reddish in the garment, or in the skin, or in the warp, or in the woof, or in any thing of skin, it is the plague of leprosy, and shall be shown unto the priest. And the priest shall look upon the plague, and shut up that which hath the plague seven days. (Leviticus 13:47-50)

Mitzvah 172 states that should someone find leprosy on his or her woolen or cotton garments, that person must present them to the priest. The priest decides whether or not to have the clothing washed or burned. The priest decides whether to have that individual quarantined.

173. THE PRECEPT THAT RITUAL CLEANSING FROM TZARA'AT AFFLICTION SHOULD BE THROUGH CERTAIN INGREDIENTS

This shall be the law of the leper in the day of his cleansing: he shall be brought unto the priest. And the priest shall go forth out of the camp; and the priest shall look, and, behold, if the plague of leprosy be healed in the leper; then shall the priest command to take for him that is to be cleansed two living clean birds, and cedar-wood, and scarlet, and hyssop. And the priest shall command to kill one of the birds in an earthen vessel over running water. As for the living bird, he shall take it, and the cedar-wood, and the scarlet, and the hyssop, and shall dip them and the living bird in the blood of

the bird that was killed over the running water. And he shall sprinkle upon him that is to be cleansed from the leprosy seven times, and shall pronounce him clean, and shall let go the living bird into the open field. And he that is to be cleansed shall wash his clothes, and shave off all his hair, and bathe himself in water, and he shall be clean; and after that he may come into the camp, but shall dwell outside his tent seven days. And it shall be on the seventh day, that he shall shave all his hair off his head and his beard and his eyebrows, even all his hair he shall shave off; and he shall wash his clothes, and he shall bathe his flesh in water, and he shall be clean. And on the eighth day he shall take two he-lambs without blemish, and one ewe-lamb of the first year without blemish, and three tenth parts of an ephah of fine flour for a meal-offering, mingled with oil, and one log of oil. And the priest that cleanseth him shall set the man that is to be cleansed, and those things, before the LORD, at the door of the tent of meeting. And the priest shall take one of the he-lambs, and offer him for a guilt-offering, and the log of oil, and wave them for a wave-offering before the LORD. And he shall kill the he-lamb in the place where they kill the sin-offering and the burnt-offering, in the place of the sanctuary; for as the sin-offering is the priest's, so is the guilt-offering; it is most holy. And the priest shall take of the blood of the guilt-offering, and the priest shall put it upon the tip of the right ear of him that is to be cleansed, and upon the thumb of his right hand, and upon the great toe of his right foot. And the priest shall take of the log of oil, and pour it into the palm of his own left hand. And the priest shall dip his right finger in the oil that is in his left hand, and shall sprinkle of the oil with his finger seven times before the LORD. And of the rest of the oil that is in his hand shall the priest put upon the tip of the right ear of him that is to be cleansed, and upon the thumb of his right hand, and upon the great toe of his right foot, upon the blood of the guilt-offering. And the rest of the oil that is

in the priest's hand he shall put upon the head of him that is to be cleansed; and the priest shall make atonement for him before the LORD. And the priest shall offer the sin-offering, and make atonement for him that is to be cleansed because of his uncleanness; and afterward he shall kill the burnt-offering. And the priest shall offer the burnt-offering and the meal-offering upon the altar; and the priest shall make atonement for him, and he shall be clean. And if he be poor, and his means suffice not, then he shall take one he-lamb for a guilt-offering to be waved, to make atonement for him, and one tenth part of an ephah of fine flour mingled with oil for a meal-offering, and a log of oil; and two turtle-doves, or two young pigeons, such as his means suffice for; and the one shall be a sin-offering, and the other a burnt-offering. And on the eighth day he shall bring them for his cleansing unto the priest, unto the door of the tent of meeting, before the LORD. And the priest shall take the lamb of the guilt-offering, and the log of oil, and the priest shall wave them for a wave-offering before the LORD. And he shall kill the lamb of the guilt-offering, and the priest shall take of the blood of the guilt-offering, and put it upon the tip of the right ear of him that is to be cleansed, and upon the thumb of his right hand, and upon the great toe of his right foot. And the priest shall pour of the oil into the palm of his own left hand. And the priest shall sprinkle with his right finger some of the oil that is in his left hand seven times before the LORD. And the priest shall put of the oil that is in his hand upon the tip of the right ear of him that is to be cleansed, and upon the thumb of his right hand, and upon the great toe of his right foot, upon the place of the blood of the guilt-offering. And the rest of the oil that is in the priest's hand he shall put upon the head of him that is to be cleansed, to make atonement for him before the LORD. And he shall offer one of the turtle-doves, or of the young pigeons, such as his means suffice for; even such as his means suffice for, the one for a sin-offering,

and the other for a burnt-offering, with the meal-offering; and the priest shall make atonement for him that is to be cleansed before the LORD. This is the law of him in whom is the plague of leprosy, whose means suffice not for that which pertaineth to his cleansing. (Leviticus 14:2-32)

Mitzvah 173 cites the procedure that the priest uses to help the leper regain purity. The Sages state that water is used in the process because before Hashem created man, the earth consisted of water. The water signifies a person's rebirth. The Sages state that Hashem commanded birds be used to regain purity since the person became a leper because he spoke Lashon Ha-Rah (negative comments both true and false). The leper had gossiped and chirped like a bird.

For a more detailed discussion of Mitzvah 173, consult the write-up of this Mitzvah in Sefer HaHinnuch.

174. THE SHAVING OF A HEALED M'TZORA ON THE SEVENTH DAY

(M'tzora means a person afflicted with a skin disorder, specifically leprosy.)

And it shall be on the seventh day, that he shall shave all his hair off his head and his beard and his eyebrows, even all his hair he shall shave off; and he shall wash his clothes, and he shall bathe his flesh in water, and he shall be clean. (Leviticus 14:9)

Mitzvah 174 states that for the leper to regain purification, every bit of hair is shaved off. This includes armpit hair and pubic hair. Humans are born without hair; therefore, the ritual shaving represents rebirth. The recovered leper is reborn; that person has atoned for his or her sins and that person is now on the path of righteousness. Their days of Lashon HaRah and committing other evil deeds are over.

175. THE PRECEPT OF RITUAL IMMERSION FOR CLEANSING THE DEFILED

And it shall be on the seventh day, that he shall shave all his hair off his head and his beard and his eyebrows, even all his hair he shall shave off; and he shall wash his clothes, and he shall bathe his flesh in water, and he shall be clean. (Leviticus 14:9)

Mitzvah 175 commands an impure person to bathe in the Ritual Mikveh bath. (Mikveh means gathering and in the case of immersion, it means the gathering of water.) The Ritual Mikveh bath cleanses the leper and cleanses a woman after menstruation.

The Ritual Mikveh bath does NOT cleanse a man who has had a bodily discharge.

And when he that hath an issue is cleansed of his issue, then he shall number to himself seven days for his cleansing, and wash his clothes; and he shall bathe his flesh in running water, and shall be clean. (Leviticus 15:13)

In Mitzvah 179, the author of Sefer HaHinnuch explains that if a man had a gonorrhea discharge, bathing in running water cleanses him.

176. THE PRECEPT OF THE OFFERING OF A M'TZORA WHEN HE IS HEALED

And on the eighth day he shall take two he-lambs without blemish, and one ewe-lamb of the first year without blemish,

and three tenth parts of an ephah of fine flour for a meal-offering, mingled with oil, and one log of oil. And the priest that cleanseth him shall set the man that is to be cleansed, and those things, before the LORD, at the door of the tent of meeting. And the priest shall take one of the he-lambs, and offer him for a guilt-offering, and the log of oil, and wave them for a wave-offering before the LORD. And he shall kill the he-lamb in the place where they kill the sin-offering and the burnt-offering, in the place of the sanctuary; for as the sin-offering is the priest's, so is the guilt-offering; it is most holy. And the priest shall take of the blood of the guilt-offering, and the priest shall put it upon the tip of the right ear of him that is to be cleansed, and upon the thumb of his right hand, and upon the great toe of his right foot. And the priest shall take of the log of oil, and pour it into the palm of his own left hand. And the priest shall dip his right finger in the oil that is in his left hand, and shall sprinkle of the oil with his finger seven times before the LORD. (Leviticus 14:10-16)

Mitzvah 176 commands the recovered leper to offer a burnt offering, a sin offering, and a guilt offering.

The three offerings are part of the process of the recovered leper humbling himself/herself before Hashem. As stated in previous Mitzvot, the individual developed leprosy due to saying and doing horrible things. Leprosy and its punishments are supposed to humble that individual.

177. THE RITUAL UNCLEANNESS OF A HOUSE CONTAMINATED WITH TZARA'AT INFECTION

When ye are come into the land of Canaan, which I give to you for a possession, and I put the plague of leprosy in a house of the land of your possession; then he that owneth the

house shall come and tell the priest, saying: 'There seemeth to me to be as it were a plague in the house.' And the priest shall command that they empty the house, before the priest go in to see the plague, that all that is in the house be not made unclean; and afterward the priest shall go in to see the house. And he shall look on the plague, and, behold, if the plague be in the walls of the house with hollow streaks, greenish or reddish, and the appearance thereof be lower than the wall; then the priest shall go out of the house to the door of the house, and shut up the house seven days. (Leviticus 14:34-38)

Mitzvah 177 commands that should a home owner see signs of leprosy in his or her house, that individual must report it to the priest. The priest would judge for himself if the house were infected or not. The signs of leprosy (actually mold, mildew or rot) are reddish or greenish spots/streaks. A bad odor usually goes with these symptoms.

The priest orders the owner to empty the house of all possessions to prevent them from contagion. If the priest determines the house is infected, the owner must scrape the plaster off the walls to remove the infection. The priest re-inspects the house. If the stones of the wall are infected, they are removed and replaced with new (clean) stones.

If the priest determines the entire house is badly infected, the house is destroyed.

Even today, we recognize that breathing in any black mold, mildew or rot growing on or inside the walls of our homes can make us sick.

178. ON THE RITUAL UNCLEANNESS OF A MAN WITH A GONORRHEAL DISCHARGE

And the LORD spoke unto Moses and to Aaron, saying: Speak unto the children of Israel, and say unto them: When any man hath an issue out of his flesh, his issue is unclean. And this shall be his uncleanness in his issue: whether his flesh run with his issue, or his flesh be stopped from his issue, it is his uncleanness. (Leviticus 15:1-3)

Mitzvah 178 states that should a man have two discharges from the opening of his generative organ (penis) in one day, he is unclean. If he has a third in the same day, he must present an offering at the Temple.

The author of Sefer HaHinnuch quotes the Sages' description of the discharged substance, resembling it to the liquid of dough from barley flour, and the white of a rotten unfertilized egg. They described semen as being the white of a sound fertilized egg. This was so the average, uneducated man would know that the discharge from the man's generative organ was not semen, but the substance just described. (Consult Sefer HaHinnuch for a more detailed description.)

Objects he touches can also become unclean:

Every bed whereon he that hath the issue lieth shall be unclean; and every thing whereon he sitteth shall be unclean. And whosoever toucheth his bed shall wash his clothes, and bathe himself in water, and be unclean until the even. And he that sitteth on any thing whereon he that hath the issue sat shall wash his clothes, and bathe himself in water, and be unclean until the even. And he that toucheth the flesh of him that hath the issue shall wash his clothes, and bathe himself in water, and be unclean until the even. And if he that hath

the issue spit upon him that is clean, then he shall wash his clothes, and bathe himself in water, and be unclean until the even. (Leviticus: 15:4-8)

179. ON THE OFFERING BY A MAN WITH A GONORRHEAL DISCHARGE, WHEN HE IS HEALED

And when he that hath an issue is cleansed of his issue, then he shall number to himself seven days for his cleansing, and wash his clothes; and he shall bathe his flesh in running water, and shall be clean. And on the eighth day he shall take to him two turtle-doves, or two young pigeons, and come before the LORD unto the door of the tent of meeting, and give them unto the priest. (Leviticus 15:13-14)

Mitzvah 179 states that when the man who had the gonorrheal discharge is cured, eight days later he must present a burnt offering and a sin offering at the Temple in order to be ritually pure again.

The following is my own interpretation as to why the man must wait eight days before he can be atoned for his actions:

A baby boy is circumcised eight days after birth. The holy ceremony makes him a member of the Jewish community. At eight days old, the circumcised infant is clean and pure. The man's atonement for his impure actions once again puts him on the same path as the circumcised infant. As mentioned above, the cured leper is immersed in water and has every body hair (including armpit hair and pubic hair) removed, because it symbolizes his (or her) rebirth. Like the cured leper, the cured man of the gonorrheal discharge is also reborn. He receives another chance to be closer with Hashem and to follow the Laws of the Torah.

180. ON THE RITUAL UNCLEANNESS OF SEMINAL FLUID

And if the flow of seed go out from a man, then he shall bathe all his flesh in water, and be unclean until the even. (Leviticus 15:16)

Mitzvah 180 states that when a man discharges semen, he is unclean for the remainder of the day. Regardless of how the seminal fluid discharged (sex or fantasizing about having sex, by accident or while sleeping), he is unclean. That night he would become clean after going to the Mikveh.

In the Days of the Temple, when a man became unclean for releasing his seminal fluid, he was not to learn Torah or put on Tefillin (phylacteries) so he could focus on fulfilling his desires. After the destruction of the Temple, the Sages allowed men to wear Tefillin and to study Torah the same day that they released seminal fluid.

181. THE PRECEPT OF THE RITUAL UNCLEANNESS OF A MENSTRUANT

And if a woman have an issue, and her issue in her flesh be blood, she shall be in her impurity seven days; and whosoever toucheth her shall be unclean until the even. (Leviticus 15:19)

Mitzvah 181 states that when a woman has her monthly period, and discharges blood (whether for one day or all seven days), she is in a state of impurity for seven days. On the eighth day she must undergo ritual immersion in water to become ritually clean again. She must abstain from sexual relations for seven days more. This Mitzvah also applies to Jewish maidservants and Canaanite slaves.

Whoever touches a woman during her menstrual period would be impure for the duration of the day. That person must also undergo ritual immersion in water to become ritually clean again.

This is a positive Mitzvah. I will cover this in greater depth when I discuss its negative counterpart in Mitzvah 207.

182. ON THE RITUAL UNCLEANNESS OF A WOMAN WITH AN IRREGULAR DISCHARGE

And if a woman have an issue of her blood many days not in the time of her impurity, or if she have an issue beyond the time of her impurity; all the days of the issue of her uncleanness she shall be as in the days of her impurity: she is unclean. (Leviticus 15:25)

Mitzvah 182 focuses on women's irregular blood discharges. The Sages state that when women menstruate, they are ritually unclean for seven days. After that they go to the Mikveh and become ritually clean again. The Sages state that if in the eleven days immediately following a woman's menstrual period, she has any discharge, then she is again considered unclean. She must be free of such discharges for a day before she can go to the Mikveh.

Should she have an irregular blood discharge two days in a row, the same law applies. However, if this irregular discharge occurs three days in a row, then she is again considered unclean. She must be free of that discharge for seven days straight before she can undergo ritual immersion at the Mikveh.

A woman who has any discharge after that eleven-day time frame is exempt from the requirement to undergo ritual immersion to become ritually clean again.

183. ON THE OFFERING BY A WOMAN WITH AN IRREGULAR DISCHARGE, WHEN SHE RECOVERS

But if she be cleansed of her issue, then she shall number to herself seven days, and after that she shall be clean. And on the eighth day she shall take unto her two turtle-doves, or two young pigeons, and bring them unto the priest, to the door of the tent of meeting. And the priest shall offer the one for a sin-offering, and the other for a burnt-offering; and the priest shall make atonement for her before the LORD for the issue of her uncleanness. (Leviticus 15:28-30)

Mitzvah 183 commands women who recover from their irregular blood discharges to present a sin offering and a burnt offering to the priest. The Sages explain that these women had irregular discharges for their wrongful deeds.

Mitzvah 179 required men who had irregular discharges to provide the exact same creatures for sacrifice. Like the women, these men had also erred.

184. THAT THE KOHANIM SHOULD ENTER THE INNER SANCTUARY ONLY FOR THE TEMPLE SERVICE

and the LORD said unto Moses: 'Speak unto Aaron thy brother, that he come not at all times into the holy place within the veil, before the ark-cover which is upon the ark; that he die not; for I appear in the cloud upon the ark-cover.' (Leviticus 16:2)

Mitzvah 184 forbids the priests from entering the Temple, except when they are required to perform Temple services.

The Temple is a holy place, the House of Hashem. The priests needed to focus all their attention on their required duties. Nobody, not even the priests, could come and go at will. If the priests had violated this Mitzvah, punishment ranged from 40 lashes of the whip to death.

185. THE PRECEPT OF THE TEMPLE SERVICE ON THE DAY OF ATONEMENT

Herewith shall Aaron come into the holy place: with a young bullock for a sin-offering, and a ram for a burnt-offering. He shall put on the holy linen tunic, and he shall have the linen breeches upon his flesh, and shall be girded with the linen girdle, and with the linen mitre shall he be attired; they are the holy garments; and he shall bathe his flesh in water, and put them on. And he shall take of the congregation of the children of Israel two he-goats for a sin-offering, and one ram for a burnt-offering. (Leviticus 16:3-5)

Mitzvah 185 requires the priests to perform burnt offerings and sin offerings on The Day of Atonement (Yom Kippur). (The priests have other responsibilities on The Day of Atonement, which are outlined in Chapter 16 of Leviticus.) On The Day of Atonement, the Children of Israel are to atone for the sins that they committed the previous year and then start fresh with a clean slate.

This Mitzvah teaches us that Hashem knows our limitations and He is ready to forgive us. In turn, we must realize that other people have limitations and we must learn to forgive them, just as Hashem forgives us. Hashem knows that we are not perfect and that is why he gave us the Torah.

186. NOT TO RITUALLY SLAY HOLY OFFERINGS OUTSIDE THE SANCTUARY FORECOURT

What man soever there be of the house of Israel, that killeth an ox, or lamb, or goat, in the camp, or that killeth it without the camp, and hath not brought it unto the door of the tent of meeting, to present it as an offering unto the LORD before the tabernacle of the LORD, blood shall be imputed unto that man; he hath shed blood; and that man shall be cut off from among his people. (Leviticus 17:3-4)

Mitzvah 186 prohibits ritual sacrifices to take place outside the designated area of the Temple. Hashem commands that the sacrifices take place in a specific area.

Under Hashem's orders, the priests cannot accept as a sacrifice any animal slaughtered outside of the designated area. They viewed it as shedding blood (killing/murder). People who violate this Mitzvah are to be severely punished. This Mitzvah is enforced when our Holy Temple exists.

187. THE PRECEPT OF COVERING THE BLOOD IN THE RITUAL SLAYING OF AN ANIMAL

And whatsoever man there be of the children of Israel, or of the strangers that sojourn among them, that taketh in hunting any beast or fowl that may be eaten, he shall pour out the blood thereof, and cover it with dust. (Leviticus 17:13)

Mitzvah 187 commands us to cover the blood of ritually slayed wild animals with earth.

If a man kills a beast or fowl with the intention of eating it, he must drain the blood from the dead creature and then cover the blood with dust / earth (bury the blood). No one is to eat the blood of ritually sacrificed beasts or fowls. (See Mitzvah 148 for a more detailed explanation.)

We do not eat or drink the blood of any beast or fowl to avoid confusion about which beasts and fowls are holy. Before we eat the animal, we must drain its blood and bury the blood as a sign of respect because it was the animal's life force.

Mitzvah 92 states that meat is the death force and milk is the life force. We do not have milk and meat together because it would be a mixture of the life force and death force together. Like milk, blood is the life force.

Burying the creature's blood is a sign of respect for the life force that comes from Hashem.

188. THE PROHIBITION OF PLEASURE WITH ANY WOMAN RANKED AS ERVAH

(Ervah means morally forbidden women. The Evrah includes a blood relative, another man's wife, or a menstruating woman.)

None of you shall approach to any that is near of kin to him, to uncover their nakedness. I am the LORD. (Leviticus 18:6)

Mitzvah 188 prohibits us from approaching morally forbidden women. To avoid the possibility of having sex with these women, we cannot engage in any type of foreplay with them. We cannot kiss them, hug them, gaze at them, smell their perfume, indulge in the pleasure of listening to their voices, or be alone with them. These actions can lead to sexual activity, just as a spark can lead to a fire. A brother and sister, a father and daughter, or a mother and son can have contact and even be alone together, but they cannot have sex or indulge in sexual foreplay with each other.

This Mitzvah sets the stage for the practice of "Shomer Negiah"–Observant Jews do not touch members of the opposite sex. Typical exceptions include brother and sister, husband and wife, mother and son, father and daughter, grandmother and grandson, or grandfather and granddaughter. Observant Jews who are Shomer Negiah will not even shake hands with members of the opposite sex because handshake can lead to a hug. A hug can lead to a kiss, and so on. Those who are Shomer Negiah pray separately from members of the opposite sex in order to focus on Hashem. Praying together can lead to distractions. For this reason, Husbands and wives also pray separately.

Some secular Jews and Gentiles ask 'where in the Torah is Shomer Negiah written?' One answer is Leviticus 18:6.

Author's Note: Hashem told Moses that the sexual practices of the people of Egypt and the people of Canaan were an abomination to Him. The Children of Israel were never to emulate those carnal relationships. The Jews were to follow Hashem's laws and customs and keep themselves holy and apart. To make sure all the Israelites understood, Hashem gave the following specifics. (Leviticus 18:1-6)

189. THE PROHIBITION ON UNCOVERING THE NAKEDNESS OF ONE'S FATHER

The nakedness of thy father, and the nakedness of thy mother, shalt thou not uncover: she is thy mother; thou shalt not uncover her nakedness. (Leviticus 18:7)

Mitzvah 189 forbids a father and son to have sexual relations. At least two witnesses must warn the offenders to stop; if the guilty parties ignore them, the offenders would be stoned to death.

If a son uncovered his father's nakedness inadvertently (had sexual relations not knowing it was his father), he would not be put to death. Instead, he would have to provide two sin offerings: one for sexual relations with his father and the other for having carnal relations with another man.

190. THE PROHIBITION ON UNCOVERING ONE'S MOTHER'S NAKEDNESS

The nakedness of thy father, and the nakedness of thy mother, shalt thou not uncover: she is thy mother; thou shalt not uncover her nakedness. The nakedness of thy father's wife shalt thou not uncover: it is thy father's nakedness. (Leviticus 18:7-8)

Mitzvah 190 forbids us from having sexual relations with our mothers. Punishment for this abomination is death by stoning.

At least two witnesses must warn the offenders to stop; if the guilty parties ignore them, the offenders would be stoned to death.

If a man had sex with his mother inadvertently (had sexual relations not knowing it was his mother), no death sentence would be carried out, however, he would have to provide a sin offering.

We cannot lie carnally with our mothers, even if our fathers are dead, because our mothers will always be our fathers' wives.

Other cultures also condemn this practice. One classic example is the Greek tale of Oedipus. Unbeknownst to him and his wife, Jocasta, they were mother and son. When they learned the truth, she hung herself and he gouged out both his eyes and lived out the remainder of his life in exile.

If Jocasta and Oedipus had been Jews at the time that this Mitzvah was applicable, Hashem would have forgiven them as long as they provided a sin offering because they did not know that they were mother and son.

191. THE PROHIBITION ON CONJUGAL INTIMACY WITH ONE'S FATHER'S WIFE EVEN IF SHE IS NOT HIS MOTHER

The nakedness of thy father's wife shalt thou not uncover: it is thy father's nakedness. (Leviticus 18:8)

Mitzvah 191 forbids intimacy between a man and his step-mother because it shows flagrant disrespect to the man's father. It violates the commandment of honoring our parents.

Ignoring the witnesses' warnings to stop would lead to death by stoning. If the act had been inadvertent, then forgiveness comes after providing a sin offering.

If a father and a stepmother divorce, or if a father dies, the son is still forbidden from having carnal relations with his step-mother because she will always be his father's wife.

192. NOT TO UNCOVER A SISTER'S NAKEDNESS, IF SHE IS ONE'S SISTER IN ANY WAY

The nakedness of thy sister, the daughter of thy father, or the daughter of thy mother, whether born at home, or born abroad, even their nakedness thou shalt not uncover. (Leviticus 18:9)

Mitzvah 192 forbids a brother to be sexually intimate with his sister or his half-sister (incest). Hashem has forbidden any sexual intercourse between blood relatives or near kinsmen.

If a man had sex with his sister inadvertently (had sexual relations not knowing it was his sister), no death sentence would be carried out, however, he would have to provide two sin offerings.

In today's society, Jews and non-Jews forbid incest–sexual intimacy between parent and child, between siblings, or between blood relatives. (See also the story of Amnon and Tamar in Second Samuel, Chapter 13, and Avot, Chapter 5, Mishnah 16.)

193. THE PROHIBITION OF CONJUGAL INTIMACY WITH THE DAUGHTER OF A SON

The nakedness of thy son's daughter, or of thy daughter's daughter, even their nakedness thou shalt not uncover; for theirs is thine own nakedness. (Leviticus 18:10)

Mitzvah 193 forbids a grandfather from having conjugal relations with his son's daughter (his granddaughter). Punishment for ignoring witnesses' warnings is death by swallowing molten liquid. If the act had been accidental, he must provide a sin offering.

194. THE PROHIBITION OF CONJUGAL INTIMACY WITH A DAUGHTER'S DAUGHTER

The nakedness of thy son's daughter, or of thy daughter's daughter, even their nakedness thou shalt not uncover; for theirs is thine own nakedness. (Leviticus 18:10)

Mitzvah 194 forbids one from having conjugal intimacy with his daughter's daughter (his granddaughter). Punishment for ignoring witnesses' warnings is death by swallowing molten liquid. If the act had been accidental, he must provide a sin offering.

195. THE PROHIBITION OF CONJUGAL INTIMACY WITH A DAUGHTER

No Torah verse forbids conjugal relations with one's daughter. In Sefer HaHinnuch, it states that no such Torah verse was necessary. Leviticus 18:10 states: The nakedness of thy son's daughter, or of thy daughter's daughter, even their nakedness thou shalt not uncover; for theirs is thine own nakedness.

Mitzvah 195 forbids a father from having sex with his daughter and his daughter's children. The Sages reasoned that because a man cannot have sex with the daughter of his son, nor can he have sex with the daughter of his daughter, therefore, a man cannot have sex with his daughter.

The passage, *"theirs is thine own nakedness,"* can be interpreted as the fruits of your loins are your sons, your daughters and all their children. Being sexually intimate with your grandchildren would be just as reprehensible as being sexually intimate with your children, for they are flesh of your own flesh (closely-tied blood relatives).

Ignoring witnesses' warnings to stop will lead to death by burning. If the act were unintentional, he must provide a sin offering.

196. THE PROHIBITION OF CONJUGAL RELATIONS WITH A SISTER ON THE FATHER'S SIDE WHO IS THE FATHER'S WIFE'S DAUGHTER

The nakedness of thy father's wife's daughter, begotten of thy father, she is thy sister, thou shalt not uncover her nakedness. (Leviticus 18:11)

Mitzvah 196 forbids us to have sex with the daughters of our fathers and stepmothers. This Mitzvah protects half-sisters and their mothers. The stepmother knows that her stepson is forbidden from sexually assaulting her daughter (his stepsister). If he committed the act deliberately, he receives divine severance of existence. If the act had been unintentional, he must provide two sin offerings.

197. THE PROHIBITION OF CONJUGAL INTIMACY WITH A FATHER'S SISTER

Thou shalt not uncover the nakedness of thy father's sister: she is thy father's near kinswoman. (Leviticus 18:12)

Mitzvah 197 forbids us from fornicating with our paternal aunts (near kinswoman). Doing it deliberately brings about divine severance of existence. If it were accidental, a sin offering is required.

198. THE PROHIBITION OF CONJUGAL INTIMACY WITH A MOTHER'S SISTER

Thou shalt not uncover the nakedness of thy mother's sister; for she is thy mother's near kinswoman. (Leviticus 18:13)

Mitzvah 198 forbids us from fornicating with our maternal aunts (near kinswoman).

The consequences are identical to those described in Mitzvah 197: doing it deliberately brings about divine severance of existence. If it were accidental, a sin offering is required.

199. THE PROHIBITION OF CARNAL RELATIONS WITH A FATHER'S BROTHER

Thou shalt not uncover the nakedness of thy fathers brother, thou shalt not approach to his wife: she is thine aunt. (Leviticus 18:14)

Mitzvah 199 forbids carnal relations with a father's brother. This constitutes two offenses: having sexual relations with a paternal uncle, and having sexual relations with another man. (See Mitzvah 209 for a more detailed discussion about Hashem's prohibition of homosexuality.)

Ignoring the witnesses' warnings to stop this abomination would lead to death by stoning. If the act had been inadvertent, the guilty parties must bring two sin offerings to the Temple.

200. THE PROHIBITION OF CONJUGAL RELATIONS WITH THE WIFE OF A FATHER'S BROTHER

Thou shalt not uncover the nakedness of thy fathers brother, thou shalt not approach to his wife: she is thine aunt. (Leviticus 18:14)

Mitzvah 200 forbids us from lying carnally with the wife of a father's brother (your aunt or your step-aunt). This applies even if the uncle divorces his wife or the uncle dies.

If a man intentionally had intercourse with his aunt while his uncle was alive, and the guilty parties ignored the witnesses' repeated warnings to stop, BOTH the guilty parties would be put to death by strangulation.

If a man intentionally had intercourse with his aunt after his uncle died, and the guilty parties ignored the witnesses' repeated warnings to stop, the man would be whipped.

If the act had been an accident, a sin offering must be provided.

The Sages added the prohibition of (1) lying carnally with a paternal uncle's wife (who is his father's half-brother from their mother's side) and (2) lying carnally with a maternal uncle's wife. Because either of these two scenarios is not a Torah prohibition, the punishment is less severe. If done intentionally, and if witnesses' repeated warnings go unheeded, the guilty party receives a whipping. If performed unintentionally, then nobody gets punished.

201. THE PROHIBITION OF CONJUGAL RELATIONS WITH THE WIFE OF A SON

Thou shalt not uncover the nakedness of thy daughter-in-law: she is thy son' wife; thou shalt not uncover her nakedness. (Leviticus 18:15)

Mitzvah 201 prohibits lying carnally with a son's wife, even if the son divorces her or the son dies.

If this act were committed intentionally, and the son ignored witnesses' warnings to stop, he is guilty and would be put to death by stoning. If done accidentally, one sin offering would be required.

The Sages extended this prohibition to also forbid a man to have sexual relations not just with his son's wife (daughter-in-law) or his grandson's wife, but down through the generations of all his male descendants. The Sages also extended this prohibition of forbidding a man to have sexual relations with his daughter's daughter-in-law; but didn't extend the prohibition to subsequent generations. For willful violations of these Rabbinic extensions, the punishment was whipping.

202. THE PROHIBITION OF CONJUGAL RELATIONS WITH A BROTHER'S WIFE

Thou shalt not uncover the nakedness of thy brother's wife: it is thy brother's nakedness. (Leviticus 18:16)

Mitzvah 202 prohibits having sexual relations with a brother's wife (your sister-in-law). Uncovering her nakedness is uncovering the nakedness of your brother because she is his wife, a part of him.

If lying with your brother's wife had been accidental, a sin offering would be required. A flagrant and willful violation of this Mitzvah results in death by strangulation, if the violation occurred while she was still married to your brother. (Strangulation is carried out for the general prohibition of being sexually intimate with another man's wife.)

If your brother had died and they already had children, punishment for breaking this Mitzvah is divine severance.

However, if your brother had died and they had no children, another brother is obligated to marry the widow in a levirate marriage. See Mitzvah 598 for a more detailed discussion about the levirate marriage.

203. THE PROHIBITION OF CONJUGAL RELATIONS WITH BOTH A WOMAN AND HER DAUGHTER

Thou shalt not uncover the nakedness of a woman and her daughter; thou shalt not take her son's daughter, or her

daughter's daughter, to uncover her nakedness: they are near kinswomen; it is lewdness. (Leviticus 18:17)

Mitzvah 203 forbids lying carnally with both a woman and her daughter.

If a man marries a woman, he cannot lie carnally with his wife's daughter (his stepdaughter).

If a man marries a woman's daughter, he cannot lie carnally with the daughter's mother (his mother-in-law).

If the guilty parties were sexually intimate, and they ignored witnesses' warnings to stop, they would be put to death by swallowing molten liquid.

If the immoral act were accidental, a sin offering would be required.

If a man is married to either of these two women, he is forbidden to have sexual relations with the other one because the 3 of them are closely related kin. This prohibition continues even after the man's wife dies. Violating this Mitzvah results in divine severance of existence for the man.

The Sages added that if a man lies with a woman without being married to her, he cannot marry any of her immediate relatives because should the immoral woman visit them, he might have memories and desires to rekindle an immoral relationship.

204. THE PROHIBITION OF CONJUGAL INTIMACY WITH BOTH A WOMAN AND HER SON'S DAUGHTER

Thou shalt not uncover the nakedness of a woman and her daughter; thou shalt not take her son's daughter, or her daughter's daughter, to uncover her nakedness: they are near kinswomen; it is lewdness. (Leviticus 18:17)

Mitzvah 204 prohibits lying carnally with both a woman and her son's daughter (her granddaughter). If a man is married to the woman or to her granddaughter, having carnal relations with the other is forbidden.

If the guilty parties intentionally or willfully violate this Mitzvah, and ignore at least two witnesses' repeated warnings to stop, the punishment for both parties is death by swallowing molten liquid. If the sexual act happened accidentally or unintentionally, a sin offering is required.

If a man is married to one of the two women, and she dies, the prohibition of lying carnally with the surviving woman remains in place. The punishment for both parties is divine severance of existence.

The Sages added the prohibition of lying carnally with the daughter of a woman's son's son (her great-granddaughter). If a man violates this edict, he is to receive a whipping.

205. THE PROHIBITION OF CONJUGAL INTIMACY WITH BOTH A WOMAN AND HER DAUGHTER'S DAUGHTER

Thou shalt not uncover the nakedness of a woman and her daughter; thou shalt not take her son's daughter, or her

daughter's daughter, to uncover her nakedness: they are near kinswomen; it is lewdness. (Leviticus 18:17)

Mitzvah 205 prohibits lying carnally with both a woman and her daughter's daughter (her granddaughter). If a man is married to the woman or to her granddaughter, having carnal relations with the other is forbidden.

If the guilty parties intentionally or willfully violate this Mitzvah, and ignore at least two witnesses' repeated warnings to stop, the punishment for both parties is death by swallowing molten liquid. If the sexual act happened accidentally or unintentionally, a sin offering is required.

If a man is married to one of the two women, and she dies, the prohibition of lying carnally with the surviving woman remains in place. The punishment for both parties is divine severance of existence.

The Sages added the prohibition of lying carnally with the daughter of her daughter's daughter (her great-granddaughter). If a man violates this edict, he receives a whipping.

206. THE PROHIBITION OF CONJUGAL RELATIONS WITH TWO SISTERS WHILE BOTH ARE ALIVE

And thou shalt not take a woman to her sister, to be a rival to her, to uncover her nakedness, beside the other in her lifetime. (Leviticus 18:18)

Mitzvah 206 forbids a man from marrying a woman and her sister. He cannot marry both sisters.

If he divorces one woman, he cannot marry her sister while his former wife is alive. Once his former wife dies, then he can marry her sister. If sisters did not have this propensity to be jealous of each other, Hashem would not have put this prohibition in place.

The Sages took this prohibition one step further: If the oldest brother were married and dies without having children, his younger brother must marry his widow.

If the younger brother releases the widow from this obligation, and never actually marries her, he still cannot marry her sister. The Sages believed that would spark rivalry and resentment between the two sisters.

Another possible reason for this Mitzvah is that jealousy and resentment have the potential to interfere with some of a woman's important responsibilities such as being like Hashem by creating life. In addition, it can prevent her from focusing on exposing her children to Yiddishkeit. She can do that with an angry and bitter heart, but she would do a much better job if she were happy and had no feelings of anger, resentment, or jealousy.

According to the author of Sefer HaHinnuch, Hashem wants his human creations to live peacefully and harmoniously with one another. How can one live in tranquility with a jealous heart? Therefore, Hashem prohibited marrying two sisters where the potential for jealousy and discord is great.

207. THE PROHIBITION OF CONJUGAL INTIMACY WITH A MENSTRUOUS WOMAN

And thou shalt not approach unto a woman to uncover her nakedness, as long as she is impure by her uncleanness. (Leviticus 18:19)

Mitzvah 207 forbids sexual intimacy with a woman when she has her monthly period. In Mitzvah 181, the Sages determined that a woman's menstrual period (whether she bleeds for one day or all seven days) makes her impure for seven days. She is forbidden to have sexual relations with her husband during those seven days. After the woman undergoes ritual immersion, she is now ritually clean and able to have intercourse with her husband.

Due to the normal intimacy that exists between a husband and wife the Sages instituted several safeguards to ensure that they do not have sexual relations during the menstrual period. He may not eat from the same plate as his wife. He may not speak words leading to foreplay or intimacy. During that time of the month, her husband cannot touch her in any way, whatsoever. If a husband needs to hand his wife an object, he puts it down on a table and then she picks it up. Their hands do not touch.

During menstruation, a woman's body is eliminating blood and body fluids often accompanied by cramping muscles, and varying degrees of discomfort and pain. She can easily become upset because her body hurts. Some husbands find that the interior temperature of their wife's body is too hot to sustain their erection.

It is a time when she needs to talk. Since a husband cannot touch her during that time, he ends up listening to what she has to say. This builds verbal communication between husband and wife.

Conjugal relations during menstruation rarely result in pregnancy. So her husband has wasted his seed and not fulfilled Hashem's command to be fruitful and multiply.

After she ritually immerses herself in the Mikveh and can lie with her husband again, their reunification is comparable to a second honeymoon. Some Rabbis have said that the divorce rate would be much lower if all couples, Jews and non-Jews, would follow the practice of abstaining from sexual relations for the two weeks of each month coinciding with the wife's menstrual period.

The following passage from Avot, Chapter 5, Mishnah 19 applies here: "Any love that is dependent on a specific cause, when that cause is gone, love is gone. But if love does not depend on the specific cause, that love will never cease." When my Partner in Torah explained this specific Mishnah to me, he told about one of the Chasidic Rabbis who saw a man enjoying himself by gobbling up a tasty dish of fish. The Rabbi asked him, "why are you eating the fish?" The man was surprised, but he responded, "because I love fish." The Rabbi said, "if you really love the fish, you would have let it live in the water. You're eating it because you love yourself and the fish gratifies your appetite." People often think of love as what does the other person do for me? However, the concept of love in Judaism is based on the love and devotion to Hashem. Just as there's devotion to Hashem, which is not self-centered, there can also be love and/or devotion for another person. A classic example is the love that David and Jonathan had for each other. Their love was unconditional. The strength of the relationship between two people is in a marriage for example. It is determined by the level of devotion that one spouse has for the other, and not dependent on the fulfillment of one's sexual desires. In many cases, what we call a loving relationship does bring gratification to people involved–even things like making supper and/or doing the laundry. A person should not keep score of all the things the spouse did for him/her. Keeping score can lead to disappointment. According to the Jewish understanding, the feeling of love is derived from the concept of Chessed–loving kindness.

On a final note, saying a woman is unclean or impure during her cycle of menstruation, coupled with her husband not lying with her during that time of the month, does not mean that she is guilty of a wrongful deed. Some people have believed that being unclean and impure is bad. In some cases, that is correct, but not in the case of a woman going through her monthly period. The restrictions imposed on her during that time of the month are for her benefit.

208. NOT TO GIVE ANY OF OUR CHILDREN TO THE IDOL MOLECH

And thou shalt not give any of thy seed to set them apart to Molech, neither shalt thou profane the name of thy God: I am the LORD. (Leviticus 18:21)

Mitzvah 208 forbids offering our children to the idol Molech.

A pagan custom was for a father to hand his child to the pagan priest who would then hold the child up to the Idol Molech. The priest would say a prayer, then hand the child back to the father. They would build a fire and the father would pass his child through or over the fire.

RAMBAM, RASHI, and RAMBAN did not believe that the act of Molech-worship involved burning the child. RAMBAM is the acronym for Rabbi Moses Ben Maimon who lived 1135-1204 CE. (I identified RASHI in Mitzvah 5 and RAMBAN in Mitzvah 166.)

In ancient times, the desire to worship idols and to pass children through / over fires was so tempting that prohibitions were established to prevent these practices.

209. THE PROHIBITION OF CARNAL RELATIONS WITH ANY MALE

Thou shalt not lie with mankind, as with womankind; it is abomination. (Leviticus 18:22)

Mitzvah 209 prohibits two men lying carnally together. Willfully violating this mitzvah results in death by stoning.

Hashem created us to fulfill the first Mitzvah, to be fruitful and multiply. Homosexuality wastes the seed that was intended to populate the world. For this reason, women are not to marry young boys not capable of producing children; and men are not to marry barren women.

If a man has desires to fornicate with another man, or has desires to lie with children, yet successfully resists the temptation, he is to be commended for controlling his passions. One cannot stop certain desires, yet with Hashem's help, one can keep from fulfilling such loathsome wishes.

The Sages praised Joseph for successfully refusing to lie with Potiphar's wife. She frequently threw herself at him, yet Joseph never succumbed. (Potiphar's wife is not named in the Tora. She is given the name Zuleikha, in the mediaeval **Sefer HaYashar,** a commentary on the Torah.)

I wondered why there was no law in the Torah forbidding two women from having carnal relations. After researching, I found a few possible answers: Mitzvah 209 forbids homosexuality because Hashem's seed is wasted. However, women cannot emit semen. They are unable to be planters. This is why only men are required to fulfill the first Mitzvah.

The Rabbis have traditionally condemned lesbianism. According to Rabbi Gershon, the ancient Rabbis sought to rule against lesbianism but the Sanhedrin refused to carry out that request. Their refusal is summed up in their statement: "What the Torah allows, man cannot disallow." (See the link http://home.earthlink.net/~ecorebbe/id3.html for a more detailed discussion.)

RAMBAM argued that lesbianism is forbidden because it was a "practice of Egypt" and because it constituted rebelliousness. See http://www.jewfaq.org/sex.htm for more information.

Because the topic of wasting the seed is covered in this Mitzvah, it should be noted that Hashem has a dim view of masturbation. See the following passage from Genesis:

And Judah said unto Onan: 'Go in unto thy brother's wife, and perform the duty of a husband's brother unto her, and raise up seed to thy brother.' And Onan knew that the seed would not be his; and it came to pass when he went in unto his brother's wife, that he spilled it on the ground, lest he should give seed to his brother. And the thing which he did was evil in the sight of the LORD; and He slew him also. (Genesis 38:8-10)

210. THE PROHIBITION OF CARNAL RELATIONS WITH ANIMALS

And thou shalt not lie with any beast to defile thyself therewith; neither shall any woman stand before a beast, to lie down thereto; it is perversion. (Leviticus 18:23)

Mitzvah 210 forbids lying carnally with animals.

Hashem never intended man to mate with animals. This is evident in the following passages from Genesis:

And God said: 'Let the earth put forth grass, herb yielding seed, and fruit-tree bearing fruit after its kind, wherein is the seed thereof, upon the earth.' And it was so. (Genesis 1:11) And God created the great sea-monsters, and every living creature that creepeth, wherewith the waters swarmed, after its kind, and every winged fowl after its kind; and God saw that it was good. And God blessed them, saying: 'Be fruitful, and multiply, and fill the waters in the seas, and let fowl multiply in the earth.' (Genesis 1:21-22) And God said: 'Let the earth bring forth the living creature after its kind, cattle, and creeping thing, and beast of the earth after its kind.' And it was so. And God made the beast of the earth after its kind, and the cattle after their kind, and every thing that creepeth upon the ground after its kind; and God saw that it was good. And God said: 'Let us make man in our image, after our likeness; and let them have dominion over the fish of the sea, and over the fowl of the air, and over the cattle, and over all the earth, and over every creeping thing that creepeth upon the earth.' (Genesis 1:24-26)

Hashem's repeated phrase, "after its kind" was clearly indicative that He intended for specific creatures to mate with creatures of their own kind.

If a male adult makes love to an animal and ignores at least two witnesses' repeated warnings to stop, both the guilty man and animal are stoned to death. If this were done unwittingly, then the beast is not killed. The male offender must provide a sin offering.

If a boy older than 9-years-old, were to have had carnal relations with an animal, the animal would be killed, but he would just be chastised. If a boy younger than 9-years of age had sex with an animal, then the animal's life would be spared. One possible explanation is that the boy would be incapable of producing seminal fluid. He cannot waste his seed because at that young age, he has none to waste.

211. THE PROHIBITION ON CARNAL INTIMACY BY A WOMAN WITH AN ANIMAL

And thou shalt not lie with any beast to defile thyself therewith; neither shall any woman stand before a beast, to lie down thereto; it is perversion. (Leviticus 18:23)

Mitzvah 211 forbids a woman to lie carnally with animals.

If a girl, 12-years-old or older lies carnally with an animal, both she and the creature are stoned to death. If performed unwittingly, the beast is not killed, and she must provide a sin offering. If she performs this act from ages three, up until her 12th birthday, then she is chastised, but the creature is stoned to death. However, if she lies with the creature, and has not yet reached her third birthday, then the creature goes free.

212. THE MITZVAH REVERENCE FOR FATHER AND MOTHER

Ye shall fear every man his mother, and his father, and ye shall keep My sabbaths: I am the LORD your God. (Leviticus 19:3)

Mitzvah 212 commands us to have a reverential fear of our parents. Having this fear prevents us from contradicting them, sitting in their place, or speaking from their place (i.e., preempting their response). If a parent strikes their adult son or adult daughter, neither grown child can strike back. However, the Talmud forbids parents to hit their grown children.

213. NOT TO TURN ASTRAY AFTER IDOL-WORSHIP IN THOUGHT OR WORD

Turn ye not unto the idols, nor make to yourselves molten gods: I am the LORD your God. (Leviticus 19:4)

Mitzvah 213 forbids us from looking at idols, thinking about them, and studying them. We are to keep our minds free of such thoughts. Observing this Mitzvah reduces the temptation to worship idols.

214. TO MAKE NO IDOL, FOR ONESELF OR FOR ANYONE ELSE

Turn ye not unto the idols, nor make to yourselves molten gods: I am the LORD your God. (Leviticus 19:4) The graven images of their gods shall ye burn with fire; thou shalt not covet the silver or the gold that is on them, nor take it unto thee, lest thou be snared therein; for it is an abomination to the LORD thy God. And thou shalt not bring an abomination into thy house, and be accursed like unto it; thou shalt utterly detest it, and thou shalt utterly abhor it; for it is an accursed thing. (Deuteronomy 7:25-26) Cursed be the man that maketh a graven or molten image, an abomination unto the LORD, the work of the hands of the craftsman, and setteth it up in secret. And all the people shall answer and say: Amen. (Deuteronomy 27:15)

Mitzvah 214 forbids us to make idols for ourselves or for Non-Jews.

There was a time in history when worshipping idols was extremely tempting and addicting. Hashem did away with the Jewish peoples' desires to worship idols, but He simultaneously abolished prophecy. Prior to Hashem's actions, the temptation to worship idols was so great that there was a need for this Mitzvah.

215. THE PROHIBITION OF EATING LEFT-OVER MEAT OF SACRIFICES

It shall be eaten the same day ye offer it, and on the morrow; and if aught remain until the third day, it shall be burnt with fire. And if it be eaten at all on the third day, it is a vile thing; it shall not be accepted. But every one that eateth it shall bear his iniquity, because he hath profaned the holy thing of the LORD; and that soul shall be cut off from his people. (Leviticus 19:6-8)

Mitzvah 215 states that we can eat the meat of a sacrificed animal for a designated time-period of 2 days. After that, no one can eat it.

The time-period for eating the meat of a sacrificed animal was briefly mentioned in Mitzvah 144. Mitzvah 144 forbids a priest to sacrifice an animal if, during the offering, he thought about eating its meat after the expired time period.

Mitzvah 215 is the actual prohibition of eating the meat of a properly sacrificed animal after the specific time-period of 2 days.

216. THE MITZVAH OF LEAVING AN EDGE OF ONE'S FIELD UNREAPED, FOR THE POOR

And when ye reap the harvest of your land, thou shalt not wholly reap the corner of thy field, neither shalt thou gather the gleaning of thy harvest. And thou shalt not glean thy vineyard, neither shalt thou gather the fallen fruit of thy vineyard; thou shalt leave them for the poor and for the stranger: I am the LORD your God. (Leviticus 19:9-10)

Mitzvah 216 requires landowners to leave food grown from the earth on a corner of their fields (called Peah) for poor people. This Mitzvah applies to food grown from the ground that is gathered all at once, and that would normally be moved to a different location for storage. These foods include grapes, olives, dates, almonds, nuts, carobs, legumes, and grains. Because the Torah did not state what specific amount should be left for the poor, the Sages decided that the designated amount would be one sixtieth. According to Tractate Peah, Chapter 1, Mishnah 1, there is no fixed amount for Peah mentioned in the Torah. But, according to the Rabbis, Mishnah 2 does spell out the minimum. See also Shabbat, Folio 1 to 7A.

Landowners are not required to leave Peah from figs because figs are not gathered all at one time. Nor do they have to leave Peah from green vegetables because they are not moved to another location, away from the field for storage.

This Mitzvah teaches us that we are the caretakers of the crops and the fields, but Hashem is the ultimate owner. Everything we have on earth is only ours to "borrow".

Leaving food for the poor reminds us that some people are less fortunate and need our help, just as we need Hashem's help. In addition, the Book of Job demonstrates that anyone can be healthy and wealthy and in the blink of an eye become ill and destitute.

217. NOT TO REAP THE VERY LAST END OF ONE'S FIELD

And when ye reap the harvest of your land, thou shalt not wholly reap the corner of thy field, neither shalt thou gather the gleaning of thy harvest. (Leviticus 19:9)

Mitzvah 217 is the negative commandment of Mitzvah 216. Should the person reap his entire field, without leaving Peah, he is still required to provide one sixtieth of his produce to the poor. If all his produce was lost or burned before he could rectify his error, he would be subject to lashes.

218. THE PRECEPT OF LEAVING THE GLEANINGS OF THE HARVEST FOR THE POOR

And thou shalt not glean thy vineyard, neither shalt thou gather the fallen fruit of thy vineyard; thou shalt leave them for the poor and for the stranger: I am the LORD your God. (Leviticus 19:10)

Mitzvah 218 states that poor people can claim whatever falls from the sickle during reaping or from the hands during picking.

The Sages stated that poor people may claim one or two ears of grain. Should three or more ears drop from the sickle or from the picker's hands, they still belong to the owner.

The Sages may have placed this limit on the amount that the poor can claim because Hashem told Moses that the owner was to leave some produce that the poor could eat; and that the poor were to leave some produce for the animals to eat.

219. NOT TO GATHER STALKS OF GRAIN THAT FELL AWAY DURING THE HARVEST

And when ye reap the harvest of your land, thou shalt not wholly reap the corner of thy field, neither shalt thou gather the gleaning of thy harvest. (Leviticus 19:9)

Mitzvah 219 is the negative commandment of Mitzvah 218, not to pick up the ears of grain that fell from your bundle during the harvesting. Violating Mitzvah 219 means the guilty party receives lashes of the whip.

220. THE PRECEPT OF LEAVING PART OF A VINEYARD UNREAPED, FOR THE POOR

And thou shalt not glean thy vineyard, neither shalt thou gather the fallen fruit of thy vineyard; thou shalt leave them for the poor and for the stranger: I am the LORD your God. (Leviticus 19:10)

Mitzvah 220 commands vineyard owners to leave a portion of grapes for poor people to claim. This continues the Mitzvah of Peah by other crops. The owner was to leave some grapes on the vine and not remove grapes that had fallen to the ground so that poor people and strangers (travelers) could eat them.

221. THE PROHIBITION OF REAPING ABSOLUTELY ALL THE FRUIT OF A VINEYARD

And thou shalt not glean thy vineyard, neither shalt thou gather the fallen fruit of thy vineyard; thou shalt leave them for the poor and for the stranger: I am the LORD your God. (Leviticus 19:10)

Mitzvah 221 is a prohibition against picking every last bit of fruit from one's vineyard.

Hashem had said that after harvest, poor people can take grapes that are in a corner of the field, left on the vine, or fallen on the ground.

RAMBAN believed that in addition to the corners, poor people have a claim to the grapes that do not grow in full bunches. Whether such grapes are in the field's corner or not, the poor person can claim them.

222. THE PRECEPT OF LEAVING FALLEN GRAPES IN A VINEYARD, FOR THE POOR

And thou shalt not glean thy vineyard, neither shalt thou gather the fallen fruit of thy vineyard; thou shalt leave them for the poor and for the stranger: I am the LORD your God. (Leviticus 19:10)

Mitzvah 222 commands us to leave grapes that drop from our bundles during harvesting for poor people to claim. This continues the Mitzvah of Peah for the poor from Mitzvah 220 and Mitzvah 221.

223. THE PROHIBITION OF GATHERING THE FALLEN GRAPES IN A VINEYARD

And thou shalt not glean thy vineyard, neither shalt thou gather the fallen fruit of thy vineyard; thou shalt leave them for the poor and for the stranger: I am the LORD your God. (Leviticus 19:10)

Mitzvah 223 is the prohibition against picking up individual grapes that fall from gathered bundles (this is the negative version of Mitzvah 222). Those grapes become the poor person's property.

224. THE PROHIBITION ON THE THEFT OF ANYTHING OF VALUE

Ye shall not steal; neither shall ye deal falsely, nor lie one to another. (Leviticus 19:11)

Mitzvah 224 prohibits stealing anything that has monetary value. Even if the person intends to return it, he or she cannot steal it. In most cases, a thief must repay a double sum to the victim. (In Mitzvah 54, I explained why stealing is regarded as a double crime.)

Mitzvah 224 also prohibits the purchase of stolen goods because that enhances wrongdoing.

225. NOT TO DENY IT WHEN SOMETHING OF VALUE THAT BELONGS TO ANOTHER IS IN OUR POSSESSION

Ye shall not steal; neither shall ye deal falsely, nor lie one to another. (Leviticus 19:11)

Mitzvah 225 states that if someone agreed to watch over another person's possession(s), then the bailee cannot deny that the owner deposited the item(s) with him. If the owner wants to reclaim his or her possession(s), the bailee cannot deny ever having them.

226. NOT TO SWEAR OVER A FALSE DENIAL ABOUT SOMETHING OF VALUE

Ye shall not steal; neither shall ye deal falsely, nor lie one to another. And ye shall not swear by My name falsely, so that thou profane the name of thy God: I am the LORD. (Leviticus 19:11-12)

Mitzvah 226 takes Mitzvah 225 one step further. Mitzvah 225 states that if someone agreed to watch over another person's possessions, then the bailee cannot deny receiving those items from their owner. Mitzvah 226 also states that the bailee is forbidden to use Hashem's name to swear that the falsehoods he told are true, either in the street or in court.

If it is proved in court that the bailee lied under oath, it is a serious offense because the bailee broke 2 rules: (1) he lied to another person and (2) he used Hashem's name to swear in court that the lie he told was true. His punishment would be lashes of the whip.

227. THE PROHIBITION AGAINST SWEARING FALSELY

And ye shall not swear by My name falsely, so that thou profane the name of thy God: I am the LORD. (Leviticus 19:12)

Mitzvah 227 is the prohibition against swearing falsely.

The Talmud lists four ways of swearing falsely, two dealing with the past and two dealing with the future:

Example One: "I performed that Mitzvah," but the person lied.

Example Two: "I did not have enough money last month to pay back the man who kindly lent me some," but that person lied.

Example Three: "I will pay my debts next month," and then that person lies.

Example Four: "I will not shower tomorrow," and then he breaks that promise.

Other Torah passages stress the importance of fulfilling vows:

When thou shalt vow a vow unto the LORD thy God, thou shalt not be slack to pay it; for the LORD thy God will surely require it of thee; and it will be sin in thee. But if thou shalt forbear to vow, it shall be no sin in thee. That which is gone out of thy lips thou shalt observe and do; according as thou hast vowed freely unto the LORD thy God, even that which thou hast promised with thy mouth. (Deuteronomy 23:22-24)

At the beginning of Yom Kippur (The Day of Atonement), the congregation chants Kol Nidre. This prayer absolves us of past and future vows to Hashem, not to other people. In the past, certain Gentiles twisted its meaning. They stated that Jews could not be trusted because they were absolving themselves of fulfilling their obligations to other people. Such lines from the prayer include:

"All personal vows we are likely to make, all personal oaths and pledges we are likely to take between this Yom Kippur and the next Yom Kippur, we publicly renounce. Let them all be relinquished and abandoned, null and void, neither firm nor established. Let our personal vows, pledges and oaths be considered neither vows nor pledges nor oaths." (Translation by Philip Birnbaum, from High Holyday Prayer Book, Hebrew Publishing Company, NY, 1951)

(See the full article on the link, http://www.torah.net/eng/parsha/02-002.htm)

That link also provides the article, YOM KIPPUR: ON THE RECITATION OF KOL NIDREY

Taken from a weekly publication of Hammaayan Institutes.

Translated by Rabbi Shabtai Teicher.

The author wrote:

"If one made a vow and forgot to abide by its terms, he has jeopardized the atonement he seeks on Yom Kippur. His only recourse is the advance repeal of future vows by which he may fail to abide; and thereby he may enter Yom Kippur without bearing the sin of violated vows. In addition to the repeal of future vows, Kol Nidrey also retroactively repeals all the vows which one might have made during the course of the previous year, but which he had forgotten."

The Kol Nidre Prayer proved to be ritually cleansing for Jews forced to convert to Christianity, and for those Jews who feared that they would convert in order to avoid death at the hands of the Gentiles.

One of the worst vows to Hashem can be found in the Book of Judges Chapter 11 verses 30-35.

30 And Jephthah vowed a vow to the Lord, and said, "If You will indeed deliver the children of Ammon into my hand,

31 And it will be, whatever comes forth, that shall come forth from the doors of my house towards me, when I return in peace from the children of Ammon, shall be to the Lord, and I will offer him up for a burnt-offering."

32 And Jephthah passed over to the children of Ammon to fight against them; and the Lord delivered them into his hand.

33 And he struck them from Aroer until you come to Minnith, twenty cities, and up to Abel Cheramim, a very great slaughter. And the children of Ammon were subdued before the children of Israel.

Abel Cheramim: The plain of vineyards [after Targum Jonathan].

34 And Jephthah came to Mizpah, to his house, and behold, his daughter was coming out towards him with timbrels and with dances, and she was an only child, he had from her neither a son nor a daughter.

35 And it was, when he saw her, that he rent his clothes, and said, "Alas, my daughter! You have made me fall and you have become one of those that trouble me; and I have opened my mouth to the Lord and I cannot go back." (Cited at http://www.chabad.org/library/bible_cdo/aid/15819/jewish/Chapter-11.htm)

A problem with Jephthah's vow is that Hashem hates human sacrifice.

Thou shalt not do so unto the LORD thy God; for every abomination to the LORD, which He hateth, have they done unto their gods; for even their sons and their daughters do they burn in the fire to their gods. (Deuteronomy 12:31)

My Partner in Torah explained to me that there is extensive debate among the commentators regarding two aspects of Jephthah's vow:

First: The language of the vow in verse 31 is vague: Did he intend to include people in the vow, or was he thinking about possible animals that would come out first? When he lived, animal sacrifices were permitted. Jephthah's intent was unclear.

Second: It is debatable, whether or not Jephthah had his daughter actually killed or just sequestered permanently.

228. NOT TO WITHHOLD ANOTHER PERSON'S PROPERTY WRONGLY

Thou shalt not oppress thy neighbour, nor rob him; the wages of a hired servant shall not abide with thee all night until the morning. (Leviticus 19:13)

Mitzvah 228 is the prohibition against withholding something from someone that rightfully belongs to him. A person cannot procrastinate in returning something that he borrowed from someone.

This Mitzvah also deals with the prohibition against withholding owed wages. If an employer or a borrower owes money to his employees or lenders, he must provide financial compensation with no delay, once the obligation has come due.

229. THE PROHIBITION AGAINST COMMITTING ROBBERY

Thou shalt not oppress thy neighbour, nor rob him; the wages of a hired servant shall not abide with thee all night until the morning. (Leviticus 19:13)

There is a difference between robbing and stealing. Robbing is taking another person's possessions in the victim's presence. Stealing is taking something without the victim seeing it happen.

Mitzvah 229 is the prohibition against robbing another human being. This Mitzvah pertains strictly to the prohibition against committing robbery.

This Mitzvah forbids us to rob any other human being, including Jews, non-Jews, Jews who converted to other religions, and Jews who try to persuade other Jews to convert. The Talmud states that this prohibition also extends to foreign enemies, even those whom we are permitted to destroy.

The Sages forbid us from robbing foreign enemies of their possessions because those people might have righteous descendants. The best example of this is Ruth. She was a righteous Moabite who converted to Judaism, and became the great-grandmother of King David. Ruth was also a direct descendant of the Moabite king, Balak.

Balak's intentions to harm the Children of Israel are in the following passages:

And Moab said unto the elders of Midian: 'Now will this multitude lick up all that is round about us, as the ox licketh up the grass of the field.'—And Balak the son of Zippor was king of Moab at that time.— And he sent messengers unto Balaam the son of Beor, to Pethor, which is by the River, to the land of the children of his people, to call him, saying: 'Behold, there is a people come out from Egypt; behold, they cover the face of the earth, and they abide over against me. Come now therefore, I pray thee, curse me this people; for they are too mighty for me; peradventure I shall prevail, that we may smite them, and that I may drive them out of the land; for I know that he whom thou blessest is blessed, and he whom thou cursest is cursed.' And the elders of Moab and the elders of Midian departed with the rewards of divination

in their hand; and they came unto Balaam, and spoke unto him the words of Balak. (Numbers 22:4-7)

(Hashem forced Balaam to bless the Children of Israel.)

Consult http://dafyomi.shemayisrael.co.il/parsha/balak3.htm for more information.

230. THAT PAYMENT OF A HIRED MAN IS NOT TO BE DELAYED

Thou shalt not oppress thy neighbour, nor rob him; the wages of a hired servant shall not abide with thee all night until the morning. (Leviticus 19:13)

Mitzvah 230 commands employers to pay their day laborers, promptly. If an employee works during the day, the boss must pay him that night (before the next day).

This passage from Deuteronomy commands employers to pay their night workers before the next night.

In the same day thou shalt give him his hire, neither shall the sun go down upon it; for he is poor, and setteth his heart upon it: lest he cry against thee unto the LORD and it be sin in thee. (Deuteronomy 24:15)

Both day laborers and night laborers need food to survive. Their employers must financially compensate them immediately. Many of the workers are poor and cannot go without payment.

Employers must provide immediate payment to their workers, whether they are Jewish or not, or whether they believe in idols or not, whether they are adults or children. It should be noted that workers can agree to accept different payment arrangements. This Mitzvah also applies to leased items, such as animals or utensils, for which the fees must be paid on a timely basis.

231. THE PROHIBITION ON CURSING ANY JEW, MAN OR WOMAN

Thou shalt not curse the deaf, nor put a stumbling-block before the blind, but thou shalt fear thy God: I am the LORD. (Leviticus 19:14)

Mitzvah 231 exhorts us to be compassionate–do not curse a deaf man.

This prohibition is also extended to forbid us cursing another Jew, whether or not that person can hear. Words hit like a fist. An insult can scar someone for life. A deaf Jew is still alive and a member of the Jewish nation. Cursing someone can lead the foulmouthed individual to physically harm his or her victim. Verbal taunts can progress to violence.

Should someone curse a deaf person, that individual might not hear the insults, but other people might, and relay the message to the hearing-impaired individual. It's not just emotional pain the Torah is concerned about but curses can inflict negative metaphysical effects as well.

232. NOT TO MAKE A TRUSTING PERSON STUMBLE THROUGH MISLEADING ADVICE

Thou shalt not curse the deaf, nor put a stumbling-block before the blind, but thou shalt fear thy God: I am the LORD. (Leviticus 19:14)

Mitzvah 232 contains metaphors. Although this Mitzvah clearly forbids us from literally placing a stumbling block in a blind person's path, it extends to forbidding us from misleading others. For example, one cannot persuade another to make a bad investment such as selling his entire field for a donkey, only to find out that the donkey is on the verge of death. Misleading someone is like intentionally causing a blind person to fall into a pit.

This Mitzvah also forbids someone to try to persuade a Nazir to consume alcohol. (As mentioned in Mitzvah 129, a Nazir cannot consume alcohol.) RAMBAM argued that if someone tries to corrupt a Nazir in that manner, the culprit is metaphorically blind for allowing his desire to cloud his true judgment.

To continue this discussion, consult:

"You Shall Not Place a Stumbling Block Before the Blind": Chazal's Metaphoric Approach by Rav Elchanan Samet

You can find it on the link, http://www.vbm-torah.org/parsha.63/30kedoshim.htm

233. NOT TO PERVERT JUSTICE IN A CIVIL JUDGMENT

Ye shall do no unrighteousness in judgment; thou shalt not respect the person of the poor, nor favour the person of the mighty; but in righteousness shalt thou judge thy neighbour. (Leviticus 19:15)

Mitzvah 233 prohibits us from corrupting judgment.

Judges must judge cases fairly. They must follow the law and cannot distort the law or show partiality. Judges cannot delay making a ruling after hearing the case; they must rule immediately. However, a capital punishment case requires judges to wait overnight before ruling. Once the judges make their ruling, and if the person is found guilty, the judgment / punishment must be carried out promptly.

A judge must be considerate. He has to hear all the arguments and think through all the pros and cons, and above all, judge in accordance with the precepts of the Torah.

234. NOT TO HONOR AN EMINENT PERSON AT A TRIAL

Ye shall do no unrighteousness in judgment; thou shalt not respect the person of the poor, nor favour the person of the mighty; but in righteousness **shalt thou judge thy neighbour. (Leviticus 19:15)**

Mitzvah 234 prohibits judges from granting honor or favor to a wealthy or a distinguished person and ignoring the rights of a poor person.

If two people go before a judge and one is wealthy or from an influential family, while the opposing party is poor and/or "ordinary," the judge cannot show extra favor or honor to the distinguished person. In the course of the preceding, the judge cannot give that person any favors in the process of hearing the case.

When a judge presides over cases, he is fulfilling Hashem's will. In the eyes of Hashem, all men are equal. A judge cannot favor anyone; no amount of wealth or fame can influence his decision. Judges must remember that poor people can be as righteous and as pleasing to Hashem as wealthy people.

If a judge were permitted to favor certain parties, he could make unfair rulings, or carry out gross miscarriages of justice.

Fulfilling this Mitzvah also prevents a judge from accepting bribes from wealthy people who want the judge to rule in their favor.

235. THE PRECEPT THAT A JUDGE SHOULD RENDER JUDGMENT WITH RIGHTEOUSNESS

Ye shall do no unrighteousness in judgment; thou shalt not respect the person of the poor, nor favour the person of the mighty; but in righteousness shalt thou judge thy neighbour. (Leviticus 19:15)

Mitzvah 235 is a positive commandment requiring judges to preside over cases fairly; both parties should receive equal treatment during the court proceeding.

The Sages stated that if one party comes to court wearing a fancy suit, while the other dresses in rags, the judge must command the wealthier man to clothe the poorer man in similar attire; and if the well-dressed man cannot oblige, he must then wear rags when the judge presides over the case. This makes both parties equal in the eyes of the judge, who is Hashem's instrument. We are equal in the eyes of Hashem.

A judge cannot allow one party to take his time in presenting his case, while forcing his opponent to tell his side quickly. A judge cannot allow one party to sit, while forcing the other to stand. Even affording one side a psychological advantage is not permitted. In sum, the judge must preside over the case with righteousness because he represents Hashem in providing justice.

If a judge has a number of cases to hear during a specific time-period and if some of them involve women, widows, or orphans, the judge must hear their cases first before hearing the men's cases because women, widows, and orphans are more vulnerable. They are in greater need of the judge's succor.

In Avot, Chapter 1, Mishnah 8, Yehudah, ben (son of) Tabbai, wrote that judges should never act as lawyers.

Another component of this Mitzvah is the requirement to give others the benefit of the doubt.

Once both parties accept the judge's ruling, the judge should view them both as innocent from this time forward. Though the guilty party suffers the consequences, the judge must not view him with contempt because that person can repent and become an upstanding citizen.

236. THE PROHIBITION ON GOSSIPING SLANDEROUSLY

Thou shalt not go up and down as a talebearer among thy people; neither shalt thou stand idly by the blood of thy neighbour: I am the LORD. (Leviticus 19:16)

Mitzvah 236 forbids us from gossiping; we must not listen to it, or encourage the gossiper.

Technically, this Mitzvah has been defined as follows: if a person hears "A" say something negative about "B", the person may not go to B to tell him what A said (unless it is to avoid injury or stop a quarrel).

This Mitzvah also includes the prohibition against the popularly known Lashon HaRah – evil speech, gossip and/or slander. We should emphasize that by definition this prohibition applies when what is being said is true. Spreading lies about another person is a violation of other precepts.

Speaking ill of someone creates a negative mental image of that person in the listener's mind.

Gossiping can lead to animosity and even bloodshed. Because Hashem wants us to live together in peace, because of the commandment, "Kol Yisrael Areivim Zeh Ba Zeh (All Jews are responsible for each other), we are forbidden to gossip. This ties in with thou shalt love thy neighbour as thyself (Leviticus 19:18).

Speaking positively of someone can be just as repugnant as speaking ill of them. To praise or flatter someone excessively can lead to Lashon HaRah because listeners may be tempted to counter with negative comments.

Talking Torah prevents gossiping. A conversation not involving Torah can lead to idle chitchat and gossip.

237. NOT TO STAND IDLY BY WHEN SOMEONE'S BLOOD IS SHED

Thou shalt not go up and down as a talebearer among thy people; neither shalt thou stand idly by the blood of thy neighbour: I am the LORD. (Leviticus 19:16)

Mitzvah 237 does not allow us to stand idly by while another Jew's life is in mortal danger. It is our obligation to save a Jew: "Kol Yisrael Areivim Zeh Ba Zeh" (All Jews are responsible for each other).

Whether or not we agree with his or her views, whether or not we have had trouble with that Jew in the past, it is our obligation to save that Jew's life.

238. THE PROHIBITION AGAINST HATING ONE'S BRETHREN

Thou shalt not hate thy brother in thy heart; thou shalt surely rebuke thy neighbour, and not bear sin because of him. (Leviticus 19:17)

Mitzvah 238 does not allow us to hate another Jew. Just the mere feeling can be a violation of this Mitzvah. The hatred people harbor inside can be quite destructive. Hating a fellow Jew can lead the hater to harm the person who is the object of his antipathy. Therefore, we must not hate or have bad feelings toward other Jews.

This Mitzvah states: "You are forbidden to hate your brethren;" the positive commandment is: "love thy neighbor."

239. THE RELIGIOUS DUTY TO REBUKE A FELLOW-JEW FOR IMPROPER BEHAVIOR

Thou shalt not hate thy brother in thy heart; thou shalt surely rebuke thy neighbour, and not bear sin because of him. (Leviticus 19:17)

Mitzvah 239 states that if a person were to witness a fellow Jew behave inappropriately or wickedly, he or she must take the offending party aside and rebuke him or her in a respectful manner. We are not to embarrass the offending party because that might cause him or her to continue to act shamefully. We cannot stand idly by either because that might cause us to build up anger and then possibly lead to hatred for the culprit. This Mitzvah even commands children to rebuke adults who act disgracefully.

One of the most tragic events in Jewish history occurred because of the violation of this Mitzvah. Rabbis stood idly by while one Jew publicly disgraced another. They did not rebuke the guilty party.

The Babylonian Talmud (BT), Tractate Gittin, 55b-56a, tells the tragic story of Kamtza and Bar Kamtza.

Shortly before the destruction of the Second Temple, a wealthy Jewish man in Jerusalem had a friend Kamtza and an enemy named Bar Kamtza. (They were both Jews.) The man held a party and told his servant to bring Kamtza, but the servant mistakenly brought Bar Kamtza. When the host saw his enemy there, he told him to leave.

Bar Kamtza said to him, "Once I have come, leave me be and I will pay for everything I eat and drink."

"No!"

"I will pay for half the party."

"No!"

"I will pay for the entire party."

"No!"

He took Bar Kamtza by the hands, picked him up and threw him out.

Bar Kamtza said: "Since the Rabbis were sitting there and did not protest, it seems that they were pleased with what happened. I will go and slander them before the emperor."

Bar Kamtza told Caesar that the Jews were rebelling against Rome.

When Caesar asked for proof, Bar Kamtza advised him to offer them a healthy calf for them to sacrifice to their G-D.

Caesar obliged, but Bar Kamtza surreptitiously placed a blemish on the animal's upper lip. The Jews were unable to sacrifice that animal because of its blemish.

The Jews' refusal to accept the animal insulted and infuriated the Romans, which inevitably led to them attacking Jerusalem and destroying the Second Temple. (For more information, consult the **Babylonian Talmud, Tractate Gittin, 55b-56a**. Also log onto http://www.sacred-texts.com/jud/tgm/tgm12.htm)

In sum, the Rabbis at the party were at fault for allowing the host to humiliate Bar Kamtza. They did not rebuke their host for mistreating a fellow Jew.

Their violation of this Mitzvah led to the Second Temple's destruction.

240. THE PROHIBITION AGAINST SHAMING A JEW

Thou shalt not hate thy brother in thy heart; thou shalt surely rebuke thy neighbour, and not bear sin because of him. (Leviticus 19:17)

Mitzvah 240 prohibits us from shaming a fellow Jew. If it is necessary to rebuke him or her, do it in private. A public rebuke causes embarrassment. We cannot embarrass a fellow Jew.

if one rebukes a fellow Jew in private multiple times for the same reason and the offending party does not repent, it may become a religious duty to rebuke him or her in public so that he may repent and return to good conduct.

The prophets ultimately rebuked our ancestors publicly because of their refusal to repent and follow Hashem's teachings.

241. THE PROHIBITION AGAINST TAKING REVENGE

Thou shalt not take vengeance, nor bear any grudge against the children of thy people, but thou shalt love thy neighbour as thyself: I am the LORD. (Leviticus 19:18)

Mitzvah 241 prohibits us from taking revenge on a fellow Jew. For example, if X asks Y to borrow something and Y refuses, X cannot subsequently take revenge against Y. If Y then asks X to borrow something, X cannot say, "No, because you didn't lend me your item when I asked to borrow it."

Not taking revenge allows us to realize that things happen because Hashem willed it. It is not Y's fault that X did not borrow his property. Hashem had a reason for Y to say 'no' to X.

Not seeking revenge, not holding grudges, overcoming slights allows us to live in peace with our Jewish brethren.

242. THE PROHIBITION AGAINST BEARING A GRUDGE

Thou shalt not take vengeance, nor bear any grudge against the children of thy people, but thou shalt love thy neighbour as thyself: I am the LORD. (Leviticus 19:18)

Mitzvah 242 forbids us to bear grudges against our Jewish brethren. This goes a step further than Mitzvah 241 – not only can we not take revenge; we may not even bear a grudge against our Jewish brethren.

For example, if X asks Y to borrow something and Y refuses; then the next day, Y asks X to borrow something, X cannot say: "I will lend it to you, even though you did not lend me what I needed yesterday. I'm not selfish like you." X is bearing a grudge, which violates Hashem's commandment.

As mentioned in Mitzvah 241, Y said no to X because Hashem willed it. Therefore, X is not to bear a grudge against Y by reminding him of his "selfish" behavior.

243. THE PRECEPT OF AFFECTION FOR A FELLOW JEW

Thou shalt not take vengeance, nor bear any grudge against the children of thy people, but thou shalt love thy neighbour as thyself: I am the LORD. (Leviticus 19:18)

Mitzvah 243 commands us to love our fellow Jews as we love ourselves. We are to treat them in the same manner that we wish to be treated. This Mitzvah is also the basis for many other Mitzvot between man and his fellowman, e.g., not charging interest, not oppressing others, etc. If someone does not like to be criticized in public, then he is not to criticize a fellow Jew in public. If someone dislikes being teased, then he is not to tease his fellow Jew.

244. THE PROHIBITION ON MATING TWO ANIMALS OF DIFFERENT SPECIES

Ye shall keep My statutes. Thou shalt not let thy cattle gender with a diverse kind; thou shalt not sow thy field with two kinds of seed; neither shall there come upon thee a garment of two kinds of stuff mingled together. (Leviticus 19:19)

Mitzvah 244 is the prohibition against mating two different animals together. Anyone caught violating this Mitzvah receives lashes.

Crossbreeding, mating creatures of two different species violates Hashem's intentions, which He stated in Genesis:

And God said: 'Let the earth bring forth the living creature after its kind, cattle, and creeping thing, and beast of the earth after its kind.' And it was so. And God made the beast of the earth after its kind, and the cattle after their kind, and every thing that creepeth upon the ground after its kind; and God saw that it was good. (Genesis 1:24-25)

245. NOT TO SOW DIFFERENT KINDS OF SEED TOGETHER, ETC. IN THE LAND OF ISRAEL

Ye shall keep My statutes. Thou shalt not let thy cattle gender with a diverse kind; thou shalt not sow thy field with two kinds of seed; neither shall there come upon thee a garment of two kinds of stuff mingled together. (Leviticus 19:19)

Mitzvah 245 prohibits us from growing two different types of food plants in the same location. Two different food plants must be planted or sowed one and a half handbreadths apart.

We cannot plant wheat and barley together because they will crossbreed. The prohibition about planting different species in proximity applies only in the Land of Israel.

This Mitzvah also forbids grafting fruit trees of two different species. We cannot take a plum tree branch and graft it onto a pear tree's roots. Hashem forbids the grafting of fruit trees anywhere in the world.

The following passage from Genesis explains why Hashem created this separation:

And God said: 'Let the earth put forth grass, herb yielding seed, and fruit-tree bearing fruit after its kind, wherein is the seed thereof, upon the earth.' And it was so. And the earth brought forth grass, herb yielding seed after its kind, and tree bearing fruit, wherein is the seed thereof, after its kind; and God saw that it was good. (Genesis 1:11-12)

Everything Hashem does is perfect. If He had intended for the food plants to be mixed, He would have mixed them. Violating this Mitzvah undermines Hashem, which explains why all guilty parties, both men and women, are subject to lashes.

We can eat the food that results from mixing the food plants because nowhere in the Torah does it say that we cannot do that.

246. NOT TO EAT THE FIRST THREE YEARS' PRODUCE OF A TREE

And when ye shall come into the land, and shall have planted all manner of trees for food, then ye shall count the fruit thereof as forbidden; three years shall it be as forbidden unto you; it shall not be eaten. (Leviticus 19:23)

Mitzvah 246 forbids us to eat fruit from a tree for the first three years of the tree's life. For the first three years, the fruit is "Orlah" (forbidden or uncircumcised).

Some scholars believe that the fruit produced during the first three years of the tree's life is not nutritious. It is small, rather tasteless and has little scent. Some trees do not produce any fruit at all until the fourth year after planting. Scholars believe that the tree's fruit comes into full glory in the fourth year, and should be offered to Hashem before people eat it.

One reason RAMBAN gives: "The fruit of the first three years of a tree's growth are like unripe fruit that is detrimental to one's health. And it is a further truth that the fruit (that grows) at the beginning of a tree's planting has excess moisture which is harmful for the body and is not good for eating."

(To see RAMBAN's comments on this discussion, consult http://vbm-torah.org/archive/parsha68/30-68kedoshim.htm)

My Partner in Torah explained that in the fourth year of a tree's life, its fruit has a special level of holiness. Therefore, we can only eat the fourth year's fruit in Jerusalem. In the fifth year, we can eat the tree's fruit anywhere in the world.

My Partner in Torah explained how to calculate the age of the fruit tree using Rosh Hashanah as the start of each new year of the tree's life.

If a tree was planted a minimum of 45 days before Rosh Hashanah, its second year of life would start on Rosh Hashanah, 45 days after the tree's planting.

If the tree was planted 80 days before Rosh Hashanah, its second year of life begins on Rosh Hashanah, 80 days after the tree's planting.

In both cases, the tree's third year would start on the following Rosh Hashanah. Each Rosh Hashanah, the tree would age another year.

If the tree was planted <u>less</u> than 45 days before Rosh Hashanah, its second year of life begins on the following Rosh Hashanah, more than one year after the tree's planting.

247. THE PRECEPT OF THE FRUIT OF A TREE'S FOURTH YEAR

And when ye shall come into the land, and shall have planted all manner of trees for food, then ye shall count the fruit thereof as forbidden; three years shall it be as forbidden unto you; it shall not be eaten. And in the fourth year all the fruit thereof shall be holy, for giving praise unto the LORD. (Leviticus 19:23-24)

Mitzvah 247 states that in the fourth year of a tree's life, its fruit is holy and can only be eaten in Jerusalem. Prior to the fourth year, the fruit is "Orlah" (forbidden).

One reason the fruit is holy in the fourth year is that it is the first year that we can eat it. It is a time of joy and blessing. The most appropriate place to honor and thank Hashem for the tree's completion is in Jerusalem, the City of Hashem's Holy Temple. And the best time to give thanks is when the fruit offerings are due during the second tithe.

If an individual is unable to carry his or her fruit to Jerusalem, that person must redeem the fruit by selling it, add one fifth of its value and use the money from the sale to buy food in Jerusalem. The sold fruit loses its holiness.

According to Ellicott's Commentary for English Readers:

Like the second tithes the fruits of the fourth year were taken up to Jerusalem, and there eaten by the owner, in company with the poor and needy whom he invited to the repast. The owner, however, was also allowed to redeem them. In this case he had to add the fifth part of their value, take up the money to the holy city, and there spend it in a repast to which he invited the poor. The grapes of the vineyards within a distance of a day's journey of Jerusalem had, however, to be taken up to decorate the streets of the holy city. Vineyards of the fourth year were exempt from the law laid down in Leviticus 19:9-10 as well as from the law of first-fruits, tithes, and second tithes.

Cited at https://biblehub.com/commentaries/ellicott/leviticus/19.htm

248. NOT TO EAT OR DRINK IN THE MANNER OF A GLUTTON OR DRUNKARD

Ye shall not eat with the blood; neither shall ye practice divination nor soothsaying. (Leviticus 19:26)

Mitzvah 248 prohibits eating and drinking to excess.

In Sefer HaHinnuch, the author asserts that food is the "dough" (nourishment) for the body; and wise thought, reflection on the fear of Hashem, and understanding His precepts is the "dough" of the spirit. The spirit and the body are opposites, yet both are required for us to exist in the physical world. Overeating, obsessing over food and drink, and drinking excessively can malnourish the spirit as well as the body. A malnourished spirit (an absence of Torah occupying the spirit) can cause a man to do horrible things. "Don't Eat on the Blood" means don't eat in a way that could cause you to spill blood. This also ties into the prohibition of eating part of an animal before its life expires.

(For a more detailed discussion, see Mitzvah 248 in Sefer HaHinnuch.)

249. THE PROHIBITION AGAINST PRACTICING DIVINATION

Ye shall not eat with the blood; neither shall ye practice divination nor soothsaying. (Leviticus 19:26)

Mitzvah 249 is the prohibition against omens or superstitions. Everything that happens is because Hashem wills it.

We cannot say that something we observed (a black cat, an eclipse of the sun, et cetera) is the cause of some totally unrelated action / accident we have had.

For example: if a person is crossing the street with a loaf of bread, spots a black cat, and then drops the bread, that person cannot say "the black cat was an omen / a sign of bad luck and made me drop the bread."

Some examples of superstitions are:
- opening an umbrella inside a building causes bad luck
- a rabbit's foot brings good luck when you are taking a test
- fear of Friday the 13th

Believing in these signs / omens can cause a parson to stray from having faith in Hashem. Everything that happens is because Hashem wills it. It is not because of a black cat, opening an umbrella inside a building, possessing a rabbit's foot, or the number 13.

Violators of this Mitzvah who continue these actions despite warnings from witnesses, receive lashes of the whip.

250. THE PROHIBITION AGAINST SOOTHSAYING OR CONJURING

Ye shall not eat with the blood; neither shall ye practice divination nor soothsaying. (Leviticus 19:26)

Mitzvah 250 forbids designating certain time periods as "good luck" or "bad luck." Jews cannot designate a particular time of the month as when good things or bad things would happen. We cannot "only do special tasks on the days around the new moon because they are 'good luck' days." We cannot put off tasks that must be done because today is Friday the 13th and it brings "bad luck."

Violators of this Mitzvah receive lashes.

251. THE PROHIBITION AGAINST ROUNDING OFF THE TEMPLES OF THE HEAD

Ye shall not round the corners of your heads, neither shalt thou mar the corners of thy beard. (Leviticus 19:27)

Mitzvah 251 prohibits us from cutting / removing the hair at our temples so the remainder is a straight even line of hair above the ears.

We cannot cut or shave our hair or another Jew's hair in a way that makes a straight even line of hair above the ears. We cannot cut our hair in the shape of an upside down bowl. We are not to wear our hair in the same manner as the idol worshippers and their priests wore their hair. Hashem has commanded us to be separate and apart from them.

Even though the Torah forbids using a razor to cut our hair, it does not forbid using scissors to cut our hair.

This Mitzvah applies to men only and does not apply to women because of the Leviticus 19:27 reference to beards: neither shalt thou mar the corners of thy beard.

252. THE PROHIBITION AGAINST MARRING THE EDGES OF THE BEARD

Ye shall not round the corners of your heads, <u>neither shalt thou mar the corners of thy beard</u>. (Leviticus 19:27)

Mitzvah 252 prohibits men from "destroying" the edges of their beards. The beard has five edges: The upper and lower cheek on the right side, the upper and lower cheek on the left side, and the pointed end of the beard–the place where the cheeks join below the chin. Every edge that a man shaves off with a razor, results in him receiving a set of lashes. If he were to shave off all five edges at once, he receives five sets of lashes of the whip.

Sefer HaHinnuch points out that this Mitzvah ensured that our ancestors distanced themselves from the idol worshippers and their priests because those people often cut their hair and shaved their beards.

Jewish men are forbidden to have a razor touch the skin of their face because it results in "complete destruction" of the hair. Jewish men can cut the edges of their beards with scissors, because scissors do not get as close to the face as the razor does. Jewish men are allowed to shave with an electric razor that employs a scissor-like cutting mechanism.

A woman cannot use a razor to shave a man's facial hair because, according to this Mitzvah, a razor cannot touch a man's face.

Women can use a razor to remove their facial hair. According to Tirzah Meacham, author of "Legal-Religious Status of the Jewish Female," a woman can shave herself with a razor, because, "these (prohibitions) were directed to men, who normally have facial hair."

For a more in depth discussion, consult http://jwa.org/encyclopedia/article/legal-religious-status-of-jewish-female

253. THE PROHIBITION AGAINST INSCRIBING ANY TATTOO IN ONE'S FLESH

Ye shall not make any cuttings in your flesh for the dead, nor imprint any marks upon you: I am the LORD. (Leviticus 19:28)

Mitzvah 253 forbids all Jews from cutting their skin or tattooing their skin as "mourning" when a loved one dies or at any other time.

In antiquity, pagan mourning rites / rituals often included shaving the head and bodily mutilation (gashing one's flesh with a knife).

Jews cannot have tattoos because pagans and idol worshippers had them. Those people honored their gods by placing tattoos on their bodies.

Jews cannot emulate those people in any way whatsoever. We cannot worship their idols, we cannot dress like them, we cannot wear our hair like them, we cannot have tattoos because they wore tattoos. We have maintained this condemnatory stance on tattoos throughout time.

Under certain circumstances, guilty parties are punished.

Scenario #1: If a person incises / cuts his or her skin, but does not mark up the edges of the incision with permanent ink or paint, then that person does not receive lashes.

Scenario #2: If a person marked his or her body with temporary ink or paint, but did not make an incision, then that person does not receive lashes.

Scenario #3: if a person cuts his or her skin or pierces it with a needle, and then marks their skin with permanent paint or ink, then that person is subject to lashes.

Scenario #4: If other people incised and then marked a Jew's skin against his or her free will, then that Jew does not receive lashes.

One of the many insults that the Nazis inflicted upon their Jewish prisoners was to tattoo numbers on their arms. Those Jews were clearly NOT guilty of violating this Mitzvah.

Scenario #5: If one person assists another person in incising and marking the other's skin, the "helper" receives lashes. A Jew cannot get around this Mitzvah by asking someone else to tattoo him or her.

254. THE PRECEPT OF REVERENT AWE FOR THE SANCTUARY

Ye shall keep My sabbaths, and reverence My sanctuary: I am the LORD. (Leviticus 19:30)

Mitzvah 254 is the obligation to be respectful and deferential to Hashem inside His Holy Temple. The Temple is the manifestation of His presence on earth.

When one enters the Temple, he or she must be humble and reverent. No one should never enter with a walking stick. A passage from Yevamot 6a-b explains that the word "revere" "means that one must not enter the Temple Mount with a walking stick."

One must not enter the Temple Mount wearing shoes. Yevamot 6a-b states that we cannot enter the Temple with one's shoes on, or with dust on our feet, and this commandment applies even when the Temple no longer exists." (Consult Entering The Temple Mount In Our Time, from Va'ad Halakha English Summaries; cited from the website: http://www.responsaforto-day.com/engsums/1_1.htm

Shoes often contained dust from walking, and contaminating Hashem's Holy Temple with dust is a flagrant display of disrespect.

The act of removing one's shoes before entering the Temple, Hashem's holy sanctuary, stems from the passage in which Hashem first spoke to Moses:

And He said: 'Draw not nigh hither; put off thy shoes from off thy feet, for the place whereon thou standest is holy ground.' (Exodus 3:5)

Other prohibited activities inside the Temple include expectoration, excretion, and discharging bodily fluids.

255. THE PROHIBITION AGAINST ACTING AS AN 'OV- A MEDIUM

Turn ye not unto the ghosts, nor unto familiar spirits; seek them not out, to be defiled by them: I am the LORD your God. (Leviticus 19:31)

Mitzvah 255 prohibits Jews from acting as an 'Ov (a medium) and forbids us from consulting a medium.

These "mediums" claim to foretell the future–they practice divination. Their actions have an element of idolatry.

They burn a certain incense. Then they do various actions. This play-acting tricks the unsuspecting person into imagining that he or she hears human speech from under the medium's armpit or from an "other worldly" source. When the unsuspecting person asks questions about his or her future or current predicament, the "other worldly" voice provides answers to all problems.

In truth, Hashem is the only one who truly knows the future. Everything happens because He wills it. Consulting with a fortuneteller, a medium, or anyone who claims that he or she can predict the future is an affront to Hashem.

In The First Book of Samuel, Chapter 28, Verse 6, King Saul committed this affront when he consulted a witch at Endor.

Because Saul had previously defied Hashem, He abandoned Saul. Saul was worried about the pending battle against the Philistines, and was desperate to know his fate. Despite Saul's rationale, he still disrespected Hashem by consulting a witch. Saul died in battle the next day.

If someone performs the actions of the Ov and, and ignores two witnesses' warnings to stop, that individual is stoned to death.

If no one warns the "medium" to stop, he or she would receive a divine severance of existence.

Should someone unknowingly perform the actions of an Ov, that person is spared from being stoned to death. However, that individual must provide a sin offering.

256. NOT TO FUNCTION AS A YID'ONI, A KIND OF WIZARD

Turn ye not unto the ghosts, nor unto familiar spirits; seek them not out, to be defiled by them: I am the LORD your God. (Leviticus 19:31)

Mitzvah 256 prohibits us from acting like a Yid'oni, a certain type of wizard.

These "wizards" claim to make predictions, or to foretell the future. Their actions have an element of idolatry.

Sefer HaHinnuch gives this description: A person, the Yid'oni, puts a bone from a dead yaddo'a (a certain type of fowl) in his mouth and then his play-acting begins. The Yid'oni burns incense, chants oaths, appears to be ill and suddenly falls to the ground. Then a strange voice is heard, supposedly coming from the dead bird. It forecasts the future or makes predictions.

This play-acting often tricks the unsuspecting person into abandoning Hashem's commandments and following pagan beliefs and worshiping idols.

If two witnesses warn the guilty party to stop, but their warnings go unheeded, the individual is stoned to death. If there were no witnesses, then the "wizard" suffers a divine severance of existence.

For more information about a Yid'oni, consult Mitzvah 256 in Sefer HaHinnuch.

257. THE MITZVAH OF HONORING WISE SCHOLARS

Thou shalt rise up before the hoary head, and honour the face of the old man, and thou shalt fear thy God: I am the LORD. (Leviticus 19:32)

Mitzvah 257 requires us to show respect for honorable elderly persons and elderly persons who have acquired wisdom. (i.e. hoary head = white haired, and old man)

This Mitzvah tells us to honor them by standing up when they enter a room, and always showing them curtesy and respect.

The Sages extended this Mitzvah to command us to honor elderly, and very wise Torah scholars. Although young Torah scholars also deserve our respect, the older ones deserve it to a greater degree because they have more Torah knowledge than the younger ones.

No one is exempt from fulfilling this Mitzvah, not even elderly wise Torah Scholars. They too must honor other Torah scholars.

Examples of showing them honor include, rising when they enter a room, giving them your chair so they do not have to stand, never disputing or contradicting them, and never sitting where they usually sit.

The Mishnah states that in certain cases, if one has the choice between assisting his father or his Torah teacher, his teacher of Torah comes first, "for his father brought him into this world, whereas his teacher who taught him wisdom brings him to the World to Come" (Tractate Bava Metzia, Chapter 2, Mishnah 11). (The Hebrew term for the world to come is Olam Haba.)

My friend Joseph Bernstein, a student of Rabbi David Aaron, a Kabbalah scholar/Founder of the Learning Center, Israelite, told me: "Our Torah teacher gives us Olam Haba because the only part of us that remains in the next world is the part that is spiritual. And the spiritual part gets brought to life through connecting to Hashem by learning Torah and being involved with Torah."

Teaching Torah is one of the greatest acts of giving, far beyond any kindness this world has to offer. (Consult the link, http://www.torah.org/learning/pirkei-avos/Chapter6-3.html for a more detailed discussion.)

Various portions of the Mishnah stress similar points.

In Tractate Avot, Chapter 3, Mishnah 1, Rabbi Akavia ben Mahalalel says:

"Consider three things and you will not come into the grip of sin: Know from where you came, where you will go, and before whom you will give justification and reckoning."

He states that we came from a putrid drop (the result of sexual intercourse). We are going to a place of dust, worms, and maggots (when we are dead and buried). We will ultimately have to give justification to Hashem.

If we truly believe that there is a greater purpose than just the physical world, we will be less likely to sin, because we know that we have to answer to Hashem.

In Tractate Avot, Chapter 1, Mishnah 6, Yoshuah ben Perachyah says, "appoint a Torah teacher for yourself." It means that one must put as much care and effort into appointing a Torah teacher as one does in appointing/hiring a doctor or lawyer. A Torah teacher provides spiritual wellbeing, which is just as important (if not more) as a doctor's job of keeping us healthy.

258. THE PROHIBITION AGAINST CHEATING WITH ANY KIND OF MEASURE

Ye shall do no unrighteousness in judgment, in meteyard, in weight, or in measure. (Leviticus 19:35)

Mitzvah 258 is the prohibition against cheating people with weights and measures. This Mitzvah tells us "You shall do no wrong in measuring any length, weight or quantity."

Sefer HaHinnuch defines "measures" to include liquid and dry measures as well as measuring cloth for garments or measuring land.

If a buyer purchases a specific amount of land, the seller cannot cheat that buyer. The same rule applies today.

The guilty party does not receive lashes for cheating his customer. Instead, he must give the buyer the amount that he is entitled to receive.

This prohibition also protects non-Jews, and even idol worshippers.

259. THE PRECEPT THAT SCALES, WEIGHTS AND MEASURES SHOULD BE MADE CORRECT

Just balances, just weights, a just ephah, and a just hin, shall ye have: I am the LORD your God, who brought you out of the land of Egypt. (Leviticus 19:36)

(Ephah denotes dry measure, and Hin means liquid measure.)

Mitzvah 259 bids us to make our instruments used as weights, measures, and scales to be as accurate as possible and to maintain them well so we do not cheat any buyer.

Jews cannot make weights out of iron and lead because they rust. We are to use stone or glass instead. Broken instruments must be destroyed. We are to test them for accuracy and re-calibrate them often to ensure that all our transactions are done fairly and honestly.

260. THE PROHIBITION AGAINST CURSING ONE'S FATHER OR MOTHER

For whatsoever man there be that curseth his father or his mother shall surely be put to death; he hath cursed his father or his mother; his blood shall be upon him. (Leviticus 20:9)

Mitzvah 260 is the prohibition against cursing our father or our mother. The penalty is death. This applies even after the parent dies.

The disrespectful offspring might only receive lashes if the cursing is less severe and they did not did not use Hashem's name when cursing.

The Rabbis have extended this Mitzvah to prohibit a convert to Judaism from cursing his or her parents, even though once he or she converts, they are not his or her parents anymore from a Halachaic perspective.

Although the Torah uses the term "man" in this Mitzvah, it applies to women as well. Women are also forbidden from showing their parents disrespect. The author of Sefer HaHinnuch states that this law "is enforced, everywhere, at every time for both man and woman, Tumtum (one of uncertain gender) and a hermaphrodite."

261. THE PRECEPT THAT WHOEVER INCURS DEATH BY BURNING IS TO BE BURNED

And if a man take with his wife also her mother, it is wickedness: they shall be burnt with fire, both he and they; that there be no wickedness among you. (Leviticus 20:14)

Mitzvah 261 obligates the court to carry out a sentence of "death by burning." Here "burning" is defined as "forcing the guilty party to swallow molten liquid that burns the innards." This practice is carried out if the culprit's crime is severe enough to warrant it.

A son-in-law (daughter's husband) fornicating with his mother-in-law (daughter's mother) is a severe crime punishable by death by burning.

If two witnesses catch a son-in-law and his mother-in-law in this forbidden activity, the two witnesses must implore the guilty parties to stop. If the pleas of the two witnesses go unheeded, the court is required to sentence BOTH the guilty people to death by burning.

To carry out the death sentence, the guilty party must be immersed up to the knees in dung (immobilized). Then a hard cloth was wrapped inside a soft cloth, and fastened around the guilty party's neck. The two witnesses participate–one pulls on the end of the hard cloth and the other pulls on the end of the soft cloth to force the guilty party's mouth open. Molten liquid–melted tin, alloy, and/or lead–is then poured down the guilty party's throat, burning their innards and causing death.

This Mitzvah is enforced only in Israel, because that is the only place where true judgment and justice is settled. The Sages only had the capacity to implement capital punishment in Israel.

Today this Mitzvah is not practiced because the Sanhedrin dissolved a few hundred years after the destruction of the Second Temple.

262. THE PROHIBITION AGAINST FOLLOWING CUSTOMS AND WAYS OF THE AMORITES

And ye shall not walk in the customs of the nation, which I am casting out before you; for they did all these things, and therefore I abhorred them. (Leviticus 20:23)

Mitzvah 262 prohibits us from emulating the Amorites' behaviors and practices. Jews must distance themselves from all heathen nations. We cannot dress like them, wear our hair like them, nor even share their interests. Interacting with them could lead a Jew away from worshipping Hashem to worshipping idols.

263. AN ORDINARY KOHEN SHOULD MAKE HIMSELF RITUALLY UNCLEAN ONLY AT THE DEATH OF CERTAIN RELATIVES

And the LORD said unto Moses: Speak unto the priests the sons of Aaron, and say unto them: There shall none defile himself for the dead among his people; except for his kin, that is near unto him, for his mother, and for his father, and for his son, and for his daughter, and for his brother; and for his sister a virgin, that is near unto him, that hath had no husband, for her may he defile himself. (Leviticus 21:1-3)

"Defile himself" means "make himself ritually unclean."

Mitzvah 263 prohibits priests from touching the body (corpse) of a dead person because it will make the priest ritually unclean. Defilement from a corpse lasts seven days.

The reason for this Mitzvah was that priests are to remain pure (ritually clean) to serve Hashem in his Temple.

Our ancient Jewish ancestors believed that the physical body (flesh and blood) with all its wants, desires, and urges was the root cause of sin. The Torah says the soul is the spirit from Hashem for goodness, truth and control of all physical desires. When a person dies, his/her soul leaves the body. The physical body minus the soul "possesses the utmost intensity of uncleanness."

A priest is forbidden to touch a corpse ("defilement by touch") with his hand, foot, fingernail, or any other body part. A priest is forbidden from transporting a corpse ("defilement by carrying") in a wheelbarrow or any other type of modern day vehicle–even if he does not touch the corpse itself (the body is wrapped in something and is not exposed). A priest is forbidden to be under the same roof with a dead body ("defilement in a tent").

But it is also a religious duty for any man to properly bury his closely related kin (blood relatives). This Mitzvah specifically states that a priest may come in contact with the dead bodies of close relatives: His mother, his father, his son, his daughter, his brother, and his sister only if she were an unmarried virgin. It is also a religious duty for a husband to properly bury his dead wife, so a priest is obligated to bury his dead spouse.

Note: If the priest's sister were married, it is the duty of the sister's husband (the priest's brother-in-law) to bury his dead wife.

The word, 'wife' is not obviously included in the list of dead relatives. However, the Sages interpreted the phrase, "except for his kin" to mean his wife. Although the word wife is not used in Leviticus 21:3, the passage "except for his kin, that is near unto him" implies that wives are to be included in this list.

Rabbis who operate the website, http://www.chabad.org, explained to me that the Midrash says that the words, "except for his relative who is close to him," refers to "his wife." The Talmud gives the priest permission to come in contact with his dead spouse. (Consult http://www.wordiq.com/definition/Kohanim for more information.)

The Sages also extended this Mitzvah to include:
that the utterly righteous do not cause defilement when dead;
that shaking or budging a corpse using an object (moving with a stick, etc) causes defilement;
that infants who do not survive birth cause defilement;
that even a tiny amount of flesh from a corpse, or any limb or organ removed from a human body causes defilement;
that under certain circumstances bones from a corpse may not cause defilement;
and many other scenarios.
See Sefer HaHinnuch, Mitzvah 263 for a more complete explanation.

Some Rabbis from www.chabad.org cited another extension of this Mitzvah: If a passer-by sees an abandoned corpse and no one else is around or is available to bury it, then it becomes the duty of the person who found the body to bury it. The duty to bury an abandoned corpse also extends to a priest.

This Mitzvah is in effect everywhere, at every time.

264. THAT A KOHEN SHOULD DEFILE HIMSELF, AND A JEW SHOULD MOURN, FOR A DECEASED CLOSE RELATIVE

And the LORD said unto Moses: Speak unto the priests the sons of Aaron, and say unto them: There shall none defile himself for the dead among his people; except for his kin, that is near unto him, for his mother, and for his father, and for his son, and for his daughter, and for his brother; and for his sister a virgin, that is near unto him, that hath had no husband, for her may he defile himself. (Leviticus 21:1-3)

Mitzvah 264 is a positive Mitzvah/commandment for priests and Israelites to mourn for close relatives (blood kin). Even though the mourner becomes ritually impure, that must not deter the individual from grieving. Even for a priest, the religious obligation of mourning for a dead relative takes precedence over remaining ritually pure.

The Sages have said that Moses instituted the custom of seven days of mourning. The Torah stated that the first day of mourning was obligatory, and the remaining six days came from a ruling by the Sages.

See Sefer HaHinnuch, Mitzvah 264 for a discussion of the rituals and customs associated with mourning a close relative.

This Mitzvah is in effect everywhere, at every time.

265. THAT A KOHEN DEFILED FOR A DAY WHO UNDERGOES RITUAL IMMERSION SHOULD NOT SERVE AT THE SANCTUARY TILL SUNSET

They shall be holy unto their God, and not profane the name of their God; for the offerings of the LORD made by fire, the bread of their God, they do offer; therefore they shall be holy. (Leviticus 21:6)

Mitzvah 265 implies that after a priest ritually immerses himself because he has been ritually unclean, he has to wait until sunset before he can once again perform his duties inside the Temple.

Waiting until sunset or until the following day before serving inside the Temple ensures that the priest has no vestige of impurities left over and that the offerings he touches will not become impure.

"...Perhaps the spirit of uncleanness does not leave him until the setting of the sun." (Cited in Sefer HaHinnuch; Mitzvah 265.)

In Judaism, sunset is when a new day begins. This derives from the passage from Genesis:

And God said: 'Let there be light.' And there was light. And God saw the light, that it was good; and God divided the light from the darkness. And God called the light Day, and the darkness He called Night. And there was evening and there was morning, one day. (Genesis 1:3-5)

This Mitzvah applies to male Kohanim at the time the Temple exists. Violators would incur death at Heaven's hands.

266. THAT A KOHEN IS PROHIBITED FROM MARRYING A WANTON

They shall not take a woman that is a harlot, or profaned; neither shall they take a woman put away from her husband; for he is holy unto his God. (Leviticus 21:7)

Mitzvah 266 prohibits regular priests and High Priests from marrying women who are harlots, profaned women or divorced women (collectively referred to as "wanton women") because every aspect of a priest's life was to be clean and holy in Hashem's eyes.

A priest is consecrated to Hashem and must remain holy in all aspects of his life. A priest is held to a higher standard of conduct that an ordinary person. These three mitzvot (#266, 267, and 268) define what types of women a male priest can / cannot marry to preserve his holiness to Hashem.

The Sages defined "wanton women" as women whom priests were forbidden to marry ("take") because their temperament was bad and bitter, and as a wife, she might lead the priest astray.

In the author's discussion of Mitzvah 266 in Sefer HaHinnuch, "wanton women" include all non-Jewish women, Jewish women who engage in relations with men that are universally prohibited, and a Jewish woman who has relations (even permitted) with an invalidated Kohen.

If an unmarried Jewish woman were promiscuous, but did not engage in any forbidden relations, that would not make her "wanton." A Jewish man and/or priest could still marry her. (A High Priest can only marry a Jewish virgin, thus making the promiscuous woman off limits to him.)

A priest violates this Mitzvah when he marries the wanton woman and becomes conjugally intimate with her. After the marriage is consummated, the both the priest and the woman receive lashes.

267. THAT A KOHEN IS PROHIBITED FROM MARRYING A PROFANED WOMAN

They shall not take a woman that is a harlot, or profaned; neither shall they take a woman put away from her husband; for he is holy unto his God. (Leviticus 21:7)

Mitzvah 267 prohibits a Kohen (priest) and a Kohen Gadol (High Priest) from marrying "profaned" women.

Because the priest's role is to embody Hashem's teachings and guide Hashem's chosen people by his example, a priest is held to a higher standard of conduct than an ordinary person.

A Kohen Gadol (High Priest) is held to the highest standard of conduct.

The Sages defined "profaned women" to be women the priests were forbidden to marry because of the circumstances of that woman's birth.

Example 1: A Kohen (or a Kohen Gadol) has conjugal relations with a forbidden woman, and their union produces a daughter, that daughter is considered a "profaned woman." An ordinary man can marry that daughter, but a Kohen (or a Kohen Gadol) is forbidden to marry her.

Example 2: if a Kohen (or a Kohen Gadol) marries a widow, which is not allowed, and their union produces a daughter, that daughter is off limits to any other Kohen seeking a wife.

Example 3: if a regular Kohen marries a divorcee, which is not allowed, and they give birth to a daughter, that daughter cannot marry a Kohen.

These restrictions are essential because a Kohen and a Kohen Gadol must maintain a high level of Kedusha (holiness).

268. THAT A KOHEN IS PROHIBITED FROM MARRYING A DIVORCED WOMAN

They shall not take a woman that is a harlot, or profaned; neither shall they take a woman put away from her husband; for he is holy unto his God. (Leviticus 21:7)

Mitzvah 268 prohibits Kohanim (priests) from marrying divorcees. A divorcee experienced a broken marriage, thus scarring her for life. On some level, her heart is bitter. At the same time, the Kohanim must be happy while serving in the Temple.

Marrying a divorcee can affect his state of happiness and his ability to serve Hashem. For this reason, divorced women are off limits to the Kohanim.

Rabbi Shaul Rosenblatt added another reason: Unfortunately, a divorced woman acquires a name, so to speak, of 'someone else's reject.' Her situation is looked upon as pagan, or similar to the physical blemishes that a Kohen cannot serve with. In practice it is wrong for a Priest of G-d to take in a woman who was 'not good enough for someone else.'

269. THE PRECEPT OF THE SANCTIFICATION OF AARON'S DESCENDANTS

Thou shalt sanctify him therefore; for he offereth the bread of thy God; he shall be holy unto thee; for I the LORD, who sanctify you, am holy. (Leviticus 21:8)

Mitzvah 269 commands us to consecrate the descendants of Aaron to the service of Hashem. We accord them preferential status when it comes to reading the Torah and leading blessings such as the Birkat Hamazon (Grace after Meals).

When reading Torah portions in the synagogue, the Kohen goes first, followed by the Levite and then an Israelite. This preferential treatment is still practiced today.

Unfortunately, it is difficult for many Jews to know for certain if they are truly descendants of Aaron. It is also difficult to determine if they are truly descendants from the Tribe of Levi. (Aaron and Moshe were from the Tribe of Levi.) For these purposes, we rely on their family tradition of their lineage.

I have seen Jews whose last names were Cohen read the Torah first followed by Jews whose last names happened to be

Levy, Levi, or something similar. However, they had no way of knowing for sure about their lineage.

When it comes to reading the Torah to the Congregation, a Kohen must not follow a fellow Kohen. The exact rule applies to Levites. Doing so, might indicate that his predecessor erred or did not have a valid status.

270. THAT A KOHEN GADOL IS PROHIBITED FROM ENTERING THE TENT OF A DEAD MAN

***neither shall he go in to any dead body*, nor defile himself for his father, or for his mother; (Leviticus 21:11)**

Mitzvah 270 prohibits the Kohen Gadol (High Priest) from coming in contact with any corpse or by entering a tent or a house where a corpse is present.

Unlike the ordinary Kohanim, the Kohen Gadol cannot even come into contact with any of his own dead relatives. (For information about which dead relatives the ordinary Kohanim can come into contact with, consult Mitzvah 263.)

This restriction applies to the Kohen Gadol because he is considered the holiest of the holy. Even though the High Priest still possesses a physical body, his spirit should abide constantly among the supernal Divine ministers. (Cited in Sefer HaHinnuch.)

If a Kohen Gadol violates this Mitzvah, even if he comes in contact with his deceased father or mother, he is to receive lashes.

This Mitzvah is applicable only when the Temple is extant.

271. THAT A KOHEN GADOL SHOULD NOT MAKE HIMSELF RITUALLY UNCLEAN OVER ANY DEAD MAN

neither shall he go in to any dead body, nor defile himself for his father, or for his mother; (Leviticus 21:11)

Mitzvah 271 prohibits the Kohen Gadol from becoming ritually impure from contact with any corpse in any manner. He cannot touch it (defilement by touch), move it, or help transport it (defilement by carrying).

Mitzvah 270 forbids the Kohen Gadol from entering the same room as the departed. Mitzvah 271 forbids the Kohen Gadol from having any physical contact with a corpse.

If a Kohen Gadol intentionally violates this Mitzvah, he would receive lashes.

This Mitzvah is applicable only when the Temple is extant.

272. THE PRECEPT THAT THE KOHEN GADOL SHOULD TAKE A VIRGIN FOR A WIFE

And he shall take a wife in her virginity. (Leviticus 21:13)

Mitzvah 272 is a positive commandment. It instructs the Kohen Gadol to marry only a Jewish virgin. A divorced or widowed Jewish woman could still have fixed thoughts on past men.

The Jewish virgin's heart must be pure and belong exclusively to the Kohen Gadol. This will make it even easier for him to fulfill his sacred duties to Hashem.

If the Jewish virgin desires another man, but does not get involved with that person, she can still marry the Kohen Gadol. As stated in Mitzvah 209, if a man desires another man, but does not act out that desire, he does not face repercussions, because nothing happened. He did not waste Hashem's seed. The same is true for a female Jewish virgin. She is not prohibited from marrying the Kohen Gadol for secretly desiring someone else.

However, once she becomes intimate with someone else, then she loses her right to marry the Kohen Gadol.

273. THAT A KOHEN GADOL IS PROHIBITED FROM MARRYING A WIDOW

***A widow,* or one divorced, or a profaned woman, or a harlot, these *shall he not take*; but a virgin of his own people shall he take to wife. (Leviticus 21:14)**

Mitzvah 273 forbids a Kohen Gadol from marrying a widow. Even if the widow never consummated her marriage with her last husband, the Kohen Gadol cannot marry her.

The Kohen Gadol's bride must be an unwed Jewish virgin. Had she already been married or had lost her virginity, she could easily think of past men, while being romantic with the Kohen Gadol.

"If a young bachelor marries a widow, there are three minds in the bed ... if a divorced man married a divorced woman, there are four minds in the bed ..." (Cited in Talmud Pesachim 112a.)

If a Kohen Gadol marries a widow, or he has sexual intercourse with a widow without marrying her, he is subject to lashes. He receives lashes because he profaned the widow and his seed (i.e., his descendants who would be offspring of such a union).

Once a widow is intimate with or marries a Kohen Gadol, she loses her right to marry a regular Kohen, should the Kohen Gadol die before her, because it is her punishment for violating this Mitzvah.

274. THAT CONJUGAL INTIMACY WITH A WIDOW IS FORBIDDEN TO A KOHEN GADOL

And he shall not profane his seed among his people; for I am the LORD who sanctify him. (Leviticus 21:15)

Mitzvah 274 forbids the Kohen Gadol to be conjugally intimate with a widow outside the framework of marriage. One reason is that the only type of female that the Kohen Gadol can be intimate with is an unwed Jewish virgin. Being intimate with a widow profanes his seed (i.e., his descendants). This also profanes the widow because she is no longer allowed to marry a Kohen. This costs a Kohen a potential mate. Violating this Mitzvah subjects the Kohen Gadol to lashes.

275. THAT A KOHEN WITH A BLEMISHING DEFECT SHOULD NOT SERVE AT THE SANCTUARY

Speak unto Aaron, saying: Whosoever he be of thy seed throughout their generations that hath a blemish, let him not approach to offer the bread of his God. For whatsoever man he be that hath a blemish, he shall not approach: a blind man, or a lame, or he that hath any thing maimed, or anything too long, or a man that is broken-footed, or broken-handed, or crook-backed, or a dwarf, or that hath his eye overspread, or is scabbed, or scurvy, or hath his stones crushed; no man of

the seed of Aaron the priest, that hath a blemish, shall come nigh to offer the offerings of the LORD made by fire; he hath a blemish; he shall not come nigh to offer the bread of his God. (Leviticus 21:17-21)

Mitzvah 275 forbids a Kohen with a disfiguration from serving in the Temple.

The visible disfiguration makes him unattractive. Even if the deformed Kohen had a pure heart, his appearance can easily distract people. They would stop and stare at the deformed Kohen instead of fulfilling their duties.

There are practical reasons, not mentioned in Sefer HaHinnuch why priests with blemishes cannot serve in the Temple. How can a blind Kohen tell if an animal that is to be sacrificed has a blemish? Animals with any type of blemish cannot be sacrificed. A priest with a bad back might have great difficulty lifting a heavy animal slated for sacrifice. Similarly, if a learned and respected Rabbi has a bad back or trouble standing, he should not lift Hashem's Torah.

It cannot be stated strongly enough that a Kohen is NOT a bad person if he has a blemish and cannot serve in the Temple. Isaac, Jacob, and Moses, three of the greatest men in Jewish history, had physical defects.

Both Isaac and Jacob were blind in their old age. Jacob walked with a limp after he fought the angel. (See my write-up of Mitzvah Three.) Moses was slow of speech and had a slow tongue.

However, a Kohen with a disfigurement is still entitled to receive a share in the sacrificial meats along with his brethren during the weeks that his family group serves in the Temple.

For more details about which blemishes disqualify a Kohen from serving in the Temple, consult Mitzvah 275 in Sefer Ha-Hinnuch.

276. THAT A KOHEN WITH A TEMPORARY BLEMISH IS FORBIDDEN TO SERVE AT THE SANCTUARY

no man of the seed of Aaron the priest, that hath a blemish, shall come nigh to offer the offerings of the LORD made by fire; he hath a blemish; he shall not come nigh to offer the bread of his God. (Leviticus 21:21)

Mitzvah 276 forbids a Kohen to serve in the Temple, while he has a temporary disfiguration. Examples include boils, eye infections, scurvies, and scabrous itches.

When the Kohen is serving in Hashem's Temple, his performance must be perfect. He must also look as perfect as possible. Having blemishes, temporary or permanent, keep him from looking like he is at perfect.

If a Kohen intentionally serves in the Temple, while he has a temporary or permanent blemish, he receives lashes of the whip.

277. THAT A KOHEN WITH A BLEMISHING DEFECT IS NOT TO ENTER THE HOLY TEMPLE

Only he shall not go in unto the veil, nor come nigh unto the altar, because he hath a blemish; that he profane not My holy places; for I am the LORD who sanctify them. (Leviticus 21:23)

Mitzvah 277 forbids a Kohen with a disfiguration and/or blemish from entering the Sanctuary section of Temple, to the area that houses the Altar. Not only is he forbidden to approach the Altar, he is also forbidden to walk down the corridor that leads to the Altar.

Sefer HaHinnuch states that the Altar is a place of wholeness and perfection. It is wrong for a Kohen or any person with a blemish to stand in that area.

278. THAT A RITUALLY UNCLEAN KOHEN IS FORBIDDEN TO SERVE AT THE HOLY TEMPLE

Speak unto Aaron and to his sons, that they separate themselves from the holy things of the children of Israel, which they hallow unto Me, and that they profane not My holy name: I am the LORD. Say unto them: Whosoever he be of all your seed throughout your generations, that approacheth unto the holy things, which the children of Israel hallow unto the LORD, having his uncleanness upon him, that soul shall be cut off from before Me: I am the LORD. What man soever of the seed of Aaron is a leper, or hath an issue, he shall not eat of the holy things, until he be clean. And whoso toucheth any one that is unclean by the dead; or from whomsoever the flow of seed goeth out; or whosoever toucheth any swarming thing, whereby he may be made unclean, or a man of whom he may take uncleanness, whatsoever uncleanness he hath; the soul that toucheth any such shall be unclean until the even, and shall not eat of the holy things, unless he bathe his flesh in water. And when the sun is down, he shall be clean; and afterward he may eat of the holy things, because it is his bread. That which dieth of itself, or is torn of beasts, he shall not eat to defile himself therewith: I am the LORD. They shall therefore keep My charge, lest they bear sin for

it, and die therein, if they profane it: I am the LORD who sanctify them. (Leviticus 22:2-9)

Mitzvah 278 forbids a Kohen from serving in the Temple while he is ritually impure from any unclean source.

In order for the Kohen to serve, he must be at a high level of excellence in every way. Being unclean and/or having a blemish removes him from that high level, thus making him unfit to serve in Hashem's Holy Temple.

If an impure Kohen serves in the Temple, he would die at the hands of Hashem because such actions profane the Holy Temple and Hashem's name.

279. THAT A RITUALLY UNCLEAN KOHEN IS FORBIDDEN TO EAT T'RUMAH

What man soever of the seed of Aaron is a leper, or hath an issue, he shall not eat of the holy things, until he be clean. And whoso toucheth any one that is unclean by the dead; or from whomsoever the flow of seed goeth out; (Leviticus 22:4)

They shall therefore keep My charge, lest they bear sin for it, and die therein, if they profane it: I am the LORD who sanctify them. (Leviticus 22:9)

Mitzvah 279 prohibits an impure Kohen from eating T'rumah. T'rumah is the Kohen's portion of produce.

Jews are required to give the Kohanim portions of their crops.T'rumah is specific types of food including fruits, vegetables, wine, and oil given to Kohanim.

If an impure Kohen eats sanctified T'rumah, he receives lashes of the whip and is struck down dead at the Hands of Hashem.

If an impure Kohen eats impure T'rumah, there is only the lesser punishment of lashes because impure T'rumah is no longer hallowed / sanctified.

My Partner in Torah explained to me what makes T'rumah and a Kohen impure:
coming into contact with a dead person or a dead animal;
coming into contact with dead rodents such as a mouse, weasel, turtle, or snake;
coming into contact with a woman during her period.

If an impure person touches a utensil, it becomes impure. If the now impure utensil touches food, the food becomes impure.

If something impure touches the T'rumah, the T'rumah becomes impure. Therefore, the crop grower and the Kohen need to prevent the T'rumah from touching anything impure.

280. THAT ANY AND EVERY NON-KOHEN IS FORBIDDEN TO EAT T'RUMAH

There shall no common man eat of the holy thing; a tenant of a priest, or a hired servant, shall not eat of the holy thing. (Leviticus 22:10)

Mitzvah 280 forbids non-Kohanim from eating T'rumah. The Kohen is allowed to share his T'rumah with the permanent members of his household: his wife,his children, his animals and his non-Jewish slaves.

The animals and the non-Jewish slaves permanently belong to the Kohen and are considered part of his household; therefor they can eat T'rumah.

Jewish slaves (indentured servants) do NOT permanently belong to the Kohen because a Jewish slave must be freed after seven years of service. Jewish slaves cannot eat T'rumah.

The Kohen's female non-Jewish slaves and his circumcised male non-Jewish slaves can eat T'rumah. But, the Kohen's uncircumcisedmale non-Jewish slaves cannot eat T'rumah.

Genesis 17:12-13 states that Jewish masters are obligated to circumcise their male non-Jewish slaves:

"And he that is eight days old shall be circumcised among you, every male throughout your generations, he that is born in the house, or bought with money of any foreigner, that is not of thy seed. He that is born in thy house, and he that is bought with thy money, must needs be circumcised; and My covenant shall be in your flesh for an everlasting covenant."

Mitzvah 282 explains why uncircumcised males cannot eat T'rumah.

Punishment for violating Mitzvah 280 is death:

They shall therefore keep My charge, lest they bear sin for it, and die therein, if they profane it: I am the LORD who sanctify them. (Leviticus 22:9)

Anyone eating the T'rumah who is forbidden to do so, is struck down by the Hands of Heaven.

281. THAT NEITHER A PERMANENT NOR A TEMPORARY HEBREW SLAVE OF A KOHEN IS TO EAT T'RUMAH

There shall no common man eat of the holy thing; a tenant of a priest, or a hired servant, shall not eat of the holy thing. (Leviticus 22:10)

Mitzvah 281 prohibits the Kohen's Hebrew slaves (Jewish indentured servants), whether permanent or temporary, from eating T'rumah, because he did not purchase them.

Jewish slaves (Hebrew indentured servants) do NOT permanently belong to the Kohen because a Jewish slave must be freed after seven years of service. They are not permanent members of the Kohen's household.

The Kohen is also forbidden to share his T'rumah with his friends, houseguests,or employees.

282. THAT AN UNCIRCUMCISED PERSON IS FORBIDDEN TO EAT T'RUMAH

There shall no common man eat of the holy thing; a tenant of a priest, or a hired servant, shall not eat of the holy thing. (Leviticus 22:10)

Mitzvah 282 forbids all uncircumcised males,Jewish and non-Jewish, from eating T'rumah because they are "outsiders." They never entered the Jewish covenant of circumcision. Circumcision is the sign–the mark–that makes one part of the Jewish nation. It is a holy bond.

There are instances when Jewish males may remain uncircumcised. If one's older brother died as a result of circumcision, he is excused from circumcision. However, he still cannot eat T'rumah.

The Sages state that if a circumcised man appears to be uncircumcised, he cannot eat T'rumah. (Consult the link http://www.hinnuch.com/season-two/class-18/class-notes—-class-18 for a more detailed discussion.)

Violators of this Mitzvah receive lashes of the whip.

283. THAT A PROFANED WOMAN IS FORBIDDEN TO EAT HALLOWED FOOD

And if a priest's daughter be married unto a common man, she shall not eat of that which is set apart from the holy things. (Leviticus 22:12)

Mitzvah 283 forbids any profaned woman from eating sanctified food.

Mitzvah 283 forbids a priest's daughter to eat T'rumah, or the breasts and thighs of sacrificed animals, after she has had sexual relations with a man forbidden to her.

The Sages of Old assigned the "status of Kohen" to a priest's daughter (female descendants of Aaron) which held her behavior to a higher standard. It also restricted her choice of acceptable husbands to other priests ("men not forbidden to her").

Growing up as a virgin living in her father's house (the Kohen's house), she is allowed to eat T'rumah, as well as the breasts and thighs of sacrificed animals.

T'rumah is entirely the Kohen's (her father's) property ("the bread of her father"), and she is allowed to eat it.

The Priest's portion from the animal sacrifices was the meat from the breast and the thigh. It is not regarded as her father, the Kohen's property–it is more like a "special holy gift" to the Kohen. The Kohen may share the breast and thigh with other members of his household who have the status of Kohen.

By marrying or having sexual relations with a "common man" (a man who is not an acceptable husband or not a priest), she loses her status as a Kohen. When she loses her status as Kohen, (1) she is permanently forbidden from eating the breasts and thighs of sacrificed animals; and (2) she is forbidden to eat T'rumah as long as she is married to a man who is not an acceptable husband or not a priest.

However, the priest's daughter CAN eat T'rumah again if ALL of the following conditions are true:

1) her husband dies or divorces her
2) she has NO children by him
3) she returns to live with her father as a member of his household

This is based on the Torah passage *Leviticus 22:13*

But if a priest's daughter be a widow, or divorced, and have no child, and is returned unto her father's house, as in her youth, she may eat of her father's bread; but there shall no common man eat thereof.

Once she has children with her husband who is not a priest, she cannot resume eating T'rumah even if he dies, because their children make her a permanent part of his non-Kohen family.

If she ate the T'rumah and/or the sacrificed breasts and thighs at a time when these holy foods were forbidden to her, she would receive lashes of the whip.

For a more detailed discussion of the prohibitions listed in Mitzvah 283, consult the following sources:

See the discussion of this prohibition in Sefer HaHinnuch.
See the comments in Mitzvah 283.
Consult TB Kiddushin 2B, ShM Negative Precept 137.
Also consult TB Yevamoth 68b.

284. NOT TO EAT TEVEL–PRODUCE FROM WHICH T'RUMAH AND THE TITHES WERE NOT SEPARATED

And they shall not profane the holy things of the children of Israel, which they set apart unto the LORD; (Leviticus 22:15)

Mitzvah 284 is the prohibition against eating crops or produce that have not had the holy portions (T'rumah) and tithes taken out. The idea is that holy food should not be profaned while it is still mixed with non-holy food.

The anglicized Hebrew term for such crops is Tevel. The original crop is considered Tevel and no one can eat it until aftertheholy portions and the tithes have been separated out. If Tevel is mixed with other food, then that other food becomes forbidden.

My Partner in Torah explained that this procedure to separate out the holy portions is called T'rumah Ma'aser(the T'rumah of the Tithe). It is portioned out as follows:

A man who harvests 100 bushels of wheat must take 2 bushels out to give to the Kohen.

Of the 98 bushels remaining, the man must give 10 bushels to a Levite. (That Levite must separate a tenth of his tithe and present it to a Kohen.)

Of the 88 bushels remaining, the man must take out 9 bushels (one tenth of the remainder) for the Second Tithe which the owner eats in Jerusalem.

According to Sefer HaHinnuch, specific Torah passages say that eating Tevel results in "Death at Heaven's Hands." However, if a man ate some of the remainder AFTER the T'rumah portion had already been removed, but BEFORE the Tithe portions had been removed, that man would receive a whipping–not death. (See the discussion of Mitzvah 284 in Sefer HaHinnuch for details.)

285. THE PROHIBITION OF CONSECRATING BLEMISHED ANIMALS FOR OFFERINGS

But whatsoever hath a blemish, that shall ye not bring; for it shall not be acceptable for you. (Leviticus 22:20)

Mitzvah 285 forbids us to consecrate blemished or disfigured animals for possible sacrifice. Not only can we not sacrifice these types of animals, we cannot even consecrate them or even verbally consider placing them on the Altar.

286. THAT AN ANIMAL OFFERING IS TO BE WHOLE, WITHOUT BLEMISH OR DISFIGUREMENT

And whosoever bringeth a sacrifice of peace-offerings unto the LORD in fulfilment of a vow clearly uttered, or for a freewill-offering, of the herd or of the flock, it shall be perfect

to be accepted; there shall be no blemish therein. (Leviticus 22:21)

Mitzvah 286 commands that animals slated for sacrifice to Hashem be perfect and unblemished.

Just like the Kohen who must be unblemished to serve in Hashem's Temple, the animal must be unblemished to merit the honor of giving it to Hashem.

287. THAT WE SHOULD NOT MAKE A BLEMISHING DEFECT IN CONSECRATED ANIMALS

And whosoever bringeth a sacrifice of peace-offerings unto the LORD in fulfilment of a vow clearly uttered, or for a free-will-offering, of the herd or of the flock, it shall be perfect to be accepted; there shall be no blemish therein. (Leviticus 22:21)

Mitzvah 287 prohibits us from creating a blemish and/or a defect on an animal after it becomes designated for sacrifice. Committing this act results in a sound whipping. This Mitzvah is enforced when the Temple is extant.

288. NOT TO SPRINKLE THE BLOOD OF DEFECTIVE ANIMALS ON THE ALTAR

Blind, or broken, or maimed, or having a wen, or scabbed, or scurvy, ye shall not offer these unto the LORD, nor make an offering by fire of them upon the altar unto the LORD. (Leviticus 22:22)

Mitzvah 288 forbids us to sprinkle the blood of a blemished animal on the Altar used to sacrifice animals. This Mitzvah is enforced when the Temple is extant.

289. THE PROHIBITION ON RITUALLY SLAYING DEFECTIVE ANIMALS FOR HOLY OFFERINGS

Blind, or broken, or maimed, or having a wen, or scabbed, or scurvy, ye shall not offer these unto the LORD, nor make an offering by fire of them upon the altar unto the LORD. (Leviticus 22:22)

Mitzvah 289 prohibits the ritual slaughter of blemished and/or defective animals for sacrificial purposes. They are not allowed to be sacrificed to Hashem, therefore, they are not to be ritually slaughtered for that purpose. The only time that this Mitzvah is applicable is when Hashem's Holy Temple stands.

290. THAT WE SHOULD NOT BURN THE PORTIONS FOR THE ALTAR FROM DEFECTIVE ANIMALS

Blind, or broken, or maimed, or having a wen, or scabbed, or scurvy, ye shall not offer these unto the LORD, nor make an offering by fire of them upon the altar unto the LORD. (Leviticus 22:22)

Mitzvah 290 prohibits the offering up of any part of the animal on the Altar if the animal has a blemish. This Mitzvah is in effect when the Holy Temple is extant.

291. NOT TO EMASCULATE ANY CREATURE OUT OF ALL THE ANIMAL SPECIES

That which hath its stones bruised, or crushed, or torn, or cut, ye shall not offer unto the LORD; neither shall ye do thus in your land. (Leviticus 22:24)

Mitzvah 291 is the prohibition against castrating or sterilizing male humans and male animals.

When Hashem created the universe, He commanded males of all species to be fruitful and multiply. (See Mitzvah 1 for a more detailed explanation.) Making a male impotent interferes in the natural biological order of reproducing. Jewish men are forbidden from making themselves sterile or making any other male human or male animal sterile.

Jewish women are forbidden from sterilizing men or male animals.

Women are allowed to make themselves barren (sterile), or have other people perform the act on them.It is also permissible to sterilize female animals to prevent them from giving birth.

Mitzvah 1 exempts all female creatures, humans and animals, from the precept "be fruitful and multiply," because male creatures are the planters, not female creatures.

292. NOT TO OFFER UP A DEFECTIVE OFFERING RECEIVED FROM A HEATHEN

Neither from the hand of a foreigner shall ye offer the bread of your God of any of these, because their corruption is in them, there is a blemish in them; they shall not be accepted for you. (Leviticus 22:25)

Mitzvah 292 prohibits Kohanim from accepting blemished animals from non-Jews for sacrifice.

Jews and non-Jews are forbidden to offer blemished animals for sacrifice. If a Kohen violates this prohibition, he would receive whiplashes. This Mitzvah is enforced when all Jews live in Israel, and when Hashem's Holy Temple is extant.

293. THE PRECEPT THAT AN ANIMAL OFFERING SHOULD BE AT LEAST EIGHT DAYS OLD

When a bullock, or a sheep, or a goat, is brought forth, then it shall be seven days under the dam; but from the eighth day and thenceforth it may be accepted for an offering made by fire unto the LORD. (Leviticus 22:27)

Mitzvah 293 requires animals to be at least eight days old in order to be sacrificed.

A sacrificed animal must be in perfect form like Hashem. Kohanim performing the sacrifice must also be in perfect form like Hashem. An animal under eight days old is not suitable for sacrifice because it is not yet in perfect form.

When an animal is born, there is uncertainty if it will survive or develop into an animal healthy enough to eat. After a week, it can be determined, whether or not the animal is healthy enough to be sacrificed and eaten.

Violating this Mitzvah does not subject the guilty party to lashes because this is a positive precept and lashes are only given to those who violate negative Mitzvot.

294. THE PROHIBITION AGAINST RITUALLY SLAYING BOTH AN ANIMAL AND ITS YOUNG IN ONE DAY

And whether it be cow or ewe, ye shall not kill it and its young both in one day. (Leviticus 22:18)

Mitzvah 294 prohibits the slaughter of an animal and its offspring on the same day. One reason for this prohibition is to remind us that Hashem is concerned about the well-being, not just of humans, but all His creatures.

To slaughter a dam and her offspring in one day can lead the slaughterer to develop cruel traits. This limitation instills the slaughterer with mercy and compassion.

This Mitzvah generally applies to the dam and her offspring, but not the sire (the animal's male parent) because it is sometimes difficult to determine the specific father from a group of male animals. However, if one is certain that a particular male animal is the offspring's sire, then both sire and offspring cannot be slaughtered on the same day.

Note that if a dam's female offspring (dam's daughter) gives birth, then the newborn and its grandmother (the dam) can be slaughtered on the same day because the prohibition only applies to the mother and its direct offspring. Violating this Mitzvah subjects the guilty party to a whipping.

This Mitzvah forbids us from slaughtering more than one animal family member in the same day to prevent wiping out entire animal family groups and causing the extinction of that animal species.

295. TO DO NOTHING BY WHICH THE DIVINE NAME WILL BE PROFANED OR DESECRATED AMONG MEN

***And ye shall not profane My holy name;* but I will be hallowed among the children of Israel: I am the LORD who hallow you, (Leviticus 22:32)**

Mitzvah 295 forbids profaning or desecrating Hashem's holy name.

Deliberately violating any Mitzvot desecrates Hashem's holy name. This sin is enormous and the violator could receive whiplashes or a death sentence.

During times of persecution, if a Jew were threatened with death if he refused to violate a Mitzvah (and profane Hashem's name), it is the Jew's duty to refuse to violate the Mitzvah (and refuse to profane Hashem's holy name). The Jew is duty-bound to give up his life (die) rather than violate the Mitzvah.

But if that same Jew decided to violate the Mitzvah (and to profane Hashem's name) to stay alive, the court would not order him whipped because the Jew's actions were coerced (forced upon him).

If a Jew intentionally chose to profane Hashem's name and/ or bow down to false gods with the intention of angering the Almighty, that Jew earns a whipping because the Jew acted of his own free will.

296. THE MITZVAH OF SANCTIFYING THE ALMIGHTY'S NAME

And ye shall not profane My holy name; but I will be hallowed among the children of Israel: I am the LORD who hallow you, (Leviticus 22:32)

Mitzvah 296 obligates us to sanctify Hashem's name. It is only fitting because He created us to serve him. Following His Mitzvot and Torah also sanctify His name.

In times of non-persecution, a Jew is duty-bound to die (give up his life) rather than break a fundamental religious precept. The Sages said there are three Mitzvot a Jew must never transgress: the three cardinal Mitzvot of adultery, idolatry and murder.

Author's Note:

The Holy Days on the Jewish Lunar Calendar:

In the Jewish calendar, the moon's orbit around the earth is the basis for delineating the months. The beginning of the month is when the New Moon appears. When Jews first see the New Moon, it marks a new month–a new lunar month.

Hashem commands us to celebrate Passover in the spring. The lunar calendar needs some adjustments to keep Passover in the spring. The Jewish calendar adds seven leap months in every 19-year cycle (so there are 7 leap years in that 19-year cycle).

Hashem explained to Moses how to calculate the Jewish calendar (and the holy days), and Moses passed that information on to Joshua, who then passed it onto a select group of Sages.

The great Sage, Hillel II, wrote down the calculations for the lunar year (and the holy days on the Jewish calendar) so everyone would know.This eliminated the need for the two witnesses' monthly testimony before a learned judge. And it eliminated the need to send messengers to all the Jews living outside of Israel to tell them when the holy days started.

In the fourth century CE, Hillel II instituted the perpetual calendar in anticipation of the disbandment of the Sanhedrin. He also incorporated leap years into that calendar.

Hillel II knew, that because there was a smaller pool of educated Jews, there were fewer people who could calculate the lunar calendar. Another factor was the Diaspora–many Jews were living outside of Israel and messengers sent to them might arrive much later or much earlier than the actual start of the holy day. Therefore, to preserve the knowledge of the Jewish lunar calendar, he wrote down the calculations, so that every Jew would know when to celebrate the holidays and the beginning of the new lunar month.

Yom Tov in Eretz Yisrael (Special Holy Days in the Land of Israel):

The first and last days of Pesach (Passover)
The one day of Shavuot
The two Days of Rosh Hashanah
The one day of Yom Kippur
The first day of Sukkot
The one day of Sh'mini Atzeret (Simchat Torah)

Yom Tov outside of Eretz Yisrael (Special Holy Days outside the Land of Israel):

The first two days and last two days of Pesach (Passover)
The two days of Shavuot
The two days of Rosh Hashanah
The one day of Yom Kippur
The first two days of Sukkot
The two days of Sh'mini Atzeret and Simchat Torah

Cited in "Laws of Yom Tov (Advanced)," by Rabbi Moshe Lazarus. To read the article, consult the website: http://ohr.edu/holidays/pesach/laws_and_customs/3467

Hashem never decreed that two consecutivedays have a special level of holiness. The Sages added the "required second day" to most of the Jewish holy days, SPECIFICALLY FOR JEWS LIVING OUTSIDE OF ISRAEL because of the distances messengers would have to travel and the uncertainty of observing the holy day on the proper day.

Although Sukkot and Passover last a week, traditionally, the first day and last day of these holidays have a greater degree of holiness than the days in between.

We celebrate Rosh Hashanah in Israel for two days because it begins on the first day of the seventh month, Tishri. Because this holy day lands on the first day of the new lunar month, and verifying a new lunar month is a process filled with uncertainty, the chances of observing Rosh Hashanah on the wrong day are greater than the chances of observing the other holy days on the wrong day. Rosh Hashanah is the only holy day that starts on the first day of a new lunar month. The other holidays do not land on the first day of the new lunar month.

My Partner in Torah explained to me that the Rabbinic nature of the second day of Rosh Hashanah differs from the second days of other holidays. The second day of Rosh Hashanah was established as a continuation of the first day, as if the "first day celebrations, rituals and practices" lasted 48 hours.The second days of other major holidays were established as exact 24-hour duplicates of their first days.

Although Hanukkah has eight days, it does not have an additional day outside of Israel because this only applies to Torah commanded holidays.

Yom Kippur, which falls on the 10th Day of Tishri, only lasts one day because of the obligation to fast. We can become sick if we attempt to fast for 48 hours. Fasting means we cannot eat or drink anything; not even a drop of water.

Yom Tov means a special holy day. The term Yom Tov can be substituted for the name of any major holiday. Yamim Tovim is the plural of Yom Tov and mean special holy days.

NOTE: Leviticus 23:7-14 specifically refers to Passover and Mitzvot # 297 through # 305 are based on these verses.

297. THE PRECEPT OF RESTING FROM WORK ON THE FIRST DAY OF PASSOVER

***In the first day ye shall have a holy convocation;* ye shall do no manner of servile work. (Leviticus 23:7)**

In Mitzvah 297, Hashem commands us to sanctify the first day of Passover and keep it holy. Jews keep this day holy by praying in the Temple and resting from work.

Obeying this positive precept encourages us to think about the great miracles that Hashem performed when He freed us from Egypt and encourages us to learn more about the laws of Passover. It also encourages us to teach our children what we have learned from the Torah and the Mitzvot.

Passover starts on the15th of day of Nisan, the first month of the year on the Jewish lunar calendar.

Note: Mitzvah 300 commands us to keep holy the SEVENTH day of Passover by resting from work and praying in the Temple. All the positive precepts that apply to Mitzvah 297 for the FIRST day of Passover also apply to Mitzvah 300 for the SEVENTH day of Passover.

298. THE PROHIBITION OF DOING WORK ON THE FIRST DAY OF PASSOVER

In the first day ye shall have a holy convocation; ye shall do no manner of servile work. (Leviticus 23:7)

Mitzvah 298 prohibits us from doing servile work on the First Day of Passover. Heavy work / servile work / laborious work includes harvesting crops, grinding flour and the like. Mitzvah 298 is negative.

On Passover and the other holy holidays, we can only cook-food in the amount that will be eaten that day. We cannot cook additional food that will be eaten tomorrow or eaten on any other day.

This stems from the Torah passage: ***And in the first day there shall be to you a holy convocation, and in the seventh day a holy convocation; no manner of work shall be done in them, save that which every man must eat, that only may be done by you. (Exodus 12:16)***

Unlike the holy holidays, we cannot cook anyfood on Shabbat (also referred to as the Sabbath, meaning Friday night thru Saturday night).

This derives from Exodus, 20:9: ***but the seventh day is a Sabbath unto the LORD thy God, in it thou shalt not do any manner of work, thou, nor thy son, nor thy daughter, nor thy man-servant, nor thy maid-servant, nor thy cattle, nor thy stranger that is within thy gates; (Exodus 20:9)***

A common question is: "Suppose the special holy day falls on Friday? Normally we do all our cooking for Shabbat (Sabbath/ Saturday) on Friday. There would be TWO special holy days in a row where we are not allowed to cook. What can we do?"

My Partner in Torah explained that if the special holy day falls on Friday, followed by Shabbat on Saturday, we would perform Eruv Tavshilin, which means "combining and mixing foods."

On Thursday, before the special holy day starts on Friday, we completely cook all the food we will eat on Friday for the special holy day.

Also on Thursday, we BEGIN the cooking process for the food we will eat on Shabbat (Saturday). Jews are allowed to make any food, as well as combine or mix together any ingredients that will not spoil by being kept over 24 hours on Friday. These foods / mixtures are blessed, stored separately and designated for use on Shabbat only. We establish Eruv Tavshilin by reciting a blessing over these foods / mixtures that includes a specific paragraph where we state our intention to finish cooking these items on the special holy day Friday and promise that these items will only be eaten on Shabbat (Saturday).

If the Eruv (the foods made Thursday, blessed and set aside for Shabbat) gets lost or eaten before Shabbat starts, then the Eruv is invalidated.

A Rabbi performs this Mitzvah for BOTH his family and his community. Rabbis set aside the Eruv (the foods made Thursday, blessed and set aside for Shabbat)for their community to benefit any Jews who forget to make their own Eruv.

Eruv Tavshilin is applicable any time the special holy day is on Friday.

299. THE PRECEPT OF MUSAF OFFERING ALL THE SEVEN DAYS OF PASSOVER

(Musaf means additional.)

<u>And ye shall bring an offering made by fire unto the LORD seven days</u>; in the seventh day is a holy convocation; ye shall do no manner of servile work. (Leviticus 23:8)

Mitzvah 299 is the obligation to bring an additional burnt-offering (Musaf offering) on all seven days of Passover to remind us that these days are especially holy and not like ordinary days.

The Musaf offering is in addition to the two daily offerings normally made on each day of Passover.

Because we no longer have the Holy Temple, we recite the Musaf Service in Shul on holidays including Passover, Shabbat and Rosh Chodesh. The Musaf service reinforces that the days of Passover are special holy days when we should contemplate the favors, blessings, and miracles Hashem has bestowed on us.

300. THE PRECEPT OF RESTING FROM WORK ON THE SEVENTH DAY OF PASSOVER

And ye shall bring an offering made by fire unto the LORD seven days; <u>in the seventh day is a holy convocation</u>; ye shall do no manner of servile work. (Leviticus 23:8)

In Mitzvah 300, Hashem commands us to sanctify the seventh day of Passover and keep it holy. Jews keep this day holy by praying in the Temple and resting from work.

Obeying this positive precept encourages us to think about the great miracles that Hashem performed when He freed us from Egypt and encourages us to learn more about the laws of Passover. It also encourages us to teach our children what we have learned from the Torah and the Mitzvot.

The Seventh day of Passover is on the 21st of day of Nisan, the first month of the year on the Jewish lunar calendar.

Note: Mitzvah 300 commands us to keep holy the SEVENTH day of Passover by resting from work and praying. All the positive precepts that apply to Mitzvah 300 for the SEVENTH day of Passover also apply to Mitzvah 297 for the FIRST day of Passover.

301. THE PROHIBITION AGAINST DOING WORK ON THE SEVENTH DAY OF PASSOVER

And ye shall bring an offering made by fire unto the LORD seven days; in the seventh day is a holy convocation; ye shall do no manner of servile work. (Leviticus 23:8)

Mitzvah 301 prohibits us from doing servile work on the Seventh Day of Passover. Heavy work / servile work / laborious work includes harvesting crops, grinding flour and the like. The seventh day of Passover is the 21st Day of Nisan. Mitzvah 301 is a negative Mitzvah.

On Passover and the other holy holidays, we can only cook food in the amount that will be eaten that day. We cannot cook additional food that will be eaten tomorrow or eaten on any other day.

This stems from the Torah passage: ***And in the first day there shall be to you a holy convocation, and in the seventh day a holy convocation; no manner of work shall be done in them, save that which every man must eat, that only may be done by you. (Exodus 12:16)***

Note: Mitzvah 298 commands us to do no work on the FIRST day of Passover. All the negative precepts that apply to Mitzvah 298 for the FIRST day of Passover also apply to Mitzvah 301 for the SEVENTH day of Passover.

302. ON THE OFFERING OF THE 'OMER OF BARLEY ON THE SECOND DAY OF PASSOVER

Speak unto the children of Israel, and say unto them: When ye are come into the land which I give unto you, and shall reap the harvest thereof, then ye shall bring the sheaf of the first-fruits of your harvest unto the priest. And he shall wave the sheaf before the LORD, to be accepted for you; on the morrow after the sabbath the priest shall wave it. And in the day when ye wave the sheaf, ye shall offer a he-lamb without blemish of the first year for a burnt-offering unto the LORD. (Leviticus 23:10-12)

Mitzvah 302 states that on the second day of Passover, the 16th of Nisan, we are to provide a special offering of a sheaf of barley. Making this offering is our way of thanking Hashem for allowing the grains to grow, ripen, and provide food to sustain us.

On the second day of Passover, we offer a male lamb in his first year of life as an 'Olah (burnt offering) and one sheaf ('Omer) of barley called the "sheaf of the wave-offering." (An 'omer is a dry measure used in biblical times and equals a few cups intoday's system of volume measurement.)

The offering of a sheaf of barley is in addition to the two daily offerings and the Musaf Offering made on Passover. At the time of the Temple, our ancestors brought barley because it is a grain crop that ripens and is harvested in the spring.

The sheaf of the wave-offering takes place on the second day of Passover to keep it separate from the offerings on the first day of Passover; because the first day of Passover is devoted to celebrating and retelling how Hashem freed us from Pharaoh.

303. TO EAT NOTHING OF THE NEW CROP OF CEREAL GRAINS BEFORE THE END OF THE 16TH OF NISAN

And ye shall eat neither bread, nor parched corn, nor fresh ears, until this selfsame day, until ye have brought the offering of your God; it is a statute for ever throughout your generations in all your dwellings. (Leviticus 23:14)

Mitzvah 303 prohibits us from eating anything from the new grain (i.e., grain planted after the prior Passover) until the following year–at the end of the 16th of Nisan, the Second Day of Passover.

On the Second Day of Passover, the required offerings must be made before eating any of the new grains- specifically the Omer offering described in Mitzvah 302. The blessing of these offerings reminds us that Hashem provided grains for our benefit.

The Sages taught that there were only five grains included under the prohibition of "do not eat the new crops:" wheat, barley, spelt, oats, and rye.

304. TO EAT NO PARCHED GRAIN FROM THE NEW CROP TILL THE END OF THE 16TH OF NISAN

And ye shall eat neither bread, nor parched corn, nor fresh ears, until this selfsame day, until ye have brought the offering of your God; it is a statute for ever throughout your generations in all your dwellings. (Leviticus 23:14)

Mitzvah 304 prohibits us from cooking with grains or eating parched (roasted) grainsfrom the new crops until the Second Day of Passover. Mitzvah 304 is an extension of Mitzvah 303.

In simple layman's terms, any grain planted or grown after the Second Day of Passover in the year 2018, cannot be eaten until the Second Day of Passover in the year 2019.

305. TO EAT NO FRESH GRAIN FROM THE NEW CROP UNTIL THE END OF THE 16TH OF NISAN

And ye shall eat neither bread, nor parched corn, nor fresh ears, until this selfsame day, until ye have brought the offering of your God; it is a statute for ever throughout your generations in all your dwellings. (Leviticus 23:14)

Mitzvah 305 is the prohibition against eating raw grain from the new crop until the Second day of Passover. Mitzvah 305 is an extension of Mitzvah 303.

In simple layman's terms, any grain planted or grown after the Second Day of Passover in the year 2021, cannot be eaten until the Second Day of Passover in the year 2022.

NOTE: Leviticus 23:15-22 specifically refers to Shavuot, the Feast of Weeks, and Mitzvot # 306 through # 309 are based on these verses.

306. THE PRECEPT OF COUNTING THE 'OMER

And ye shall count unto you from the morrow after the *Day of Rest*, from the day that ye brought the sheaf of the waving; seven weeks shall there be complete; even unto the morrow after the seventh week shall ye number fifty days; and ye shall present a new meal-offering unto the LORD. (Leviticus 23:15-16)

Seven weeks shalt thou number unto thee; from the time the sickle is first put to the standing corn shalt thou begin to

number seven weeks. And thou shalt keep the *Feast of Weeks* unto the LORD thy God after the measure of the freewill-offering of thy hand, which thou shalt give, according as the LORD thy God blesseth thee. (Deuteronomy 16:9-10)

Mitzvah 306 commands us to count 50 days from the 16th of Nisan (the Second Day of Passover) to the Sixth of Sivan, which is the day we celebrate Shavuot, the start of the wheat harvest. It is also the day the Jews received Hashem's Torah.

On the 16th of Nisan, our ancestors brought an Omer of barley (a specific measure of barley) to the Temple for the sheaf of the wave offering. Fifty days later, on Shavuot, they brought wheat to the Temple to ask blessings for the start of the wheat harvest. This 50-day counting period is called Sefirat HaOmer, "counting the sheaves to Shavuot."

Sefirat HaOmer also honors the spiritual cleansing that our ancestors experienced after Hashem liberated them from Egypt to make them worthy to receive Hashem's Torah.

According to Midrash Rabbah Parashat Emor, the Children of Israel had reached 49 levels of impurity when they left Egypt and needed 49 days to undergo a spiritual cleansing before they became holy enough to receive Hashem's Torah.

We always celebrate Shavuot on the Sixth of Sivan, because we now have a fixed calendar. In ancient times, when the monthly calendar was established by the testimony of witnesses who had sighted the New Moon, Shavuot sometimes fell as early as the Fifth of Sivan (if both Nisan and Iyar had 30 days that year) or as late as the Seventh of Sivan (if both Nisan and Iyar had 29 days). For further details, consult the link:http://www.chabad.org/library/article_cdo/aid/70779/jewish/Emor.htm

Although the Temple no longer exists, we still count the Omer. Every night of Sefirat HaOmer we say the blessing:

BARUCH ATAH HSHEM E-LOHEINU MELEKH HA-OLAM ASHER KID'SHANU B'MITZVOTAV V'TZIVANU AL S'FIRAT HA-OMER.

("Blessed are You, Lord our God, King of the Universe, Who has sanctified us with His commandments and commanded us to count the Omer.")

The 33 Days of Mourning for Rabbi Akiba's students:

For first 33 days of Sefirat HaOmer, we mourn the death of tens of thousands of Rabbi Akiba's students who died from a plague during Sefirat HaOmer in ancient times. Jews refrain from getting haircuts, we refrain from listening to music and no wedding celebrations take place.

On Lag Ba'Omer, the thirty-third day of the Counting of the Omer, Rabbi Akiba's students stopped dying. On that day, Jews stop mourning and resume normal activities.

For additional information about the plight of Rabbi Akiba's students, consult the Babylonian Talmud, Yevamot 62B.

Due to fluctuations in the lunar calendar, not all Jews observe these days of mourning during Sefirat HaOmer on the exact same date.

Because Hashem did not command us to refrain from joyous activities during Sefirat HaOmer, there is no universal agreement about when (which dates) we should refrain from joyous activities. There is no Torah law on this. Many Rabbis will perform marriage ceremonies on Lag Ba'Omer only, but not on the other days of Sefirat HaOmer. If a Jewish couple wishes to marry on Lag Ba'Omer, they should secure the Rabbi's services several months in advance before he is too booked up.

According to Rabbi Alpert, there are numerous customs for how to count the 33 Days of Mourning. The Sephardim do weddings on the 34th Day. Some Rabbis perform weddings on Israel Independence Day, the 5th of Iyar, and Jerusalem Reunification Day, the 28th of Iyar. Some even start the count from Rosh Chodesh Iyar.

307. THE PRECEPT OF THE MEAL-OFFERING OF NEW WHEAT ON SHAVU'OT

even unto the morrow after the seventh week shall ye number fifty days; and ye shall present a new meal-offering unto the LORD. Ye shall bring out of your dwellings two wave-loaves of two tenth parts of an ephah; they shall be of fine flour, they shall be baked with leaven, for first-fruits unto the LORD. (Leviticus 23:16-17)

And ye shall present with the bread seven lambs without blemish of the first year, and one young bullock, and two rams; they shall be a burnt-offering unto the LORD, with their meal-offering, and their drink-offerings, even an offering made by fire, of a sweet savour unto the LORD. And ye shall offer one he-goat for a sin-offering, and two he-lambs of the first year for a sacrifice of peace-offerings. And the priest shall wave them with the bread of the first-fruits for a wave-offering before the LORD, with the two lambs; they shall be holy to the LORD for the priest. (Leviticus 23:18-20)

Mitzvah 307 commands us to bring a special wheat offering of the finest flour to the Temple, where it was baked into 2 loaves and used as a wave-offering to Hashem.

Afterwards, the Kohen Gadol received the first loaf to eat on Shavuot and the other priests split the second loaf. (Mitzvah 91 discusses our obligation to give the Kohanim our first fruits on Shavuot.)

Like the Omer offering, this is a communal offering, meaning that not every individual had to bring it himself. There was one offering brought on behalf of the entire Jewish people.

In addition, Hashem commanded us to provide the following for the Musaf service on Shavuot:

Also in the day of the first-fruits, when ye bring a new meal-offering unto the LORD in your feast of weeks, ye shall have a holy convocation: ye shall do no manner of servile work; but ye shall present a burnt-offering for a sweet savour unto the LORD: two young bullocks, one ram, seven he-lambs of the first year; and their meal-offering, fine flour mingled with oil, three tenth parts for each bullock, two tenth parts for the one ram, a several tenth part for every lamb of the seven lambs; one he-goat, to make atonement for you. Beside the continual burnt-offering, and the meal-offering thereof, ye shall offer them—they shall be unto you without blemish—and their drink-offerings. (Numbers 28:26-31)

308. THE PRECEPT OF RESTING FROM WORK ON SHAVUOT

And ye shall make proclamation on the selfsame day; <u>there shall be a holy convocation unto you</u>; ye shall do no manner of servile work; it is a statute forever in all your dwellings throughout your generations. (Leviticus 23:21)

In Mitzvah 308, Hashem commands us to sanctify Shavuot and keep it holy. Jews keep this day holy by praying in the

Temple and resting from work.

Obeying this positive precept encourages us to think about the great miracles that Hashem performed for us and encourages us to learn more about Shavuot. It also encourages us to teach our children what we have learned from the Torah and the Mitzvot.

Jews are permitted to cook human food on Shavuot that will be eaten that day. The same restrictions that apply for Passover (see Mitzvah 297) also apply to Shavuot.

309. THE PROHIBITION AGAINST DOING WORK ON THE SHAVUOT FESTIVAL

And ye shall make proclamation on the selfsame day; there shall be a holy convocation unto you; ye shall do no manner of servile work; it is a statute for ever in all your dwellings throughout your generations. (Leviticus 23:21)

Mitzvah 309 prohibits us from doing servile work on Shavuot. Heavy work / servile work / laborious work includes harvesting crops, grinding flour and the like. Mitzvah 309 is a negative Mitzvah.

Keeping Shavuot holy means to observe it as a day separated from others days, keeping it as a segment of time belonging especially to Hashem. No manual labor, no servile work, no heavy labor is permitted.

On Shavuot and the other holy holidays, we can only cook food in the amount that will be eaten that day. We cannot cook additional food that will be eaten tomorrow or eaten on any other day. The same restrictions that apply for Passover (see Mitzvah 298) also apply to Shavuot.

NOTE: Leviticus 23:24-25 pertain to Rosh Hashanah and Mitzvot # 310 through # 312 derive from these verses.

310. THE PRECEPT OF RESTING FROM WORK ON ROSH HASHANAH

Speak unto the children of Israel, saying: <u>In the seventh month, in the first day of the month, shall be a solemn rest unto you, a memorial proclaimed with the blast of horns, a holy convocation.</u> Ye shall do no manner of servile work; and ye shall bring an offering made by fire unto the LORD. (Leviticus 23:24-25)

In Mitzvah 310, Hashem commands us to sanctify Rosh Hashanah and keep it holy. A blast of horns calls Jews to pray in the Temple and do no work (rest from work).

Obeying this positive precept encourages us to think about the great miracles that Hashem performed for us and encourages us to learn more about Rosh Hashanah. It also encourages us to teach our children what we have learned from the Torah and the Mitzvot.

Jews are permitted to cook human food on Rosh Hashanah that will be eaten that day. The same restrictions that apply for Passover (see Mitzvah 297) also apply to Rosh Hashanah.

311. THE PROHIBITION OF DOING WORK ON ROSH HASHANAH

Speak unto the children of Israel, saying: In the seventh month, in the first day of the month, <u>shall be a solemn rest unto you</u>, a memorial proclaimed with the blast of horns, a holy convocation. <u>Ye shall do no manner of servile work;</u>

and ye shall bring an offering made by fire unto the LORD. (Leviticus 23:24-25)

Mitzvah 311 prohibits us from doing servile work on Rosh Hashanah. Heavy work / servile work / laborious work includes harvesting crops, grinding flour and the like. Mitzvah 311 is a negative Mitzvah.

Keeping Rosh Hashanah holy means to observe it as a day separated from others days, keeping it as a segment of time belonging especially to Hashem. No manual labor, no servile work, no heavy labor is permitted.

On Rosh Hashanah and the other holy holidays, we can only cookfood in the amount that will be eaten that day. We cannot cook additional food that will be eaten tomorrow or eaten on any other day. The same restrictions that apply for Passover (see Mitzvah 298) also apply to Rosh Hashanah.

My Partner in Torah explained that we cannot work on Rosh Hashanah because Hashem judges every human being–Jews and non-Jews–individually on that day. How can one possibly work when Hashem is judging every person?

Eliyahu Kitov, author of Book of our Heritage quoted the Talmud, Tractate Rosh Hashanah when he mentioned that Hashem places every person into one of three categories: The completely righteous, the completely wicked, or somewhere in between.

On Rosh Hashanah, Hashem seals the completely righteous people in the Book of Life, and He decides on Rosh Hashanah to exclude the completely wicked individuals. Those people in between have until the end of Yom Kippur to repent. When they do, Hashem seals them in the Book of Life. Wicked people always have the opportunity to repent.

Not one person knows if he or she will be sealed in the Book of Life, therefore it is advantageous to behave kindly toward others and to ask Hashem for forgiveness during the high holidays.

312. THE PRECEPT OF THE MUSAF OFFERING ON ROSH HASHANAH

Speak unto the children of Israel, saying: In the seventh month, in the first day of the month, shall be a solemn rest unto you, a memorial proclaimed with the blast of horns, a holy convocation. Ye shall do no manner of servile work; and ye shall bring an offering made by fire unto the LORD. (Leviticus 23:24-25)

Mitzvah 312 commands us to make an additional burnt-offering (the Musaf offering) on Rosh Hashanah. It is a positive Mitzvah.

Because we no longer have the Temple, we cannot sacrifice animals, therefore, on Rosh Hashanah, as on other major holidays, our Musaf Service is an additional prayer service.

NOTE: Leviticus 23:27-32 pertain to Yom Kippur, the Day of Atonement and Mitzvot # 313 through # 317 derive from these verses.

313. THE PRECEPT OF FASTING ON THE 10TH OF TISHRI (YOM KIPPUR)

Howbeit on the tenth day of this seventh month is the day of atonement; there shall be a holy convocation unto you,

and ye shall afflict your souls; and ye shall bring an offering made by fire unto the LORD. And ye shall do no manner of work in that same day; for it is a day of atonement, to make atonement for you before the LORD your God. For whatsoever soul it be that shall not be afflicted in that same day, he shall be cut off from his people. (Leviticus 23:27-29)

Mitzvah 313 commands us to keep Yom Kippur (the Day of Atonement) holy by praying in the temple and bringing a Musaf offering (an additional offering) made by fire. Hashem commands us to do no work and to focus on asking Hashem to forgive us our sins.

Yom Kippur is our last appeal to Hashem to seal us in the Book of Life. We ask Hashem to forgive us our sins. Hashem does not automatically forgive us for our sins against other human beings. First, we must ask the person we sinned against to forgive us; then we can ask Hashem to forgive us.

If the person we sinned against does NOT forgive us the first time we ask, we can ask that person two additional times. If the person we sinned against grants forgiveness, Hashem can still decide not to forgive our sin because Hashem is the ultimate judge.

The learned Sages and Rabbis extended the meaning of these verses to include the precept that we should fast on Yom Kippur, the Day of Atonement. This means no eating or drinking; not even water. We may not wash ourselves or use deodorant. These things are pleasurable, and excessive pleasures can lead one to sin. By refraining from these activities, we are free to focus on cleansing our souls.

Even though fasting is mandatory, a person in poor health, or a dying individual is allowed to eat and drink. Preserving life takes priority over fulfilling this Mitzvah.

Girls are required to fast after their 12th birthday and boys are required to fast after their 13th birthday. Jews teach their children how to fast in a gradual process over the years. For example, a nine-year-old child might skip breakfast, and a ten-year old child might skip breakfast and lunch, but still eat a snack.

This Mitzvah is applicable today.

The author of Sefer HaHinnuch wrote that we cannot wear leather shoes on Yom Kippur because the leather sandal plays a part in releasing one from a levirate marriage. On Yom Kippur, only Hashem can spare us, no human being has that authority on that day. Married couples cannot be intimate on Yom Kippur.

314. THE PRECEPT OF THE MUSAF OFFERING ON THE DAY OF ATONEMENT

Howbeit on the tenth day of this seventh month is the day of atonement; there shall be a holy convocation unto you, and ye shall afflict your souls; <u>and ye shall bring an offering made by fire unto the LORD</u>. (Leviticus 23:27)

Mitzvah 314 commands us to make an additional burnt-offering (the Musaf offering) on Yom Kippur. It is a positive Mitzvah.

Because we no longer have the Temple, we cannot sacrifice animals, therefore, on Yom Kippur, as on other major holidays, our Musaf Service is an additional prayer service.

315. THE PROHIBITION AGAINST DOING WORK ON THE TENTH OF TISHRI

Howbeit on the tenth day of this seventh month is the day of atonement; there shall be a holy convocation unto you, and

ye shall afflict your souls; and ye shall bring an offering made by fire unto the LORD. And ye shall do no manner of work in that same day; for it is a day of atonement, to make atonement for you before the LORD your God. For whatsoever soul it be that shall not be afflicted in that same day, he shall be cut off from his people. And whatsoever soul it be that doeth any manner of work in that same day, that soul will I destroy from among his people. (Leviticus 23:27-30)

Mitzvah 315 prohibits us from working on Yom Kippur. It is a day for praying, asking forgiveness for our sins, fasting, and asking Hashem to seal us in The Book of Life.

Yom Kippur is a very holy day reserved for spiritual endeavors and cooking food is not permitted (ye shall do no manner of work).

However, there is one exception: According to Sefer HaHinnuch, the Sages allowed us to clean and trim vegetables on Yom Kippur in order to eat them after the holiday ends. However, the Sages stated we have to wait for the conclusion of the Minhah (afternoon) service before we can tend to our vegetables. This manner of work is permitted on Yom Kippur, but not on Shabbat.

316. THE PROHIBITION AGAINST EATING OR DRINKING ON THE DAY OF ATONEMENT

For whatsoever soul it be that shall not be afflicted in that same day, he shall be cut off from his people. (Leviticus 23:29)

Mitzvah 316 is the negative side of Mitzvah 313.

Mitzvah 313 is a positive commandment obligating us to fast.

Mitzvah 316 is a negative Mitzvah. It tells us that Hashem will punish anyone who eats or drinks on Yom Kippur by cutting him off from his people (excommunication or even exile).

A person in poor health, or a dying individual is allowed to eat and drink without fear of punishment. Preserving life takes priority over fasting.

317. THE PRECEPT OF RESTING FROM WORK ON THE DAY OF ATONEMENT

It shall be unto you a Sabbath of solemn rest, and ye shall afflict your souls; in the ninth day of the month at even, from even unto even, shall ye keep your Sabbath. (Leviticus 23:32)

Mitzvah 317 commands us to rest on Yom Kippur. It is the Sabbath of Sabbaths (Shabbat Shabbaton).

When the author of Sefer HaHinnuch wrote about Mitzvah 317, he compared the punishment for working on Yom Kippur to working on Shabbat. The punishment for the former is a spiritual death and the punishment for the latter is physical death by stoning. Violating Shabbat is a more serious offense than violating Yom Kippur because Shabbat has a higher level of sanctity. Various Torah passages remind us to keep Shabbat:

Remember the sabbath day, to keep it holy. Six days shalt thou labour, and do all thy work; but the seventh day is a sabbath unto the LORD thy God, in it thou shalt not do any manner of work, thou, nor thy son, nor thy daughter, nor thy man-servant, nor thy maid-servant, nor thy cattle, nor thy stranger that is within thy gates; for in six days the LORD

made heaven and earth, the sea, and all that in them is, and rested on the seventh day; wherefore the LORD blessed the sabbath day, and hallowed it. (Exodus 20:-10)

Observe the sabbath day, to keep it holy, as the LORD thy God commanded thee. Six days shalt thou labour, and do all thy work; but the seventh day is a sabbath unto the LORD thy God, in it thou shalt not do any manner of work, thou, nor thy son, nor thy daughter, nor thy man-servant, nor thy maid-servant, nor thine ox, nor thine ass, nor any of thy cattle, nor thy stranger that is within thy gates; that thy man-servant and thy maid-servant may rest as well as thou. And thou shalt remember that thou was a servant in the land of Egypt, and the LORD thy God brought thee out thence by a mighty hand and by an outstretched arm; therefore the LORD thy God commanded thee to keep the sabbath day. (Deuteronomy 5:11-14)

Shabbat existed long before Yom Kippur. After Hashem created the world in six days, He rested on the seventh. When we rest on Shabbat, we emulate Hashem.

According to Sefer HaHinnuch, the Sages allowed us to clean and trim vegetables on Yom Kippur in order to eat them after the holiday ends. However, the Sages stated we have to wait for the conclusion of the Minhah (afternoon) service before we can tend to our vegetables. This manner of work is permitted on Yom Kippur, but not on Shabbat.

NOTE: Leviticus 23:34-43 specifically refers to Sukkot and Mitzvot # 318 through # 325 are based on these verses.

318. THE PRECEPT OF RESTING FROM WORK ON THE FIRST DAY OF SUKKOT

Speak unto the children of Israel, saying: On the fifteenth day of this seventh month is the feast of tabernacles for seven days unto the LORD. On the first day shall be a holy convocation; ye shall do no manner of servile work. (Leviticus 23:34-35)

Mitzvah 318 commands us to refrain from working on the First Day of Sukkot. This is a positive Mitzvah. In my write-up of Mitzvah 298, I discussed the type of work that we can do on Sukkot and other major holidays. There are other types of work that we can do on Sukkot such as carrying things transferring a flame and cooking as long as the day does not fall on Shabbat. On Shabbat, these activities are prohibited. See the commentary to Mishnah Betza, Chapter 5, Mishnah 1, and Mishnah Megillah, Chapter 1, Mishnah 5.

319. THE PROHIBITION AGAINST DOING WORK ON THE FIRST DAY OF SUKKOTH

Speak unto the children of Israel, saying: On the fifteenth day of this seventh month is the feast of tabernacles for seven days unto the LORD. On the first day shall be a holy convocation; ye shall do no manner of servile work. (Leviticus 23:34-35)

Mitzvah 319 forbids us to work on the First Day of Sukkot. Unlike Mitzvah 318, which is positive, Mitzvah 319 is negative. What I wrote about in my discussions of Mitzvot 298 and 318 applies here.

320. THE PRECEPT OF THE MUSAF OFFERING ON EACH DAY OF SUKKOT

Seven days ye shall bring an offering made by fire unto the LORD; on the eighth day shall be a holy convocation unto you; and ye shall bring an offering made by fire unto the LORD; it is a day of solemn assembly; ye shall do no manner of servile work. (Leviticus 23:36)

Mitzvah 320 requires that additional (Musaf) sacrifices take place on all seven days of Sukkot.

When I was a student at Aish HaTorah Yeshiva in The Old City of Jerusalem, I learned that at the time of the Temple, the priests sacrificed 70 bullocks on Sukkot, because the 70 bullocks represented the nations of the world.

Sukkot is a happy holiday because Hashem had forgiven us for our sins on Yom Kippur, which takes place five days before Sukkot begins. We are happy with Hashem and He is happy with us. We share the happiness with the 70 nations of the world. The sacrifices on behalf of the 70 nations is our way of asking Hashem to bless them. The sacrifices are to atone for the nations. It is also a way of beseeching Hashem to look out for their welfare. We pray that the other nations will live in peace instead of having wars. The nations don't have to know that the Jewish people perform these sacrifices on their behalf.

At the time that these sacrifices took place, there were only 70 nations in the world. On the first day, the priests sacrificed 13 bullocks. The second day they sacrificed 12 bullocks. On the third day, the number of sacrificed bullocks dropped to 11. Then the fourth day they sacrificed 10 bullocks. On the fifth day, the number of sacrificed bullocks dropped to nine. On the sixth day, the number decreased to eight and finally on the seventh day, the number of sacrificed bullocks was seven. (For more details about the diminishing number of bullocks sacrificed each day on Sukkot, consult Numbers Chapter 29, verses 12-34.) At Aish HaTorah, the Rabbis explained that the reduction of sacrificed bullocks each day symbolized the fewer number of enemies against Israel.

My Partner in Torah and I discussed the sacrifices on behalf of the 70 nations and consulted Book of Our Heritage by Eliyahu Kitov. We learned that there is great significance to the number 70. One case in point is in regard to this Mitzvah. According to Kitov, Ishmael was the father of 35 nations, while Esau was the father of the other 35 nations. They are both descendants of Abraham, who was not only the Father of the Jewish people, but of a multitude of nations. Abraham's Hebrew name, Avraham derives from two words: Av, meaning father and Raham meaning multitude. (Rabbi Alpert explained that technically the correct word for father of a multitude of nations is Av Hamohn Goyim.) When Jacob and his household of 70 went down to Egypt, they were a united Jewish nation. In sum, Jacob's household of 70, Ishmael and Esau together being the fathers of a total of 70 nations, coupled with them descending from Abraham, demonstrates that bonds between the Jewish people and the nations of the world are present.

When I first learned about the obligation of slaughtering a decreasing number of animals as Sukkoth progresses, I simultaneously studied Hillel's and Shammai's opposing views about lighting candles on the eight nights of Hanukkah. Shammai argued that we should light eight candles on the First Night and then light one less candle each night of the holiday. By The Eighth Night, we would only light one candle. Hillel had the opposite view. He believed that we should light one candle on The First Night and by The Eighth Night, light eight candles. Shammai's opinion was based on the idea that Hanukkah was a second-chance Sukkot because he perceived the connection to the Karbonot (sacrifices) of Sukkot.

Shammai believed that as a holiday progresses, people feel less excited about it. He said that the diminished number of candles would symbolize our reduced excitement. Hillel was convinced that we should light Hanukkah candles, based on how we are supposed to feel, not on how we actually feel. Hillel believed that as Hanukah progresses, we should feel more excited about the holiday. (It's about us ascending in holiness, Ma'ahlin BaKodesh.)

When it comes to lighting Hanukkah candles, we follow HIllel. The lighting of Eight Hanukkah candles is a beautiful sight. As we light additional Hanukkah candle each day, we see that the scene looks prettier and prettier. We look forward to the eighth day when the beauty of all eight lighted candles finally climaxes. Imagine following Shammai and the scene of lighting fewer candles each day! The diminished number of lit candles would make the Hanukkah experience depressing.

For more details about Hillel and Shammai's opinions about lighting Hanukkah candles, consult the link, http://www.morim.org/contents.aspx?id=2002

When my Partner in Torah and I discussed the Eighth Day of Hanukkah and its special level of holiness, I viewed it as additional ammunition to support Hillel's argument.

The Eighth Day is Zot Hanukkah, (This is Hanukkah). On The Eighth Day, we always read the Torah portion, which includes Numbers, Chapter 7, verse 84: This was the dedication-offering of the altar, in the day when it was anointed, at the hands of the princes of Israel: twelve silver dishes, twelve silver basins, twelve golden pans;

(In Hebrew the passage contains the words Zot Hanukah.)

Seven is the natural order, like Seven Days of the Week. Eight is above and beyond the natural order. There is an additional level of holiness surrounding the number eight. We take the joy of the Seven Days of Hanukkah and combine all of it into the Eighth Day. (Similarly, the Eighth Day of Sukkot, has a special level of holiness not present on the other seven days. This day, Shemini Atzeret, is a special day for just the Jewish people and Hashem to be together.)

In sum, the priests sacrificed fewer bullocks each Day of Sukkot because that symbolized reduced strife with the other nations. However, we light more candles each Night of Hanukkah because that symbolizes the beauty of the light and the holiday's greatness.

321. THE PRECEPT OF RESTING FROM WORK ON THE EIGHTH DAY OF SUKKOT

Seven days ye shall bring an offering made by fire unto the LORD; on the eighth day shall be a holy convocation unto you; and ye shall bring an offering made by fire unto the LORD; it is a day of solemn assembly; ye shall do no manner of servile work. (Leviticus 23:36)

Mitzvah 321 commands us to rest on The Eighth Day of Sukkot, Shemini Atzeret (The Eighth Day of Assembly). It falls on the 22nd of Tishri. However, we can cook food on Shemini Atzeret if we were to eat it that day.

322. THE PRECEPT OF THE MUSAF OFFERING ON THE EIGHTH DAY OF SUKKOT

Seven days ye shall bring an offering made by fire unto the LORD; <u>on the eighth day shall be a holy convocation unto you; and ye shall bring an offering made by fire unto the LORD</u>; it is a day of solemn assembly; ye shall do no manner of servile work. (Leviticus 23:36)

Mitzvah 322 requires a Musaf offering on Shemini Atzeret. More details about Shemini Atzeret will be covered in Mitzvah 323.

323. THE PROHIBITION AGAINST DOING WORK ON THE EIGHTH DAY OF SUKKOT

Seven days ye shall bring an offering made by fire unto the LORD; on the eighth day shall be a holy convocation unto you; and ye shall bring an offering made by fire unto the LORD; <u>it is a day of solemn assembly; ye shall do no manner of servile work.</u> (Leviticus 23:36)

Mitzvah 323 forbids us to work on the Eighth Day of Sukkot. It is a negative Mitzvah.

In Sefer HaHinnuch, the author states that Hashem is sad to see us, the Jewish people- His chosen people- leave Jerusalem at the end of Sukkot. As a result, He commands us to remain an extra day. During the Seven Days of Sukkot, the 70 nations are represented, via the gradual daily reduction of sacrificed bullocks. (Consult my write-up of Mitzvah 320 for more details.) However, on The Eighth Day of Sukkot, no such representation of the other nations takes place. It is a day just for the Jewish people and Hashem to be together.

My Partner in Torah explained that according to most customs, we eat our meals in our Sukkah(s) (branched covered huts) on Shemini Atzeret, as we do on the First Seven Days of the holiday, we do not say the blessing for sitting in our Sukkah(s). We say the blessing for the first seven days. During the seven days, we dwell in our Sukkot. We relax, eat, sleep, and enjoy snacks in our Sukkot, but not on Shemini Atzeret.

324. THE PRECEPT OF TAKING UP THE LULAV ON THE FIRST DAY OF SUKKOT

And ye shall take you on the first day the fruit of goodly trees, branches of palm-trees, and boughs of thick trees, and willows of the brook, and ye shall rejoice before the LORD your God seven days. (Leviticus 23:40)

Mitzvah 324 commands us to shake the Lulav on Sukkot. (Lulav means palm branch.)

The Lulav must be accompanied by two willow and three myrtle branches. We also have to carry the Etrog (citron). We must carry these four species in order to complete this Mitzvah, which we still fulfill today.

According to Midrash **Vayikra Rabbah** 30:12, these four species represent four different categories of the Jewish people. The Etrog, which smells great and is edible, represents the Jew who studies Torah and who performs good deeds. The Lulav has taste but no aroma. This represents the Jew who studies Torah, but who refrains from practicing good deeds. The myrtle, which has aroma but no taste, represents the Jew who performs good deeds, but who refrains from Torah study. Finally, the willow has neither taste nor aroma, thus representing the Jew who neglects Torah study and the performance of doing good deeds. Shaking the Lulav represents bringing these four groups of Jews together.

My Partner in Torah added that these four species also represent body parts: The Etrog represents the heart, the Lulav represents the spine, the willow represents the lips, and the myrtle represents the eyes. The Lulav symbolically brings these body parts together in order to better serve Hashem.

When the Temple existed, the Jewish people shook their Lulavim on the First Day of Sukkot, and outside of Jerusalem only on the first day. However, after its destruction, the Rabbis commanded that Lulavim be shaken every day of the holiday, except Shabbat, in order to remember the Temple. (See Tractate Rosh Hashanah, Chapter 4, Mishnah 3, and parallels.)

No one may carry a Lulav on Shabbat. The Rabbis passed this decree to prevent people from carrying them in places without Eruvin. (The Eruv defines an area as an enclosed residential communal entity thus allowing people to carry from their homes to the street. The plural for Eruv is Eruvin.) For more information about the prohibition of carrying a Lulav on Shabbat, consult the link: http://www.askmoses.com/en/article/266,2057008/Why-dont-we-shake-the-Four-Species-on-Shabbat.html Also consult Chapter Four, Mishnah Two of Tractate Sukkah.

Before we shake our Lulavim, we say the following blessing:

(In Hebrew, the prayer reads from right to left)

Barukh Atah Hashem, Eloheinu, Melekh Ha-Olam Asher Kidshanu B'mitz'votav V'tzivanu Al N'tilat Lulav.

Blessed are you, Lord, our God, King of the universe Who has sanctified us with His commandments and commanded us to take up the Lulav.

325. THE MITZVAH OF DWELLING IN A SUKKAH

Ye shall dwell in booths seven days; all that are home-born in Israel shall dwell in booths; that your generations may know that I made the children of Israel to dwell in booths, when I brought them out of the land of Egypt: I am the LORD your God. (Leviticus 23:42-43)

Mitzvah 325 commands us to dwell in a Sukkah for all Seven Days of the Holiday. During Sukkot, we sit, eat, and sleep in our Sukkah.

A Sukkah is an outdoor hut with an opened roof. (The plural for Sukkah is Sukkot.) There are stringent rules about what can and cannot be used to build a Sukkah. For more information, consult the discussion of Mitzvah 325 in Sefer HaHinnuch. Also consult Book of our Heritage by Eliyahu Kitov.

According to Sefer HaHinnuch, we dwell in our Sukkot during the holiday in order to remember the miracles that Hashem did for the children of Israel while they were in the Wilderness for 40 years. The covering that we put on the Sukkah reminds us of Hashem's protective cloud cover that He provided them from the time they left Egypt until they entered the Land of Canaan. They lived in Sukkot while they were in the wilderness.

Some Rabbis told me that dwelling in a Sukkah reminds us that nothing lasts forever, except Hashem. Being in the Sukkah reminds us that our houses and possessions come from Hashem, and that they are not here forever.

Dwelling in our Sukkot for seven days also reminds us that no one is better than anyone else. It is easy for a rich person to mistakenly think that he is better than a poor person because he has wealth and riches and a great abundance of food. However, when he lives in his Sukkah, he is now on the same playing field as poor people. Sukkot is the one time out of the year where he does not live in his expensive house, nor does he enjoy his wealth. It is a reminder that we are all equal in the eyes of Hashem.

Sukkot is in the fall in Israel and in places in the Northern Hemisphere. Dwelling in our Sukkot in the fall is more challenging than doing so in the spring because the weather is colder in autumn. True, in South America, Sukkot comes in the spring. However, Hashem established this Torah commandment long before the Diaspora.

326. THE PROHIBITION AGAINST WORKING THE EARTH DURING THE SABBATICAL YEAR

But in the seventh year shall be a sabbath of solemn rest for the land, a sabbath unto the LORD; thou shalt neither sow thy field, nor prune thy vineyard. (Leviticus 25:4)

Mitzvah 326 prohibits us from working the Land of Israel in the seventh year of the seven-year cycle. Violators of this Mitzvah are to receive lashes of the whip. This Mitzvah is in effect when the Holy Temple is extant.

I discussed reasons for the sabbatical year in my write-up of Mitzvah 84.

327. THE PROHIBITION ON DOING WORK ON TREES DURING THE SABBATICAL YEAR

But in the seventh year shall be a sabbath of solemn rest for the land, a sabbath unto the LORD; thou shalt neither sow thy field, nor prune thy vineyard. (Leviticus 25:4)

Mitzvah 327 prohibits us from doing work on trees in the sabbatical year. This Mitzvah is applicable when the Temple is extant.

328. THE PROHIBITION AGAINST HARVESTING WHAT GROWS WILD IN THE SABBATICAL YEAR

That which groweth of itself of thy harvest thou shalt not reap, and the grapes of thy undressed vine thou shalt not gather; it shall be a year of solemn rest for the land. (Leviticus 25:5)

Mitzvah 328 is the prohibition against harvesting in the seventh year of the seven-year cycle, crops that one grew in the sixth year and/or crops that grew without human assistance in the seventh year. There is no prohibition against eating these fruits, but no one may harvest, store, nor sell them.

329. NOT TO GATHER THE FRUIT OF TREES IN THE SABBATICAL YEAR AS IT IS GENERALLY GATHERED

That which groweth of itself of thy harvest thou shalt not reap, and the grapes of thy undressed vine thou shalt not gather; it shall be a year of solemn rest for the land. (Leviticus 25:5)

Mitzvah 329 forbids us from picking fruit from trees in the seventh year with the intention of storing or selling them. We can pick fruit from trees in the seventh year to eat them. All the fruit from trees are to be ownerless. Therefore, we cannot gather or handle fruit the way we would in other years when we harvest them. In the other six years, those fruits are our possessions. Because the fruit is ownerless in the seventh year, we must handle them differently. For example, we cannot use special fig knives to cut figs off trees, but we can use ordinary knives. We cannot stomp on grapes in wine presses, yet we can do that in kneading basins. We cannot use olive presses to squeeze them out, yet we can use small pressing basins. Handling the fruit differently in the seventh year reminds us that they are ownerless.

330. THE PRECEPT OF COUNTING SEPTENNATES-CYCLES OF SEVEN YEARS

And thou shalt number seven sabbaths of years unto thee, seven times seven years; and there shall be unto thee the days of seven sabbaths of years, even forty and nine years. (Leviticus 25:8)

Mitzvah 330 commands us to count seven seven-year cycles. After the completion of the 49th year begins the Jubilee Year. In the Jubilee Year, which is the 50th, purchased land is returned to the original owners, and Jewish slaves are set free.

Returning land reminds us that Hashem is the true and permanent owner of everything. Freeing the Jewish slaves is a reminder that the Jewish people are Hashem's chosen ones. As mentioned in Mitzvah 280, both Jewish and non-Jewish slaves must be treated humanely. For more details, consult my write-up of Mitzvah 280.

331. THE PRECEPT OF SOUNDING THE SHOFAR ON THE DAY OF ATONEMENT IN A JUBILEE YEAR

Then shalt thou make proclamation with the blast of the horn on the tenth day of the seventh month; in the day of atonement shall ye make proclamation with the horn throughout all your land. And ye shall hallow the fiftieth year, and proclaim liberty throughout the land unto all the inhabitants thereof; it shall be a jubilee unto you; and ye shall return every man unto his possession, and ye shall return every man unto his family. (Leviticus 25:9-10)

Mitzvah 331 commands us to blow the Shofar on Yom Kippur in the Jubilee Year because it signifies that all Jewish slaves are now free. It also signifies that purchased land goes back to the original owners.

My Partner in Torah and I covered this topic while consulting the discussion of Mitzvah 331 in Sefer HaHinnuch.

At the time of the Temple and the Bet Din and, when the Jubilee Year was enforced, the Shofar blast occurred during Yom Kippur, but not at the end of the holiday. If Yom Kippur fell on Shabbat during the Jubilee Year, the Shofar was blown in the Bet Din. The prohibition to blow the Shofar on Shabbat is a Rabbinic law, not a Torah law. The Rabbis made this decision to prevent the Jewish people from carrying their Shofars in areas without Eruvs. For that reason, we do not blow the Shofar on Rosh Hashanah if the holiday falls on Shabbat.

There is no preventive measure to blow the Shofar on Yom Kippur if it falls on Shabbat of a Jubilee Year because it is so infrequent; one time every 50 years, and Yom Kippur does not always fall on Shabbat.

Today we blow the Shofar at the end of Yom Kippur, because it serves as an announcement that the fast is over.

332. THE PRECEPT OF SANCTIFYING THE JUBILEE YEAR

And ye shall hallow the fiftieth year, and proclaim liberty throughout the land unto all the inhabitants thereof; it shall be a jubilee unto you; and ye shall return every man unto his possession, and ye shall return every man unto his family. (Leviticus 25:10)

Mitzvah 332 commands us to sanctify the Jubilee Year. The Jubilee Year is quite similar to the Sh'mittah Year in that we cannot work the land in either year. Another similarity is that in both cases, all debts are cancelled. A difference is that in the Jubilee Year, unlike the Sh'mittah Year, Jewish slaves are set free and land, including that which was purchased, is returned to original owners. (For more information about the Jubilee Year, consult my write-up of Mitzvah 330. For more information about the Sh'mittah Year, consult my write-up of Mitzvah 84.)

The author of Sefer HaHinnuch points out that the Jubilee Year is not counted as one of the seven years in the seven-year cycle. The process of counting septennate-cycles of seven years commences after the end of the Jubilee Year.

333. THE PROHIBITION AGAINST FARMING THE LAND IN A JUBILEE YEAR

A jubilee shall that fiftieth year be unto you; ye shall not sow, neither reap that which groweth of itself in it, nor gather the grapes in it of the undressed vines. (Leviticus 25:11)

Mitzvah 333 prohibits us from farming the land in the Jubilee Year. Just like the Sh'mittah Year, this prohibition reminds us that the land does not belong to us, but to Hashem. Hashem makes this abundantly clear in Leviticus 25:23: "And the land shall not be sold in perpetuity; for the land is Mine; for ye are strangers and settlers with Me."

334. THAT WE SHOULD NOT HARVEST WILD-GROWING PRODUCE IN A JUBILEE YEAR

***That which groweth of itself* of thy harvest thou shalt not reap, and the grapes of thy undressed vine thou shalt not gather; it shall be a year of solemn rest for the land. (Leviticus 25:5)**

Mitzvah 334 forbids us to harvest wild growing produce in the Jubilee Year. The reasons for this prohibition are identical to the reasons for not harvesting during the Sh'mittah Year. I discussed this in my write-ups of Mitzvot 84 and 328.

335. NOT TO GATHER THE FRUIT OF TREES IN THE ORDINARY WAY DURING A JUBILEE YEAR

A jubilee shall that fiftieth year be unto you; ye shall not sow, neither reap that which groweth of itself in it, nor gather the grapes in it of the undressed vines. (Leviticus 25:11)

Mitzvah 335 prohibits us from picking fruit from trees with the purpose of storing or commercializing it during the Jubilee Year, as in the Sh'mittah Year. In the Jubilee Year and the Sh'mittah Year, we can pick fruit to eat it at the time we pick it, but we cannot pick the fruit for any other reason.

336. THE PRECEPT OF EFFECTING JUSTICE BETWEEN BUYER AND SELLER

And if thou sell aught unto thy neighbour, or buy of thy neighbour's hand, ye shall not wrong one another. (Leviticus 25:14)

Mitzvah 336 requires proper legal structure for buyers and sellers. The requirements are necessary because it keeps people from cheating one another. This Mitzvah makes it possible for neighbors to live in peace and it fulfills the commandment cited in Leviticus 19:18: thou shalt love thy neighbour as thyself.

337. THE PROHIBITION AGAINST WRONGING ANYONE IN BUYING AND SELLING

And if thou sell aught unto thy neighbour, or buy of thy neighbour's hand, ye shall not wrong one another. (Leviticus 25:14)

Mitzvah 337 prohibits the act of cheating one another in regard to buying and selling items. Overcharging a buyer is forbidden, just as intentionally not paying the seller the full value of his or her product. This Mitzvah applies to buying and selling chattel, but not land because the latter does not have a defined market value.

This Mitzvah prevents people from taking advantage of other individuals' ignorance. It also strengthens the chances of harmonious relationships between neighbors.

Violating this Mitzvah does not result in receiving lashes of the whip. Rather, the cheater must compensate his or her victim.

338. THE PROHIBITION AGAINST OPPRESSING A JEW WITH WORDS

And ye shall not wrong one another; but thou shalt fear thy God; for I am the LORD your God. (Leviticus 25:17)

Mitzvah 338 forbids a Jew from verbally tormenting his or her fellow Jew. This includes no teasing or insulting one another. If a Jew had previously been a criminal and now repented, another Jew cannot remind him or her of those bad days. In my write-up of Mitzvah 63, I mentioned that Rabbi Yochanan did Reish Lakish a serious injustice by reminding him of his days as a robber. Treating fellow Jews respectfully includes not providing false information. For example, if traveling merchants need food for their donkeys, no one can intentionally advise them to go to a specific address if that person knows that the people at that place cannot be accommodating. One cannot pretend to be interested in buying specific items from a particular vendor, if not really interested.

Observing this Mitzvah allows Jews to live together without strife. This goes back to "Kol Yisrael Areivim Zeh Ba Zeh (All Jews are responsible for each other).

Although this Mitzvah commands Jews to treat other Jews respectfully, one should treat another person (Jew and non-Jew) as he or she would like to be treated. (See Tractate, Bava Metzia, Chapter 4, Mishnah 10.)

339. THE PROHIBITION AGAINST SELLING A FIELD PERMANENTLY IN THE LAND OF ISRAEL

And the land shall not be sold in perpetuity; for the land is Mine; for ye are strangers and settlers with Me. (Leviticus 25:23)

Mitzvah 339 forbids the permanent sale of land in Israel. Not one bit of land can be sold in perpetuity because all of Eretz Yisrael (The Land of Israel) belongs to Hashem.

If a buyer and seller of land in Israel agree that the buyer can possess the land for 60 years, for example, the buyer does not have to return the land in the Yovel–the Jubilee Year, because that particular property will inevitably go back to the owner at the end of the 60-year period. The reason for this allowance is that there was no permanent transaction of the land.

340. THE PRECEPT OF RETURNING LAND TO ITS ORIGINAL OWNER AT THE JUBILEE

And in all the land of your possession ye shall grant a redemption for the land. (Leviticus 25:24)

Mitzvah 340 is the obligation to return property to the original owner in the Jubilee Year. Houses in open fields and in villages also go back to the original owners in the Jubilee Year because homes are included as property. However, houses in walled cities, such as the Holy City of Jerusalem, is another story. If a vendor sells his or her house and does not redeemit within a year, then the house belongs to the new owner, permanently. Not even the Jubilee Year allows the vendor to reclaim it. An explanation is that homes in walled cities have a special holiness. The owner should love the house so much that he would do anything to get it back. If a year passes and the owner takes no action to reclaim it, then the penalty is that he lost all claims to it, permanently. (The laws of the Jubilee Year take place in Israel and only when all the Jews are living there.) For more information about the irrevocability of purchased houses in walled cities, consult the discussion of Mitzvah 340 in Sefer HaHinnuch.

The Levites, unlike the rest of the tribes, can reclaim their houses in walled cities at any time. As stated in Leviticus 25:32: But as for the cities of the Levites, the houses of the cities of their possession, the Levites shall have a perpetual right of redemption.

Special privileges given to the Levites will be given more attention in Mitzvah 342.

341. THE PRECEPT OF REDEEMING LAND IN A WALLED CITY WITHIN A YEAR

And if a man sell a dwelling-house in a walled city, then he may redeem it within a whole year after it is sold; for a full year shall he have the right of redemption. And if it be not redeemed within the space of a full year, then the house that is in the walled city shall be made sure in perpetuity to him that bought it, throughout his generations; it shall not go out in the jubilee. (Leviticus 25:29–30)

Mitzvah 341 allows a vendor to buy back his house in a walled city before the one-year anniversary of the purchase. Within a year, the vendor can buy back the house by giving the buyer a full refund. When the buyer sells the vendor his house back, the former cannot charge the latter interest. A vendor can repurchase the house by either simply returning the money, or the vendor can sell his other properties in order to pay for the house. He cannot borrow money to buy the house back because that transaction leads to additional money being spent. He cannot buy back the house by paying in installments. He must give the buyer the lump sum of money. If the vendor dies before the one-year anniversary of the sale, then his son can buy back the house until the end of the first year. The Levites, unlike the other tribes, can reclaim their houses any time.

342. NOT TO ALTER THE OPEN LAND AROUND THE LEVITES' CITIES, OR THEIR FIELDS

But as for the cities of the Levites, the houses of the cities of their possession, the Levites shall have a perpetual right of redemption. And if a man purchase of the Levites, then the house that was sold in the city of his possession, shall go out in the jubilee; for the houses of the cities of the Levites are their possession among the children of Israel. But the fields of the open land about their cities may not be sold; for that is their perpetual possession. (Leviticus 25:32–34)

Mitzvah 342 states that pieces of land distributed to the Levites cannot be changed. If a Levite is given open land, it cannot be used as a field and vise versa. In addition, if a Levite is given land in a city, that land cannot be used as open land in the country or as fields.

Hashem distributed land to the other eleven tribes of Jacob for them to cultivate. However, because Hashem assigned the Levites to work in His Holy Temple in Jerusalem, they had no time to take care of land. Therefore, Hashem granted the Levites pieces of land in specified areas. Some of the Levites' land was in 48 specific cities, six being cities of refuge. Other portions extended to fields and open areas. The open area was a thousand cubits wide, while the fields were two thousand cubits wide.

343. THE PROHIBITION AGAINST LENDING AT INTEREST

Thou shalt not give him thy money upon interest, nor give him thy victuals for increase. (Leviticus 25:37)

Thou shalt not lend upon interest to thy brother: interest of money, interest of victuals, interest of any thing that is lent upon interest. Unto a foreigner thou mayest lend upon interest; but unto thy brother thou shalt not lend upon interest; that the LORD thy God may bless thee in all that thou puttest thy hand unto, in the land whither thou goest in to possess it. (Deuteronomy 23:20-21)

Mitzvah 343 is the prohibition against charging a Jew interest on a monetary loan. This prohibition extends to food and other objects. For example, if a Jew lends a fellow Jew three eggs, he cannot demand four eggs in return. Implied interest is also forbidden. An example of implied interest: A Jew cannot promise to reduce a fellow Jew's debt if he repays it early, and he cannot charge interest if the debt is past due.

A Jew can charge a non-Jew interest. On the surface, that might seem inhumane, but that is not the case. If someone works for Company A and needs heath-coverage, he should have Company A provide it, not Company B. It is not Company B's responsibility to provide for him. If a father has only enough money to lend one person and the choice is between his son and a stranger, he would naturally help his son. Other nations need to help their own kinsmen before helping outsiders. Families need to help their relatives before helping outsiders. Jews need to help fellow Jews before helping non-Jews. Similarly, Jews should give to Jewish charities and to Israel before giving money to non-Jewish causes and to other countries.

My Partner in Torah explained how charging fellow Jews interest, is similar to "Lashon HaRah (speaking with an evil tongue–gossiping)."

He referenced The Power of Speech by Yehuda Cahn.

According to Cahn, those who charge interest show that they are unwilling to wait for the reward of performing the Mitzvah of lending money to help the poor. It is an implicit denial of Hashem. Just as usurers display impatience by demanding an immediate reward–people often speak Lashon HaRah because they also are too impatient to wait and ascertain the accurate details. Instead, they jump to conclusions.

Chapter six, Mishnah six, of Tractate Avot states that one of the 48 prerequisites for success in Torah study is to have faith in the Sages. Because the Rabbis are responsible for the transmission of the Oral Torah from generation to generation, they must have the trust of the Jewish nation. One who does not trust them cannot believe in the validity of the Torah. The Torah entrusts the leadership of the Jewish nation to righteous Torah scholars. Such leaders must also render controversial decisions and since qualified leaders have deep knowledge and insight, the Sages caution that one must accept their rulings even when what they say contradicts one's own opinion. Because some people may fail to fully understand the Rabbis' teachings or the basis for those teachings, they might be tempted to speak Lashon HaRah about their Torah leaders.

344. THAT WE SHOULD NOT HAVE A HEBREW MANSERVANT DO CONTEMPTIBLE WORK LIKE A HEATHEN SLAVE

And if thy brother be waxen poor with thee, and sell himself unto thee, thou shalt not make him to serve as a bondservant. (Leviticus 25:39)

Mitzvah 344 forbids us to have our Hebrew slaves do contemptible work like heathen slaves. For example, if the master usually sits on a rag or cushion, he cannot have the Hebrew slave carry it around for him. He cannot have the Hebrew slave carry his toiletries to the bathhouse.

The master should treat his Hebrew slave better than he treats himself. For example, if there is only one pillow, the Hebrew slave uses it.

The purpose of this Mitzvah is to remind ourselves that we must treat our fellow Jews with the utmost respect, even if they have to be slaves for a seven–year period. This also reminds the master that any Jew, including himself, might have an unforeseen predicament that would cause him to end up a slave, therefore, the master must be kind and compassionate.

This Mitzvah is no longer applicable because we do not have the Jubilee Year anymore.

345. THE PROHIBITION OF SELLING A HEBREW MANSERVANT AT THE SLAVES' SELLING-BLOCK

For they are My servants, whom I brought forth out of the land of Egypt; they shall not be sold as bondmen. (Leviticus 25:42)

Mitzvah 345 prohibits us from selling a Hebrew/Jewish slave in a public manner. It is humiliating enough for him or her to have to be a slave, therefore the public sale adds to the humiliation. This also falls in line with loving all fellow Jews.

This Mitzvah is no longer applicable because we no longer observe the Jubilee Year.

346. NOT TO WORK A HEBREW MANSERVANT AT HARD LABOR

Thou shalt not rule over him with rigour; but shalt fear thy God. (Leviticus 25:43)

Mitzvah 346 is the prohibition against giving the Jewish slave useless work, just for the sake of keeping him or her busy. For example, he cannot have his slave chop trees for no reason. This Mitzvah prevents the master from mistreating and taking advantage of a fellow Jew.

This Mitzvah is not applicable today because the Jubilee Year is no longer in effect. In addition, Jews no longer have any type of slaves, neither Jewish nor non-Jewish.

347. THE PRECEPT OF KEEPING A HEATHEN SLAVE PERMANENTLY

Moreover of the children of the strangers that do sojourn among you, of them may ye buy, and of their families that are with you, which they have begotten in your land; and they may be your possession. And ye may make them an inheritance for your children after you, to hold for a possession: of them may ye take your bondmen for ever; but over your brethren the children of Israel ye shall not rule, one over another, with rigour. (Leviticus 25:45-46)

Mitzvah 347 obligates us to keep a non-Jewish slave permanently. This includes passing the slave to the owner's heirs after the owner dies.

The origins of this decree date back to Ham's mistreatment of his father Noah.

The following passages, Genesis 9:21-27 explain the circumstances.

And he drank of the wine, and was drunken; and he was uncovered within his tent. And Ham, the father of Canaan, saw the nakedness of his father, and told his two brethren without. And Shem and Japheth took a garment, and laid it upon both their shoulders, and went backward, and covered the nakedness of their father; and their faces were backward, and they saw not their father's nakedness. And Noah awoke from his wine, and knew what his youngest son had done unto him. And he said: Cursed be Canaan; a servant of servants shall he be unto his brethren. And he said: Blessed be the LORD, the God of Shem; and let Canaan be their servant. God enlarge Japheth, and he shall dwell in the tents of Shem; and let Canaan be their servant.

There are arguments about why the punishment was severe: One possibility is that Ham saw his father naked, and then castrated him. Another argument is that Ham sodomized his mother, Noah's wife Naamah. The child born was Canaan. The discussion about Noah's castration and the sodomizing of Noah's wife can be found at the link http://en.allexperts.com/q/Orthodox-Judaism-952/sons.htm For additional details, consult Sanhedrin 70a] \b 23\b0.

(According to the Midrash, Genesis Rabbah, (23.3), Noah's wife's name was Naamah.)

A Canaanite slave is a non-Jew who can come from any heathen nation, according Sefer HaHinnuch.

Although a Jew is commanded to keep his Canaanite slave forever, there are circumstances when the slave must be set free:

Knocking out a slave's tooth, and/or removing an eye or any other limb that cannot grow back are grounds for freeing the slave. The master must also provide financial compensation. According to Sefer HaHinnuch, if a master has his heathen slave wearT'fillin (phylacteries) or read at least three verses of Torah to a congregation, the slave is set free because these actions are things that free men do. Another case where a non-Jewish slave can be freed is when 10 men are needed for a Minyan, but only nine of them and the slave are present. (In order for a traditional Jewish service to take place, 10 Jewish men must be present.) Under these circumstances, the slave must be set free, made a Jew and be included in the Minyan. The author of Sefer HaHinnuch wrote that forming a Minyan takes precedence over keeping a heathen a slave for life. The 10th man, the former slave, makes it possible for the others to worship and to serve Hashem.

In sum, a Jew can give a heathen slave menial work, but he still has to treat the non-Jewish slave with compassion. Treating Jewish and non-Jewish slaves in the same manner that slaves were treated in the United States would be reprehensible.

348. NOT TO LET A HEATHEN PUT A HEBREW MANSERVANT TO HARSH WORK

As a servant hired year by year shall he be with him; he shall not rule with rigour over him in thy sight. (Leviticus 25:53)

Mitzvah 348 prohibits us from allowing a heathen master from having his Hebrew/Jewish slave do harsh work. If we see a heathen subjecting a fellow Jew to doing contemptible work, we are obligated to stop it. We do this because Hashem commands all Jews to love each other.

349. THE PROHIBITION AGAINST PROSTRATING OURSELVES ON A FIGURED STONE

Ye shall make you no idols, neither shall ye rear you up a graven image, or a pillar, neither shall ye place any figured stone in your land, to bow down unto it; for I am the LORD your God. (Leviticus 26:1)

Mitzvah 349 forbids us to prostrate ourselves on stones, even when praying to Hashem because idol worshippers did that while praying to their gods.

At the time of the Holy Temple, we were allowed to prostrate ourselves there because it was G-d's house.

Today when we say the prayer, Aleinu (it is upon us), we bow at the waist during a certain section, and when we recite Aleinu during the High Holiday Musaf Amida service, we go down on our knees and bow at certain parts of the prayer. My Partner in Torah told me that in order to avoid the possibility of violating this prohibition, many have the custom to place a cloth or paper on the floor as they kneel on the High Holidays.

350. THE PRECEPT OF ONE WHO VOWS A PERSON'S VALUATION, THAT HE SHOULD GIVE HIS PRESCRIBED PRICE

Speak unto the children of Israel, and say unto them: When a man shall clearly utter a vow of persons unto the LORD, according to thy valuation, then thy valuation shall be for the male from twenty years old even unto sixty years old, even thy valuation shall be fifty shekels of silver, after the shekel of the sanctuary. And if it be a female, then thy valuation shall be thirty shekels. (Leviticus 27:2–4)

Mitzvah 350 pertains to fulfilling a specific type of monetary vow called an Erech (literally, "valuation").If either a man or a woman vows to donate money to the Temple in the form of an Erech, they would have to fulfill that promise. The specific amount of money the person taking the vow would have to donate depends on the age and gender of the object of the Erech. Thus, for example, the Torah prescribes that the Erech of a man who is between 20 and 60 years old is 50 shekels. In this case, someone making a vow to pay the Erech of such a person must donate that amount.

In my write-up of Mitzvah 105, I mentioned that all males, 20 and over must give half a shekel to the Temple every year. That was mandatory. In this case, if an individual does not vow to donate the monetary sum based on his or her market value or fixed value, then that person is not required to make that donation.

The crux of this Mitzvah is not making a financial contribution to the Temple, but rather it is to fulfill a vow to donate to the Temple, if such a vow were made.

Fulfilling vows is mandatory. In my write-up of Mitzvah 63, I stated that we can commit physical sins such as killing, just like animals. However, unlike the animals, Hashem gave us the ability to speak. Speaking separates us from animals and places us closer to Hashem. Being able to speak is Hashem's gift to us. Not fulfilling our vows shows disrespect to Hashem, who gave us the gift of speech.

351. THE PROHIBITION AGAINST EXCHANGING ANIMALS CONSECRATED FOR HOLY OFFERINGS

He shall not alter it, nor change it, a good for a bad, or a bad for a good; and if he shall at all change beast for beast, then both it and that for which it is changed shall be holy. (Leviticus 27:10)

Mitzvah 351 prohibits the animal's owner from swapping it for another animal after the animal had been selected for sacrifice. If animal A is designated to be sacrificed, then Animal B cannot go in Animal A's place. Once an animal is chosen to be sacrificed, it acquires holiness.

If one makes the exchange and ignores two witnesses' repeated warnings to stop, then that person receives lashes of the whip because violating this Mitzvah involves dishonoring a vow. In my write-up of Mitzvah 350, I explained why dishonoring vows is a serious offense.

If animal A were exchanged for animal B in violation of this precept, then animal B acquires a level of sanctity and both are to be sacrificed. (See Mitzvah 352 for more details.)

352. THAT IF ONE EXCHANGES AN ANIMAL CONSECRATED FOR AN OFFERING, BOTH ANIMALS ARE CONSECRATED

He shall not alter it, nor change it, a good for a bad, or a bad for a good; and if he shall at all change beast for beast, then both it and that for which it is changed shall be holy. (Leviticus 27:10)

Mitzvah 352 states that if one animal designated for sacrifice were to be exchanged for another, then both animals are to be sacrificed.

If one swaps the animals and ignores two witnesses' repeated warnings to stop, then the culprit is subject to lashes. The first animal does not lose its holiness, while the second animal gains holiness. If the second animal were a mixed breed, if it were born by caesarian section, or if it were ill or wounded, then these circumstances disqualify the animal altogether.

353. THE PRECEPT THAT ONE WHO VOWS AN ANIMALS' VALUATION SHOULD GIVE AS THE KOHEN VALUES IT

And if it be any unclean beast, of which they may not bring an offering unto the LORD, then he shall set the beast before the priest. And the priest shall value it, whether it be good or bad; as thou the priest valuest it, so shall it be. (Leviticus 27:11–12)

Mitzvah 353 states that if an individual expresses intent to consecrate his or her animal to the Temple, then he or she must keep their word. If the animal is of the type that is permitted to be offered as a sacrifice, then the consecrated animal would be offered as a sacrifice. However, if the animal is not fit to be sacrificed, then the value of the animal is donated to the Temple. The person presents the animal to the Kohen, the Kohen assesses the animal's monetary worth, and then that individual must donate that sum of money to the Temple. This Mitzvah is only applicable when the Temple is extant.

354. THAT IF ONE VOWS THE EVALUATION OF A HOUSE HE SHOULD GIVE THE KOHEN'S VALUATION PLUS A FIFTH

And when a man shall sanctify his house to be holy unto the LORD, then the priest shall value it, whether it be good or bad; as the priest shall value it, so shall it stand. And if he that sanctified it will redeem his house, then he shall add the fifth part of the money of thy valuation unto it, and it shall be his. (Leviticus 27:14 -15)

Mitzvah 354 states that if one consecrates his house, but then wishes to redeem it, the Kohen determines its valuation. The person must then pay the Kohen that specific amount and an additional fifth. My Partner in Torah told me that a third party who redeems a consecrated item does not pay the extra fifth.

355. THAT IF ONE VOWS A FIELD'S VALUATION, HE SHOULD GIVE THE VALUE SET BY SCRIPTURE

And if a man shall sanctify unto the LORD part of the field of his possession, then thy valuation shall be according to the sowing thereof; the sowing of a homer of barley shall be valued at fifty shekels of silver. (Leviticus 27:16)

Mitzvah 355 states that if someone donates/consecrates his field and then wants it back, he has to pay the amount specified in the Torah, which is based on the production of the land. The individual gives that monetary sum to the priests who use the funds to make necessary repairs to the Temple.

For more details about Mitzvah 355, consult Sefer HaHinnuch.

356. THE PROHIBITION AGAINST CHANGING CONSECRATED ANIMALS FROM ONE KIND OF OFFERING TO ANOTHER

Howbeit the firstling among beasts, which is born as a firstling to the LORD, no man shall sanctify it; whether it be ox or sheep, it is the LORD'S. (Leviticus 27:26)

Mitzvah 356 forbids us from changing the type of sacrifice that a specific animal is to have. For example, if an animal is supposed to be offered up as a guilt offering, its status cannot change to a peace offering and vice versa. This is something that cannot be tampered with at any time.

357. THE PRECEPT THAT IF ONE VOWS A HEREM ON PROPERTY OF HIS, IT GOES TO THE KOHANIM

(Herem is Hebrew for a proscriptive vow of devotement.)

Notwithstanding, no devoted thing, that a man may devote unto the LORD of all that he hath, whether of man or beast, or of the field of his possession, shall be sold or redeemed; every devoted thing is most holy unto the LORD. None devoted, that may be devoted of men, shall be ransomed; he shall surely be put to death. (Leviticus 27:28-29)

Mitzvah 357 commands us to surrender our possessions to the Kohanim if we vow a Herem on them. For example, if one owns a field and vows to destroy it, he must turn it over to the Kohanim because in truth the field belongs to Hashem. All our possessions come from Hashem, so in reality, we are the possessions' caretakers. If that person does not want his possession, if he vows to destroy it, the Kohanim get it because they are Hashem's representatives.

358. THAT LAND PUT UNDER A HEREM BY ITS OWNER IS NOT TO BE SOLD BUT TO BE GIVEN TO THE KOHANIM

Notwithstanding, no devoted thing, that a man may devote unto the LORD of all that he hath, whether of man or beast, or of the field of his possession, shall be sold or redeemed; every devoted thing is most holy unto the LORD. None devoted, that may be devoted of men, shall be ransomed; he shall surely be put to death. (Leviticus 27:28-29)

Mitzvah 358 prohibits us from selling land that is put under Herem. This also applies to movable objects that the owner puts under Herem.

All our possessions, both movable and unmovable belong to Hashem. Putting Hashem's possession under Herem, forfeits our right to continue being the item's caregiver, therefore it goes to Hashem's representatives, the Kohanim.

359. THE PRECEPT THAT LAND UNDER A VOW OF HEREM IS NOT TO BE REDEEMED

Notwithstanding, no devoted thing, that a man may devote unto the LORD of all that he hath, whether of man or beast, or of the field of his possession, shall be sold or redeemed; every devoted thing is most holy unto the LORD. None devoted, that may be devoted of men, shall be ransomed; he shall surely be put to death. (Leviticus 27:28-29)

Mitzvah 359 states that after an object and/or land are put under a vow of Herem, that individual can never redeem it. In addition, if the priest were to sell that field, in the Jubilee Year, the field goes back to the priest and not to the previous owner who put it under a vow of Herem.

360. THE PRECEPT OF THE TITHE OF PERMISSIBLE DOMESTIC ANIMALS TO BE GIVEN EVERY YEAR

And all the tithe of the herd or the flock, whatsoever passeth under the rod, the tenth shall be holy unto the LORD (Leviticus 27:32)

Mitzvah 360 is the obligation to take a tenth of the kosher animals born every year and give them holiness and the honor of being sacrificed. The process to determine which animal is the "tenth" is that the owner is to put the new-born animals in the pen and have a narrow gate. For example, if he has fifty lambs, he has each lamb walk through a narrow opening one at a time. He paints a red stripe on the 10th, 20th, 30th, 40th, and 50th lamb. If he has 32 lambs, he would place the stripe on the 10th, 20th and 30th; that's rounding down to the nearest 10th. Those lambs have acquired a high level of holiness, where they receive the honor of being sacrificed and eaten by the owner in Jerusalem. We cannot eat them anywhere else in the world.

My Partner in Torah explained that the rationale for the Mitzvah is that people obsess about making a living, and neglect Torah. This Mitzvah forces the individual to come to Jerusalem, where he can sacrifice the animals and eat part of them there. (He cannot eat the animal's fatty parts or their blood.) In Jerusalem, he experiences a great level of holiness that he cannot experience anywhere else. It helps bring him closer to Hashem.

We carry out this Mitzvah in the month of Elul because the Mitzvah applies on an annual basis. We begin preparing this ritual in the month of Tishri by including all animals born since that time, and it comes to fruition in Elul.

361. THAT THE TITHE OF ANIMALS BUT ONLY EATEN IN JERUSALEM

He shall not inquire whether it be good or bad, neither shall he change it; and if he change it at all, then both it and that for which it is changed shall be holy; it shall not be redeemed. (Leviticus 27:33)

Mitzvah 361 prohibits us from selling animals designated as the 10th, 20th etc. As discussed in Mitzvah 360, these specific animals receive a special level of holiness and must be sacrificed in Jerusalem. The Kohanimsacrifice these animals, which we then eat in Jerusalem. However, we do not have to share this meal with the Kohanim.

Mitzvot from Numbers

362. THE PRECEPT OF SENDING THE RITUALLY UNCLEAN OUTSIDE THE CAMP OF THE SHECHINIAH

(The Shechinah means The Divine Presence.)

'Command the children of Israel, that they put out of the camp every leper, and every one that hath an issue, and whosoever is unclean by the dead; both male and female shall ye put out, without the camp shall ye put them; that they defile not their camp, in the midst whereof I dwell.' (Numbers 5:2 -3)

Mitzvah 362 commands us to send out from The Tent of Meeting and from the Holy Temple, all lepers, and individuals with impurities. (The Tent of Meeting was applicable when the Children of Israel were in the desert for 40 years.)

Leprosy and impurities weaken one's intelligent spirit, thus making it difficult to serve Hashem. Therefore, priests must avoid contact with such individuals, until they fully recover. Causes of impurity include coming in contact with corpses and dead rodents, emitting seminal fluids, giving birth and menstruating.

363. THAT A RITUALLY DEFILED PERSON SHOULD NOT ENTER ANYWHERE IN THE SANCTUARY

'Command the children of Israel, that they put out of the camp every leper, and every one that hath an issue, and whosoever is unclean by the dead; both male and female shall ye put out, without the camp shall ye put them; that they defile not their camp, in the midst whereof I dwell.' (Numbers 5:2–3)

Mitzvah 363 prohibits ritually unclean people from entering the Temple and it prevents them from entering the court that leads into the Temple.

While the Children of Israel were in the wilderness for 40 years, the Tabernacle served as Hashem's Temple. Impure individuals could not enter the Tabernacle until undergoing ritual immersion. At the time of the First and Second Temple, ritual immersion allowed one to reenter the Holy Sanctuary. The more severe types of impurity, such as that derived from a corpse, required a more elaborate purification process, including the obligation to bring certain sacrifices.

364. THE PRECEPT OF CONFESSION OVER SINS

and it shall be, when he shall be guilty in one of these things, that he shall confess that wherein he hath sinned; (Leviticus 5:5)

Speak unto the children of Israel: When a man or woman shall commit any sin that men commit, to commit a trespass against the LORD, and that soul be guilty; then they shall confess their sin which they have done; and he shall make restitution for his guilt in full, and add unto it the fifth part thereof, and give it unto him in respect of whom he hath been guilty. (Numbers 5:6–7)

Mitzvah 364 obligates us to repent and to confess our sins to Hashem. At the time when Hashem's holy Temple stood, our ancestors not only performed sin offerings to atone for their misdeeds, but they also were required to confess to Hashem. The confession is a verbal acknowledgment that a person has done something wrong, and it constitutes the first step of the Teshuva (repenting) process. The verbal confession forced them, and it forces us today, to acknowledge Hashem's omniscience.

365. THE PRECEPT OF SOTAH, A STRAYING WOMAN, SUSPECTED OF INFIDELITY

Speak unto the children of Israel, and say unto them: If any man's wife go aside, and act unfaithfully against him, and a man lie with her carnally, and it be hid from the eyes of her husband, she being defiled secretly, and there be no witness against her, neither she be taken in the act; and the spirit of jealousy come upon him, and he be jealous of his wife, and she be defiled; or if the spirit of jealousy come upon him, and he be jealous of his wife, and she be not defiled; then shall the man bring his wife unto the priest, and shall bring her offering for her, the tenth part of an ephah of barley meal; he shall pour no oil upon it, nor put frankincense thereon; for it is a meal-offering of jealousy, a meal-offering of memorial, bringing iniquity to remembrance. (Numbers 5:12–15)

Mitzvah 365 pertains to the wayward wife. If a husband suspects his wife of infidelity, but there are no witnesses, he warns her to stop interacting with the other man. However, if she ignores his warning and/or he is still suspicious, he brings her to the Kohen. There, she has to uncover her hair. First, the Kohen attempts to persuade her to admit to adultery. If the wife admits to her adultery, she would be executed, and if she refuses to confess, the Kohen makes her drink a bitter type of water. If it kills her, it means that she is guilty, but if she survives, then she is declared innocent. If found innocent, the water serves as a blessing because it replaces mistrust and suspicion with love and closeness.

366. TO PUT NO OIL IN THE MEAL-OFFERING OF A SOTAH

then shall the man bring his wife unto the priest, and shall bring her offering for her, the tenth part of an ephah of barley meal; he shall pour no oil upon it, nor put frankincense thereon; for it is a meal-offering of jealousy, a meal-offering of memorial, bringing iniquity to remembrance. (Numbers 5:15)

Mitzvah 366 forbids oil to be added to the Sotah's meal-offering. Oil symbolizes light and goodness. This situation is not an auspicious occasion. Adding oil makes the sacrifice more desirable, and in this case, her deed is undesirable and unworthy of having extra niceties provided.

367. TO PUT NO FRANKINCENSE IN THE MEAL-OFFERING OF A SOTAH

then shall the man bring his wife unto the priest, and shall bring her offering for her, the tenth part of an ephah of barley meal; he shall pour no oil upon it, nor put frankincense thereon; for it is a meal-offering of jealousy, a meal-offering of memorial, bringing iniquity to remembrance. (Numbers 5:15)

Mitzvah 367 prohibits frankincense to be added to the Sotah's meal-offering. (As mentioned in Mitzvah 365, a Sotah is a woman whose husband suspects her of infidelity.) Like oil, frankincense is used to celebrate auspicious events. This is an unhappy occasion, thus making frankincense and oil completely inappropriate.

368. THAT A NAZIR IS FORBIDDEN TO DRINK WINE OR ANY STRONG WINE DRINK

Speak unto the children of Israel, and say unto them: When either man or woman shall clearly utter a vow, the vow of a Nazirite, to consecrate himself unto the LORD, he shall abstain from wine and strong drink: he shall drink no vinegar of wine, or vinegar of strong drink, neither shall he drink any liquor of grapes, nor eat fresh grapes or dried. (Numbers 6:2 -3)

Mitzvah 368 forbids a Nazir to drink wine, and any other grape-based beverage. (A person becomes a Nazir when he or she take a vow of abstention in order to get closer to Hashem. There are three basic prohibitions applicable to a Nazir, discussed in the next several Mitzvot). Alcohol impairs one's judgment and a Nazir must be 100 percent focused on serving Hashem. A person can be a Nazir for 30 days or more. When one vows to be a Nazir for a specific period of time, that individual is obliged to follow through. Violations of this oath subjects the guilty party to receive lashes of the whip.

The key way a Nazir serves Hashem is by stripping away physical pleasures and striving for spiritual pleasure, which brings the Nazir closer to Hashem.

369. THAT A NAZIR IS PROHIBITED FROM EATING FRESH GRAPES

he shall abstain from wine and strong drink: he shall drink no vinegar of wine, or vinegar of strong drink, neither shall he drink any liquor of grapes, nor eat fresh grapes or dried. (Numbers 6:3)

Mitzvah 369 prohibits the Nazir from eating fresh grapes because wine derives from grapes. Violating this Mitzvah subjects the Nazir to a flogging.

370. THAT A NAZIR IS PROHIBITED FROM EATING DRIED GRAPES

he shall abstain from wine and strong drink: he shall drink no vinegar of wine, or vinegar of strong drink, neither shall he drink any liquor of grapes, nor eat fresh grapes or dried. (Numbers 6:3)

Mitzvah 370 prohibits the Nazir from eating dried grapes, aka raisins. The reasons for this prohibition were discussed in Mitzvah 368 and 369. Violating this Mitzvah subjects the culprit to a whipping.

371. THAT A NAZIR IS PROHIBITED FROM EATING GRAPE SEEDS

All the days of his Naziriteship shall he eat nothing that is made of the grape-vine, from the pressed grapes even to the grapestone. (Numbers 6:4)

Mitzvah 371 forbids the Nazir from eating grape seeds. Consult Mitzvah 369 for the reasons and consequences for violating this Mitzvah.

372. THAT A NAZIR IS FORBIDDEN TO EAT GRAPE SKINS

All the days of his Naziriteship shall he eat nothing that is made of the grape-vine, from the pressed grapes even to the grapestone. (Numbers 6:4)

Mitzvah 372 forbids the Nazir from eating grape skins. Consult Mitzvah 369 for more information.

373. THAT A NAZIR IS PROHIBITED FROM SHAVING HIS HAIR ALL HIS DAYS AS A NAZIR

All the days of his vow of Naziriteship there shall no razor come upon his head; until the days be fulfilled, in which he consecrateth himself unto the LORD, he shall be holy, he shall let the locks of the hair of his head grow long. (Numbers 6:5)

Mitzvah 373 forbids the Nazir from cutting his hair. The female counterpart is called a Nezirah. Samson's great strength was not his only characteristic that made him standout. His long hair was another, and he kept it long because he was a Nazir.

Samuel and Absalom were also Nazirites. (See Second Samuel Chapter 15, verse 7, and Second Samuel Chapter 14, verse 26.)

The author of Sefer haHachinuch states that a Nazir needs to be 100 percent focused on serving Hashem. Tending to appearance, cutting one's hair, distracts him/her from serving Hashem.

(See Samuel tractate Nazir, Chapter 9, Mishnah 5.)

A Kohen cannot consume alcohol while serving Hashem at the Temple. In that respect, the Kohen and the Nazir are similar. Unlike a Nazir, a Kohen keeps his hair short while on duty because he must look good while interacting with individuals. He is Hashem's messenger. The Nazir does not have that responsibility. A Nazir should not worry about his appearance.

Violating this Mitzvah results in a flogging.

374. THE PRECEPT OF LETTING A NAZIR'S HAIR GROW LONG

All the days of his vow of Naziriteship there shall no razor come upon his head; until the days be fulfilled, in which he consecrateth himself unto the LORD, he shall be holy, he shall let the locks of the hair of his head grow long. (Numbers 6:5)

Mitzvah 374 obligates the Nazir to allow his or her hair to grow long. The individual must honor that commitment while serving as a Nazir. I explained why in my write-up of Mitzvah 373.

375. THAT A NAZIR SHOULD NOT ENTER A DEAD MAN'S TENT

All the days that he consecrateth himself unto the LORD he shall not come near to a dead body. (Numbers 6:6)

Mitzvah 375 prohibits the Nazir to enter a structure where a corpse is located. Doing so will make the Nazir impure. As discussed in Mitzvah 362, impurity weakens one's intelligent spirit, thus making it difficult to serve Hashem.

376. THAT A NAZIR SHOULD NOT BECOME DEFILED BY A DEAD PERSON OR ANY OTHER UNCLEANNESS

He shall not make himself unclean for his father, or for his mother, for his brother, or for his sister, when they die; because his consecration unto God is upon his head. (Numbers 6:7)

Mitzvah 376 forbids the Nazir to come in contact with corpses, even if the corpses were close relatives. (It should be noted that Mitzvah 375 focuses exclusively on prohibiting

a Nazir from entering an inside structure if a corpse were there. Mitzvah 376 forbids the Nazir from having any contact with corpses, whether inside or outside.)

A Nazir must keep away from his dead relatives, including the immediate ones, because:

All the days of his Naziriteship he is holy unto the LORD. (Numbers 6:8)

Unlike a Nazir, a Kohen can have contact with his dead immediate relatives. According to Sefer HaHinnuch, the Kohen has leeway in this situation because he sometimes has a lesser degree of holiness than a Nazir. The kohanim are from the Tribe of Levi. Hashem decreed that the Levites serve Him in the Temple:

And they shall have no inheritance among their brethren; the LORD is their inheritance, as He hath spoken unto them. (Deuteronomy 18:2)

The Kohanim have no choice but to serve Hashem. However, the Nazir chooses to be one, and must honor that vow. (The Kohen Gadol cannot come in contact with his dead relatives because he is at a higher level of holiness than the Kohanim.)

If a person chooses to be a Nazir, it would be for a specific time period, like 30 days. If during the 30-day period, the Nazir has contact with a corpse or violates any of the other prohibitions mentioned in previous Mitzvot, the previous days that he or she served in that capacity are erased. The Nazir would have to start his or her 30-day period over again. Thirty days serving as a Nazir means 30 continuous days. Sixty days serving as a Nazir means 60 continuous days. It is one unit of time.

377. THE PRECEPT OF SHAVING A NAZIR'S HAIR AND BRINGING HIS OFFERINGS

And this is the law of the Nazirite, when the days of his consecration are fulfilled: he shall bring it unto the door of the tent of meeting; (Numbers 6:13)

Mitzvah 377 obligates the Nazir to shave his head at the end of the time-period serving in that capacity. According to Sefer HaHinnuch, a Nazir must not fix or trim his hair while serving as a Nazir because that can potentially lead to vanity and neglecting Hashem. A head shave at the end of the period continues to prevent the former Nazir from becoming vain. In general, a bald head and/or uncombed long hair could be quite unattractive. Looking that way can help keep the former Nazir focused on Hashem and not his outer appearance.

The Torah also commands the Nazir to provide sacrifices at the end of his or her term of service.

and he shall present his offering unto the LORD, one he-lamb of the first year without blemish for a burnt-offering, and one ewe-lamb of the first year without blemish for a sin-offering, and one ram without blemish for peace-offerings, and a basket of unleavened bread, cakes of fine flour mingled with oil, and unleavened wafers spread with oil, and their meal-offering, and their drink-offerings. (Numbers 6:14–Numbers 6:15)

A common question is, "why would one have to provide a sin offering after serving as a Nazir?"

While serving Hashem and becoming closer to Him, the Nazir deprives himself of many of the benefits that Hashem provides for us, such as wine. Hashem created the world and He created us so we can experience pleasure and happiness.

378. THE PRECEPT OF THE BLESSING OF THE KOHANIM EVERY DAY

'Speak unto Aaron and unto his sons, saying: On this wise ye shall bless the children of Israel; ye shall say unto them: The LORD bless thee, and keep thee; The LORD make His face to shine upon thee, and be gracious unto thee; (Numbers 6:23 -25)

Mitzvah 378 commands the Kohanim to bless the Children of Israel, the Jewish people, every day. The daily blessing reinforces that Hashem truly loves us.

379. THE PRECEPT OF CARRYING THE HOLY ARK ON THE SHOULDERS

But unto the sons of Kohath he gave none, because the service of the holy things belonged unto them: they bore them upon their shoulders. (Numbers 7:9)

Mitzvah 379 commands the Levites to carry the Holy Ark on their shoulders. That is the ONLY way it can be moved. The Levites were tasked with transporting all thecomponents of the Tabernacle, for which they were given oxen and wagons. However,the only way that they couldtransport the Ark was carrying it by hand.

The Holy Ark is a sacred representation of what separates us from the other nations. Because the Kohanim are Hashem's representatives, they are the ones to carry the Holy Ark.

380. THE PRECEPT OF THE "SECOND PASSOVER" OFFERING ON THE 14TH OF IYAR

in the second month on the fourteenth day at dusk they shall keep it; they shall eat it with unleavened bread and bitter herbs; they shall leave none of it unto the morning, nor break a bone thereof; according to all the statute of the passover they shall keep it. (Numbers 9:11 -12)

Mitzvah 380 commands individuals who failed to bring their Passover offerings to the Temple on the 14th of Nisan to do so one month later on the 14th of Iyar. This is the Second Passover, and it lasts one day. There is no obligation to dispose of Hametz. Like the First Passover, sacrificial food eaten during the Second Passover cannot be saved for the following day.

On the Second Passover, there is no reduction or stoppage of work.

Women can fulfill this Mitzvah, but they are not obligated. If men fail to fulfill this Mitzvah, they will suffer a spiritual death.

This Mitzvah is in effect only when the Temple is extant.

381. THAT THE "SECOND PASSOVER" OFFERING IS TO BE EATEN WITH MATZAH AND BITTER HERBS

in the second month on the fourteenth day at dusk they shall keep it; they shall eat it with unleavened bread and bitter herbs; (Numbers 9:11)

Mitzvah 381 commands that matzah and bitter herbs be eaten even with the Passover offering. A requirement of observing The Second Passover is to eat unleavened bread and bitter herbs.

382. TO LEAVE OVER NOTHING OF THE SECOND PASSOVER OFFERING UNTIL THE NEXT DAY

they shall leave none of it unto the morning, nor break a bone thereof; according to all the statute of the Passover they shall keep it. (Numbers 9:12)

Mitzvah 382 prohibits saving any portion of the Passover offering for the next day. This prohibition is identical to that of the first Passover. I explained the reason for this prohibition in my write-up of Mitzvah 8.

383. THE PROHIBITION AGAINST BREAKING ANY OF THE BONES OF THE SECOND PASSOVER OFFERING

they shall leave none of it unto the morning, nor break a bone thereof; according to all the statute of the passover they shall keep it. (Numbers 9:12)

Mitzvah 383 forbids breaking bones of the Secondary Passover sacrifice. The exact prohibition is applicable during the First Passover. I covered the reasons for the prohibition in my write-up of Mitzvah 16.

384. THE PRECEPT OF SOUNDING TRUMPETS AT THE SANCTUARY AND IN BATTLE

And when ye go to war in your land against the adversary that oppresseth you, then ye shall sound an alarm with the trumpets; and ye shall be remembered before the LORD your God, and ye shall be saved from your enemies. 10,10 Also in the day of your gladness, and in your appointed seasons, and in your New Moons, ye shall blow with the trumpets over your burnt-offerings, and over the sacrifices

of your peace-offerings; and they shall be to you for a memorial before your God: I am the LORD your God.' (Numbers 10:9 -10)

Mitzvah 384 commands the blowing of the trumpets while animals are being sacrificed, and when Israel goes into battle against enemy nations. In both cases, a minimum of two trumpets must be sounded simultaneously, according to Sefer HaHinnuch.The author of Sefer HaHinnuch states that the sounding of the trumpets jolts the Kohanim into concentrating on performing perfect sacrifices.

When Israel goes into battle, Her fighters must concentrate on asking Hashem for assistance.

The Temple must exist in order for this Mitzvah to be applicable.

385. THE PRECEPT OF HALLAH, A PORTION OF DOUGH SET ASIDE FOR THE KOHEN

Speak unto the children of Israel, and say unto them: When ye come into the land whither I bring you, then it shall be, that, when ye eat of the bread of the land, ye shall set apart a portion for a gift unto the LORD. Of the first of your dough ye shall set apart a cake for a gift; as that which is set apart of the threshing-floor, so shall ye set it apart. Of the first of your dough ye shall give unto the LORD a portion for a gift throughout your generations. (Numbers 15:18 -21)

Mitzvah 385 commands us to separate a portion of dough from a batch to give to a Kohen. The separated portion is called Hallah. Most of the world lives on bread. It is a vital part of our meals. I learned at Aish haTorah that when we eat food without bread, it does not count as a meal. Bread fuels our bodies and spirits. The Kohanim require this fuel in order to serve Hashem.

Today, Rabbinic law still requires that we separate a portion of dough that we create if it is above a minimum quantity (5 lbs.). A blessing is made on the performance of this Mitzvah. The portion that is separated is burned because it contains a level of impurity and cannot be eaten by a Kohen. Moreover, when Jews returned to Israel at the time of Ezra, the bread still contained a level of impurity because Hashem did not bring them back. (Consult Numbers 15:18–15:19, listed above.) Another reason for burning a portion of Hallah is to remember this Mitzvah.

For more information, consult Mishneh Torah and go to the link, http://www.chabad.org/library/article_cdo/aid/1002531/jewish/Chapter-5.htm.

When my Partner in Torah and I studied Tractate Avot, Chapter 5, Mishnah 8, he explained to me that violating this specific Mitzvah is one of the seven transgressions that would cause punishment to come to the world. In Chapter 5, Mishnah 10, it states that a famine caused by a fatal drought will ensue for failure to separate out a portion of Hallah.

386. THE PRECEPT OF TZITZIT, TASSELS ON A FOUR-CORNERED GARMENT

'Speak unto the children of Israel, and bid them that they make them throughout their generations fringes in the corners of their garments, and that they put with the fringe of each corner a thread of blue. And it shall be unto you for a fringe, that ye may look upon it, and remember all the

commandments of the LORD, and do them; and that ye go not about after your own heart and your own eyes, after which ye use to go astray; (Numbers 15:38 -39)

Mitzvah 386 commands us to wear Tzitzit, strings that are strung on four-corner garments made of wool or linen. We wear them because they serve as a reminder to fulfill the 613 Mitzvot. The tzitzit is a representation of 613. The alphanumeric value of the Hebrew word Tzitzit is 600. In addition, in each tassel or fringe, there are eight threads tied with five knots, totaling 613.

The Tzitzit must be blue and white. (We also wear the Tallit, a blue and white prayer shawl, over our shoulders during morning services.) According to Sefer Hachinuch, white alludes to the body, which was originally of the earth (Adam). Blue represents the sky, and the sky resembles Hashem's throne of glory.

We wear Tzitzit during the day because seeing them reminds us of the 613 Mitzvot. However, Rabbinic law commands us to wear them one night out of the year, during the Kol Nidre service, because it is a token of special reverence for Yom Kippur. Kol Nidre also begins before sundown, so we are already wearing it, but we leave it on after it is dark. All males, 13 and older, are required to fulfill this Mitzvah.

My Partner in Torah added that Biblically, this is a conditional Mitzvah. If one wears a four-cornered garment, he must one put Tzitzit on it. However, the Sages made it obligatory to wear such a garment in order for people to fulfill this Mitzvah. Blind men are not exempt, because they are to also experience the greatness of this Mitzvah.

While discussing this Mitzvah with Rabbi Alpert, he mentioned that the blue thread, which in Hebrew is Tekhelet, is less available than the white.

According to Chabd.org, the unique blue dye was made from a byproduct of a sea creature known as the C*hilazon.* This creature was rarely spotted. According to the Radziner Rebbe, Rabbi Gershon Henoch Leiner (1839–1891) the cuttlefish was the lost C*hilazon*, and produced and distributed from this fish. Not all rabbis agree with Rabbi Leiner. Rabbi Sholom DovBer, the fifth Rebbe of Lubavitch, maintained that the C*hilazon* will not reemerge until the Messiah comes.

For more details about this discussion of the Tekhelet, consult https://www.chabad.org/library/article_cdo/aid/530127/jewish/Tekhelet-The-Mystery-of-the-Long-Lost-Biblical-Blue-Thread.htm

Women are exempt from this Mitzvah because it is a positive time bound one. They are exempt from the majority of positive time-bound Mitzvot.

"A positive time-bound commandment is defined as one that could be physically fulfilled at any time, but that the Torah has mandated is to be done only at specific times: if not fulfilled at that specific time, there is no way to "make up" the Mitzvah."

Cited at *https://www.myjewishlearning.com/article/women-and-the-fulfillment-of-positive-time-bound-commandments/*

In addition, see the Bartenura Commentary to Tractate Kiddushin, Chapter 1, Mishnah 7. BT, Kiddushin, 34a, points out that women are obligated to dwell in the Sukkah. Women are also obligated to hear the Megillah reading on Purim because they were part of the great miracle of being saved from annihilation. Those are positive time-bound Mitzvot. See Babylonian Talmud Megillah 4a.

This Mitzvah is applicable today.

387. NOT TO GO STRAYING AFTER ONE'S HEART AND EYES

And it shall be unto you for a fringe, that ye may look upon it, and remember all the commandments of the LORD, and do them; and that ye go not about after your own heart and your own eyes, after which ye use to go astray; (Numbers 15:39)

Mitzvah 387 prohibits following inner desires if they are inappropriate. Examples include:

Longing to drive on Shabbat; longing for a ham sandwich because one sees non-Jews enjoying it, longing to seduce a non-Jew. The list is endless.

Observing this Mitzvah prevents sinning.

This Mitzvah is applicable to all men and women in every generation.

388. THE PRECEPT OF GUARDING THE SANCTUARY

And they shall be joined unto thee, and keep the charge of the tent of meeting, whatsoever the service of the Tent may be; but a common man shall not draw nigh unto you. (Numbers 18:4)

Mitzvah 388 commands 24 men, three Kohanim and 21 Levites to guard the Temple at night. The three Kohanim guard three locations inside the Temple, while the 21 Levites guard at 21 different locations outside the Temple. The reason for guarding the Temple has nothing to do with fending off enemies. Hashem protects us under these circumstances. This Mitzvah allows the Levites and the Kohanim to honor, exalt, and to glorify the Temple.

This law requires a man of the Temple Mount to inspect all 24 areas throughout the night. When he approaches a sentry (Kohen/Levite), the sentry must be standing. He says, "Man of the Temple Mount, peace abide with you." If the sentry is not standing, or does not greet him with those words, or is asleep, the Man of the Temple Mount has the right to strike him with a staff and then set fire to his cloak, until it would be said in Jerusalem, "What is the sound in the Temple Court?"

"It is the sound of a Levite being beaten and his clothing burnt because he slept at his watch."

This Mitzvah is applicable to the Levites when the Temple exists.

389. THAT THE KOHANIM SHOULD NOT DO THE LEVITES' SACRED TASKS, NOR VICE-VERSA

but thus do unto them, that they may live, and not die, when they approach unto the most holy things: Aaron and his sons shall go in, and appoint them every one to his service and to his burden (Numbers 4:19) And they shall keep thy charge, and the charge of all the Tent; only they shall not come nigh unto the holy furniture and unto the altar, that they die not, neither they, nor ye. (Numbers 18:3)

Mitzvah 389 forbids the Levites to do the Kohanim's work and vice versa. All the tasks assigned to the Levites and Kohanim are meaningful and honorable, and to guarantee that everyone takes their roles seriously, nobody can trade jobs.

If a Levite performed one of the Kohen's duties, he would incur death because the Kohen's service is more sacred in that it involves being Hashem's representative. However, if a Kohen performed a Levite's task, he would just receive a whipping because the Levite's job is less sacred. Levites cannot switch roles with other Levites. The penalty is death. If a Kohen switches roles with another Kohen, then he incurs the penalty of death.

This Mitzvah is in effect when the Temple is extant.

390. THAT ONE WHO IS NOT A KOHEN SHOULD NOT WORK AT THE SANCTUARY

And they shall be joined unto thee, and keep the charge of the tent of meeting, whatsoever the service of the Tent may be; but a common man shall not draw nigh unto you. (Numbers 18:4)

Mitzvah 390 prohibits non-Kohanim to work in the Temple. A non-Kohen who performs the following jobs faces death at heaven's hands: Sprinkling the blood of sacrificed animals, burning parts of the offerings on the Altar, and pouring libations of water and wine.

The non-Kohen can perform certain tasks such as slaughtering the animal for sacrifice, bringing the wood for the Altar fire, and kindling the menorah's lights.

391. NOT TO PUT AN END TO THE GUARDING OF THE SANCTUARY

And ye shall keep the charge of the holy things, and the charge of the altar, that there be wrath no more upon the children of Israel. (Numbers 18:5)

Mitzvah 391 does not allow Levites to refrain from patrolling the Temple at night. This Mitzvah is the negative flipside to Mitzvah 388. I covered the reasons for this Mitzvah in my write-up of Mitzvah 388.

392. THE PRECEPT OF REDEEMING A FIRST BORN HUMAN CHILD

Every thing that openeth the womb, of all flesh which they offer unto the LORD, both of man and beast, shall be thine; howbeit the first-born of man shalt thou surely redeem, and the firstling of unclean beasts shalt thou redeem. (Numbers 18:15)

Mitzvah 392 obligates us to redeem the first born male son. This applies only if the son is the first baby to emerge from his mother's womb. If the mother's first child is a girl, followed by a boy, then this Mitzvah would not be applicable. I explained the reasons for this Mitzvah in my write-up of Mitzvah 18.

393. NOT TO REDEEM THE FIRSTLING OF A KOSHER DOMESTIC ANIMAL

But the firstling of an ox, or the firstling of a sheep, or the firstling of a goat, thou shalt not redeem; they are holy: thou shalt dash their blood against the altar, and shalt make their fat smoke for an offering made by fire, for a sweet savour unto the LORD. (Numbers 18:17)

Mitzvah 393 forbids us to redeem the firstling of a domestic kosher animal. Those animals are sacred by birth and unredeemable. I covered this topic in my write-up of Mitzvah 18.

394. THE PRECEPT OF THE LEVITE'S SERVICE AT THE SANCTUARY

But the Levites alone shall do the service of the tent of meeting, and they shall bear their iniquity; it shall be a statute for ever throughout your generations, and among the children of Israel they shall have no inheritance. (Numbers 18:23)

Mitzvah 394 requires the Levites to serve in the Temple. Their jobs include opening the Temple's gates in the morning and closing them at night. Their principal role is to chant Psalms over the Olah (burnt offerings) for the entire community, and during the peace offerings, and the pouring of the wine. A minimum of twelve Levites must chant in order to fulfill this Mitzvah, yet there is no maximum number. Hundreds of Levites can chant during the sacrifices. Instruments can accompany the Levites' Psalms, but they are not required.

Before the Levites could serve in the Temple, they have a five-year apprenticeship.

When the Levites age and their singing voices deteriorate, they can no longer chant during the sacrifices. They can still serve as gatekeepers and patrol the Temple.

395. THE PRECEPT OF THE FIRST TITHE, FOR THE LEVITES

For the tithe of the children of Israel, which they set apart as a gift unto the LORD, I have given to the Levites for an inheritance; therefore I have said unto them: Among the

children of Israel they shall have no inheritance.' (Numbers 18:24) And all the tithe of the land, whether of the seed of the land, or of the fruit of the tree, is the LORD'S; it is holy unto the LORD. (Leviticus 27:30)

Mitzvah 395 requires us to give 1/10 of a crop, our first tithe, to a Levite. (The first 2 percent of the crops go to the priests.) The obligation kicks in once the person harvests his crops. After the crop is harvested, he then places it in a container for storage. It cannot be eaten until a 10th is given to a Levite. Once the tenth is given to the Levites, anyone can eat that specific 1/10th crop. This specific portion does not have a special status of sanctity. It is not at the same holy level as the portion (T'rumah) given to the priests.

The reason for this Mitzvah is that the Levites cannot own land. Their primary focus is to serve Hashem. Our obligation to provide them with sustenance, frees them from having to work the land, thus allowing them to focus on being Hashem's servants.

396. THE OBLIGATION OF THE LEVITES TO GIVE A TITHE OF THE TITHE

'Moreover thou shalt speak unto the Levites, and say unto them: When ye take of the children of Israel the tithe which I have given you from them for your inheritance, then ye shall set apart of it a gift for the LORD, even a tithe of the tithe. (Numbers 18:26)

Mitzvah 396 commands the Levites to take a 10th of the tithe that the Israelites give them and give that portion (1/100 of the original crop) to the Kohanim. Although the Levites have a special status (see Mitzvah 395), performing this Mitzvah reinforces their realization that the Kohanim have an even greater status; serving Hashem in His Holy Temple. The Kohanim have a close relationship with Hashem, therefore they understand that He is superior to them, as He is Master of the universe.

397. THE PRECEPT OF THE RED HEIFER

This is the statute of the law which the LORD hath commanded, saying: Speak unto the children of Israel, that they bring thee a Red Heifer, faultless, wherein is no blemish, and upon which never came yoke. And ye shall give her unto Eleazar the priest, and she shall be brought forth without the camp, and she shall be slain before his face. (Numbers 19:2-3)

Mitzvah 397 commands that a Red Heifer be slaughtered and burned. Afterwards, its ashes are mixed in special water from a flowing stream, and then sprinkled onto an individual who came in contact with a dead Jewish person. Jews have a special level of holiness, but death suppresses it, thus causing impurity. A Jew would not be impure for coming in contact with a non-Jewish corpse because a non-Jew never had that spiritual level of Holiness.

Requirements for the Red Heifer to perform this Mitzvah include being entirely red, and never having worked in its life.

According to my Partner in Torah, the Talmud states that this Mitzvah was performed only nine times, from the time of Moses up until the destruction of the Second Temple. To be able to find a Red Heifer was a rarity. As a result, its ashes could be used over many years. My Partner also explained that the Mitzvah of the Red Heifer is impossible to understand. Not even King Solomon could comprehend it. The only person whoever understood it was Moses, and that was due to Hashem explaining its significance to him.

398. THE PRECEPT OF THE RITUAL UNCLEANNESS OF THE DEAD

This is the law: when a man dieth in a tent, every one that cometh into the tent, and every thing that is in the tent, shall be unclean seven days. (Numbers 19:14)

Mitzvah 398 states that one becomes impure after coming in contact with a corpse. I covered this topic in my write-ups of Mitzvot 159 and 263.

399. THE PRECEPT OF THE LUSTRAL WATER, THAT IT DEFILES A RITUALLY CLEAN MAN AND PURIFIES ONLY ONE DEFILED BY THE DEAD

And the clean person shall sprinkle upon the unclean on the third day, and on the seventh day; and on the seventh day he shall purify him; and he shall wash his clothes, and bathe himself in water, and shall be clean at even. (Numbers 19:19)

Mitzvah 399 commands that the water mixture of the Red Heifer's ashes get sprinkled on an individual who becomes impure as a result of coming in contact with a corpse. The sprinkled ashes remove the impurity. However, the person who sprinkles the ashes is now impure, but that individual can regain purity the next day without the sprinkled ashes. He just needs to go to the Mikveh. The sprinkled ashes are reserved for those people who come in contact with corpses.

400. THE PRECEPT OF THE LAWS OF INHERITANCE

And thou shalt speak unto the children of Israel, saying: If a man die, and have no son, then ye shall cause his inheritance

to pass unto his daughter. And if he have no daughter, then ye shall give his inheritance unto his brethren. And if he have no brethren, then ye shall give his inheritance unto his father's brethren. And if his father have no brethren, then ye shall give his inheritance unto his kinsman that is next to him of his family, and he shall possess it. And it shall be unto the children of Israel a statute of judgment, as the LORD commanded Moses.' (Numbers 27:8–11)

Mitzvah 400 states that sons are to inherit their father's possessions. However, if the father only had daughters, then they receive the inheritance. If the father had sons and daughters, then his sons receive the inheritance, not his daughters. If there are no daughters or sons, the deceased's brothers inherit the possessions. No brothers, then the inheritance goes to his father's brothers, not his mother's brothers.

401. THE PRECEPT OF THE REGULAR OLAH OFFERING, SACRIFICED EVERY DAY

Command the children of Israel, and say unto them: My food which is presented unto Me for offerings made by fire, of a sweet savour unto Me, shall ye observe to offer unto Me in its due season. And thou shalt say unto them: This is the offering made by fire which ye shall bring unto the LORD: he-lambs of the first year without blemish, two day by day, for a continual burnt-offering. The one lamb shalt thou offer in the morning, and the other lamb shalt thou offer at dusk; (Numbers 28:2–4)

Mitzvah 401 obligates the community to bring a regular sacrifice every day to the Temple. This consists of two lambs, one sacrificed in the morning and the other in the evening. Those are the traditional times that we eat our meals. This Mitzvah reminds us that our efforts to provide food for ourselves should not be greater than providing food for Hashem. This Mitzvah is in effect when the Temple is standing.

402. THE PRECEPT OF THE MUSAF OFFERING OF THE SABBATH

And on the sabbath day two he-lambs of the first year without blemish, and two tenth parts of an ephah of fine flour for a meal-offering, mingled with oil, and the drink-offering thereof. (Numbers 28:9)

Mitzvah 402 requires the community to bring an additional (Musaf) sacrifice to the Temple on Shabbat. This additional sacrifice consists of two male lambs in their first year of life. These lambs must be brought to the Temple before sundown Friday night. A blemish disqualifies the lamb from this honor of being sacrificed to Hashem.

As discussed in Mitzvah 299, the Musaf offering takes place on holidays, Rosh Chodesh, and Shabbat because they are holier than all other days.

403. THE PRECEPT OF THE MUSAF OFFERING EVERY Rosh Chodesh

And in your New Moons ye shall present a burnt-offering unto the LORD: two young bullocks, and one ram, seven he-lambs of the first year without blemish; (Numbers 28:11)

Mitzvah 403 requires the community to bring an additional sacrifice on Rosh Chodesh. This consists of two bullocks, one ram, and seven he-lambs in their first years of life.

As mentioned in Mitzvah 299 and 402, we provide Musaf offerings on Rosh Chodesh because of the day's holiness.

404. THE PRECEPT OF THE MUSAF OFFERING ON THE SHAVUOT FESTIVAL

Also in the day of the first-fruits, when ye bring a new meal-offering unto the LORD in your feast of weeks, ye shall have a holy convocation: ye shall do no manner of servile work; but ye shall present a burnt-offering for a sweet savour unto the LORD: two young bullocks, one ram, seven he-lambs of the first year; (Numbers 28:26 -27)

Mitzvah 404 requires the Musaf offering on Shavuot. This consists of two bullocks, one ram, and seven he-lambs in their first year of life.

I explained why we have the Musaf offerings in my write-up of Mitzvah 299.

405. THE PRECEPT OF THE SHOFAR ON ROSH HASHANAH

And in the seventh month, on the first day of the month, ye shall have a holy convocation: ye shall do no manner of servile work; it is a day of blowing the horn unto you. (Numbers 29:1)

Mitzvah 405 commands us to hear the Shofar on Rosh Hashanah.

My Partner in Torah and I found 10 explanations in Book of our Heritage by Eliyahu Kit'Ovon why we hear the Shofar on Rosh Hashanah.

1. We reinforce our acceptance of Hashem as king. Trumpets are blown for coronation ceremonies of kings, and Hashem is our king.

2. It serves as a warning for people to repent.
3. It is a reminder of the revelation on Mount Sinai when the Children of Israel heard the sound of the Shofar.
4. The Shofar reminds us of the words of the prophets who encouraged us to follow the path of Hashem. The words of the prophets are comparable to the sound of the Shofar.
5. The Shofar reminds us of the destruction of the Temple because during battle, the sound of trumpets and bugles blasted. Hearing the sound of the Shofar blasting during our services remind us to ask Hashem to rebuild the Temple.
6. It recalls the binding of Isaac, where he was ready to give up his life. We are trying to reach the same level of dedication to Hashem as Isaac had. At the end of the binding, the ram was sacrificed in Isaac's place. The Shofar is the ram's horn.
7. Hearing the sound of the Shofar causes us to humble ourselves, and to submit and to tremble before Hashem.
8. To remind us of the awesome judgment that is happening on Rosh Hashanah. Rosh Hashanah is the Day of Judgment.
9. To remind us of the gathering of the exiles that will happen in the future. This will help us long for those days to come.
10. To remind us that one day Hashem will resurrect the dead.

There are three specific Shofar sounds we hear on Rosh Hashanah: ***Tekiah*** (which is rooted), *S***hevarim (broken into pieces),** and T***eruah*****(broken and incomplete).**

Tekiah is one long sound. **Shevarim** consists of three medium wailing sounds, and **Teruah** is nine quick blasts in succession.

In Hebrew, the word Rosh Hashanah is not used. ***Yom Teruah*** is used in its place. As mentioned, ***Teruah*** refers to something, incomplete or broken. ***Teruah*** is a humbling sound. We have to break down our spirit and become humble, which makes it possible for us to repent.

The Shofar is a spiritual battle cry. The Shofar must be longer than a person's fist. The horn of the Shofar can be from any kosher animal except the cow, because it is a reminder of the sin of the golden calf.

406. THE PRECEPT OF THE LAW OF NULLIFYING VOWS

When a man voweth a vow unto the LORD, or sweareth an oath to bind his soul with a bond, he shall not break his word; he shall do according to all that proceedeth out of his mouth. Also when a woman voweth a vow unto the LORD, and bindeth herself by a bond, being in her father's house, in her youth, and her father heareth her vow, or her bond wherewith she hath bound her soul, and her father holdeth his peace at her, then all her vows shall stand, and every bond wherewith she hath bound her soul shall stand. (Numbers 30:3–5)

Mitzvah 406 pertains to nullifying vows. We do not have free reign to nullify vows. This can be done in certain situations:

If a woman is married, her husband can nullify the vow, but she cannot do that. He can nullify it, only if her fulfillment of the vow were to have a negative effect on him.

A father can nullify a vow that his daughter makes. That is the same thing with the husband and the wife. Nullifying the vow means lifting the restriction that the vow would have imposed. The husband and the father can nullify the vows only within 24 hours after they were made.

Another example is if someone wanted to nullify a vow because he realized that he never should have made it. He can go before three people, present his case, and they can nullify it.

At the beginning of Yom Kippur, just before sunset, we chant the Kol Nidre (all vows) prayer. In this prayer, we ask Hashem to release us from vows we made to Him.

407. THAT WE SHOULD NOT BREAK OUR WORD IN VOWS THAT WE MAKE

When a man voweth a vow unto the LORD, or sweareth an oath to bind his soul with a bond, he shall not break his word; he shall do according to all that proceedeth out of his mouth. (Numbers 30:30)

Mitzvah 407 is the prohibition against breaking vows. If someone vows to do something (or not to do something), that individual must keep that promise.

The nullifying of vows, which is discussed in 406, is not the same as breaking a vow. Nullifying means cancelling the vow, while breaking it means violating a valid vow. There are circumstances when vows can be nullified. I covered this topic in my write-up of Mitzvah 227.

408. TO GIVE THE LEVITES CITIES TO DWELL IN, AND TO GIVE REFUGE TO THE UNINTENTIONAL MANSLAYER

'Command the children of Israel, that they give unto the Levites of the inheritance of their possession cities to dwell in; and open land round about the cities shall ye give unto the Levites. And the cities shall they have to dwell in; and their open land shall be for their cattle, and for their substance,

and for all their beasts. And the open land about the cities, which ye shall give unto the Levites, shall be from the wall of the city and outward a thousand cubits round about. And ye shall measure without the city for the east side two thousand cubits, and for the south side two thousand cubits, and for the west side two thousand cubits, and for the north side two thousand cubits, the city being in the midst. This shall be to them the open land about the cities. And the cities which ye shall give unto the Levites, they shall be the six cities of refuge, which ye shall give for the manslayer to flee thither; and beside them ye shall give forty and two cities. All the cities which ye shall give to the Levites shall be forty and eight cities: them shall ye give with the open land about them. (Numbers 35:2–7)

Mitzvah 408 requires the Children of Israel to give 48 cities in the Land of Israel to the Levites. Unlike the other tribes, the Levites do not own land because of their obligation to serve Hashem in His Temple. Of these 48 cities, there are 6 specific ones that serve as Cities of Refuge for individuals who inadvertently killed another human being. According to the author of Sefer HaHinnuch, the Levites have a special relationship with Hashem, thus making them less likely to condemn and mistreat these manslayers.

409. NOT TO EXECUTE A GUILTY PERSON WHO DESERVES DEATH, BEFORE HE STANDS TRIAL

And the cities shall be unto you for refuge from the avenger, that the manslayer die not, until he stand before the congregation for judgment. (Numbers 35:12)

Mitzvah 409 states that if witnesses see someone commit murder, then they are not to slay that individual. Instead, that person is brought before 23 judges of the Sanhedrin, who decide the defendant's fate. (Of course, the witnesses are required to try to stop the murder.) If judges witnessed the murder, then they are not to preside over the case because that could possibly prevent them from wanting to look for reasons why the murderer's life should be spared. They might be too upset from seeing the murder that they would resist developing an argument of defense. As discussed in Mitzvah 261, the Torah places more importance on life than anything else. If all 23 judges decide that the slayer be put to death, then that individual goes free because it means that no one truly tried to prepare a suitable defense.

410. THE DUTY OF THE COURT TO MAKE AN UNINTENTIONAL KILLER GO TO A CITY OF REFUGE. AND HIS DUTY TO GO THERE

(That wording appeared in the English translation of Sefer HaHinnuch.)

and the congregation shall deliver the manslayer out of the hand of the avenger of blood, and the congregation shall restore him to his city of refuge, whither he was fled; and he shall dwell therein until the death of the High Priest, who was anointed with the holy oil. (Numbers 35:25)

Mitzvah 410 commands the Sanhedrin to send a Jew to a City of Refuge if he or she unintentionally committed murder. In order for the sentence to be carried out, the victim must die immediately after receiving the blow, otherwise the Sanhedrin cannot exile the killer. Exile to a City of Refuge is a serious punishment because the killer is separated from friends and family in unfamiliar surroundings.

The Cities of Refuge were put in place for only Jews to derive safety and benefit. They were not put in place to help non-Jews.

If a heathen (non-Jew) kills a Jew, whether intentional or not, then that individual is put to death. My Partner in Torah gave me an explanation. The Gentiles do not have 613 Mitzvot to fulfill, just seven. They are the Noahide laws. One of the seven prohibits murder. These seven laws are quite strict without room for interpretation. (See the seven laws at the bottom of this Mitzvah write-up.)

If a heathen kills another heathen unintentionally, then the death penalty applies.

The Seven Noahide Laws

(Cited from the link: http://www.auburn.edu/~allenkc/noahide.html)

Idolatry is forbidden.

1. Man is commanded to believe in Hashem alone and worship only Him.
2. Incestuous and adulterous relations are forbidden. Human beings are not sexual objects, nor is pleasure the ultimate goal of life.
3. Murder is forbidden. The life of a human being, formed in G-d's image, is sacred.
4. Cursing the name of G-d is forbidden. Besides honoring and respecting G-d, we learn from this precept that our speech must be sanctified, as that is the distinctive sign which separated man from the animals.
5. Theft is forbidden. The world is not ours to do with as we please.
6. Eating the limb of a living animal (including the flesh) is forbidden. This teaches us to not to be cruel to animals. (This was commanded to Noah for the first time along

with the permission of eating meat. The rest were already given to Adam in the Garden of Eden.)

7. Mankind is commanded to establish courts of justice and a just social order to enforce the first six laws and enact any other useful laws or customs.

411. THAT A WITNESS WHO TESTIFIES IN A TRIAL FOR A CAPITAL CRIME SHOULD NOT SPEAK IN JUDGMENT

Whoso killeth any person, the murderer shall be slain at the mouth of witnesses; but one witness shall not testify against any person that he die. (Numbers 35:30)

Mitzvah 411 forbids a witness to a capital case from rending any sort of judicial opinion. A witness can tell the court what he saw, but he cannot be one of the 23 judges. The reasons can be found in my write-up of Mitzvah 409.

412. TO TAKE NO RANSOM TO SAVE A KILLER FROM HIS DEATH SENTENCE

Moreover ye shall take no ransom for the life of a murderer, that is guilty of death; but he shall surely be put to death. (Numbers 35:31)

Mitzvah 412 prohibits us from accepting financial compensation from a killer on trial, in exchange for acquittal. The killer must stand trial and be sentenced. If a killer can buy his way out, then rich people could then get away with murder. This Mitzvah reminds us that wealth does not make one superior.

413. TO TAKE NO RANSOM FROM SOMEONE SENTENCED TO BANISHMENT, TO FREE HIM FROM IT

And ye shall take no ransom for him that is fled to his city of refuge, that he should come again to dwell in the land, until the death of the priest. (Numbers 25:32)

Mitzvah 413 states that if a person unintentionally commits murder and is then sentenced to a City of Refuge, the guilty party cannot bribe his way out of the sentence. As mentioned in Mitzvah 412, possessing wealth does not mean that one is superior to those less wealthy. In the eyes of Hashem, we are all the same. Accepting bribes would make it easier for killers (whether they murdered intentionally or not) to get away with murder.

Mitzvot from Deuteronomy

414. NOT TO APPOINT ANY JUDGE WHO IS UNLEARNED IN THE TORAH, EVEN IF HE IS GENERALLY LEARNED

Ye shall not respect persons in judgment; ye shall hear the small and the great alike; ye shall not be afraid of the face of any man; for the judgment is God's; and the cause that is too hard for you ye shall bring unto me, and I will hear it.' (Deuteronomy 1:17)

Mitzvah 414 forbids the appointment of judges who lack a thorough background in Torah. That person should be well respected and accomplished, but that does not qualify him to preside as a judge. Torah knowledge, and practicing Torah, ensures fair rulings. The Torah teaches us to be compassionate, humble, and to love and fear Hashem. A learned man without Torah knowledge could possibly preside without these traits, which can bring about unfair and unjust rulings.

415. THAT A JUDGE PRESIDING AT A TRIAL SHOULD NOT FEAR ANY EVIL MAN

Ye shall not respect persons in judgment; ye shall hear the small and the great alike; ye shall not be afraid of the face of any man; for the judgment is God's; and the cause that is

too hard for you ye shall bring unto me, and I will hear it.' (Deuteronomy 1:17)

Mitzvah 415 forbids judges to fear litigants. Even if the person on trial could cause bodily harm to the judge, he should not automatically rule in favor of such a person, unless proven innocent. Hashem is the only one we need to fear. Fearing anyone else is indicative of lack of faith and gratitude to Hashem for creating us. Fearing intimidating litigants violates Hashem's commandment in Deuteronomy 1:17 cited above.

416. NOT TO DESIRE WHAT BELONGS TO OUR FELLOW JEWS

Neither shalt thou covet thy neighbour's wife; {S} neither shalt thou desire thy neighbour's house, his field, or his man-servant, or his maid-servant, his ox, or his ass, or any thing that is thy neighbour's. (Deuteronomy 5:17)

Mitzvah 416 is the prohibition against desiring other persons' property or money. It differs from Mitzvah 38 in that that Mitzvah forbids acting upon one's desire, while Mitzvah 416 forbids the act, or feeling, of desiring itself. Fulfilling Mitzvah 416 prevents jealousy, resentment, and robbery. Hashem gave us the ability to control our desires.

417. THE PRECEPT OF THE ONENESS OF THE ETERNAL LORD

Hear, O Israel: the LORD our God, the LORD is one. (Deuteronomy 6:4)

Mitzvah 417 commands us to believe in the singularity of G-d. He has no Partners. There is no trinity because G-d is perfect. Deuteronomy 6:4 is also the opening lines of our pledge of allegiance to Hashem, which is known as the Shema. When we say the Shema, we affirm our belief that Hashem is one. He's the supreme being. Mitzvah 417 is the core belief in one God. A person would need to sacrifice his or her life instead of violating this Mitzvah. Violating this Mitzvah means violating Hashem's Torah.

418. THE PRECEPT OF LOVE FOR THE ETERNAL LORD

And thou shalt love the LORD thy God with all thy heart, and with all thy soul, and with all thy might. 6,6 And these words, which I command thee this day, shall be upon thy heart; (Deuteronomy 6:5)

Mitzvah 418 commands us to love Hashem with all our heart, all our soul, and all our might. These lines are in the Shema.

The Torah requires us to say the Shema twice a day:

and thou shalt teach them diligently unto thy children, and shalt talk of them when thou sittest in thy house, and when thou walkest by the way, and when thou liest down, and when thou risest up. Deuteronomy 6:7)

By immersing ourselves in Torah, by saying the Shema, we come to appreciate Hashem. The things that we think are most precious, should pale in comparison to our love of Hashem. He should be on our minds, constantly.

Hillel and Shammai debated over many issues pertaining to Judaism, including the Shema.

The School of Shammai taught, "In the evening, everyone should lie down in order to recite (the Shema), and in the morning (each person) must stand, for it is written, **'when you lie down and when you rise up.'"** However, Hillel disagreed. He taught: "Each person recites the Shema according to his preferred manner (that is, one can do so while sitting or standing, while laying down or walking." According to Hillel, the references to waking and laying down are only indicative of the times of day to recite the Shema, not the manner in which it must be said.To review this argument in more detail, consult Mishnah (Berakhot Chapter 1, Mishnah 3).

419. THE PRECEPT OF TORAH STUDY

and thou shalt teach them diligently unto thy children, and shalt talk of them when thou sittest in thy house, and when thou walkest by the way, and when thou liest down, and when thou risest up. (Deuteronomy 6:7)

Mitzvah 419 commands us to teach Torah to our children. Children includes sons and students.

According to Sefer HaHinnuch, only sons are required to learn Torah, which is based on Deuteronomy 11:19:

And ye shall teach them your sons, talking of them, when thou sittest in thy house, and when thou walkest by the way, and when thou liest down, and when thou risest up."

Today many English translations of Deuteronomy 11:19 replaced the word sons with children. According to Sefer Ha-Hinnuch, women are allowed to learn Torah, but they are not obligated to do so. The author of Sefer HaHinnuch elaborated: "the Sages ordained that a man should not teach his daughter Torah, for women are light-minded, and they will apply the words of Torah to matters of nonsense in their paucity of understanding."

When I learned at Aish HaTorah Yeshiva in the Old City of Jerusalem, I initially thought that observant (Orthodox) Jews discriminated against women by not allowing them to read from the Torah. I thought it unfair that they could not wear Tefillin, Kippot (Yarmulkes), and Tallitot (prayer shawls). Some Aish Rabbis and observant women who worked there explained to me that men are spiritually weaker than women, and therefore are the ones who need to pray. Kippot, Tallitot, and Tefillin remind men to focus on learning Torah and to be mindful of Hashem. These people at Aish HaTorah elaborated that women are on a higher level because like Hashem, they bring life into the world.

420. THE MITZVAH OF RECITING THE SHEMA EVERY MORNING AND EVENING

Hear, O Israel: the LORD our God, the LORD is one. (Deuteronomy 6:4)

Mitzvah 420 commands us to read and recite the Shema twice a day. Doing this indicates our acceptance of Hashem's singular kingship. The last words we should say every night before going to sleep is the Shema. When we wake up in the morning, we should also say the Shema. This reinforces our performance of the Mitzvah.

While the Romans were executing the great Rabbi Akiva, his students asked why he was reciting the Shema. He answered: "All my days I have been troubled by the verse [of the Shema] 'with all my soul' [Deut. 6:5], which I interpret 'even if God takes my soul.' I thought 'When shall I have the opportunity of fulfilling this? Now that I have the opportunity, shall I not fulfill it?" The last words that left Rabbi Akiva's lips were from the shema. For more information about the Shema and Rabbi Akiva's death, consult http://www.dailykos.com/story/2012/08/03/1116207/-D-var-Torah-Va-Etchanan.

See Tractate Berakhot, Chapter 9, Mishnah 5, and BBabylonian Talmud Berakhot, 61B.

421. THE PRECEPT OF THE TEFILLIN OF THE HAND

And thou shalt bind them for a sign upon thy hand, and they shall be for frontlets between thine eyes. (Deuteronomy 6:8)

Mitzvah 421 commands us to place Tefillin (the phylactery) on our arm when we pray to Hashem during the day. The Oral Torah instructs us on how to use Tefillin.

On a side note, it is unadvisable to study the written Torah without the Oral Torah. The written Torah states commandments and Mitzvot, while the Oral Torah fills in the gaps. For example, the Written Torah does not explain how we are to slaughter animals or how to put on Tefillin, but the Oral Torah does.

In regard to Tefillin, one wraps it around the arm, then the other Tefillin is placed on the head. After that, we resume wrapping the arm-Tefillin around the palm and the middle finger.

When we take off our Tefillin, we first unwrap the fingers, then we remove the head-Tefillin, and then we finish unwrapping the arm-Tefillin.

Putting on and taking off Tefillin must be done in this order, as it says in Deuteronomy 6:8. That Torah passage is at the top of this Mitzvah write-up.

Sefer HaHinnuch states that by keeping Tefillin on the arm longer than the head, it will keep us from straying from Hashem for a longer period of time. (Time here does not refer to days, months, or years, but to minutes and hours.) For example, if a man desires another man's wife, he would most likely not pursue her, while wearing the Tefillin on his arm. The Tefillin for the arm is symbolic of our deeds. The deeds we do with the arm need to be done in accordance with the Torah. When the arm is in its natural position, it is adjacent to the heart. The heart is the source of the person's desire. Having the Tefillin on the arm reminds us that we need to restrain our deeds in accordance with the Torah. The Tefillin on the head corresponds with the brain. A person's deeds are more indicative than the person's thoughts.

I heard another argument for putting on and taking off Tefillin in this order: The head Tefillin is holier than the arm Tefillin. Out of respect for Hashem, we put the head portion on last and we take it off first because we should not wear it longer than necessary.

When I was a camper at Camp Ramah, a camp sponsored by the Conservative movement, my counselor told my bunkmates and me to take off our Tefillin because we were going to begin the Musaf portion of the Rosh Chodesh service.

Initially, I was annoyed because I was still learning how to put on Tefillin and that day I had a hard time putting it on correctly.

I ignored him, thinking that he would eventually overlook it, but I was wrong.

He walked over to me and said:

"We're doing Musaf, take off your Tefillin."

"Why?"

"I'll explain later."

I took off my Tefillin. After the service, he explained why I had to do it. I recently looked up answers on line, some of which corresponded with his explanations.

Rabbi Baruch S. Davidson wrote: "In many communities, the liturgy for the Musafkedushah begins with the words "Keter Yitnu L'cha," ("A crown is given to You, L-rd our G-d..."). This is a reference to the supernal crown which the angels on high, and the Jews below, bestow upon G-d. The Tefillin are also considered to be a crown, and therefore, the Zohar explains, it would be disrespectful for an individual to wear his own "crown" while crowning G-d." (Cited in http://www.chabad.org/library/article_cdo/aid/563495/jewish/Why-do-we-remove-tefillin-on-Rosh-Chodesh-before-Musaf.htm) This also explains why we do not wear t'fillin on holidays and Shabbat.

According to Sefer HaHinnuch, women are not obligated to wear Tefillin because they are exempt from positive time-bound Mitzvot. However, a woman is not forbidden from observing this Mitzvah either. As mentioned in Mitzvah 386, women are NOT exempt from all positive time-bound Mitzvot.

This Mitzvah is applicable today.

422. THE PRECEPT OF THE TEFILLIN OF THE HEAD

And thou shalt bind them for a sign upon thy hand, and they shall be for frontlets between thine eyes. ((Deuteronomy 6:8)

Mitzvah 422 commands us put Tefillin on our heads. This relates to our core belief in Hashem's mastery of the world. For more details, consult Sefer HaHinnuch. A more lengthy discussion of Tefillin was covered in Mitzvah 421.

Today, we still observe this Mitzvah.

423. THE PRECEPT OF THE MEZUZAH ON THE DOORPOST

And thou shalt write them upon the door-posts of thy house, and upon thy gates. (Deuteronomy 6:9)

Mitzvah 423 commands us to place a Mezuzah on the doorposts of our homes. If you are unfamiliar with the term, a Mezuzah is a parchment inscribed with certain passages from the Torah and placed in a case that is attached to the doorpost of a Jewish house as a sign of faith. (Consult http://www.thefreedictionary.com/mezuzah. Also consult Deuteronomy 6:4-9 and Deuteronomy 11:13-21.)

In order for one to be obligated to place a Mezuzah in his or her house, the house must fulfill the following requirements:

1. Its area should be sufficient to make a square of four cubits by four cubits
2. The house should have two doorposts
3. A lintel
4. A ceiling.
5. Doors.
6. The gate entrance should be ten handbreadths high or more.
7. The house should be non-holy.

8. It should be made for human occupancy.
9. It should be made for dignified occupancy.
10. It should be made for permanent occupancy.

The Mezuzah has a scroll inside of it, which contains the first two paragraphs of the Shema. Like the passages inside the Tefillin, the Mezuzah must be written by a scribe on parchment. A scribe must inspect our Mezuzot twice in a seven-year period to make sure that their letters are still intact.

We place Mezuzot on our doorposts to remind us of our obligations to Hashem when we enter and leave our homes.

This Mitzvah is applicable today.

424. NOT TO TEST A TRUE PROPHET TO AN UNDUE DEGREE

Ye shall not try the LORD your God, as ye tried Him in Massah. (Deuteronomy 6:16) (For information about the Massah incident, consult Exodus 17:7)

Mitzvah 424 prohibits us from challenging a true prophet excessively. The Torah tells us to watch out for false prophets. However, after the prophet's legitimacy is established, no one should test him or her. A key reason is that at the time of prophecy, Hashem infrequently appeared to many of them. Another reason is that if people keep testing certain prophets, the prophet would be forced to repeatedly prove that his or her forecasts are true. Seeing a prophet repeatedly demonstrate his or her authenticity can make certain individuals jealous that Hashem does not appear to them. They would then ignore the prophets' warnings. Most important, the prophets' duties do not consist of them showing the masses repeatedly that they have favor with Hashem. Their primary task is to make the Children of Israel follow Hashem's commandments.

This Mitzvah is enforced when there is prophecy.

Over the years, I have heard certain secular Jews tell Christians that although they do not believe in Jesus, they still acknowledge him as a prophet. They either said that to bond with the Christians or they just did not know the truth. In truth, Jesus was not a prophet because when he lived, there was no more prophecy. Jesus was just a man.

425. THE PRECEPT OF WIPING OUT THE SEVEN NATIONS

When the LORD thy God shall bring thee into the land whither thou goest to possess it, and shall cast out many nations before thee, the Hittite, and the Girgashite, and the Amorite, and the Canaanite, and the Perizzite, and the Hivite, and the Jebusite, seven nations greater and mightier than thou; and when the LORD thy God shall deliver them up before thee, and thou shalt smite them; then thou shalt utterly destroy them; thou shalt make no covenant with them, nor show mercy unto them; (Deuteronomy 7:1-2)

Mitzvah 425 commands us to destroy the seven nations, cited above, that occupied the Land of Israel when Joshua led our ancestors there. Although we are also commanded to destroy the Amalekites, they are not included in this Mitzvah because they did not occupy the Land of Israel.

The seven nations were idol worshippers, while the Amalekites wanted every Jew annihilated. (Amalek was Esau's grandson. See Genesis 36:12.)

A common question is why would Hashem create these nations if He wanted them destroyed? The seven nations and the Amalekites, like everyone else Hashem created, has free will. They chose to do things that Hashem detested. Another common question is why would Hashem bring us to the Land of Israel if he allowed us to be driven from it? The answer is free will. In Leviticus 26:3-43, and in Deuteronomy 28:1-68, Hashem promises us good fortune and happiness if we serve and obey Him, and He warns us of terrible times to come if we go astray.

We cannot practice this Mitzvah today because of the uncertainty of who belongs to which nation, however, the Mitzvah itself is still theoretically applicable.

426. TO SHOW NO MERCY TO IDOL WORSHIPPERS

and when the LORD thy God shall deliver them up before thee, and thou shalt smite them; then thou shalt utterly destroy them; thou shalt make no covenant with them, nor show mercy unto them (Deuteronomy 7:2)

Mitzvah 426 prohibits us from caring for idol worshippers. We cannot grant them any type honor or benefit, nor can we say anything nice about them; not one word of kindness. The reason is that this can lead us to become idol worshippers. The first step that leads to action is a person's thoughts and speech. To prevent this spark from growing into a flame, we cannot think favorably of or say nice things to or about idol worshippers. Thinking and saying leads to doing.

Today this Mitzvah might seem extreme. However, before the destruction of the First Temple, the temptation to worship idols was as tempting as the desire for sex still is today. The "Yetzer Hara" (evil inclination) for idol worship was more powerful than we can possibly fathom.

Members of the Sanhedrin asked Hashem to remove the "Yetzer Hara" in regard to idol worship. Hashem granted their request, but in so doing that, He also abolished prophecy.

For more information about the abolishment of the desire to worship idols and the abolishment of prophecy, consult Avoda Zarah (Idolatry by Rabbi Dr. Hillel Ben David (Greg Killian). See also Babylonian Talmud Yoma 69B.

427. TO FORM NO MARITAL BOND WITH IDOL-WORSHIPPERS

neither shalt thou make marriages with them: thy daughter thou shalt not give unto his son, nor his daughter shalt thou take unto thy son. (Deuteronomy 7:3)

Mitzvah 427 prohibits us from marrying non-Jews. Marrying a non-Jew could lead one from abandoning Hashem for idol worship. Marrying non-Jews was a huge concern as far back as Genesis. In Genesis, Rebecca feared that Jacob would marry an idol worshipper:

And Rebekah said to Isaac: 'I am weary of my life because of the daughters of Heth. If Jacob take a wife of the daughters of Heth, such as these, of the daughters of the land, what good shall my life do me?' (Genesis 27:46)

428. NOT TO DERIVE BENEFIT FROM ANY ORNAMENTATION OF AN IDOL

The graven images of their gods shall ye burn with fire; thou shalt not covet the silver or the gold that is on them, nor take it unto thee, lest thou be snared therein; for it is an abomination to the LORD thy God. (Deuteronomy 7:25)

Mitzvah 428 prohibits us from deriving benefit from ornaments on idols and/or objects used for idol worship. We must distance ourselves from anything associated with idols. If an ornament from an idol were on something not forbidden to us such as an animal, tree, or mountain, we still cannot have benefit from that ornament. As mentioned in Deuteronomy 7:25, Hashem forbade our ancestors from taking the silver and valuables from the seven nations after conquering them.

429. NOT TO TAKE ANY OBJECT FROM IDOLATRY INTO OUR POSSESSION, TO DERIVE BENEFIT FROM IT

And thou shalt not bring an abomination into thy house, and be accursed like unto it; thou shalt utterly detest it, and thou shalt utterly abhor it; for it is a devoted thing. (Deuteronomy 7:26)

And there shall cleave nought of the devoted thing to thy hand, that the LORD may turn from the fierceness of His anger, and show thee mercy, and have compassion upon thee, and multiply thee, as He hath sworn unto thy fathers; (Deuteronomy 13:18)

Mitzvah 429 forbids us to derive benefit from things used to worship idols. For example, should certain people worship a specific tree, then we cannot use the wood from that tree to heat up our houses or to light fires. We cannot use that tree because its essence became corrupted as a result of it being used for idol worship.

430. THE PRECEPT OF BLESSING THE ALMIGHTY FOR THE FOOD WE RECEIVE

And thou shalt eat and be satisfied, and bless the LORD thy God for the good land which He hath given thee. (Deuteronomy 8:10)

Mitzvah 430 requires us to say blessings after meals (Birkat HaMazon). We say this blessing when we are satiated. Our meals must consist of bread in order for us to be required to say Birkat HaMazon.

The Sages established shorter blessing for eating things without bread. Grains without bread require a specific blessing. Eating just fruit requires its own blessing, just as eating sweets. The blessing we say after eating corresponds with the blessing we say beforehand. The after blessing has a shorter version, which applies to items like a glass of water, eggs, yogurt, or fruits.

If we drink wine without bread, we say a second after blessing.

If a person is uncertain whether he said the "Birkat HaMazon," he must say it because there cannot be uncertainty. The Birkat HaMazon, unlike the other blessings before and after food, is a Torah commandment, while the others are Rabbinic obligations and placed on a lower level of importance. This is comparable to the Second Holy Days of our holidays, which the Sages established, not Hashem. (In my write-up of Mitzvah 298, I explained why the Sages did this.) The blessings we say before we eat are Rabbinic obligations, not Torah. Nowhere in the Torah does Hashem command us to say a blessing before meals. The Sages required us to say the before blessings and the after blessings, not counting the Torah required Birkat Hamazon, in order for us to remember that everything we eat comes from Hashem. Not giving thanks to Hashem before and after meals is comparable to animals' behavior. Animals do not speak. They just devour their food. To further separate us from the animals, our behavior must not be likened to theirs. Saying the blessings strengthens the realization that we have Hashem to thank for the food that we are about to receive and then thank Him afterwards. This also prevents us from taking our food for granted.

Rabbi Yehuda Shurpin of Chabad.org shared with me the article, "Why a Blessing?" where it explains why before blessings are said: "Chassidic teachings explain that all food contains a G-dly spark of holiness. When we say a blessing before eating, and eat with the intention to serve G-d, we actually elevate the physical substance of the food into holiness and reunite it with its Divine source." (To read the article:
http://www.chabad.org/library/article_cdo/aid/90550/)

The only Torah commanded before blessing we say is the one for studying Torah. We say the required blessing before learning because we know that we are about to do something holy and spiritually rewarding. When my Partner in Torah taught me this blessing, I asked him if there was an after blessing and he said no because we can never be satiated from Torah study.

In the article, "The Blessings on the Torah," Aryey Citron points out that: "The RAMBAN (Nachmanides) includes this Mitzvah in his listing of the 613 Mitzvot.4 The RAMBAM, however, does not count it as a one of the 613 Mitzvot. In his opinion, the blessings on the Torah are of Rabbinic origin. … The Aruch Hashulchan (s. 47:2) contends that the RAMBAM agrees that these blessings are a Torah obligation, but it is not counted as a separate Mitzvah, as it is part of the Mitzvah of Torah study. To read this article, go to the link, http://www.chabad.org/library/article_cdo/aid/986857/

Before learning Torah, one must recite the required blessings:

BA-RUCH A-TAH A-DONAI ELOHEINU MELECH HA-OLAM ASHER KID-DE-SHANU B'MITZ-VO-TAV VE-TZI-VANU LA-A-SOAK B'DIVREI TORAH. V'HA-AREV NA ADONAI ELOHEINU ETDDIVREI TO-RA-T'CHA B'FINU U-VE-FI AM'CHA BAIT YISRAEL, V'NIH-YEH ANACHNU V'TZE-E-TZA-EINU V'TZE-E-TZA-EI AM'CHA BAIT YISRAEL, KULANU YOD'EI SHMECHA V'LOME-DEI TORATECHA LISHMA. BARUCH ATAH ADONAI HA-M'LAMAID TORAH L'AMO YISRAEL.

BARUCH ATAH ADONAI ELOHEINU MELECH HA-OLAM ASHER BACHAR BANU MIKOL HA-AMIM V'NA-TAN LANU ET TORATO. BARUCH ATAH ADONAI NOTAIN HA-TORAH.

Y'VA-RE-CHE-CHA ADONAI V'YISHME-RECHA. YA-AIR ADONAI PANAV AILECHA VI-CHU-NEKA. YI-SA ADONAI PANAV AILECHA VE-YA-SAIM LE-CHA SHALOM.

The following link contains the same exact prayer, but in Hebrew:
http://www.hebrew4christians.com/Blessings/Daily_Blessings/Torah_Study/b4torahstudy.pdf

Rabbi Shaul Rosenblatt sent me the following email with his own explanations about the reasons for before and after blessings:

"The Rabbis say that blessings before meals are obvious–that's why they were not written in the Torah. But they nevertheless felt they should make it clear to people that it was necessary, by making it a Rabbinic Mitzvah…I believe there is dispute about whether "Birkat HaTorah" is a Torah Mitzvah. If so, I guess maybe it is not so obvious to bless over the Torah, so the Torah felt it necessary to point it out."

431. THE PRECEPT OF LOVE FOR CONVERTS TO JUDAISM

Love ye therefore the stranger; for ye were strangers in the land of Egypt. (Deuteronomy 10:19)

Mitzvah 431 commands us to love converts to Judaism. The convert is as vulnerable as an orphan and widow. In certain cases, the convert is separated from his or her family and native land. We must defend the convert against injustices. Not only are we to love converts to Judaism because of the obligation to love your fellow Jew, but because we need to remember that we were strangers in the Land of Egypt.

I provided more content about how we are supposed to treat converts in my write-up of Mitzvah 63.

432. THE PRECEPT OF REVERENT AWE FOR THE ETERNAL LORD

Thou shalt fear the LORD thy God; Him shalt thou serve; and to Him shalt thou cleave, and by His name shalt thou swear. (Deuteronomy 10:20)

Mitzvah 432 obligates us to fear Hashem. Having a reverent fear of Hashem keeps us from sinning. This is a constant Mitzvah, unlike many of the others, which are episodic. Every minute of every day, we must observe this Mitzvah.

An example of observing this Mitzvah is refraining from saying Hashem's name, except when we pray to Him. Another example is that we omit the letter o when we write G-d. Doing these things takes His name in vain and it diminishes our reverent awe of Him.

Although we are supposed to fear Hashem, we are also supposed to love Him. We do not fear Him like we might a tyrant. Hashem is no tyrant. He chose us from all the nations of the world to receive His Torah and to observe His Mitzvot. He loves us. Fear and love should not preclude one another.

This Mitzvah is applicable today and will be for all time, and it applies to every human being, both Jew and Gentile.

433. THE PRECEPT OF PRAYER TO THE ALMIGHTY

Thou shalt fear the LORD thy God; Him shalt thou serve; and to Him shalt thou cleave, and by His name shalt thou swear. (Deuteronomy 10:20)

Mitzvah 433 commands us to serve Hashem with all our heart and soul.

And it shall come to pass, if ye shall hearken diligently unto My commandments which I command you this day, to love the LORD your God, and to serve Him with all your heart and with all your soul, that I will give the rain of your land in its season, the former rain and the latter rain, that thou mayest gather in thy corn, and thy wine, and thine oil. (Deuteronomy 11:13-11:14)

Prior to the Temple's destruction, Jews served Hashem by sacrificing animals to Him. That was our primary way of staying in relationship with Him. Without the Temple, we now have to maintain our relationship with Him through prayer.

We pray to Him when we need help, and we also pray when everything is going great. We have to always thank Him because this teaches us not only to be grateful to Him, but we learn to never take what we have for granted. This includes our ability to see, hear, speak, walk, and to relieve ourselves. This reminds us that there are people who would like nothing better than to see perfectly, to have a healthy colon, and to walk without pain. Being able to do these seemingly simple tasks is a gift from Hashem. That is why we are to thank him when we relieve ourselves, when we wake up in the morning, and when we take a sip of water.

Consult the write-up of Mitzvah 433 in Sefer HaHinnuch for a more detailed discussion.

434. THE MITZVAH OF ASSOCIATING WITH TORAH SCHOLARS AND ADHERING TO THEM

Thou shalt fear the LORD thy God; Him shalt thou serve; and to Him shalt thou cleave, and by His name shalt thou swear. (Deuteronomy 10:20)

Mitzvah 434 commands us to associate with Torah scholars. This obligation derives from the Sages' interpretation of Deuteronomy 10:20, where the words "cleave to" are used. The Sages interpreted "cleave to" to mean associate with Hashem's representatives, Torah scholars. When one stays close to Torah scholars, it fulfills the obligation to stay close to Hashem. It is a way to learn proper behavior. The Torah scholars are a mirror of Hashem's behavior.

In Avot, Chapter 1, Mishnah 16, Rabbi Gamaliel tells us that we should appoint for ourselves a Torah teacher. Besides having the benefit of learning Torah, a Torah teacher makes prudent decisions. We know that we can trust his judgment.

In Avot, Chapter 1, Mishnah 4, Rabbi Yosay Ben Yoezer of Tzredah tells us to sit at the dust of the feet of Torah scholars and drink their words thirstily. This means that our homes should be a gathering place for Torah scholars. Of course, not everyone can offer this service to Torah scholars, so under those circumstances, that individual should make places of Torah study his additional home.

I once heard a Rabbi discuss Avot, Chapter 1, Mishnah 4 with 15 and 16-year-old yeshiva students. One of the students protested that anyone who would sit at the dust of the feet of another person, even Torah scholars, had to be an idiot.

The Rabbi replied that literally sitting at the dust of the feet of Torah scholars is a wise thing to do because it helps prevent that person from following idol worshippers and becoming Idol worshippers.

435. THAT WHOEVER NEEDS TO TAKE AN OATH SHOULD SWEAR BY THE NAME OF THE ETERNAL LORD

Thou shalt fear the LORD thy God; Him shalt thou serve; and to Him shalt thou cleave, and by His name shalt thou swear. (Deuteronomy 10:20)

Mitzvah 435 commands us to swear in the name of Hashem if we need to resort to an oath to establish something. Then we must use the name of Hashem/swear in the name of Hashem to help establish the oath. If one takes an oath to diet, that person would take the oath in the name of Hashem.

Oaths invoke the name of Hashem. Vows, on the other hand, do not always invoke His name. For that reason, it is preferred that people take oaths sparingly. This prevents us from unnecessarily using the name of Hashem.

See my write-up of Mitzvah 30 for more details.

436. THE PRECEPT TO DESTROY AN IDOL AND ALL THAT SERVES IT

Ye shall surely destroy all the places, wherein the nations that ye are to dispossess served their gods, upon the high mountains, and upon the hills, and under every leafy tree. 12,3 And ye shall break down their altars, and dash in pieces their pillars, and burn their Asherim with fire; and ye shall hew down the graven images of their gods; and ye shall destroy their name out of that place. (Deuteronomy 12:2-12-3)

Mitzvah 436 is the obligation to destroy objects of idol worship and any secondary items that are used in its service. If the idol is on a tray, then the tray must be destroyed along with the idol. That is one example of fulfilling this Mitzvah. Any type of destruction is appropriate, whether by burning, chopping, as long as the items are destroyed. We are prohibited from receiving any benefit from idol worship. If an idol is a natural formation, such as a mountain or the sky, we are not obligated to destroy them. We can receive natural benefits from those things, and even if others worship those items does not prohibit them.

437. NOT TO ERASE HOLY WRITINGS OR WRITTEN NAMES OF THE HOLY ONE, NOR DESTROY THE TEMPLES OF HOLY WORSHIP

Ye shall not do so unto the LORD your God. (Deuteronomy 12:4)

(It states in Deuteronomy 12:2-3, that we must destroy items associated with idols. See my write-up of Mitzvah 436 for more details.)

Mitzvah 437 prohibits us from destroying objects that spell out Hashem's name in Hebrew, such as the Torah scroll.

If a Jew who worships idols wrote a portion of the Torah, it must be destroyed, but if a non-Jew were to do that, we would only need to hide and/or bury it.

Rabbi Yehuda Shurpin of Chabad.org explained to me why we are to react differently.

He emailed me the following explanation:

"The issue is that if a Jew who worships idols wrote a Torah, we assume that he had whatever is his belief in mind when he wrote. However, if a non-Jew wrote it, it is only not kosher, due a technicality (i.e. it needs to be written by a Jew)."

He elaborated that Christian Bibles, which contain the Tanakh, should also be buried, and hidden if written by a Non-Jew and destroyed if a Jew penned it.

The Tanakh consists of the Torah, the Nevi'im (prophets), and the Ketuvim (writings). Tanakh is an acronym, consisting of the first Hebrew letter of Torah, Nevi'im, and Ketuvim.

438. TO BRING ALL OBLIGATORY OR VOLUNTARY OFFERINGS AT THE FIRST PILGRIMAGE FESTIVAL THAT COMES ALONG

But unto the place which the LORD your God shall choose out of all your tribes to put His name there, even unto

His habitation shall ye seek, and thither thou shalt come; and thither ye shall bring your burnt-offerings, and your sacrifices, and your tithes, and the offering of your hand, and your vows, and your freewill-offerings, and the firstlings of your herd and of your flock; (Deuteronomy 12:5-6)

Mitzvah 438 states that if we vow to bring an offering to the Temple for the next pilgrimage, then it is preferred that we bring it for the next possible pilgrimage. If one makes this vow, and then the next pilgrimage is Passover, he should not wait for the one after that. I mentioned that at the time of the Temple, three specific times a year, Jews had to make pilgrimages to Jerusalem, which were Passover, Shavuot, and Sukkot. If he makes the vow and then misses the next two pilgrimages, he is not in violation of this Mitzvah. However, he is in violation if he misses the third pilgrimage.

439. THE PROHIBITION AGAINST SACRIFICING HOLY OFFERINGS OUTSIDE THE SANCTUARY

Take heed to thyself that thou offer not thy burnt-offerings in every place that thou seest; but in the place which the LORD shall choose in one of thy tribes, there thou shalt offer thy burnt-offerings, and there thou shalt do all that I command thee. (Deuteronomy 12:13-14)

Mitzvah 439 forbids us to offer sacrifices outside the Temple. This is a negative commandment. Mitzvah 440 is its positive flipside.

In Sefer HaHinnuch, it states that the word "all" in Deuteronomy 12:14 means the other sacrifices. Deuteronomy 12:13 deals specifically with the burnt offerings.

I covered the subject of the prohibition of making sacrifices outside the Temple in my write-up of Mitzvah 186.

440. THE PRECEPT TO SACRIFICE ALL OFFERINGS AT THE SANCTUARY, AND NOT ANYWHERE OUTSIDE IT

but in the place which the LORD shall choose in one of thy tribes, there thou shalt offer thy burnt-offerings, and there thou shalt do all that I command thee. (Deuteronomy 12:14)

Mitzvah 440 commands us to perform all sacrifices inside the Temple. This is the positive flipside to Mitzvah 439. A violation of a negative Mitzvah can often subject the culprit to be flogged.

441. TO REDEEM ANIMALS CONSECRATED FOR OFFERINGS WHICH BECOME BLEMISHED

Notwithstanding thou mayest kill and eat flesh within all thy gates, after all the desire of thy soul, according to the blessing of the LORD thy God which He hath given thee; the unclean and the clean may eat thereof, as of the gazelle, and as of the hart. (Deuteronomy 12:15)

Mitzvah 441 obligates us to redeem any animal designated for sacrifice that develops the type of blemish that disqualifies it. The developed blemish means that the animal loses the honor of being brought to the altar and sacrificed to Hashem. The animal's owner is to sell that animal and use the proceeds to buy an animal more suitable for sacrifice. This is for our benefit because even though this animal had attained a level of holiness, Hashem is giving it back to us with that holiness still attached for us to derive pleasure from it. Even though it is no longer suitable for Hashem, the animal is still good enough for us to eat. Deriving benefit (eating a kosher animal) is pleasurable and Hashem wants us to experience that. My Partner in Torah said that redemption for purposes of eating is the only permitted benefit. It cannot be kept for breeding or for producing wool.

442. THE PROHIBITION AGAINST EATING THE SECOND TITHE OF GRAIN OUTSIDE JERUSALEM

Thou mayest not eat within thy gates the tithe of thy corn, or of thy wine, or of thine oil, or the firstlings of thy herd or of thy flock, nor any of thy vows which thou vowest, nor thy freewill-offerings, nor the offering of thy hand; but thou shalt eat them before the LORD thy God in the place which the LORD thy God shall choose, thou, and thy son, and thy daughter, and thy man-servant, and thy maid-servant, and the Levite that is within thy gates; and thou shalt rejoice before the LORD thy God in all that thou puttest thy hand unto. (Deuteronomy 12:17-18)

Mitzvah 442 prohibits us from eating the Second Tithes outside of Jerusalem. After one separates out the First Tithe that goes to the Levites, then he has to take out Second Tithes, which belong to him. He is obligated to eat them in Jerusalem. This Mitzvah is the prohibition against eating them outside of Jerusalem. The tithes have a special holiness, and therefore must be eaten in Jerusalem. This also forces the animal's owner to come to Jerusalem. This Mitzvah pertains to tithes consisting of grains.

In my write-up of Mitzvah 360, I provided additional reasons why the Second Tithes must be eaten in Jerusalem.

443. THE PROHIBITION AGAINST CONSUMING THE SECOND TITHE OF WINE OUTSIDE JERUSALEM

Thou mayest not eat within thy gates the tithe of thy corn, or of thy wine, or of thine oil, or the firstlings of thy herd or of thy flock, nor any of thy vows which thou vowest, nor thy freewill-offerings, nor the offering of thy hand; but thou shalt eat them before the LORD thy God in the place which the LORD thy God shall choose, thou, and thy son, and thy daughter, and thy man-servant, and thy maid-servant, and the Levite that is within thy gates; and thou shalt rejoice before the LORD thy God in all that thou puttest thy hand unto. (Deuteronomy 12:17-18)

Mitzvah 443 forbids us from consuming the Second Tithes of wine outside Jerusalem. This Mitzvah is practically identical to Mitzvah 442, except that the former deals with grain, while the latter deals with wine. Wine is a specialized grape product that requires tithing.

444. THE PROHIBITION AGAINST CONSUMING THE SECOND TITHE OF OIL OUTSIDE JERUSALEM

Thou mayest not eat within thy gates the tithe of thy corn, or of thy wine, or of thine oil, or the firstlings of thy herd or of thy flock, nor any of thy vows which thou vowest, nor thy freewill-offerings, nor the offering of thy hand; but thou shalt eat them before the LORD thy God in the place which the LORD thy God shall choose, thou, and thy son, and thy daughter, and thy man-servant, and thy maid-servant, and the Levite that is within thy gates; and thou shalt rejoice before the LORD thy God in all that thou puttest thy hand unto. (Deuteronomy 12:17-18)

Mitzvah 444 is similar to 442 and 443 except 444 pertains to olive oil. Wine and oil derive from grapes and olives. Even though they are by-products of fruit, they have a special status because they are part of the sacrificial rituals to Hashem. Thus, even though normally the tithes are separated from the unprocessed produce, in the case of grapes and olives the tithes may be separated after they are made into wine and oil.

445. THE PROHIBITION AGAINST EATING AN UNBLEMISHED FIRST BORN ANIMAL OUTSIDE JERUSALEM

Thou mayest not eat within thy gates the tithe of thy corn, or of thy wine, or of thine oil, or the firstlings of thy herd or of thy flock, nor any of thy vows which thou vowest, nor thy freewill-offerings, nor the offering of thy hand; but thou shalt eat them before the LORD thy God in the place which the LORD thy God shall choose, thou, and thy son, and thy daughter, and thy man-servant, and thy maid-servant, and the Levite that is within thy gates; and thou shalt rejoice before the LORD thy God in all that thou puttest thy hand unto. (Deuteronomy 12:17-18)

Mitzvah 445 forbids the Kohanim from eating first born animals outside Jerusalem.

First born unblemished animals have a holier status than their younger siblings. Jerusalem is the holiest city in the world. Therefore, only the Kohanim, Hashem's servants, may eat these animals, but just in Jerusalem. If a Kohen eats the animal outside Jerusalem, he must be whipped. A non-Kohen may not eat this holy animal. Doing so earns the guilty party lashes of the whip.

For more details about this Mitzvah and the holiness of the first born, consult my write-up of Mitzvah 18.

446. NOT TO EAT OF A HATTATH OR AN ASHAM OUTSIDE THE HOLY TEMPLE

Thou mayest not eat within thy gates the tithe of thy corn, or of thy wine, or of thine oil, or the firstlings of thy herd or of thy flock, nor any of thy vows which thou vowest, nor thy freewill-offerings, nor the offering of thy hand; but thou shalt eat them before the LORD thy God in the place which the LORD thy God shall choose, thou, and thy son, and thy daughter, and thy man-servant, and thy maid-servant, and the Levite that is within thy gates; and thou shalt rejoice before the LORD thy God in all that thou puttest thy hand unto. (Deuteronomy 12:17-18)

Mitzvah 446 forbids the Kohanim from eating the flesh of a Hattat (sin-offering) and an Asham (guilt-offering) outside the Azarah (Sanctuary outside the Temple).

The author of Sefer HaHinnuch explains that the Temple and the Azarah have a high level of holiness. While eating the flesh of these specific animals, the priest must think about the sins the person committed and pray that Hashem forgives the culprit. Eating the flesh of these animals outside these areas can cause the Kohanim to lose focus. It is easier to focus on Hashem when eating in His holy sanctuary.

Peace offerings and offerings of thanksgiving are at a lower status than the sin and guilt offerings. Therefore, the peace offerings and the offerings of thanksgiving can be eaten anywhere in Jerusalem.

When my Partner in Torah first taught me this Mitzvah, my knowledge of the Temple's layout was limited. He patiently explained that the Temple had a number of rooms. There was a courtyard surrounded by a wall. The Western Wall was analogous to the courtyard. The wall surrounded the Temple Mount. The Temple Building was built inside the wall. The primary area inside the Temple was the Azarah, an area closed to everyone, except the Kohanim. It was a large hall, where the altar was located. Inside the large hall is the Holy of Holies, which is part of the Inner Sanctuary.

447. NOT TO EAT THE FLESH OF AN OLAH, A BURNT OFFERING

Thou mayest not eat within thy gates the tithe of thy corn, or of thy wine, or of thine oil, or the firstlings of thy herd or of thy flock, nor any of thy vows which thou vowest, nor thy freewill-offerings, nor the offering of thy hand; but thou shalt eat them before the LORD thy God in the place which the LORD thy God shall choose, thou, and thy son, and thy daughter, and thy man-servant, and thy maid-servant, and the Levite that is within thy gates; and thou shalt rejoice before the LORD thy God in all that thou puttest thy hand unto. (Deuteronomy 12:17-18)

Mitzvah 447 prohibits us from eating any portion of the Olah, the burnt offering. No one, not even the Kohanim, or the Kohen Gadol (High Priest) can eat any portion of this offering.

This prohibition is enforced because the Olah represents a complete submission to Hashem. He receives the entire Olah. The Oral Tradition explains that "The expression 'general pledges' refers to burnt-offerings ... The verse teaches that one who eats from a burnt-offering transgresses a prohibition — whether he does so before or after sprinkling the blood, within the curtains or outside the curtains." For more information, Consult the link, http://m.chabad.org/m/article_cdo/aid/961790 for additional information.

Olah is from the Hebrew root, Ayin-Lamed-Hei (ascension). It is the same root as the word Aliyah, which describes moving to Israel. It also means ascending to the podium to say a blessing over the Torah.

448. NOT TO EAT OF OFFERINGS OF LESSER HOLINESS BEFORE THEIR BLOOD IS SPRINKLED ON THE ALTAR

Thou mayest not eat within thy gates the tithe of thy corn, or of thy wine, or of thine oil, or the firstlings of thy herd or of thy flock, nor any of thy vows which thou vowest, nor thy freewill-offerings, nor the offering of thy hand; but thou shalt eat them before the LORD thy God in the place which the LORD thy God shall choose, thou, and thy son, and thy daughter, and thy man-servant, and thy maid-servant, and the Levite that is within thy gates; and thou shalt rejoice before the LORD thy God in all that thou puttest thy hand unto. (Deuteronomy 12:17-8)

Mitzvah 448 is the prohibition against eating the lower level offerings prior to the sprinkling of the animal's blood onto the altar. These lower level sacrifices are Sh'lamim (peace) offerings and Todah (offerings of giving thanks). A Kohen gathers up the blood of the animal from the container and sprinkles it onto the altar. This act of sprinkling the blood is a spiritual redemption or forgiveness for the person on whose behalf the sacrifice takes place.

The author of Sefer HaHinnuch states:

"It is always worthwhile for us to give preference to the benefit of our spirit over the benefit of our physical body, in every matter in the world. It is therefore not right that the body should have the enjoyment of food before the sprinkling of the blood, which is done to bring atonement to the spirit."

Violating this Mitzvah subjects the guilty party to a whipping.

For more information about this Mitzvah, consult #448 in Sefer HaHinnuch.

449. THAT THE KOHANIM SHOULD NOT EAT BIKKURIM BEFORE THEY ARE SET DOWN IN THE AZARAH, THE SANCTUARY GROUNDS

(Bikkurim means first fruits and Azarah means sanctuary outside the Temple)

Thou mayest not eat within thy gates the tithe of thy corn, or of thy wine, or of thine oil, or the firstlings of thy herd or of thy flock, nor any of thy vows which thou vowest, nor thy freewill-offerings, nor the offering of thy hand; but thou shalt eat them before the LORD thy God in the place which the LORD thy God shall choose, thou, and thy son, and thy daughter, and thy man-servant, and thy maid-servant, and the Levite that is within thy gates; and thou shalt rejoice before the LORD thy God in all that thou puttest thy hand unto. (Deuteronomy 12:17-18)

Mitzvah 449 forbids the Kohanim from eating the Bikkurim anywhere outside the Temple. When Israelites hand the Kohanim their Bikkurim, the Kohanim cannot eat them until they are inside the Temple. The Bikkurim have a high level of holiness and can only be eaten inside the Temple. Israelites may not eat the Bikkurim after they reach Jerusalem. Doing that means death by Heaven's hand. If a Kohen eats the Bikkurim outside the Temple, he is subject to lashes.

450. NOT TO NEGLECT THE LEVITES BY FAILING TO GIVE THEM THEIR GIFTS, ETC.

Take heed to thyself that thou forsake not the Levite as long as thou livest upon thy land. (Deuteronomy 12:19)

Mitzvah 450 is the prohibition against refraining from giving the Levites the gifts that are due them. At the time of the Temple, the Levites were not permitted to own land. When my Partner in Torah and I studied this Mitzvah, he told me that the Levites were given 48 cities. In that respect, the Levites owned land, but unlike the other tribes, they could not do farm work.)

Their key obligation was to serve Hashem in the Temple. The Levites were Hashem's representatives. It was the Israelites responsibility to provide the Levites with tithes. Fulfilling this Mitzvah allowed the Israelites to experience the joy of giving Tzedakah. Giving Tzedakah is obligatory. This Mitzvah makes it possible for the Levites and the Israelites to help each other and to strengthen their harmonious relationships with each other. The Israelites help the Levites by giving them tithes, while the Levites help the Israelites by sharing their Torah knowledge. These two groups benefit from each other. The Israelites gives Tzedakah to the Levites, while the Levites in return share their knowledge of Torah and prayer.

These actions are a manifestation of the assertion of Shimon HaTzaddik (The Righteous) in Tractate Avot, Chapter 1, Mishnah 2: "Upon three things the world exists: Torah, prayer and Tzedakah (love and kindness)."

It is also a fulfillment of what is commanded in Leviticus 19:17:

"Thou shalt not hate thy brother in thy heart; thou shalt surely rebuke thy neighbour, and not bear sin because of him."

There are benefits to giving Tzedakah. In Tractate Avot, Chapter 2, Mishnah 17, Rabbi Yosi said, "Let all your deeds be for the sake of heaven." My Partner in Torah told me that it means: "Tzedakah is the only thing that we can count on that provides a lasting benefit. The charity is truly yours when you give it away."

This corresponds with Numbers 5:10:

"And every man's hallowed things shall be his: whatsoever any man giveth the priest, it shall be his."

451. THE PRECEPT OF SHEHITTAH, RITUAL SLAYING

If the place which the LORD thy God shall choose to put His name there be too far from thee, then thou shalt kill of thy herd and of thy flock, which the LORD hath given thee, as I have commanded thee, and thou shalt eat within thy gates, after all the desire of thy soul. (Deuteronomy 12:21)

Mitzvah 451 commands us to slaughter animals and birds in a specific way for them to be kosher. The knife must be smooth, not serrated.

The animals have two pipes -a food and wind pipe- that pass from the mouth and nose to the neck. The knife has to go through the majority of both pipes, but with the bird, cutting through just one pipe is required.

Using the knife on the animals' pipes will drain them of their blood–the life force. Hashem forbids us to eat the animals' life force.

Using a knife on an animal in one of the following five ways will disqualify the creature from being kosher: pausing, pressing down, incising underneath ((cutting the animal from between the pipes instead of from the outsides), swerving, and tearing. These ways cause the animal great and unnecessary suffering.

For additional details on how to use the knife to properly and humanely slay an animal in order for it to be kosher, consult the write-up of Mitzvah 451 in Sefer HaHinnuch.

452. NOT TO EAT A LIMB OR PART TAKEN FROM A LIVING ANIMAL

Only be steadfast in not eating the blood; for the blood is the life; and thou shalt not eat the life with the flesh. (Deuteronomy 12:23) And ye shall be holy men unto Me; therefore ye shall not eat any flesh that is torn of beasts in the field; ye shall cast it to the dogs. (Exodus 22:30)

Mitzvah 452 prohibits us from eating the limbs of live animals. If an animal's limb was severed while it was alive, we cannot eat it because it is inhumane.

This Mitzvah is one of the seven Noachide Mitzvot that non-Jews must observe.

(In my write-up of Mitzvah 410, I list the seven Noachide Mitzvot.)

453. TO ATTEND TO BRINGING AN ANIMAL OFFERING FROM ANOTHER LAND TO THE SANCTUARY

Only thy holy things which thou hast, and thy vows, thou shalt take, and go unto the place which the LORD shall choose; and thou shalt offer thy burnt-offerings, the flesh and the blood, upon the altar of the LORD thy God; and the blood of thy sacrifices shall be poured out against the altar of the LORD thy God, and thou shalt eat the flesh. (Deuteronomy 12:26-27)

Mitzvah 453 commands us to bring our animals that are to be sacrificed to the Temple without procrastinating. Whether bringing the animal from the Land of Israel or outside The Land of Israel, there should be no delay, once the obligation to bring a sacrifice occurred. He has the following Three Festivals to fulfill his vow. If the next Festival were Sukkot, then he can either bring the animal to be sacrificed on Sukkot, Passover, or Shavuot.

The author of Sefer HaHinnuch states that animals chosen for sacrifice have the same level of holiness. One slated animal is not holier than another slated animal.

454. THE PROHIBITION AGAINST ADDING TO THE PRECEPTS OF THE TORAH

All this word which I command you, that shall ye observe to do; thou shalt not add thereto, nor diminish from it. (Deuteronomy 13:1)

Mitzvah 454 prohibits us from adding additional Mitzvot. Neither precepts nor prohibitions can be added. The total number of Mitzvot is 613 and that is how it is to remain.

The Oral and Written Torah, which Hashem gave to Moses, was perfect. Everything Hashem does is perfect. To add to the Torah would eliminate its perfection.

455. NOT TO DIMINISH THE PRECEPTS OF THE TORAH IN ANYWAY

All this word which I command you, that shall ye observe to do; thou shalt not add thereto, nor diminish from it. (Deuteronomy 13:1)

Mitzvah 455 prohibits us from reducing the scope of the Mitzvot. For example, if an animal's blood needs to be sprinkled four times, we cannot sprinkle it just one time. That would be diminishing the scope of the Mitzvah.

456. TO PAY NO HEED TO ANYONE PROPHESYING IN THE NAME OF AN IDOL OR IDOLATRY

thou shalt not hearken unto the words of that prophet, or unto that dreamer of dreams; for the LORD your God putteth you to proof, to know whether ye do love the LORD your God with all your heart and with all your soul. (Deuteronomy 13:4)

Mitzvah 456 prohibits us from heeding false prophets who claim to be prophets in the name of idols. As soon as people do that, ignore them. Do not ask them to show you signs. Do not converse with them. Do not listen to what they have to say.

457. TO HAVE NO AFFECTION FOR AN ENTICER TO IDOLATRY

thou shalt not consent unto him, nor hearken unto him; neither shall thine eye pity him, neither shalt thou spare, neither shalt thou conceal him; (Deuteronomy 13:9)

Mitzvah 457 commands us to have no affection for enticers of idolatry. Do not love, like, or show favor to someone who persuades Israelites to worship idols.

458. NOT TO RELINQUISH HATRED FOR AN ENTICER TO IDOLATRY

thou shalt not consent unto him, nor hearken unto him; neither shall thine eye pity him, neither shalt thou spare, neither shalt thou conceal him; (Deuteronomy 13:9)

Mitzvah 458 prohibits us from reducing our antipathy for enticers who persuade Jews to worship idols. We must distance ourselves from enticers. Despising them, helps fulfill this Mitzvah.

459. NOT TO RESCUE FROM DEATH AN ENTICER TO IDOL-WORSHIP

thou shalt not consent unto him, nor hearken unto him; neither shall thine eye pity him, neither shalt thou spare, neither shalt thou conceal him; (Deuteronomy 13:9)

Mitzvah 459 prohibits us from saving the lives of enticers of idol-worship. These individuals attempt to persuade Israelites to abandon Hashem, which is reprehensible.

460. THAT SOMEONE ENTICED TO IDOLATRY SHOULD NOT SPEAK IN FAVOR OF THE ENTICER

thou shalt not consent unto him, nor hearken unto him; neither shall thine eye pity him, neither shalt thou spare, neither shalt thou conceal him; (Deuteronomy 13:9)

Mitzvah 460 prohibits Israelites whom were led astray by enticers of idol-worship to speak out in favor of such individuals. When an enticer is on trial, the enticer's victim must not provide evidence that would make the guilty party appear favorable. This prohibition must be observed after it is proven that the culprit led people to idol-worship.

461. THAT A PERSON ENTICED TO IDOL-WORSHIP SHOULD NOT REFRAIN FROM SPEAKING OUT AGAINST THE ENTICER

thou shalt not consent unto him, nor hearken unto him; neither shall thine eye pity him, neither shalt thou spare, neither shalt thou conceal him; (Deuteronomy 13:9)

Mitzvah 461 prohibits Israelites, whom enticers to idolatry led astray, from withholding detrimental evidence that can be used against the enticers.

462. NOT TO ENTICE AN ISRAELITE TOWARD IDOL-WORSHIP

And all Israel shall hear, and fear, and shall do no more any such wickedness as this is in the midst of thee. (Deuteronomy 13:12)

Mitzvah 462 is the prohibition against subverting and persuading Israelites to worship idols.

If the enticer's intended victim refuses, the enticer is still brought before the Sanhedrin to be put to death because of the magnitude of the offense.

Before a person is put on trial for capital punishment, two witnesses must warn the person to stop. However, an enticer receives no warning. In all cases, the offending party would know that there are two witnesses observing him/her breaking the law. However, that is not the case with the enticer. The witnesses can conceal their presence from the enticer. Once they hear or see him/her entice an Israelite, they can bring the culprit to the Sanhedrin.

463. THE PRECEPT OF EXAMINING WITNESSES THOROUGHLY

then shalt thou inquire, and make search, and ask diligently; and, behold, if it be truth, and the thing certain, that such abomination is wrought in the midst of thee; (Deuteronomy 13:15)

Mitzvah 463 commands that witnesses receive a thorough examination.

They are asked, the year that they witnessed the crime. Other questions include:

Which septenate of the seven-year cycles in the Jubilee period did the event occur?

Of which year of the seven in the septennate did the crime take place?

What was the month?

What was the day of the month?

What was the day of the week?

What was the hour of the day?

Where did the crime take place?

If the accused is on trial for idol-worship, the witnesses are asked to describe the type of idol worshipped, how he or she worshipped the idol. In the case of working on Shabbat, the witnesses are asked to describe the type of work that the accused performed.

Secondary questions include:

What did that person wear on the day he/she committed the offense?

Not remembering can affect the outcome of the case when it comes to primary questions.

If the two witnesses' testimonies are contradictory, the case becomes null and void.

Consult Sefer HaHinnuch for more details about conflicting testimonies. Also see Tractate Sanhedrin, Chapter 5, Mishnah 1.

464. THE PRECEPT OF BURNING A CITY GONE ASTRAY INTO IDOLATRY

And thou shalt gather all the spoil of it into the midst of the broad place thereof, and shall burn with fire the city, and all the spoil thereof every whit, unto the LORD thy God; and it shall be a heap for ever; it shall not be built again. (Deuteronomy 13:17)

Mitzvah 464 commands us to destroy apostate cities in Israel that have gone astray. This means that such cities turned to idol worship. This excludes the cities on the border, the Cities of Refuge, and Jerusalem.

The idol worshippers of that city are also to be killed. It says in Deuteronomy 13:14-17:

"Certain base fellows are gone out from the midst of thee, and have drawn away the inhabitants of their city, saying: Let us go and serve other gods, which ye have not known'; then shalt thou inquire, and make search, and ask diligently; and, behold, if it be truth, and the thing certain, that such abomination is wrought in the midst of thee; thou shalt surely smite the inhabitants of that city with the edge of the sword, destroying it utterly, and all that is therein and the cattle thereof, with the edge of the sword. And thou shalt gather all the spoil of it into the midst of the broad place thereof, and shall burn with fire the city, and all the spoil thereof every whit, unto the LORD thy God; and it shall be a heap for ever; it shall not be built again."

465. NOT TO REBUILD TO ITS FORMER CONDITION A CITY GONE ASTRAY INTO IDOLATRY

And thou shalt gather all the spoil of it into the midst of the broad place thereof, and shall burn with fire the city, and all the spoil thereof every whit, unto the LORD thy God; and it shall be a heap for ever; it shall not be built again. (Deuteronomy 13:17)

Mitzvah 465 prohibits rebuilding misled cities. The reason is obvious: Abandoning Hashem to serve idols is a heinous crime. That city must be destroyed just as a poisonous snake so it does not come back.

Mitzvah 465 prohibits us from rebuilding apostate cities.

466. TO DERIVE NO BENEFIT FROM THE WEALTH OF A CITY GONE ASTRAY INTO IDOLATRY

And there shall cleave nought of the devoted thing to thy hand, that the LORD may turn from the fierceness of His anger, and show thee mercy, and have compassion upon thee, and multiply thee, as He hath sworn unto thy fathers; (Deuteronomy 13:18)

Mitzvah 466 is the prohibition against deriving benefit from the riches or other material possessions of the city that was burnt, due to idol worship. Please consult my write-up of Mitzvah 429 for more information.

467. THE PROHIBITION AGAINST GASHING ONESELF AS IDOL-WORSHIPPERS DO

Ye are the children of the LORD your God: ye shall not cut yourselves, nor make any baldness between your eyes for the dead. (Deuteronomy 14:1) Ye shall not make any cuttings in your flesh for the dead, nor imprint any marks upon you: I am the LORD. (Leviticus 19:28)

Mitzvah 467 prohibits us from cutting ourselves with knives or any instruments when mourning the loss of a loved-one or in the name of an idol. Idol-worshippers perform these deeds and we cannot emulate them in any way whatsoever. Violating this Mitzvah subjects the guilty party to receive lashes of the whip.

In the First Book of Kings Chapter 18 Verse 28 idol worshippers prayed to Baal for fire, while the Prophet Elijah prayed to Hashem. The Baal worshippers: "cried aloud, and cut themselves according to their manner with knives and lancets, till the blood gushed out upon them."

When we lose a loved-one, we are sad and we mourn, however, we understand that Hashem decides our fate. I discussed in my write-up of Mitzvah 151 that mourners must say the blessing: "Baruch Atah Hashem, Eloheinu Melekh Ha-Olam Dayan Ha-Emet." **(Blessed are thou, Lord our G-d, King of the Universe, the true Judge.) (See my write-up of Mitzvah 151 for more details.)**

468. NOT TO CAUSE BALDNESS, TEARING THE HAIR IN GRIEF OVER THE DEAD

Ye are the children of the LORD your God: ye shall not cut yourselves, nor make any baldness between your eyes for the dead. (Deuteronomy 14:1)

Mitzvah 468 forbids us to make bald spots on our heads as a sign of mourning. We cannot pull our hair out, or use an instrument to do the job. In addition, we cannot hire someone to remove our hair either. Those who violate this Mitzvah are subject to floggings.

The reasons for this prohibition are the same ones I provided in my write-up of Mitzvah 467 when I explained why we cannot gash ourselves as a way of mourning.

469. NOT TO EAT HOLY ANIMAL OFFERINGS THAT BECAME DISQUALIFIED

Thou shalt not eat any abominable thing. (Deuteronomy 14:3)

Mitzvah 469 is the prohibition against eating invalidated sacrifices. Certain processes must be followed to sacrifice an animal, and if not performed, the sacrifice becomes invalidated. There are also external occurrences that can invalidate a sacrifice. An example of this type of disqualification is a blemish on the animal. Once that is discovered, the animal cannot be eaten. It has lost its holiness.

According to the Midrash, Deuteronomy 14:3 refers to disqualified animals. For more details, consult Mitzvah 469 in Sefer HaHinnuch.

470. THE RELIGIOUS DUTY OF EXAMINING THE MARKS OF A FOWL, IF IT MAY BE EATEN

Of all clean birds ye may eat. (Deuteronomy 14:11)

Mitzvah 470 obligates us to check the signs of a kosher bird. I covered this material in my write-up of Mitzvah 157. As mentioned there, the bird must have a crop as part of his digestive system. It has to have a gizzard that we can peel. It must have a back claw transposed to its other claws. The bird cannot grasp its food in its claws when it eats. The bird does not need to have all four of these signs. One would suffice, except the Torah lists 24 species that have one or more of these signs that would make it kosher, but they are listed as not being kosher. We would eat birds that have a tradition of being kosher.

471. TO EAT NO UNCLEAN, NON-KOSHER LOCUSTS, NOR ANY WINGED INSECTS

And all winged swarming things are unclean unto you; they shall not be eaten. (Deuteronomy 14:19)

Mitzvah 471 prohibits us from eating flying insects. Insects are a different species than birds. Whatever prohibition there is about non-kosher birds, it does not apply here because ALL flying insects are non-kosher with the exception of certain locusts. These forbidden flying insects include bees, flies, and wasps.

472. NOT TO EAT THE FLESH OF ANY KOSHER ANIMAL THAT DIED OF ITSELF

Ye shall not eat of any thing that dieth of itself; thou mayest give it unto the stranger that is within thy gates, that he may eat it; or thou mayest sell it unto a foreigner; for thou art a holy people unto the LORD thy God. Thou shalt not seethe a kid in its mother's milk. (Deuteronomy 14:21)

Mitzvah 472 forbids us to eat a kosher animal that died through any other means than being slaughtered in a kosher manner. We can give or sell that dead animal to non-Jews for them to derive benefit if they wish to make purchase it.

473. THE PRECEPT OF THE SECOND TITHE

Thou shalt surely tithe all the increase of thy seed, that which is brought forth in the field year by year. And thou shalt eat before the LORD thy God, in the place which He shall choose to cause His name to dwell there, the tithe of thy corn, of thy wine, and of thine oil, and the firstlings of thy herd and of thy flock; that thou mayest learn to fear the LORD thy God always. (Deuteronomy 14:22-23)

Mitzvah 473 commands us to separate out the Second Tithe (Ma'aser Sheni). The First Tithe goes to a Levi; the Second Tithe gets separated out so that the owner can eat it in Jerusalem. As an alternative, the owner can exchange that tithe for money and add 20 percent to it, yet he must buy food with that sum of money in Jerusalem. Then he must eat the food he purchased with that sum of money in Jerusalem. The money is considered the Second Tithe. This Mitzvah only applies in the first, second, fourth and fifth years of the 7-year cycle.

474. THE PRECEPT OF THE TITHE FOR THE POOR, IN PLACE OF THE SECOND TITHE IN THE THIRD YEAR

At the end of every three years, even in the same year, thou shalt bring forth all the tithe of thine increase, and shall lay it up within thy gates. (Deuteronomy 14:28)

Mitzvah 474 commands us to separate out the tithes for poor people. This is complimentary to Mitzvah 473 in that this takes place in the third and sixth years of the 7-year cycle. A difference in how the owner gives his primary tithe to the Levi and this tithe to the poor is that the owner can choose which Levi will benefit. However, that is not the case with the poor. If a poor person asks for a portion of the tithe, the owner must oblige. He needs to give the poor person a meal's worth. That portion should be enough to satisfy the owner himself if he were hungry. If several poor people pass and want the tithe, the owner does not choose. He leaves the tithe there for the poor people to distribute amongst themselves.

475. NOT TO DEMAND PAYMENT FOR A LOAN OVER WHICH THE SEVENTH YEAR SH'MITTAH HAS PASSED

And this is the manner of the release: every creditor shall release that which he hath lent unto his neighbour; he shall not exact it of his neighbour and his brother; because the LORD'S release hath been proclaimed. (Deuteronomy 15:2)

Mitzvah 475 commands us not to demand debt payments in the sh'mittah Year.Loans are cancelled with the end of the Sh'mittah Year. It prohibits the lender from claiming payment for the loan.

When my Partner in Torah and I covered this Mitzvah, he told me that the lender can assign the loan to a Jewish court of Law and that the court can collect at any time, even during the seventh year. (This is the Prozbol procedure, established by the Sage Hillel so as to encourage lenders not to refrain from lending close to Sh'mittah.

See Tractate Sheviit, Chapter 10, Mishnayot 3-4.)

Violating this negative Mitzvah does not require the culprit to receive lashes because a violation does not involve physical action, just verbal.

476. THE PRECEPT OF EXACTING A LOAN RIGOROUSLY FROM A HEATHEN

Of a foreigner thou mayest exact it; but whatsoever of thine is with thy brother thy hand shall release. (Deuteronomy 15:3)

Mitzvah 476 commands us to collect our debts from Non-Jews in a timely fashion. This forces Non-Jews to pay their debts on time. We should not give them extensions on paying the loans or have compassion for them. The author of Sefer HaHinnuch states that extending the loan and having compassion might tempt Jews to emulate non-Jews, which includes idol worship.

477. THE PRECEPT OF RELINQUISHING MONEY OWED IN THE SEVENTH YEAR

Of a foreigner thou mayest exact it; but whatsoever of thine is with thy brother thy hand shall release. (Deuteronomy 15:3)

Mitzvah 477 forbids us from demanding money from the people who owe it to us in the Seventh (Sh'mittah) Year of the

Seven-Year cycle. In the Sh'mittah Year, we release these people from the obligation of having to repay their loans.

This Mitzvah helps instill generosity. It also forces us to practice the Mitzvah of loving fellow Jews. There are exceptions. If someone works for us, that person is to be paid the money owed him, even during the seventh year. My Partner in Torah explained that forgiving debts would also reduce possible temptations on the part of the lender to steal. This Mitzvah occurs at the end of the SeventhYear, and it is still applicable today.

478. NOT TO REFRAIN FROM SUSTAINING A POOR MAN AND GIVING HIM WHAT HE NEEDS

If there be among you a needy man, one of thy brethren, within any of thy gates, in thy land which the LORD thy God giveth thee, thou shalt not harden thy heart, nor shut thy hand from thy needy brother; (Deuteronomy 17:7)

Mitzvah 478 commands us to provide financial assistance to fellow Jews in need. It forbids us to act miserly. This Mitzvah allows us to practice being generous. It also reinforces the commandment that we are to love our fellow Jews. This Mitzvah is applicable today.

479. THE MITZVAH OF CHARITY

but thou shalt surely open thy hand unto him, and shalt surely lend him sufficient for his need in that which he wanteth. (Deuteronomy 15:8)

Mitzvah 479 commands us to give charity without condescension. The recipient is already in a state of ignominy by having to rely on a handout. Under no circumstances are we to add to that person's suffering. The proper way to give charity is by handing the money to an official charity collector. He would collect the funds and distribute it to the poor. The recipient is not to know who gives him the money and the charity giver is not to know who receives his money. This prevents embarrassment. Reminding the recipient of who gave him the money can worsen his state of embarrassment. It is a vulgar display of sanctimony void of generosity. We are to give to the poor not to make ourselves feel important, rather we do it because we are commanded to love fellow Jews.

480. THAT WE SHOULD NOT AVOID LENDING MONEY TO THE POOR BECAUSE OF SH'MITTAH

Beware that there be not a base thought in thy heart, saying: 'The seventh year, the year of release, is at hand'; and thine eye be evil against thy needy brother, and thou give him nought; and he cry unto the LORD against thee, and it be sin in thee.. (Deuteronomy 15:9)

Mitzvah 480 forbids us from refusing to lend money to people in need because of the Sh'mittah year. In the Sh'mittah year, debts are cancelled. Therefore, we must not refuse to lend money because of the approach of Sh'mittah, out of concern that the loan will not be repaid. Fulfilling this Mitzvah helps prevent us from being miserly.

481. NOT TO SEND AWAY A HEBREW MANSERVANT EMPTY-HANDED WHEN HE GOES FREE

And when thou lettest him go free from thee, thou shalt not let him go empty; (Deuteronomy 15:13)

Mitzvah 481 prohibits us from sending away our newly freed Jewish manservants empty-handed. In the Sh'mittah year, we have to free our Jewish slaves. Because he will have to take care of himself, he will need money, food, and possessions such as animals. Before the destruction of the Second Temple, owning animals was advantageous because they worked our land, generated income, and were a source of food for us.

482. THE PRECEPT OF GIVING A BONUS TO A HEBREW MANSERVANT AT HIS DISCHARGE

If thy brother, a Hebrew man, or a Hebrew woman, be sold unto thee, he shall serve thee six years; and in the seventh year thou shalt let him go free from thee. And when thou lettest him go free from thee, thou shalt not let him go empty; thou shalt furnish him liberally out of thy flock, and out of thy threshing-floor, and out of thy winepress; of that wherewith the LORD thy God hath blessed thee thou shalt give unto him. (Deuteronomy 15:12-14)

Mitzvah 482 commands us to give our newly freed Hebrew manservant gifts, such as food and animals. We are to give him the means to start a new life. The Torah tries to instill in us traits of generosity and appreciation for people who had worked for us, especially as their service far outweighed the time that they served. Instructing us to give the gifts helps us develop our own fine characteristics.

The Torah does not regard cash and clothing as gifts. The animals and food help to permanently sustain the newly freed servant because these things generate wealth. A sheep provides wool; a cow provides milk. Animals can work the land, and can be sold. This Mitzvah applies to freed Hebrew manservants and freed Hebrew females, and it is in effect when the Temple is extant.

On a personal note, over 50 years ago, my parents benefited from aspects of this Mitzvah. My mother's affluent and generous cousins, Edna and Stan Tuttleman, provided her and my father with the means to start a new life in the U.S. When my parents left Cuba in 1960 because of Fidel Castro, they arrived to Philadelphia without money or a place to live. Edna and Stan provided them with an apartment and my father with a car so that he could look for work. The car made it possible for him to drive to job interviews and then to work until he could make enough money to purchase his own car. Having a place to live and a car freed him to focus on earning income.

483. TO DO NO WORK WITH ANIMALS CONSECRATED FOR OFFERINGS

All the firstling males that are born of thy herd and of thy flock thou shalt sanctify unto the LORD thy God; thou shalt do no work with the firstling of thine ox, nor shear the firstling of thy flock. (Deuteronomy 15:19)

Mitzvah 483 forbids us from making our holy animals do any form of work. Holy animals include firstlings. We must sacrifice these animals to Hashem. Therefore, these animals cannot work the land. Because they are holy, no one can shear their wool. They have a holy function to perform, being sacrificed to Hashem. Therefore, we are forbidden to do these things mentioned here that would reduce and eliminate their status of holiness.

484. NOT TO SHEAR ANIMALS CONSECRATED FOR OFFERINGS

All the firstling males that are born of thy herd and of thy flock thou shalt sanctify unto the LORD thy God; thou

shalt do no work with the firstling of thine ox, nor shear the firstling of thy flock. (Deuteronomy 15:19)

Mitzvah 484 forbids us from shearing holy animals. Consult my my write-up of Mitzvah 483 for more details.

485. NOT TO EAT HAMETZ AFTER NOON ON THE DAY BEFORE PASSOVER

Thou shalt eat no leavened bread with it; seven days shalt thou eat unleavened bread therewith, even the bread of affliction; for in haste didst thou come forth out of the land of Egypt; that thou mayest remember the day when thou camest forth out of the land of Egypt all the days of thy life. (Deuteronomy 16:3)

Mitzvah 485 is the prohibition against eating Hametz on the afternoon preceding the beginning of the holiday. Two hours before midday is when the prohibition begins. We stop eating two hours before, we burn the Hametz, one hour before midday.

Observing this Mitzvah helps put us in the proper frame of mind to observe Passover and ensures that we do not violate the prohibition of Hametz. This Mitzvah is applicable to men and women, whether or not Hashem's Temple is extant.

486. NOT TO LEAVE OVER TILL THE THIRD DAY ANY FLESH OF THE FESTIVAL OFFERING AT PASSOVER

And there shall be no leaven seen with thee in all they borders seven days; neither shall any of the flesh, which thou sacrificest the first day at even, remain all night until the morning. (Deuteronomy 16:4)

Mitzvah 486 forbids us to keep for a third straight day sacrificed animals for Passover. This does not include the Pascal lamb, which we sacrifice for Passover. (We must eat the Pascal lamb by the midnight of the first night of Passover.) This Mitzvah pertains to the other animals sacrificed for this holiday. We can eat these animals on the eve of Passover and the first full day of the holiday; the 14th and 15th of Nisan. These two days have a high level of holiness and should be celebrated by deriving benefit from these animals. These sacrifices fall into the category of peace offerings, which generally may be eaten the day of slaughtering and the following day, but may not be left over till the third day.

487. NOT TO OFFER UP THE PASSOVER OFFERING ON AN INDIVIDUAL'S PROVISIONAL ALTAR.

Thou mayest not sacrifice the passover-offering within any of thy gates, which the LORD thy God giveth thee; (Deuteronomy 16:5)

Mitzvah 487 prohibits us from sacrificing Passover offerings on private altars.

Before the Temple was built, Jews could sacrifice animals to Hashem on private altars (except during the time when the Tabernacle resided Shiloh). However, animals sacrificed for Passover, were performed exclusively on communal altars. Performing this Mitzvah shows that the animals sacrificed for Passover have a higher level of holiness than the other animals. After the Temple was built, private and communal altars were no longer used. Now all the sacrifices took place in Hashem's Holy Temple in Jerusalem.

488. THE PRECEPT OF BEING HAPPY ON THE PILGRIMAGE FESTIVALS

And thou shalt rejoice in thy feast, thou, and thy son, and thy daughter, and thy man-servant, and thy maid-servant, and the Levite, and the stranger, and the fatherless, and the widow, that are within thy gates. (Deuteronomy 16:14)

Mitzvah 488 commands us to rejoice on the days of Pilgrimage Festivals. When the Jews made their pilgrimages to Jerusalem for the three festivals, they brought peace offerings. They ate festive meals, which consisted of meat and wine, both of which are associated with happiness.

Because meat symbolizes joy, Jews refrain from it during the week of Tisha B'Av because it is a time of mourning. However, meat is allowed on the Shabbat before Tisha B'Av because Shabbat is a day of happiness. Shabbat overrides the Tisha B'Av customs, so if the 9th of Av falls on Shabbat, the fast is postponed until after Shabbat ends.

Other ways Jews displayed happiness during the Festivals was by wearing new clothing and giving out treats to the young children.

489. THE PRECEPT TO APPEAR ON THE PILGRIMAGE FESTIVALS AT THE SANCTUARY

Three times in a year shall all thy males appear before the LORD thy God in the place which He shall choose; on the feast of unleavened bread, and on the feast of weeks, and on the feast of tabernacles; and they shall not appear before the LORD empty; (Deuteronomy 16:16)

Mitzvah 489 commands us to appear at the Temple on Festival days, during the Three Festivals. When we had the First and Second Temples, Jews did not have to spend all their time in Jerusalem, but they had to be there for some of the days. Peace and burnt offerings were sacrificed to Hashem.

The author of Sefer HaHinnuch states that this Mitzvah applies to the men because they are the heads of their families. The women and children have secondary roles and are therefore excused from performing this Mitzvah.

490. NOT TO GO UP TO JERUSALEM FOR A PILGRIMAGE FESTIVAL WITHOUT AN ANIMAL OFFERING

Three times in a year shall all thy males appear before the LORD thy God in the place which He shall choose; on the feast of unleavened bread, and on the feast of weeks, and on the feast of tabernacles; and they shall not appear before the LORD empty; (Deuteronomy 16:16)

Mitzvah 490 prohibits us from appearing without a sacrifice on Festival days at the Temple. The sacrifices to Hashem demonstrate our gratitude. He gave us these joyous days to celebrate. Although Hashem is perfect and does not need our heartfelt thanks, it is vital that we express it because it teaches us not to take anything for granted. This ties in with thanking G-d after every meal. We acquire appreciation for the meal and realize that we can lose that luxury at any moment.

491. THE PRECEPT OF APPOINTING JUDGES AND OFFICERS IN EVERY SINGLE COMMUNITY IN JEWRY

Judges and officers shalt thou make thee in all thy gates, which the LORD thy God giveth thee, tribe by tribe; and they shall judge the people with righteous judgment. (Deuteronomy 16:18)

Mitzvah 491 commands us to appoint judges and court officers in every Jewish community to ensure that the laws of the Torah are obeyed. In regular towns, there needs to be a Beit Din, Rabbinical Court, consisting of 23 members. Twenty-three judges make up a small Sanhedrin. The number 23 was not picked at random. Twenty-three judges constitute a double Minyan. Verdicts cannot end in ties. In capital cases, to find someone guilty, there must be a majority of three, but we only require a majority of one to acquit a person.

For monetary matters, appointing only three judges is sufficient. (See Tractate Sanhedrin, Chapter 1, Mishnah 1.)

To be appointed to the Sanhedrin, the appointees must be upstanding citizens, worldly and knowledgeable of Torah. This ensures that Hashem's Torah will be observed.

492. THE PROHIBITION AGAINST PLANTING TREES IN THE SANCTUARY

Thou shalt not plant thee an Asherah of any kind of tree beside the altar of the LORD thy God, which thou shalt make thee. (Deuteronomy 16:21)

Mitzvah 492 forbids us to plant trees in the sanctuary. Idol worshippers used to do that so this prohibition keeps us from following their customs. Hashem forbids us to emulate those People who violate this Mitzvah. The violation leads to flogging.

493. THE PROHIBITION AGAINST ERECTING AN IDOLATROUS PILLAR

Neither shalt thou set thee up a pillar, which the LORD thy God hateth. (Deuteronomy 16:22)

Mitzvah 493 prohibits us from erecting monuments anywhere at all. Idol worshippers practiced this ritual, therefore, in order to distance ourselves from them, we cannot follow any of their customs. Violating this Mitzvah subjects the culprit to receive a flogging.

494. NOT TO PRESENT AS AN OFFERING AN ANIMAL WITH A TEMPORARY BLEMISH

Thou shalt not sacrifice unto the LORD thy God an ox, or a sheep, wherein is a blemish, even any evil thing; for that is an abomination unto the LORD thy God. (Deuteronomy 17:1)

Mitzvah 494 prohibits us from sacrificing animals to Hashem that have temporary deformities, injuries, and/or blemishes. We must wait for the animal to recover. If the deformities, injuries, and/or blemishes become permanent, then we must replace it with a one-hundred percent healthy animal. (Animals with permanent blemishes are forbidden to be sacrificed to Hashem. More details about this are covered in my Mitzvah write-up of 286.)

495. THE RELIGIOUS DUTY TO HEED EVERY GREAT SANHEDRIN, IN EVERY PERIOD

And thou shalt do according to the tenor of the sentence, which they shall declare unto thee from that place which the LORD shall choose; and thou shalt observe to do according to all that they shall teach thee. (Deuteronomy 17:10)

Mitzvah 495 commands us to abide by whatever the Beit Din dictates. We must accept their decisions, and adhere to them. Other considerations are when there are disputes. If it is a Torah matter, then we must follow the stricter rulings. That is if it pertains to Torah Matters; but in the case of Rabbinic matters, we can rely on the more lenient opinions. If a practice were established in one generation, a later generation cannot undo that practice. For example, there is a Rabbinic prohibition about taking medicine on Shabbat, that was put into place when people made their medicine by grinding. Grinding is forbidden on Shabbat. Today, even though medicine is ready-made, the prohibition is still in place, except in cases of serious illnesses.

496. NOT TO DISOBEY THE WORD OF THE GREAT BET DIN–THE SANHEDRIN

According to the law which they shall teach thee, and according to the judgment which they shall tell thee, thou shalt do; thou shalt not turn aside from the sentence which they shall declare unto thee, to the right hand, nor to the left. (Deuteronomy 17:11)

Mitzvah 496 forbids us to go against the words of the Sages. This reflects the presumption that G-d gave the power and authority to the Sages to interpret the words of the Torah.

This Mitzvah covers Torah Law and Rabbinic Law. Following the words of the Sages, would seem Rabbinic, but it is a Biblical Mitzvah to obey them.

While the Torah is encompassing, we see that Hashem understands that there will be a need to interpret the Torah because the lay person might be unable to understand all of it. If each person follows his own interpretation of the Torah, that would lead to chaos. That is why G-d built in the correcting mechanism to provide the official interpretation. The way that Sages exercise their authority can differ. Certain laws were handed down orally, while others types of laws were based on certain established principles that apply the Torah laws.

When my Partner in Torah and I covered this Mitzvah, he explained that certain laws have more stringencies than others. We also covered the concept of Muktzeh, which means that certain items cannot be moved on Shabbat. We cannot write on Shabbat, therefore, we cannot use a pen or pencil. The Sages created the concept of not being allowed to move items like the pen. Touching the pen can lead one to accidentally writing with it. Muktzehis an avenue that the Sages created to safeguard the laws of the Torah. This is an example of how Sages establish laws.

497. THE PRECEPT OF APPOINTING A KING OVER US

When thou art come unto the land which the LORD thy God giveth thee, and shalt possess it, and shalt dwell therein; and shalt say: 'I will set a king over me, like all the nations that are round about me'; thou shalt in any wise set him king over thee, whom the LORD thy God shall choose; one from among thy brethren shalt thou set king over thee; thou mayest not put a foreigner over thee, who is not thy brother. (Deuteronomy 17:14-15)

Mitzvah 497 obligates us to appoint a Jewish king. At all times, Hashem is our ultimate King. The role of the appointed king is to fulfill the socio-political needs of the nation. There are rules that apply to the king. He has to be appointed by a prophet. Special oil is used to anoint him. The title gets handed down from father to son. This is in the ideal state when the king upholds the laws of the Torah. The king cannot abuse his authority. He must do his part to uphold Hashem's laws. If anyone transgresses the king's decrees or shows him disrespect, that person faces capital punishment. The Talmud discusses several categories of people of whom respect is due. (See Babylonian Talmud Kiddushin 31B.) The son is obligated to honor and respect his father. You cannot sit in your father's chair. He can forego that rule. A father has the right to forego the honor that is due him by his children. A king, unlike an ordinary father, cannot forego the honor that is due him. No one can ride his horse, sit on his throne, or marry his widow. That is a vulgar display of disrespect. These actions lead to capital punishment.

At the same time, the King of Israel needs to be respectful of the nation of Israel.

The King of Israel's key function is to serve the Jewish people and NOT for them to serve him.

On the surface, this Mitzvah and Deuteronomy Chapter 17 verses 14-15 contradict the First Book of Samuel Chapter 8 verses 4-6.

When thou art come unto the land which the LORD thy God giveth thee, and shalt possess it, and shalt dwell therein; and shalt say: 'I will set a king over me, like all the nations that are round about me'; thou shalt in any wise set him king over thee, whom the LORD thy God shall choose; one from among thy brethren shalt thou set king over thee; thou mayest not put a foreigner over thee, who is not thy brother. (Deuteronomy 17:14-17:15)

First Book of Samuel Chapter 8 verses 4-6:

8:4 Then all the elders of Israel gathered themselves together, and came to Samuel unto Ramah, 8:5 And said unto him, Behold, thou art old, and thy sons walk not in thy ways: now make us a king to judge us like all the nations.

8:6 But the thing displeased Samuel, when they said, Give us a king to judge us. And Samuel prayed unto the LORD.

Samuel was upset not because they wanted a king, but because their request was a manifestation of their rejection of Hashem. See First Book of Samuel Chapter 8 verses 7-20:

8:7 And the LORD said unto Samuel, Hearken unto the voice of the people in all that they say unto thee: for they have not rejected thee, but they have rejected me, that I should not reign over them.

8:8 According to all the works which they have done since the day that I brought them up out of Egypt even unto this day, wherewith they have forsaken me, and served other gods, so do they also unto thee.

8:9 Now therefore hearken unto their voice: howbeit yet protest solemnly unto them, and shew them the manner of the king that shall reign over them.

8:10 And Samuel told all the words of the LORD unto the people that asked of him a king.

8:11 And he said, This will be the manner of the king that shall reign over you: He will take your sons, and appoint them for himself, for his chariots, and to be his horsemen; and some shall run before his chariots.

8:12 And he will appoint him captains over thousands, and captains over fifties; and will set them to ear his ground, and to reap his harvest, and to make his instruments of war, and instruments of his chariots.

8:13 And he will take your daughters to be confectionaries, and to be cooks, and to be bakers.

8:14 And he will take your fields, and your vineyards, and your oliveyards, even the best of them, and give them to his servants.

8:15 And he will take the tenth of your seed, and of your vineyards, and give to his officers, and to his servants.

8:16 And he will take your menservants, and your maidservants, and your goodliest young men, and your asses, and put them to his work.

8:17 He will take the tenth of your sheep: and ye shall be his servants.

8:18 And ye shall cry out in that day because of your king which ye shall have chosen you; and the LORD will not hear you in that day.

8:19 Nevertheless the people refused to obey the voice of Samuel; and they said, Nay; but we will have a king over us; 8:20 That we also may be like all the nations; and that our king may judge us, and go out before us, and fight our battles.

This portion of the First Book of Samuel demonstrates that there were no contradictions. Samuel was a righteous and learned prophet and Hashem's faithful servant. He never would have contradicted any words from G-d's Torah.

498. NOT TO APPOINT ANYONE KING OVER THE PEOPLE OF ISRAEL BUT AN ISRAELITE

thou shalt in any wise set him king over thee, whom the LORD thy God shall choose; one from among thy brethren shalt thou set king over thee; thou mayest not put a foreigner over thee, who is not thy brother. (Deuteronomy 17:15)

Mitzvah 498 forbids us to appoint a non-Jewish king. Converts to Judaism are also excluded. The king must be of Israelite descent. There are innate characteristics endowed with the Jewish people, which explain why the king must be a native-born Jew. Such characteristics include possessing mercy, and a sense of true justice. The Sages extended this to other people with positions of authority. They too would have to be naturally born Jews. One such person is in charge of the water system. The water fulfills a critical need. A position of such importance cannot be given to a convert for the exact reasons why a convert can never be king of Israel.

499. THAT THE KING SHOULD NOT ACQUIRE AN UNDULY GREAT NUMBER OF HORSES

Only he shall not multiply horses to himself, nor cause the people to return to Egypt, to the end that he should multiply

horses; forasmuch as the LORD hath said unto you: 'Ye shall henceforth return no more that way.' (Deuteronomy 17:16)

Mitzvah 499 prohibits the king from having too many horses. He can have the horses he needs for his chariot and cavalry, but he cannot have extra horses for the sake of creating an impression. This Mitzvah prevents the king from showing off his high ranking position. He can have a sufficient supply for a war. He can have spare ones, within reason. This stops him from grabbing too much honor. The Torah warns against going back to Egypt. If he fills his stable with horses and wants more, he might want to go back to Egypt. This forbids him to go back to Egypt. Too many horses might compel him to go to Egypt to get supplies to take care of the vast amount.

500. NOT TO EVER DWELL IN THE LAND OF EGYPT

Only he shall not multiply horses to himself, nor cause the people to return to Egypt, to the end that he should multiply horses; forasmuch as the LORD hath said unto you: 'Ye shall henceforth return no more that way.' (Deuteronomy 17:16)

Mitzvah 500 forbids us to dwell in the Land of Egypt on a permanent basis. The Egyptians were immoral people who enslaved us. Other Torah passages forbid us to return to Egypt. Exodus 14:13: And Moses said unto the people: 'Fear ye not, stand still, and see the salvation of the LORD, which He will work for you to-day; for whereas ye have seen the Egyptians to-day, ye shall see them again no more for ever." Leviticus 18:3-4: "After the doings of the Land of Egypt, wherein ye dwelt, shall ye not do; and after the doings of the land of Canaan, whither I bring you, shall ye not do; neither shall ye walk in their statutes. Mine ordinances shall ye do, and My statutes shall ye keep, to walk therein: I am the LORD your God."

There were times when thriving Jewish communities lived in Egypt. Even RAMBAM lived there. Although Hashem forbade the Jewish people to return to Egypt, He punished his people by sending them back there.

Deuteronomy 28:68: "And the LORD shall bring thee back into Egypt in ships, by the way whereof I said unto thee: 'Thou shalt see it no more again'; and there ye shall sell yourselves unto your enemies for bondmen and for bondwoman, and no man shall buy you."

According to Rabbi Aryeh Citron, this prohibition applied to Jews returning to Egypt, not the future generations who lived there. When RAMBAM lived in Egypt, the Jews were not rulers of the Land of Israel.

501. THAT THE KING SHOULD NOT TAKE HIMSELF AN UNDULY LARGE NUMBER OF WIVES

Neither shall he multiply wives to himself, that his heart turn not away; neither shall he greatly multiply to himself silver and gold. (Deuteronomy 17:17)

Mitzvah 501 forbids the king of Israel to have too many wives; 18 is the limit.

King David had six wives; then he wanted three times the amount, and this was used to define the parameters of unduly large numbers, mentioned in the verse.

King David was the greatest king of Israel, not because of his great fighting skills, but because of his love for Hashem. The Messiah will be King David's descendant. Therefore, future kings of Israel should emulate many of his actions, including loving Hashem and marrying no more than 18 wives. Violating this Mitzvah subjects the king to receive lashes of the whip.

It should be noted that in Judaism, the number 18 is significant because the numeric value of the Hebrew word for life "chai," adds up to 18. Numerically, the word consists of the eighth (8th) and tenth (10th) letters of the Hebrew alphabet Chet (ח) and Yud (י), adding up to eighteen. In Hebrew, the number 18 also means "Chai."

For additional information about the number 18's importance, consult the link:
http://www.shiva.com/learning-center/commemorate/chai/

502. THAT THE KING SHOULD AMASS GOLD AND SILVER INORDINATELY, BUT ONLY WHAT HE NEEDS

Neither shall he multiply wives to himself, that his heart turn not away; neither shall he greatly multiply to himself silver and gold. (Deuteronomy 17:17)

Mitzvah 502 restricts the amount of gold and silver that the king can possess. He may have sufficient gold and silver to sustain his family and servants and to protect the nation. His job is to focus on his people, not himself. The limit prevents him from becoming greedy and haughty.

503. THE KING'S OBLIGATION TO WRITE ONE TORAH SCROLL MORE THAN OTHER ISRAELITES

And it shall be, when he sitteth upon the throne of his kingdom, that he shall write him a copy of this law in a book, out of that which is before the priests the Levites. (Deuteronomy 17:18)

Mitzvah 503 commands the king of Israel to write a second Torah scroll. Mitzvah 613 commands each Jew to write one Torah scroll. The king, unlike the Israelites, must write a second Torah scroll. (People still write Torah scrolls today.)

The king must keep the second scroll with him at all times, except when he is in the bathhouse and/or relieving himself. The king has to write an extra scroll and keep it with him because it reminds him to behave morally and compassionately. Having the Torah in his presence is supposed to keep him righteous.

504. THAT THE TRIBE OF LEVI SHOULD HAVE NO INHERITANCE OF LAND IN ISRAEL

The priests the Levites, even all the tribe of Levi, shall have no portion nor inheritance with Israel; they shall eat the offerings of the LORD made by fire, and His inheritance. (Deuteronomy 18:1)

Mitzvah 504 prohibits the Levite tribe from owning land in Israel. (My Partner in Torah explained to me that Levites were allowed to own land, but they never received a portion through the formal distribution process as did the other tribes.. More details about this were covered in Mitzvah 450.)

The other tribes have portions of land. Hashem commanded the Levites to serve in His Temple. Owning and working the land would distract them from fulfilling that sacred duty. Forty-eight cities are designated for the Levites, along with areas of land outside those 48 cities, but the Levites do not have to work the land because they are required to serve Hashem in His Holy Temple.

505. THAT THE TRIBE OF LEVI SHOULD TAKE NO SHARE OF BOOTY IN THE CONQUEST OF LAND

The priests the Levites, even all the tribe of Levi, shall have no portion nor inheritance with Israel; they shall eat the offerings of the LORD made by fire, and His inheritance. (Deuteronomy 18:1)

Mitzvah 505 prohibits the Levites from getting a share of the spoils of war. After the Israelites took possession of the Land of Israel from the Canaanites, all the tribes, except the Levites, divided everything.

According to the author of Sefer HaHinnuch, the root of this Mitzvah is that because the Levites serve Hashem, it would be unseemly for them to "make use of objects, snatched from the hands of people."

506. THE PRECEPT OF GIVING THE FORELEG, CHEEKS AND MAW OF AN OFFERING TO THE KOHEN

And this shall be the priests' due from the people, from them that offer a sacrifice, whether it be ox or sheep, that they shall give unto the priest the shoulder, and the two cheeks, and the maw. (Deuteronomy 18:3)

Mitzvah 506 commands us to give specific portions of slaughtered animals (no-sacrifices) to the Kohanim; these include the foreleg, the cheek, and the stomach. This Mitzvah honors Pinchas's bravery and staunch loyalty to Hashem. Numbers 25:5–11 documents Pinchas's heroism:

25,5 And Moses said unto the judges of Israel: 'Slay ye every one his men that have joined themselves unto the Baal of Peor.' 25,6 And, behold, one of the children of Israel came and brought unto his brethren a Midianitish woman in the sight of Moses, and in the sight of all the congregation of the children of Israel, while they were weeping at the door of the tent of meeting. 25,7 And when Phinehas, the son of Eleazar, the son of Aaron the priest, saw it, he rose up from the midst of the congregation, and took a spear in his hand. 25,8 And he went after the man of Israel into the chamber, and thrust both of them through, the man of Israel, and the woman through her belly. So the plague was stayed from the children of Israel. 25,9 And those that died by the plague were twenty and four thousand. {P}

25,10 And the LORD spoke unto Moses, saying: 25,11 'Phinehas, the son of Eleazar, the son of Aaron the priest, hath turned My wrath away from the children of Israel, in that he was very jealous for My sake among them, so that I consumed not the children of Israel in My jealousy.

Pinchas struck the sinners with his forearm. We give the front legs of the animal to the Kohanim because the front legs of the animals are equivalent to humans' arms. We give the cheeks to the Kohanim to remember that Pinchas spent extra time praying for the Nation of Israel before he killed the sinners. The cow has four stomachs, and we give the Keva to the priest because that one is most similar to the human belly. Pinchas hit the sinners in their stomachs.

If the priest has an animal and slaughters it, he is exempt from giving portions to other priests.

To learn more about this Mitzvah andfor further details about the Keva, consult the website, http://kehuna.org/matanot-kehuna/zeroalechayayimandkeva/and and read the article, Zeroa, Llechayayim and Keva.

507. THE RELIGIOUS DUTY OF SEPARATING THE "GREAT T'RUMAH–THE KOHEN'S PORTION FROM PRODUCE

The first-fruits of thy corn, of thy wine, and of thine oil, and the first of the fleece of thy sheep, shalt thou give him. (Deuteronomy 18:4)

Mitzvah 507 commands us to give T'rumah (a portion of our crops) to the Kohanim. The Torah never defined the appropriate amount that we are to give them. The Sages decided that the minimum amount would be two percent. We can give more than that. We can give two and a half percent (deemed by the Sages as a generous amount). Two percent of the crops that is set aside for the kohanim is one fiftieth. The crops we give to the priests are grains, wine, and oil because these items sustain us. Those three items are at the Torah level. The items that the Sages added are at the Rabbinic level, that would be food for humans grown from the ground.

The priest's entire household is permitted to eat the donated items, including their children and their non-Jewish servants. His wife can also eat from this, even if she were born a Yisrael, she would still have the same privilege as the rest of the household. The priests' animals can also eat the T'rumah. The reason the household can eat this is that the priest, who is head of the house does not work the land. He does not have a way of producing crops like the other tribes of Israel.He cannot give any to outside company, just his household. This only applies to crops from the Land of Israel.

508. THE PRECEPT OF THE FIRST OF THE FLEECE, THAT IT SHOULD BE GIVEN TO THE KOHEN

The first-fruits of thy corn, of thy wine, and of thine oil, and the first of the fleece of thy sheep, shalt thou give him. (Deuteronomy 18:4)

Mitzvah 508 commands us to give the Kohanim our first shearings of wool.

This Mitzvah must be carried out when the owner has a minimum of five sheep.

The Torah does not specify a portion, so the Rabbis determined the amount to be one sixtieth; that equals about 1.7%.

The primary use for wool is to provide the Kohen and his entire household with clothing.

509. THE PRECEPT THAT THE KOHANIM SHOULD SERVE AT THE SANCTUARY IN WATCHES, AND ALL TOGETHER AT THE FESTIVALS

And if a Levite come from any of thy gates out of all Israel, where he sojourneth, and come with all the desire of his soul unto the place which the LORD shall choose; then he shall minister in the name of the LORD his God, as all his brethren the Levites do, who stand there before the LORD. They shall have like portions to eat, beside that which is his due according to the fathers' houses. (Deuteronomy 18:6-8)

Mitzvah 509 commands the Kohanim and the Levites who work in the Temple to split into shifts. Throughout the year, they work specific shifts, but during the festivals, all the Kohanim are required to work together there.

There are 24 shifts throughout the year. The priests would work two weeks out of the year, and then about another two weeks during the festivals. Samuel and King David devised this strategy because they knew that if many people were assigned to do jobs at once instead of a few, that could risk nothing getting done, but if fewer people had the responsibility to perform certain duties, these jobs would get done more efficiently.

Certain things have not changed much over time. For example, the 1968 (CE) Darley and Latane experiment documents that if fewer people witness an emergency, they would more than likely help than if a number of people witnessed the same thing. The victim of a mugging has a greater chance of getting help if one person witnesses it rather than if many people see it.

Consult the link:
http://www.appsychology.com/IB%20Psych/IBcontent/Studies/Latane%20and%20Darley.htm

510. THE PROHIBITION AGAINST THE PRACTICE OF DIVINATION

There shall not be found among you any one that maketh his son or his daughter to pass through the fire, one that useth divination, a soothsayer, or an enchanter, or a sorcerer, (Deuteronomy 18:10)

Mitzvah 510 prohibits us from focusing on developing powers to foretell the near future.

According to the author of Sefer HaHinnuch, developing this power requires complete concentration. Doing so can cause us to enter a spiritual realm and see the near future. They cannot see the distant future, only Hashem's prophets can. The Sages frown on Jews who learn to become fortunetellers, because they would have to put all their energy into the craft and neglect developing and strengthening themselves as a whole; physically, mentally, and intellectually to better serve Hashem. . Worse, it prevents this individual from continuing to enhance his Torah knowledge. Only Hashem knows the future and the prophets can see into the future, but only with Hashem's help.

511. NOT TO PRACTICE SORCERY

There shall not be found among you any one that maketh his son or his daughter to pass through the fire, one that useth divination, a soothsayer, or an enchanter, or a sorcerer, (Deuteronomy 18:10)

Mitzvah 511 is the prohibition against performing witchcraft. This includes not using grass or stones to perform magic.

My Partner in Torah told me that the Talmud mentioned that a Rabbinical judge has to have a working knowledge of witchcraft so that he can tell if someone's actions result from witchcraft or not, but like the Jewish nation, he cannot practice it. The only times when practicing witchcraft has been allowed was for healing sick people. However, that person could not be superstitious or carry good luck charms such as a rabbit's foot.

Consult my Mitzvah 62 write-up for additional details about this topic.

512. THE PROHIBITION AGAINST EMPLOYING CHARMS

There shall not be found among you any one that maketh his son or his daughter to pass through the fire, one that useth divination, a soothsayer, or an enchanter, or a sorcerer, 18,11

or a charmer, or one that consulteth a ghost or a familiar spirit, or a necromancer. (Deuteronomy 18:10–11)

Mitzvah 512 is the prohibition against using spells and incantations. No one can resort to these practices, not even to drive away snakes or to become free of pain. However, words of Torah can be used to reduce pain and suffering because that puts the living soul on a path to recovery; in addition, saying words of Torah can compel Hashem to intercede on the sick person's behalf. Spells and incantations can be used to heal sick people because the Torah places more importance on life than anything else. Preserving life takes precedence over observing Shabbat. To save a life, one can violate Shabbat. (See Tractate Yoma, Chapter 8, Mishnah 6.)

513. NOT TO CONSULT AN OV, A KIND OF MEDIUM

There shall not be found among you any one that maketh his son or his daughter to pass through the fire, one that useth divination, a soothsayer, or an enchanter, or a sorcerer, 18,11 or a charmer, or one that consulteth a ghost or a familiar spirit, or a necromancer. (Deuteronomy 18:10–11)

Mitzvah 513 prohibits necromancy. The author of Sefer HaHinnuch mentions that the practitioner would raise the dead person under his arm pit; the person seeking advice would ask the deceased questions, and would hear the dead person's advice through the armpit of the sorcerer. This practice is forbidden. For more details, consult Mitzvah 511. In addition, see my write up of Mitzvah 255.

514. THE PROHIBITION AGAINST CONSULTING A YID'ONI, A KIND OF WIZARD

There shall not be found among you any one that maketh his son or his daughter to pass through the fire, one that useth divination, a soothsayer, or an enchanter, or a sorcerer, 18,11 or a charmer, or one that consulteth a ghost or a familiar spirit, or a necromancer. (Deuteronomy 18:10–11)

Mitzvah 514 prohibits us from consulting a Yid'oni. This practitioner would place an animal's bone in his mouth, and then a voice would come out of the bone. We are not to rely on a Yid'oni or any wizard or corpse for guidance.

515. THE PROHIBITION AGAINST MAKING ANY ENQUIRY OF THE DEAD

There shall not be found among you any one that maketh his son or his daughter to pass through the fire, one that useth divination, a soothsayer, or an enchanter, or a sorcerer, 18,11 or a charmer, or one that consulteth a ghost or a familiar spirit, or a necromancer. (Deuteronomy 18:10–11)

Mitzvah 515 forbids us from seeking advice from the dead. According to the author of Sefer HaHinnuch, certain people would sleep in cemeteries and hope that the dead person would communicate with them. There is to be no communication with the dead, not for advice, not for anything.

516. THE PRECEPT TO HEED EVERY PROPHET, IN EVERY GENERATION, PROVIDED HE CHANGES NOTHING IN THE PRECEPTS OF THE TORAH

A prophet will the LORD thy God raise up unto thee, from the midst of thee, of thy brethren, like unto me; unto him ye shall hearken; (Deuteronomy 18:15)

Mitzvah 516 commands us to obey the true prophets. Only Hashem can appoint a true prophet. The prophet is G-d's representative. Obeying the words of a prophet is obeying Hashem.

The following passages from Deuteronomy explain how we can identify true prophets.

Deuteronomy 18:21 -22 And if thou say in thy heart: 'How shall we know the word which the LORD hath not spoken?' When a prophet speaketh in the name of the LORD, if the thing follow not, nor come to pass, that is the thing which the LORD hath not spoken; the prophet hath spoken it presumptuously, thou shalt not be afraid of him.

Another passage is ***Deuteronomy 13:2–13:6***

If there arise in the midst of thee a prophet, or a dreamer of dreams—and he give thee a sign or a wonder, and the sign or the wonder come to pass, whereof he spoke unto thee—saying: 'Let us go after other gods, which thou hast not known, and let us serve them'; thou shalt not hearken unto the words of that prophet, or unto that dreamer of dreams; for the LORD your God putteth you to proof, to know whether ye do love the LORD your God with all your heart and with all your soul. After the LORD your God shall ye walk, and Him shall ye fear, and His commandments shall ye keep, and

unto His voice shall ye hearken, and Him shall ye serve, and unto Him shall ye cleave. And that prophet, or that dreamer of dreams, shall be put to death; because he hath spoken perversion against the LORD your God, who brought you out of the land of Egypt, and redeemed thee out of the house of bondage, to draw thee aside out of the way which the LORD thy God commanded thee to walk in. So shalt thou put away the evil from the midst of thee.

In my write-up of Mitzvah 426, I explained that Hashem ultimately abolished prophecy.

517. THE PROHIBITION AGAINST PROPHESYING FALSELY

But the prophet, that shall speak a word presumptuously in My name, which I have not commanded him to speak, or that shall speak in the name of other gods, that same prophet shall die.' (Deuteronomy 18:20)

Mitzvah 517 forbids us to bear false prophecy. Nobody has the right to declare himself/herself a prophet without Hashem's approving it. We cannot speak on His behalf if He never ordered us to do so.

518. THE PROHIBITION AGAINST PROPHESYING IN THE NAME OF AN IDOL

But the prophet, that shall speak a word presumptuously in My name, which I have not commanded him to speak, or that shall speak in the name of other gods, that same prophet shall die.' (Deuteronomy 18:20)

Mitzvah 518 forbids us to bear prophecy in the name of an idol. We cannot say that an idol desires us to worship it, even if we believe that worshipping that idol would mean receiving wealth and prosperity. Committing this offense, results in capital punishment.

519. NOT TO REFRAIN FROM PUTTING A FALSE PROPHET TO DEATH, AND NOT TO BE AFRAID OF HIM

When a prophet speaketh in the name of the LORD, if the thing follow not, nor come to pass, that is the thing which the LORD hath not spoken; the prophet hath spoken it presumptuously, thou shalt not be afraid of him. (Deuteronomy 18:22)

Mitzvah 519 commands us to be intrepid when putting a false prophet to death. Hashem is the only one that we should fear. To fear a false prophet, an enemy of the Jewish people, or any person or nation more than Hashem is a vulgar display of cowardice and a lack of faith.

520. THE PRECEPT TO PREPARE SIX CITIES OF REFUGE

Thou shalt prepare thee the way, and divide the borders of thy land, which the LORD thy God causeth thee to inherit, into three parts, that every manslayer may flee thither. And this is the case of the manslayer, that shall flee thither and live: whoso killeth his neighbour unawares, and hated him not in time past; (Deuteronomy 19:3-4)

Mitzvah 520 commands for there to be six cities of refuge for people who inadvertently commit murder.

(See Mishnah Makkot, Chapter 3, Mishnayot 4-5 and the Bartenura Commentary. Also see Mishnah Shekalim, Chapter 1, Mishnah 1.)

These cities belong to the Levites. Although all 48 of the Levites' cities serve as refuge for the manslayer who intentionally enters them, these specific six also serve as refuge even if the killer does not know that he is in that city. If the killer lives in one of those six cities, he is exempt from paying rent, but he would have to pay rent if he temporarily lived in another one of the six. One of the requirements of this Mitzvah is to put up sign posts that give directions and the distance to the city. On the 15th of Adar, the Bet Din would send deputies to repair these roads. Listed below are the six cities of refuge:

(1) Kedesh in Galilee, in the mountains of Naphtali
(2) Shechem in the mountains of Ephraim
(3) Kirjath Arba (which is Hebron) in the mountains of Judah
(4) Bezer in the wilderness on the plain, from the tribe of Reuben
(5) Ramoth in Gilead, from the tribe of Gad
(6) Golan in Bashan, from the tribe of Manasseh

Cited from the link:
http://www.bridgetothebible.com/Bible%20Lists/6%20cities%20of%20refuge.htm

TB, Makkot 8b discusses how these cities of refuge are lined up like rows in a vineyard.

521. TO HAVE NO MERCY IN CORPOREAL JUDGMENT ON A PERSON WHO HAS INFLICTED INJURY

And thine eye shall not pity: life for life, eye for eye, tooth for tooth, hand for hand, foot for foot. (Deuteronomy 19:21)

Mitzvah 521 forbids us to show mercy to a murderer and to people who harm other individuals. This maintains social order and stability. Without this prohibition, people could kill and assault each other without punishment. According to the author of Sefer HaHinnuch,, "For the continued existence of the (Jewish) people is impossible if the rod is not bent constantly over the backside of fools."

522. THE PROHIBITION AGAINST OVERREACHING A BOUNDARY

Thou shalt not remove thy neighbour's landmark, which they of old time have set, in thine inheritance which thou shalt inherit, in the land that the LORD thy God giveth thee to possess it. (Deuteronomy 19:14)

Mitzvah 522 forbids us from moving a border between two peoples' property.

If someone has a post in the ground, showing it is his property, his neighbor cannot move that post in order to take away some of that property to make it his own, as it is a form of stealing. What we have is what we have. Practicing this Mitzvah prevents feuds between neighbors. This pertains to the Land of Israel. Observing this Mitzvah also reminds us that the land of Israel is not truly ours; it belongs to Hashem. Hashem allows us to live in and use His land.

523. NOT TO PASS JUDGMENT ON THE WORD OF ONE WITNESS

One witness shall not rise up against a man for any iniquity, or for any sin, in any sin that he sinneth; at the mouth of two witnesses, or at the mouth of three witnesses, shall a matter be established. (Deuteronomy 19:15)

Mitzvah 523 is the prohibition against passing judgment, based on the testimony of just a single witness. The reason is that even upstanding and honest people have the potential to bear false witness, especially if there is animosity. According to the author of Sefer HaHinnuch, there is the assumption that two honest and upstanding Torah scholars would not testify falsely. This assumption does not pertain to two lay people.

As discussed in Mitzvah 29, if someone violates a Torah prohibition where the consequence is execution, two witnesses, not one, must first warn the perpetrator repeatedly that his actions, such as worshipping idols or working on Shabbat, would mean being put to death. The person would then acknowledge that he knows what he is doing is wrong and the consequences facing him. The two witnesses would then testify in court. We cannot rely on the testimony of one witness.

524. THE PRECEPT TO DO TO SCHEMING WITNESSES AS THEY INTENDED TO HAVE DONE TO THEIR VICTIM

then shall ye do unto him, as he had purposed to do unto his brother; so shalt thou put away the evil from the midst of thee. (Deuteronomy 19:19)

Mitzvah 524 commands us to do to corrupt witnesses what they intended to do to others. For example, witnesses A and B testify against Fred. They say that Fred owes someone money. Then witnesses C and D refute A and B's testimony by averring that A and B were with them at a different location at the very time that they testified that Fred engaged in the action. C and D's testimony frees Fred of the debt and then A and B have to pay Fred what they tried to extort from him.

The same principle applies if A and B testify that Fred killed someone. Then C and D testify that A and B could not have witnessed the crime that they said Fred had committed, A and B are subsequently put to death.

A similar example takes place in the Book of Esther, Chapter 7: 9-10.

And Harbonah, one of the chamberlains, said before the king, "Behold also, the gallows fifty cubits high, which Haman had made for Mordecai, who spoken good for the king, standeth in the house of Haman." Then the king said, "Hang him thereon."

So they hanged Haman on the gallows that he had prepared for Mordecai. Then was the king's wrath pacified.

The evil that Haman intended to inflict onto Mordecai was instead inflicted onto himself.

525. NOT TO QUAIL IN FEAR BEFORE AN ENEMY IN BATTLE

Thou shalt not be affrighted at them; for the LORD thy God is in the midst of thee, a God great and awful. (Deuteronomy 7:21) When thou goest forth to battle against thine enemies, and seest horses, and chariots, and a people more than thou, thou shalt not be afraid of them; for the LORD thy God is with thee, who brought thee up out of the land of Egypt.) Deuteronomy 20:1)

(Several hundred years ago, awful used to mean being worthy of awe; awe-inspiring.)

Mitzvah 525 prohibits us from being fearful of our enemies when we are at war with them. We are NEVER to cower to them or fearfully retreat from battle. During the time of war, we must focus one hundred percent on destroying our enemies and not worry about the fate of our wives and children should we perish. Fulfilling this Mitzvah instills trust in Hashem. In the Book of Numbers, the ten spies who reported back to Moses that the Canaanites would destroy them in battle, was a vulgar display of cowardice and lack of faith in Hashem. Hashem forbade them to enter the Promised Land. However, Hashem granted entry to Joshua and Caleb because their reports were optimistic:

(The ten spies' sins are in Numbers, 13:28-29 and Numbers, 13: 31-33.)

Here is the punishment for their sins:

surely ye shall not come into the land, concerning which I lifted up My hand that I would make you dwell therein, save Caleb the son of Jephunneh, and Joshua the son of Nun. But your little ones, that ye said would be a prey, them will I bring in, and they shall know the land which ye have rejected. But as for you, your carcasses shall fall in this wilderness. And your children shall be wanderers in the wilderness forty years, and shall bear your strayings, until your carcasses be consumed in the wilderness. (Numbers 14:30–33)

526. THE PRECEPT TO ANOINT A KOHEN FOR WAR

And it shall be, when ye draw nigh unto the battle, that the priest shall approach and speak unto the people, and shall say unto them: 'Hear, O Israel, ye draw nigh this day unto battle against your enemies; let not your heart faint; fear not, nor be alarmed, neither be ye affrighted at them; for the LORD your God is He that goeth with you, to fight for you against your enemies, to save you.' (Deuteronomy 20:2–4)

Mitzvah 526 commands us to anoint a special priest at the time of war. He is to accompany the troops at the time of battle and provide encouragement. This Mitzvah was applicable when the Israelites entered the Land of Canaan.

527. THE PRECEPT TO ACT IN A WAR OF CHOICE ACCORDING TO THE RULES OF SCRIPTURE

When thou drawest nigh unto a city to fight against it, then proclaim peace unto it. And it shall be, if it make thee answer of peace, and open unto thee, then it shall be, that all the people that are found therein shall become tributary unto thee, and shall serve thee. And if it will make no peace with thee, but will make war against thee, then thou shalt besiege it. (Deuteronomy 20:10–12)

Mitzvah 527 commands us to offer peace to nations before attacking them in a non-Torah-mandated war. Before fighting commences, the inhabitants can surrender. They would have to agree to be subservient, and accept the seven Noahide laws. (These laws were covered in Mitzvah 410.) This Mitzvah shows a measure of mercy. Even though these nations' citizens are idol worshippers, they are human beings and deserve mercy. If this were a Torah war–one that Hashem commanded–then the inhabitants are still given the option to surrender before facing an attack. If the non-Jews in these cities accept these laws, they can live in peace.

The difference between Torah wars and non-Torah wars is that the former commands that everyone in that nation be destroyed if they refuse to surrender.

528. TO LET NO ONE IN THE SEVEN NATIONS OF CANAAN STAY ALIVE

Howbeit of the cities of these peoples, that the LORD thy God giveth thee for an inheritance, thou shalt save alive nothing that breatheth, (Deuteronomy 20:16)

Mitzvah 528 is the prohibition against not destroying the seven nations that Hashem commanded us to obliterate. The seven nations were listed in Mitzvah 93. According to Sefer HaHinnuch, King David came close to fulfilling this Mitzvah.

529. NOT TO DESTROY FRUIT-TREES IN SETTING SIEGE–AND SO IS ANY NEEDLESS DESTRUCTION INCLUDED IN THE BAN

When thou shalt besiege a city a long time, in making war against it to take it, thou shalt not destroy the trees thereof by wielding an axe against them; for thou mayest eat of them, but thou shalt not cut them down; for is the tree of the field man, that it should be besieged of thee? (Deuteronomy 20:19)

Mitzvah 529 is the prohibition against destroying fruit-trees because we are commanded to love what is good and beneficial. However, there are exceptions: If other fruit trees would grow better if we cut a specific fruit tree, or if the wood is more valuable than the fruit. The reasons for these exceptions are that the wood and the other fruit trees would provide a greater benefit than the tree. Had that specific tree remained standing, there would be less of a benefit. In that case, that specific tree can be cut down.

530. THE PRECEPT OF BEHEADING THE HEIFER IN A RIVERBED

If one be found slain in the land which the LORD thy God giveth thee to possess it, lying in the field, and it be not known who hath smitten him; then thy elders and thy judges shall come forth, and they shall measure unto the cities which are round about him that is slain. And it shall be, that the city which is nearest unto the slain man, even the elders of that city shall take a heifer of the herd, which hath not been wrought with, and which hath not drawn in the yoke. (Deuteronomy 21:1- 3)

Mitzvah 530 states that if a murdered victim's murderer is unidentified, the inhabitants of the city closest to where the body was found, must break a heifer's neck in order to atone for allowing the murder.

A way of preventing traveling guests departing from a city from being murdered is for the host to either accompany his guest or have someone whom he knows and trusts be the escort. The guest who is a stranger in a city risks being killed if he leaves the area unescorted. To learn more about this topic, read the article, Escorting the Traveler by Eliezer Wenger at Chabad.org. Cited at https://www.chabad.org/library/article_cdo/aid/289767/jewish/Escorting-the-Traveler.htm.

That is why there is a need for atonement. We learn from this to make sure that guests are accompanied when they leave a city. This strengthens their chances of remaining safe.

This Mitzvah only applies if the person had been stabbed. It is a limited situation. Breaking the heifer's neck takes place in a particular riverbed. The city's inhabitants witness the heifer's destruction. According to Sefer HaHinnuch, hearing the heifer's neck crack, might compel witnesses of the murder–if any–to testify.

531. NOT TO PLOUGH OR SOW IN THE COURSING

And the elders of that city shall bring down the heifer unto a rough valley, which may neither be plowed nor sown, and shall break the heifer's neck there in the valley. (Deuteronomy 21:4)

Mitzvah 531 prohibits us from ploughing and sowing in a riverbed where the heifer's neck is broken. The reason for breaking the heifer's neck was covered in Mitzvah 530. Breaking the heifer's neck and then not working that specific riverbed signify waste. This is a punishment for not pursuing the murderer (see Mitzvah 530 for details about the murderer). A human life was wasted and the killer got away with it. The human life was wasted because nobody accompanied the guest as he left the area to go home. It is just as bad as allowing a fellow Jew to be murdered or mistreated. It is a violation of the obligation of loving fellow Jews. This Mitzvah is enforced when the Temple is extant.

532. THE PRECEPT OF THE LAW OF A "BEAUTIFUL WOMAN"–CAPTURED IN WAR

and seest among the captives a woman of goodly form, and thou hast a desire unto her, and wouldest take her to thee to wife; then thou shalt bring her home to thy house; and she shall shave her head, and pare her nails; and she shall put the raiment of her captivity from off her, and shall remain in thy house, and bewail her father and her mother a full month; and after that thou mayest go in unto her, and be her husband, and she shall be thy wife. And it shall be, if thou have no delight in her, then thou shalt let her go whither she

will; but thou shalt not sell her at all for money, thou shalt not deal with her as a slave, because thou hast humbled her. (Deuteronomy 21:11 -14)

Mitzvah 532 commands Israelite soldiers who capture beautiful non-Jewish women from opposing nations in battle to observe the following process before marrying them: The soldier must bring her to his house where she shaves her head and allows her nails to grow long. If she were wearing attractive garments, then she must remove them. She is in this predicament for 30 days, where she would usually be crying over her separation from her parents.

The Rabbis explain that Hashem allows this so the men would fight their desires to have relations with that woman. If the man wants to marry her after 30 days, then he can, if she converts to Judaism. The initial 30 days is a test for him to see if he truly loves her without her beauty. If he still wants to marry her after the 30-day period, she has to go through a proper conversion to Judaism. If she had gotten pregnant before their marriage, their child would not be Jewish. If he decides after the 30 day period that he does not want to marry her, then he has to send her back home. He cannot sell her.

To state that the non-Jewish woman is given 30 days to mourn without having sexual relations because Hashem wants us to practice compassion is problematic. Hashem is responsible for the entire universe and for everything that He creates. We cannot understand His true motives.

There are obvious reasons for the 30-day mourning period: The non-Jewish woman's heart is incapable of belonging to the Jewish man who plans to marry her because she is grieving for her family. It is not a time to rejoice. The shaving of her head, allowing her fingernails to grow, and allowing her to weep make her unappealing. She stays at her captor's home in order for him to see her in this grotesque state always underfoot. Therefore, he learns whether his love for her is genuine or if it is just lust.

533. THE PROHIBITION AGAINST SELLING A "BEAUTIFUL WOMAN" CAPTURED IN WAR

And it shall be, if thou have no delight in her, then thou shalt let her go whither she will; but thou shalt not sell her at all for money, thou shalt not deal with her as a slave, because thou hast humbled her. (Deuteronomy 21:14)

Mitzvah 533 is the prohibition against selling the "beautiful woman" whom was captured in battle if she is no longer desirable. According to Sefer HaHinnuch, men of the heathen nations sold their beautiful captured women into slavery after sexually violating them. Jews are supposed to be moral and treat people with respect. Therefore, if the woman's capture chooses not to marry her, he cannot sell her, or make her a maid servant.

534. NOT TO MAKE A "BEAUTIFUL WOMAN" WORK AS A SLAVE AFTER CONJUGAL INTIMACY WITH HER

And it shall be, if thou have no delight in her, then thou shalt let her go whither she will; but thou shalt not sell her at all for money, thou shalt not deal with her as a slave, because thou hast humbled her. (Deuteronomy 21:14)

Mitzvah 534 is the prohibition against turning this woman into his own maid servant if he chooses not to marry her. The reasons for this prohibition are covered in Mitzvah 533.

535. THE PRECEPT OF THE LAW OF HANGING SOMEONE AFTER HIS EXECUTION, WHEN REQUIRED

And if a man have committed a sin worthy of death, and he be put to death, and thou hang him on a tree; (Deuteronomy 21:22)

Mitzvah 535 commands us to hang people who have committed a capital crime and who were executed by the Beit Din (hanging itself is not one of the 4 methods of capital punishment described in the Torah). Sparing them is forbidden. The person is put to death by stoning. Then the corpse is hanged that day, but only for a short while. The two sins that result in suffering from this fate are cursing Hashem and idol worship. The purpose of hanging the corpse is to show the Israelites that that can happen to them if they worship idols or curse Hashem. After the person is stoned, we erect a beam, and put him up right before sundown; take him almost down immediately. Bury him with the beam and the stones that killed him. This is done to avoid future embarrassment of the executed person.

This is a lesson of showing compassion, even to Jews who worshipped idols and/or cursed Hashem.

536. THAT SOMEONE HUNG SHOULD NOT BE LEFT OVERNIGHT ON THE GALLOWS, ETC.

his body shall not remain all night upon the tree, but thou shalt surely bury him the same day; for he that is hanged is a reproach unto God; that thou defile not thy land which the LORD thy God giveth thee for an inheritance. (Deuteronomy 21:23)

Mitzvah 536 prohibits us from leaving the corpse hung publicly for an extended period. When my Partner in Torah and I discussed this Mitzvah, he estimated that the possible time a corpse would remain hung would be 15 to 20 minutes.

This Mitzvah requires us to bury the corpse as soon as possible.

537. THE PRECEPT OF BURIAL FOR SOMEONE EXECUTED BY COURT ORDER, AND SO FOR EVERY DECEASED PERSON

his body shall not remain all night upon the tree, but thou shalt surely bury him the same day; for he that is hanged is a reproach unto God; that thou defile not thy land which the LORD thy God giveth thee for an inheritance. (Deuteronomy 21:23)

Mitzvah 537 commands us to bury the executed person on the same day that he is executed. According to Sefer HaHinnuch, if that individual's corpse remains hung on the tree for any extended period of time, he is on display. This might cause people to discuss his execution. They would ultimately mention that the guilty party was hung for either cursing Hashem or for worshipping idols. To even discuss that Hashem was shown disrespect is not allowed. To prevent this discussion, the guilty party's remains and the objects used to kill him are buried the same day. This Mitzvah also commands that all Jews who die are buried the same day, whether they committed a crime or not. Although it is required to bury the deceased within 24 hours of his/her death, some Jewish funerals occur a few days after the person dies: Reasons include that the body might need to be transported to another city or country. Immediate family might have to travel a long distance to attend the funeral. Burying the dead on Shabbat or a sacred holiday is forbidden. Therefore, if someone dies on Shabbat or on a sacred holiday, the funeral must be pushed back.

538. THE RELIGIOUS DUTY OF RETURNING A LOST OBJECT TO ITS OWNER

Thou shalt not see thy brother's ox or his sheep driven away, and hide thyself from them; thou shalt surely bring them back unto thy brother. (Deuteronomy 22:1) If thou meet thine enemy's ox or his ass going astray, thou shalt surely bring it back to him again. (Exodus 23:4)

Mitzvah 538 is the obligation to return a lost object to its owner. If the person finds something that is not his, he must announce it. He does not have to describe it. Whoever lost it needs to describe the object because that prevents other people from claiming it. This pertains to objects that can be identified. If a person sees something on the street, yet there are implications that the object is not lost, the person who "found" it cannot claim it. If the object is not identifiable at all, the finder can keep it because the owner gave up hope of recovering it.

If a person finds something at the bottom of the river, he can keep it because the owner obviously gave up owning it. Some examples of unidentified objects that a finder may keep include scattered fruit, loaves of bread, strings of fish, and scattered money. These items are so nondescript that the owner effectively renounces hope of recovery.

The key reason for having to return identifiable objects to the owner is to enhance harmony in Israel.

539. NOT TO TURN A BLIND EYE TO A LOST OBJECT

And so shalt thou do with his ass; and so shalt thou do with his garment; and so shalt thou do with every lost thing of

thy brother's, which he hath lost, and thou hast found; thou mayest not hide thyself. (Deuteronomy 22:3)

Mitzvah 539 is the prohibition against passing by a lost object and leaving it there. Reasons for this Mitzvah are covered in my write-up of Mitzvah 538.

540. NOT TO LEAVE THE BEAST OF ONE'S FELLOW MAN LYING UNDER ITS BURDEN

Thou shalt not see thy brother's ass or his ox fallen down by the way, and hide thyself from them; thou shalt surely help him to lift them up again. (Deuteronomy 22:4)

Mitzvah 540 is the prohibition against not helping a fellow Jew whose animal is falling under the weight of the burden of what it is carrying. This Mitzvah requires us to help fellow Jews, whether we know them or not, whether we like them or not. The reasons for these specific laws are covered in my write-up of Mitzvah 80.

541. THE PRECEPT FOR LIFTING UP A LOAD FOR AN ISRAELITE

Thou shalt not see thy brother's ass or his ox fallen down by the way, and hide thyself from them; thou shalt surely help him to lift them up again. (Deuteronomy 22:4)

Mitzvah 541 obligates us to assist a fellow Jew who is loading up merchandise. Today, if a Jew is loading up his car, it is required that we provide assistance.

My Partner in Torah explained to me that the owner must also help. He cannot sit back and watch while others perform the Mitzvah. The person offering help can ask for a payment.

This Mitzvah also obligates us to help a fellow Jew unload merchandise. but in this case no one can ask for money. We unload for free because at certain times, our fellow Jew and/or his animal might be suffering from carrying a heavy load. It is our obligation to help him in times of need without asking to be paid. We are required to love our fellow Jews, and to help them, even if we have personal problems with specific ones. Consult my Mitzvah 80 write-up for this Mitzvah's root reasons.

542. THAT A WOMAN IS NOT TO WEAR A MAN'S FINERY

A woman shall not wear that which pertaineth unto a man, neither shall a man put on a woman's garment; for whosoever doeth these things is an abomination unto the LORD thy God. (Deuteronomy 22:5)

Mitzvah 542 prohibits women from wearing men's clothing and from carrying men's weapons. This has a subjective component and that being this question: What is appropriate clothing for men and women? My Partner in Torah told me that women do not wear pants because it is a question of modesty. Dresses are more modest than pants. There is specific headgear that only men can wear. Women are forbidden to wear them. The reason for this Mitzvah is to maintain distinction between the two sexes. There would be chaos and immorality if men and women dressed alike.

543. THAT A MAN IS NOT TO WEAR A WOMAN'S FINERY

A woman shall not wear that which pertaineth unto a man, neither shall a man put on a woman's garment; for whosoever doeth these things is an abomination unto the LORD thy God. (Deuteronomy 22:5)

Mitzvah 543 prohibits men from wearing women's clothing. When my Partner in Torah and I covered this Mitzvah, he explained that women's clothing and men's clothing are determined by the region's customs. There was a time in history when it was the norm for men to wear skirts. Today in western countries, especially, men wear pants and women wear skirts and dresses. However, in Scotland and Ireland, it is socially acceptable for men to wear kilts, so arguably in those locales they would not be considered women's garments. Observant Jewish women wear long dresses and observant men–like most men–wear pants. That is society's custom. This can possibly raise another question: Is same-sex marriage acceptable because it is now legal in some areas?

Regardless of the law, regardless of whether society embraces it or not, the answer is no. Times might change, but not Hashem's Torah. Mitzvah 209 forbids two men to lie together because it is an abomination. (In my write-up of Mitzvah 209, I discussed why the Torah does not forbid two women to lie together.)

On another note, on Sunday, June 12, 2016, 50 people were shot to death in a gay bar in Orlando, Florida. Although their lifestyles clashes with Hashem's Torah, that still forbids killing them. There is no way that this heinous act is worth applauding. At the time of the Sanhedrin, homosexuals would have been brought before the Sanhedrin to face capital punishment. I discussed in my write-ups of Mitzvah 76, 261, and 409, that the Sanhedrin must find reasons why the guilty party should not be put to death. Today, none of the Mitzvot that require someone to face capital punishment can be enforced because the Sanhedrin no longer exists.

Mitzvah 543 also forbids men to decorate themselves; women do that–not men. Men can neither pull out their white hairs, nor can they dye their hair; these actions display vanity. Certain women do these things because they care about looking pretty. Men cannot act like women. In general, women care more about their appearances than men care about theirs. It is acceptable for women to act that way because they need to look attractive to their husbands in order for their husbands to still desire them. A man who does not desire his wife can lead to violating the first Mitzvah: Be fruitful and multiply.

544. NOT TO TAKE THE MOTHER-BIRD WITH THE YOUNG IN THE NEST

If a bird's nest chance to be before thee in the way, in any tree or on the ground, with young ones or eggs, and the dam sitting upon the young, or upon the eggs, thou shalt not take the dam with the young; (Deuteronomy 22:6)

Mitzvah 544 prohibits us from removing a mother-bird from her nest when her eggs are there; in addition, we cannot take the mother's chicks in her presence. Explanations about why this is a significant Mitzvah are covered in my write-up of 545.

545. THE PRECEPT OF SENDING THE MOTHER-BIRD AWAY FROM THE NEST

thou shalt in any wise let the dam go, but the young thou mayest take unto thyself; that it may be well with thee, and that thou mayest prolong thy days. (Deuteronomy 22:7)

Mitzvah 545 commands us to send the mother-bird away from her nest before we take her eggs. This Mitzvah generates discussion. On the surface, it appears that the root reason for this Mitzvah is that Hashem is compassionate, but that is the wrong approach. If a person tries to use this Mitzvah as evidence as Hashem's mercy, we silence him. A key reason for this Mitzvah is for us to know that Hashem's rule extends to all creatures and He is concerned with the creatures' welfare. The concern for animals demonstrates His ownership of every person and every living creature in the world. Humans, animals, and every living organism are products of His creation. By telling us a law that relates to the animals, shows that He cares about them and that everything and everyone exist because He wills it. By giving us a law like this, it shows that Hashem is Master over everything in the world. He has an interest in everything.

This Mitzvah write-up does not provide a definitive reason why Hashem established this law. We cannot understand everything in the Torah, nor can we fully fathom why Hashem permits certain things while forbidding others. In the Book of Job, 38:4-5, G-d said to him:

"Where wast thou when I laid the foundations of the earth? Declare, if thou hast the understanding. Who determined the measures thereof, if thou knowest? Or who stretched the line upon it?"

(Consult the link, http://www.mechon-mamre.org/e/et/et27.htm

There, you will find the Book of Job. This was an English translation of a Jewish Bible. As mentioned in the introduction, the English translations of the Torah passages cited in this book are from strictly Jewish sources. See also Tractate Avot, Chapter 2, Mishnah 1.)

Here, Rebbe Yehuda **haNasi said:**

"One should be as careful with a light Mitzvah as with a heavy Mitzvah. While (it is generally assumed that) the Torah contains 613 Mitzvot, they are not all equally important. The Mitzvah not to mix meat and milk cannot be equated with the

command not to murder. Nor can the prohibition of Shatnez, mixing wool and linen, be compared to the obligation to conduct one's business dealings faithfully. As a general rule, sins of commission, Mitzvot Lo Ta'aseh, are of greater import than sins of omission, Mitzvot Aseh. And within mitzvoth lo Ta'aseh, those that carry a death penalty or the punishment of Karet are clearly of greater importance."

Rebbe Yehuda haNasi tells us not to automatically give little attention to and in some cases discard what appear to us as the "lighter" Mitzvot. Although certain Mitzvot carry more weight such as not committing murder, they all have great importance. If not, Hashem would not have given our ancestors these Mitzvot when they received His Torah.

An example of a light Mitzvah juxtaposed with a heavy Mitzvah is sending the mother bird away to honoring our parents. The former is the lighter Mitzvah and the latter is the heavier one.

Honour thy father and thy mother, as the LORD thy God commanded thee; that thy days may be long, and that it may go well with thee, upon the land which the LORD thy God giveth thee. (Deuteronomy 5:15)

546. THE RELIGIOUS DUTY OF BUILDING A PARAPET

When thou buildest a new house, then thou shalt make a parapet for thy roof, that thou bring not blood upon thy house, if any man fall from thence. (Deuteronomy 22:8)

Mitzvah 546 commands us to put a fence around our roofs. This Mitzvah extends to all dangerous situations. For example, steps must have railings to keep people from falling.

My Partner in Torah told me about the argument about whether or not peoples' accidents derive from Hashem's wish or not. Some believe that if Hashem wants someone to fall, that person will fall, whether a railing is there or not. The point is to avoid potentially dangerous predicaments. We cannot expose ourselves to danger, like finding and drinking from an uncovered bottle of water. A poisonous snake might have drunk from it, or someone with a terrible cold or a contagious disease might have also used it. We are given the gift of common sense to not do certain things that could hurt and/or kill us. We know not to jump in front of a moving train or car. We know not to play with fire. In fact, that Talmud tells us that avoiding dangerous situations is more severe than avoiding forbidden actions.

This leads to the Midrashic story of King Nimrod as one of the 10 miracles that occurred to Abraham when Nimrod ordered Abraham to be thrown into a fiery furnace. Abraham survived, because Hashem willed it.

(See Bartenura's commentary on Avot Chapter 5, Mishnah 3 for further explanations about this Midrashic story.)

In the book of Daniel, his three companions were thrown into a fiery furnace and survived unharmed because Hashem was with them. Daniel was thrown into the lion's den, but the lions did him no harm.

Hashem spares the lives of these people who were victims of these injustices. These men who were victims of these injustices. That does not mean to try to do something dangerous to see if G-d will come to the rescue. These holy men had a special relationship with G-d.

A small number of Pentecostal churches in a few rural areas of the United States handle serpents during their prayer service. They are literally adhering to the Christian Bible's book of Mark:

"they will pick up snakes with their hands; and when they drink deadly poison, it will not hurt them at all; they will place their hands onsick people, and they will get well." (Mark 16:18)

A number of people died while handling serpents during their church services. As stated, most Christians do not handle serpents. We, as Jews, do NOT study these Christian texts, which Christians regard as their Bible. We do not believe in the trinity, nor that a virgin gave birth to a son and his father was Hashem. This book is not meant to refute the Christian religion. Hashem never commanded Moses to tell the Israelites to handle snakes or to drink poison. To do so, would not be following Hashem's wishes.

On a personal note, a blind Christian friend of mine had a bad experience at church. Members of the congregation assumed that if they prayed to G-d, then he would be able to see again. He seriously doubted it, but allowed them to try to restore his vision through prayer. As he suspected, he remained blind. The congregants rebuked him for not "having faith in G-d." It was "his fault that they failed; not theirs."

When my friend told me what happened, I thought that those particular congregants were arrogant. G-d does not work that way. In addition, Abraham, Isaac, Jacob, and Moses talked with G-d, yet they were incredibly humble. They did not boast that G-d was with them. They never wanted to be treated as gods or kings. They accurately viewed themselves as men, and nothing more.

The essential point here is not to put ourselves in dangerously stupid predicaments and assume that Hashem will save us.

547. NOT TO LEAVE A STUMBLING-BLOCK (KEEP A DANGEROUS OBJECT) ABOUT

When thou buildest a new house, then thou shalt make a parapet for thy roof, that thou bring not blood upon thy house, if any man fall from thence. (Deuteronomy 22:8)

Mitzvah 547 prohibits us from having dangerous items on our property such as stumbling-blocks and snares. What was said in Mitzvah 546 applies here.

548. NOT TO SOW MIXED KINDS OF SEEDS IN A VINEYARD IN ISRAEL

Thou shalt not sow thy vineyard with two kinds of seed; lest the fulness of the seed which thou hast sown be forfeited together with the increase of the vineyard. (Deuteronomy 22:9)

Mitzvah 548 is the prohibition against planting cross breeding grains. (The Hebrew word for cross breeding in the English transliteration is Kilayim.) We cannot plant both wheat and grains in the same vineyard. These species have purity, therefore to cross breed them can cause contamination. At the Biblical level, it would involve planting two different kinds of grain seeds together. On a Rabbinic level, other mixed seeds are prohibited, such as vegetable seeds with grape seeds. On the Torah level, this Mitzvah only applies in the Land of Israel, but on the Rabbinic level, it applies everywhere in the world. We cannot have benefit from things grown from cross breeding. Other explanations for this prohibition are cited in my Mitzvah write-ups 244 and 245.

549. NOT TO EAT THE PRODUCE OF MIXED SEEDS IN A VINEYARD IN ISRAEL

Thou shalt not sow thy vineyard with two kinds of seed; lest the fulness of the seed which thou hast sown be forfeited together with the increase of the vineyard. (Deuteronomy 22:9)

Mitzvah 549 forbids us to eat food that results from cross breeding (mixed planting). Things such as wine that cause us to possibly stray from Hashem and/or do improper acts are what Hashem wants us to distance ourselves from. Wine is in that border line category because it can cause a negative impact on certain people who derive too much benefit from it. It is bad enough that negative things can come out from drinking too much wine. If someone fails to realize that mixed planting took place on his property, but then discovers it, he must remove the grains immediately.

I covered these topics in my write-ups of Mitzvot 244, 245, and 548.

550. NOT TO DO WORK WITH TWO KINDS OF ANIMALS TOGETHER

Thou shalt not plow with an ox and an ass together. (Deuteronomy 22:10)

Mitzvah 550 forbids us to use two different types of animals to do the same work, simultaneously. For example, we cannot hook up an ox and a donkey to a plough at the same time. We cannot hook up two kinds of animals to the same wagon at the same time. This causes the animals discomfort about being forced to interact with a different animal. Being too close into proximity is not good for the animal. There is also the possibility that these different animals will mate. Mitzvah 244 explains why cross breed mating of animals is forbidden. For additional details, consult Mitzvot 244 and 245.

551. NOT TO WEAR CLOTH OF WOOL AND LINEN

Thou shalt not wear a mingled stuff, wool and linen together. (Deuteronomy 22:11)

Mitzvah 551 prohibits us from wearing clothes from wool and linen. (The Hebrew term for this prohibition is Shatnez.) We cannot wear both simultaneously. I discussed Shatnez in my Mitzvah 99 write-up. To reiterate a few points, idol worshipping priests used to wear wool and linen together. Refusing and refraining from dressing like them, helps us distance ourselves from them. This Mitzvah also applies to blankets. On a Rabbinic level, Shatnez also applies to seat cushions.

Thou shalt not wear a mingled stuff, wool and linen together. (Deuteronomy 22:11)

The Hebrew term for the forbidden mixture of clothing is Shatnez. Wool comes from animals and linen derives from plants.

Shatnez stems from the tragedy of Cain and Abel.

And again she bore his brother Abel. And Abel was a keeper of sheep, but Cain was a tiller of the ground. And in process of time it came to pass, that Cain brought of the fruit of the ground an offering unto the LORD. And Abel, he also brought of the firstlings of his flock and of the fat thereof. And the LORD had respect unto Abel and to his offering; but unto Cain and to his offering He had not respect. And Cain was very wroth, and his countenance fell. And the LORD said unto Cain: 'Why art thou wroth? and why is thy countenance fallen? If thou doest well, shall it not be lifted up? and if thou

doest not well, sin coucheth at the door; and unto thee is its desire, but thou mayest rule over it.' And Cain spoke unto Abel his brother. And it came to pass, when they were in the field, that Cain rose up against Abel his brother, and slew him. (Genesis 4:2 -8)

Abel's offering pertained to animals, which involved wool, and Cain's offering pertained to plants, which involved linen. Consequently, the mixture of these two substances recalls the conflict between Cain and Abel.

To learn more about Shatnez deriving from Cain and Abel's conflict, consult Midrash Tanhuma B'reishit 9:9

Evidence that the tragedy of Cain and Abel tie in with Shatnez is that the Torah juxtaposes this prohibition and the commandment to love thy neighbor. This juxtaposition is in Leviticus Chapter 19 verses 18-19:

Thou shalt not take vengeance, nor bear any grudge against the children of thy people, but thou shalt love thy neighbour as thyself: I am the LORD. Ye shall keep My statutes. Thou shalt not let thy cattle gender with a diverse kind; thou shalt not sow thy field with two kinds of seed; neither shall there come upon thee a garment of two kinds of stuff mingled together.

According to RAMBAM, Shatnez is forbidden because the Canaanites dressed that way. We are prohibited from dressing like them and emulating their actions.

For more information, read Shatnez: A Mixture of Wool and Linen Parshat Kedoshim by Aryeh Citron. Log onto http://www.chabad.org/library/article_cdo/aid/882920/jewish/Shatnez-A-Mixture-of-Wool-and-Linen.htm

Also see Wool and Linen = Shatnez
A practical guide to keeping your clothes kosher.
by Rabbi Shraga Simmons.
http://www.aish.com/jl/m/mm/48948976.html

552. THE PRECEPT OF MARRIAGE TO A WOMAN

If any man take a wife, and go in unto her … (Deuteronomy 22:13)

Mitzvah 552 is the obligation to marry a woman with a Ketubah **(marriage contract).**

"The K*etubah* is a unilateral agreement drawn by witnesses in accordance with Jewish civil law, in which they testify that the husband guarantees to his wife that he will meet certain minimum human and financial conditions of marriage." (For more details, consult the link, http://www.chabad.org/library/article_cdo/aid/465168/jewish/The-Marriage-Contract-Ketubah.htm)

The Ketubah formalizes the relationship's uniqueness between the man and woman. That is when the man and woman are officially married. In the modern Jewish wedding ceremony, placing the wedding ring on the woman's finger, and the consummation of the marriage, take place after witnesses observe the signing of the ketubah.

553. THE PRECEPT THAT THE WIFE OF ONE WHO SPREADS AN EVIL REPORT–THAT SHE WAS IMMORAL–IS TO REMAIN WITH HIM PERMANENTLY

And they shall fine him a hundred shekels of silver, and give them unto the father of the damsel, because he hath brought

up an evil name upon a virgin of Israel; and she shall be his wife; he may not put her away all his days. (Deuteronomy 22:19)

Mitzvah 553 states that if a husband falsely claims that his wife was not a virgin, he loses the right to divorce her, and she has to remain with him (however, if she agrees to a divorce then it would be valid). My Partner in Torah explained that the presumption is that he would besmirch her name in order to get rid of her. At the time of the Sanhedrin, the prevailing attitude was that the wife wanted to remain married because then she would have a harder time finding a new husband. At the time when the Temple stood, women had a harder time surviving without a husband than today. A bad husband was preferable to no husband, so it is plausible that she would be willing to remain with a husband who had falsely accused her

This Mitzvah is enforced when the Temple is extant.

554. THAT A MAN WHO SPREADS AN EVIL REPORT–THAT SHE WAS IMMORAL–IS NEVER TO DIVORCE HIS WIFE

And they shall fine him a hundred shekels of silver, and give them unto the father of the damsel, because he hath brought up an evil name upon a virgin of Israel; and she shall be his wife; he may not put her away all his days. (Deuteronomy 22:19)

Mitzvah 554 prohibits a man from divorcing his wife if his allegations that she had lost her virginity before their marriage proved to be false. The reasons were covered in Mitzvah 553.

555. THE DUTY OF THE COURT TO HAVE ANYONE WHO MERITS STONING, STONED TO DEATH

If there be a damsel that is a virgin betrothed unto a man, and a man find her in the city, and lie with her; then ye shall bring them both out unto the gate of that city, and ye shall stone them with stones that they die: the damsel, because she cried not, being in the city; and the man, because he hath humbled his neighbour's wife; so thou shalt put away the evil from the midst of thee. (Deuteronomy 22:23-24)

The hand of the witnesses shall be first upon him to put him to death, and afterward the hand of all the people. So thou shalt put away the evil from the midst of thee. (Deuteronomy 17:7)

Mitzvah 555 is the obligation to put to death by stoning people who commit specific crimes that warrant it.

Before the man's stoning commences, he is stripped naked, and placed on a platform two stories high, but before a woman is stoned, her private parts are covered for the sake of modesty.

556. NOT TO PUNISH ANYONE COMPELLED TO COMMIT A TRANSGRESSION

But unto the damsel thou shalt do nothing; there is in the damsel no sin worthy of death; for as when a man riseth against his neighbour, and slayeth him, even so is this matter. (Deuteronomy 22:26)

Mitzvah 556 prohibits us to punish an individual who unwillingly committed a sin. In certain cases, it is beyond the person's control.

My Partner in Torah and I talked about how a raped married woman is free of guilt because she was forced to have sex. If during the rape, the sex had become consensual, she would remain free of guilt, because the initial sex was against her will.

557. THE DUTY OF A RAPIST TO TAKE HIS VICTIM FOR A WIFE

If a man find a damsel that is a virgin, that is not betrothed, and lay hold on her, and lie with her, and they be found; then the man that lay with her shall give unto the damsel's father fifty shekels of silver, and she shall be his wife, because he hath humbled her; he may not put her away all his days. (Deuteronomy 22:28-29)

Mitzvah 557 commands the rapist of an Israelite virgin to marry her and to pay her father 50 silver shekels. She can refuse to marry him, but he has to marry her if she wishes. Unlike the girl, he has no choice because he robbed her of her virginity, thus making her less desirable to the male Israelites seeking a wife. Therefore, the rapist now has to take care of her for the rest of her life. According to the author of Sefer HaHinnuch, the purpose of this Mitzvah is to deter rapists from seducing the daughters of Israel.This punishment reinforces that the Jewish women must never be treated like concubines.

558. THAT A RAPIST IS NOT EVER TO DIVORCE HIS VICTIM

If a man find a damsel that is a virgin, that is not betrothed, and lay hold on her, and lie with her, and they be found; then the man that lay with her shall give unto the damsel's father fifty shekels of silver, and she shall be his wife, because he hath humbled her; he may not put her away all his days. (Deuteronomy 22:28-29)

Mitzvah 558 prohibits a man from divorcing an Israelite woman whom he raped prior to marrying her. If the rapist is an Israelite and not a Kohen, and he divorces her, he must remarry her. However, if a Kohen raped the woman and then divorced her, he cannot remarry her because the Kohanim cannot marry divorced women. Instead, he is to be whipped.

559. THAT AN EMASCULATED MAN IS NOT TO TAKE ANY ISRAELITE WOMAN IN MARRIAGE

He that is crushed or maimed in his privy parts shall not enter into the assembly of the LORD. (Deuteronomy 23:2)

Mitzvah 559 forbids an emasculated man from marrying an Israelite woman.

According to Sefer HaHinnuch, certain Israelite men allowed themselves to be emasculated in order to serve in the king's palace and attain wealth. (Kings often appointed eunuchs to take charge of the women in his palace.) This Mitzvah's objective is to discourage Jewish men from doing this. Another reason is that Hashem commanded us to be fruitful and multiply, and voluntary castration is a direct violation of this commandment.

560. THAT A BASTARD FROM AN ADULTEROUS OR INCESTUOUS UNION SHOULD NOT MARRY ANY JEWISH WOMAN

A bastard shall not enter into the assembly of the LORD; even to the tenth generation shall none of his enter into the assembly of the LORD. (Deuteronomy 23:3)

Mitzvah 560 prohibits Mamzerim (bastards–products of illegitimate marriages) from marrying into the Jewish nation. (See

Mishnah Kiddushin, Chapter 3, Mishnah 12.) To fall into this category, one must be the product of an incestuous relationship or the result of a carnal relationship between a married woman and her lover.

The author of Sefer HaHinnuch attributes this prohibition to the "Mamzerim", even though he himself did nothing wrong, as resulting from "abominable thought and sinful action. There is no doubt that the nature of the father is hidden in the son".

Bastards and converts can marry each other. A bastard is also allowed to marry a woman who has his exact status. For more details, consult the link:
http://www.jewfaq.org/marriage.htm

561. THAT NO AMMONITE OR MOABITE MAY MARRY AN ISRAELITE WOMAN

An Ammonite or a Moabite shall not enter into the assembly of the LORD; even to the tenth generation shall none of them enter into the assembly of the LORD for ever; because they met you not with bread and with water in the way, when ye came forth out of Egypt; and because they hired against thee Balaam the son of Beor from Pethor of Aram-naharaim, to curse thee. (Deuteronomy 23:4-5)

Mitzvah 561 prohibits all the Moabite and Ammonite men from marrying into the Jewish nation. The reason is that when the Israelites wandered for 40 years, the men of those two nations refused to give them food and water. Worse, the Moabites hired Balaam to curse the Israelites. These actions disqualified them from ever marrying our people.

This prohibition does not apply to women. Ruth was a Moabite.

This Mitzvah became inapplicable after Sennacherib, the king of Assyria, exiled the kingdom of Israel; he comingled the other nations. As a result, we do not know the specific nations where people were from. (See Tractate Yadayim, Chapter 4, Mishnah 4.)

562. NOT TO EVER OFFER PEACE TO AMMON OR MOAB

Thou shalt not seek their peace nor their prosperity all thy days for ever. (Deuteronomy 23:27)

Mitzvah 562 forbids us to give the nations of Ammon and Moab the option to surrender before attacking them. Mitzvah 527 commands us to give enemy nations the option to surrender before attacking them, but the Moabites and Ammonites do not have that option. The reason for this Mitzvah was covered in my write-up of Mitzvah 561.

563. NOT TO EXCLUDE THE PROGENY OF ESAU FROM INTERMARRYING WITH ISRAELITES, AFTER THEY CONVERT, PAST TWO GENERATIONS

Thou shalt not abhor an Edomite, for he is thy brother; thou shalt not abhor an Egyptian, because thou wast a stranger in his land. 23,9 The children of the third generation that are born unto them may enter into the assembly of the LORD. (Deuteronomy 23:8–9)

Mitzvah 563 forbids an Edomite (a descendant of Esau) and an Egyptian who converted to Judaism to marry one who was born Jewish. They can marry other Jewish converts. This restriction applies to them and to their children, but not to their grandchildren who can marry any Jew they want. Unlike the

Moabites' and Amonites' descendants who can never marry into the Jewish nation, the Egyptians and Edomites can after the second generation, since those nations were following Hashem's will. Even though the Egyptians and the Edomites treated us cruelly, their actions were part Hashem's plan for the Jewish nation.

564. SIMILARLY, TO EXCLUDE AN EGYPTIAN ONLY UP TO THE THIRD GENERATION, NOT INCLUDING THE THIRD

Thou shalt not abhor an Edomite, for he is thy brother; thou shalt not abhor an Egyptian, because thou wast a stranger in his land. 23,9 The children of the third generation that are born unto them may enter into the assembly of the LORD. (Deuteronomy 23:8-9)

Mitzvah 564 states that we are not to refrain from marrying third generation Egyptian converts. The reasons and details are covered in my write-up of Mitzvah 563.

565. THAT A RITUALLY UNCLEAN PERSON SHOULD NOT ENTER THE CAMP OF THE LEVITES

If there be among you any man, that is not clean by reason of that which chanceth him by night, then shall he go abroad out of the camp, he shall not come within the camp. (Deuteronomy 23:11)

Mitzvah 565 forbids impure people from entering the Levites' camp. This decree pertained to the Israelites at the time of Moses. After the building of the First and Second Temples, the restricted location became the Temple Mount. The Temple Mount is a large area surrounding the Temple.

566. THE PRECEPT TO PREPARE A PLACE OF EASEMENT IN A CAMP

When thou goest forth in camp against thine enemies, then thou shalt keep thee from every evil thing. If there be among you any man, that is not clean by reason of that which chanceth him by night, then shall he go abroad out of the camp, he shall not come within the camp.But it shall be, when evening cometh on, he shall bathe himself in water; and when the sun is down, he may come within the camp. Thou shalt have a place also without the camp, whither thou shalt go forth abroad. And thou shalt have a paddle among thy weapons; and it shall be, when thou sittest down abroad, thou shalt dig therewith, and shalt turn back and cover that which cometh from thee. For the LORD thy God walketh in the midst of thy camp, to deliver thee, and to give up thine enemies before thee; therefore shall thy camp be holy; that He see no unseemly thing in thee, and turn away from thee. (Deuteronomy 23:10-15)

Mitzvah 566 requires the Jewish men in battle to use specific areas outside the camp to take care of personal needs. Relieving one's self outside the camp area is a key example. This prevents them from taking care of these personal matters any place they choose.

When our Holy Temple stood and when the Israelite men went to war, the Shechinah (Hashem's presence) was there. That was a holy location, which had to be clean at all times. This Mitzvah applied to males at the time of the Temple when they fought wars that Hashem commanded. Women were excused from fulfilling this Mitzvah because at the time of the Temple, they did not go to war.

567. THE PRECEPT TO PREPARE A BORING-STICK–A SPADE, FOR EASEMENT–IN A CAMP

And thou shalt have a paddle among thy weapons; and it shall be, when thou sittest down abroad, thou shalt dig therewith, and shalt turn back and cover that which cometh from thee. (Deuteronomy 23:14)

Mitzvah 567 commands the Jewish men in battle to carry shovels or trowels to cover the areas where they relieve themselves. Reasons for fulfilling this Mitzvah are covered in my write-up of Mitzvah 566.

568. NOT TO RETURN A SLAVE WHO FLED FROM HIS MASTER ABROAD, INTO THE LAND OF ISRAEL

Thou shalt not deliver unto his master a bondman that is escaped from his master unto thee; (Deuteronomy 23:16)

Mitzvah 568 prohibits us from returning run-away slaves to their masters. Whether or not the slave escaped to the Land of Israel or was already there before fleeing, that person is set free. The reason for this Mitzvah is that the Land of Israel is sacred; it is a Land where our ancestors traveled after being redeemed from Egypt.

569. NOT TO OPPRESS THIS SLAVE WHO FLEES FROM HIS MASTER ABROAD INTO THE LAND OF ISRAEL

he shall dwell with thee, in the midst of thee, in the place which he shall choose within one of thy gates, where it liketh him best; thou shalt not wrong him. (Deuteronomy 23:17)

Mitzvah 569 prohibits us from oppressing the slave who has escaped into the Land of Israel. Not only are we never to return the slave to his owner, we cannot abuse him physically or verbally.

Presumably, the escaped slave is a non-Jew. He accepted upon himself allegiance to Hashem. According to the author of Sefer HaHinnuch, the slave must be treated with the exact decency that we are to treat converts to Judaism.

570. THAT THERE SHOULD BE NO "HARLOT" IN JEWRY, NO WOMAN CONJUGALLY INTIMATE OUT OF WEDLOCK

There shall be no harlot of the daughters of Israel, neither shall there be a sodomite of the sons of Israel. (Deuteronomy 23:18)

Mitzvah 570 prohibits sexual relations without the Ketubah (marriage contract).

This Mitzvah is the source for prohibiting prostitution. However, the ban extends to no sex before marriage, whether or not there is a monetary exchange.

The RAMBAM and the RAMBAN had differing views about the parameters of this Mitzvah. The RAMBAN argued that sex between two consenting adults would not violate the Mitzvah, as long as they were not forbidden to marry each other. The sexual act would be forbidden if the couple were related, or if the woman were married to another man, or if one of the parties were a non-Jew.

RAMBAM, on the other hand, said that even if the two people could marry, they would still be prohibited from having relations without the Ketubah.

571. NOT TO BRING THE WAGE OF A HARLOT OR THE EXCHANGE-PRICE OF A DOG AS A HOLY OFFERING

Thou shalt not bring the hire of a harlot, or the price of a dog, into the house of the LORD thy God for any vow; for even both these are an abomination unto the LORD thy God. (Deuteronomy 23:19)

Mitzvah 571 is the prohibition against using a harlot's wages or money received from selling a dog to purchase an animal for sacrifice.

If one receives an animal that can be sacrificed, in exchange for a dog or for a prostitute's services, that animal loses its holy status. It is no longer suitable for sacrifice. We must have pure thoughts when making sacrifices to Hashem. If the person brought an animal to the Temple that resulted from a harlot's wages, that would eliminate the holiness of the act of the sacrifice. The purpose of the sacrifice is to soften our hearts. According to the author of Sefer HaHinnuch, dogs are stubborn. One who trades their dog for a different animal cannot bring that animal to the Temple for sacrifice because that individual can easily think about the dog's strong nature and then think stubborn thoughts while inside the Temple.

572. NOT TO BORROW AT INTEREST FROM AN ISRAELITE

Thou shalt not lend upon interest to thy brother: interest of money, interest of victuals, interest of any thing that is lent upon interest. (Deuteronomy 23:20)

Mitzvah 572 is the prohibition of paying interest when borrowing from a Jew. Mitzvot 68 and 343 prohibit the lender from charging a Jew interest. This prohibition applies to the borrower.

573. THE PRECEPT OF LENDING TO A HEATHEN AT INTEREST IF HE NEEDS A LOAN, BUT NOT SO TO AN ISRAELITE

Unto a foreigner thou mayest lend upon interest; but unto thy brother thou shalt not lend upon interest; that the LORD thy God may bless thee in all that thou puttest thy hand unto, in the land whither thou goest in to possess it. (Deuteronomy 23:21)

Mitzvah 573 commands us to charge a non-Jew interest on a loan. (My write-ups of 68, 343, and 572 explain why we cannot charge our brethren interest.)

This Mitzvah obligates us to give Jews preferential treatment over non-Jews.

If we lend a non-Jew money and then he converts to Judaism, we still collect the interest because the agreement was made before his conversion. This also prevents the accusation that he converted to avoid paying interest. When one converts to Judaism, there cannot be an ulterior motive.

574. NOT TO BE TARDY WITH VOWED AND VOLUNTARY OFFERINGS

When thou shalt vow a vow unto the LORD thy God, thou shalt not be slack to pay it; for the LORD thy God will surely require it of thee; and it will be sin in thee. (Deuteronomy 23:22)

Mitzvah 574 commands that pledged vows of bringing offerings to the Temple be carried out. The timeframe to act on this promise is the next three pilgrimages to Jerusalem. If one makes this vow before Passover, he has until Sukkot to do it. If he made the commitment after Passover, he can wait until the next Passover because that would be the third festival. Although the vow should be carried out without delay, the promiser might have personal hardships, which would make it impossible for him to be prompt.

575. THE RELIGIOUS DUTY OF FULFILLING WHATEVER GOES OUT FROM ONE'S LIPS

That which is gone out of thy lips thou shalt observe and do; according as thou hast vowed freely unto the LORD thy God, even that which thou hast promised with thy mouth. (Deuteronomy 23:24)

Mitzvah 575 commands us to keep our vows.

The author of Sefer HaHinnuch, the RAMBAM and the RAMBAN give examples of vows: A commitment to bring a sacrifice to the Temple, a promise to donate to the Temple's upkeep, and to give to the poor. The question of having to fulfill the Mitzvah is not the topic here. Rather, it is the question of whether or not it is a personal vow or a vow to Hashem.

576. OUR DUTY TO ALLOW A HIRED WORKER TO EAT CERTAIN THINGS WHILE UNDER HIRE

When thou comest into thy neighbour's vineyard, then thou mayest eat grapes until thou have enough at thine own pleasure; but thou shalt not put any in thy vessel. (Deuteronomy 23:25)

Mitzvah 576 commands us to allow hired workers to eat from items with which they are working. This applies to food that grows from the ground. Practicing this Mitzvah allows us to be generous. While a person is harvesting his crops, he feels gratitude to Hashem. While he thanks G-d, he must allow employees to partake in that joy by sharing the food with them. This Mitzvah does not apply to watchmen. It only applies to workers who are actively working with the food, not to the overseers.

577. THAT A HIRED MAN SHOULD NOT RAISE A SICKLE TO HIS FELLOW-MAN'S STANDING GRAIN

When thou comest into thy neighbour's vineyard, then thou mayest eat grapes until thou have enough at thine own pleasure; but thou shalt not put any in thy vessel. (Deuteronomy 23:25)

Mitzvah 577 forbids the employee, who has the right to partake in the food based on Mitzvah 576, from taking more than what he is able to eat on the job. Although he may eat on the job, he cannot take and save for later. This eliminates the possibility of greed. This pertains to employees working with the food growing from the ground. This does not apply to store workers. The food in the stores is already packaged.

This Mitzvah strikes a balance; employers cannot be cruel to their employees by denying them to eat of the food that they are working with, and at the same time this Mitzvah prevents the employees from taking advantage of their bosses. It would be like having ten refills of coffee instead of just one.

578. THAT A HIRED HAND IS FORBIDDEN TO EAT FROM HIS EMPLOYER'S CROPS DURING WORK

When thou comest into thy neighbour's standing corn, then thou mayest pluck ears with thy hand; but thou shalt not move a sickle unto thy neighbour's standing corn. (Deuteronomy 23:26)

Mitzvah 578 prohibits employees from eating during the actual time that they should be working. Even though the workers are entitled to the food, they cannot eat it when they should be working.

My Partner in Torah explained that this Mitzvah tells us that in the absence of a specific agreement between the worker and employer, then there are parameters such as no eating on the job or taking food home.

579. THE PRECEPT THAT ONE WHO WANTS TO DIVORCE HIS WIFE SHOULD DO SO WITH A PROPER DOCUMENT

When a man taketh a wife, and marrieth her, then it cometh to pass, if she find no favour in his eyes, because he hath found some unseemly thing in her, that he writeth her a bill of divorcement, and giveth it in her hand, and sendeth her out of his house, (Deuteronomy 24:1)

Mitzvah 579 requires husbands who wish to divorce their wives to provide them with a Get, which is a written notification of divorce. The Torah recognizes that marriages can fail. The divorce needs to be a conscious decision. The husband must take the time to have the Get written. It prevents him from divorcing his wife in the heat of the moment.

The Get benefits the wife because it shows that she is divorced and can remarry. A man can divorce his wife if he finds her incompatible. She is there to be his helper, as written in Genesis Chapter 2, Verse 18:

And the LORD God said: 'It is not good that the man should be alone; I will make him a help meet for him.'

The Mishnah (Tractate Gittin, Chapter 9, Mishnah 10) states that a man can divorce his wife if she burns his dinner or if he finds a another woman more desirable. If she has extramarital affairs, then he is obligated to divorce her.

In order for the divorce to be completed, the Get must be handed to her or to her representative in the presence of two witnesses.

Although a husband can divorce his wife for any reason, she on the other hand, cannot. She would have grounds for divorce if her husband verbally or physically abuses her, if he refuses to have marital relations with her, and if he forbids her to see her family. Under these circumstances, he has a concrete obligation to give her the Get. Consult Sefer HaHinnuch for more details about divorce.

580. THAT A DIVORCED MAN SHOULD NOT TAKE BACK HIS EX-WIFE AFTER SHE HAS REMARRIED

her former husband, who sent her away, may not take her again to be his wife, after that she is defiled; for that is abomination before the LORD; and thou shalt not cause the land to sin, which the LORD thy God giveth thee for an inheritance. (Deuteronomy 24:4)

Mitzvah 580 prohibits a man from remarrying his wife if she marries another man. Even if her second husband divorces her, her first husband cannot remarry her. He can remarry her if she had remained single after they divorced.

This prohibition prevents the spread of immorality. To use a modern day term, this Mitzvah prevents legalized wife-swapping.

581. THAT A BRIDEGROOM IS NOT TO BE TAKEN FROM HOME FOR LONG DURING THE ENTIRE FIRST YEAR OF MARRIAGE

When a man taketh a new wife, he shall not go out in the host, neither shall he be charged with any business; he shall be free for his house one year, and shall cheer his wife whom he hath taken. (Deuteronomy 24:5)

Mitzvah 581 neither allows a newly married man from going on extended trips without his wife nor to serve in the army during the first year of his marriage. (The exact number of days that the husband can make the trip alone is not specified.) In the first year of marriage, the husband must make his wife happy. His attention should be on her–not other matters.

582. THE PRECEPT THAT A BRIDEGROOM SHOULD REJOICE WITH HIS WIFE IN THEIR FIRST YEAR

When a man taketh a new wife, he shall not go out in the host, neither shall he be charged with any business; he shall be free for his house one year, and shall cheer his wife whom he hath taken. (Deuteronomy 24:5)

Mitzvah 582 commands a man to put all his energy into pleasing his wife the first year of marriage. He should stay by her side, and make her happy. It also keeps him from pursuing other women. This Mitzvah sets the stage for a loving marriage. The first year is the time for the husband to know his wife and to create a life with her.

583. NOT TO TAKE IN PLEDGE ANY OBJECTS USED IN PREPARING LIFE-SUSTAINING FOOD

No man shall take the mill or the upper millstone to pledge; for he taketh a man's life to pledge. (Deuteronomy 24:6)

Mitzvah 583 forbids us from taking as collateral items that debtors need for food preparations. If that person owes money, his food prep items remain with him.

The reason for this Mitzvah is obvious: Not having the items lead to not having food. Without food, one cannot live.

584. NOT TO PLUCK OUT SIGNS OF TZARA'AT AFFLICTION

Take heed in the plague of leprosy, that thou observe diligently, and do according to all that the priests the Levites shall teach you, as I commanded them, so ye shall observe to do. (Deuteronomy 24:8)

Mitzvah 584 forbids us from removing the symptoms that show that we have leprosy. A key sign is white hairs on the afflicted body parts. If it is leprosy, then that afflicted spot changes color. Hiding or removing the signs does not cure leprosy. These signs cannot be removed. The exception is when a Jewish baby boy has his Brit Milah/ritual circumcision. (Ashkenazi Jews pronounce it bris.) A positive Mitzvah takes precedence over a negative one, and therefore, if there is a leperous sore on the foreskin it may still be removed as part of the Brit Milah

A Brit Milah overrides Shabbat, but only if it is the eighth day after the baby's birth. I covered this topic in Mitzvah 2.

585. NOT TO TAKE AN OBJECT IN PLEDGE FROM A DEBTOR BY FORCE

When thou dost lend thy neighbour any manner of loan, thou shalt not go into his house to fetch his pledge. (Deuteronomy 24:10)

Mitzvah 585 prohibits us from forcibly taking items from debtors who owe money. However, we can if the Rabbinical court authorizes it. This prevents us from accosting our neighbors; this also keeps us from accosting the debtor and taking things off his person such as watches and rings. When we have the authorization, we must wait outside the debtor's home for him to bring out the items. Otherwise, this can lead to animosity between neighbors.

586. NOT TO WITHHOLD A PAWNED OBJECT FROM ITS OWNER WHEN HE NEEDS IT

And if he be a poor man, thou shalt not sleep with his pledge; (Deuteronomy 24:12)

Mitzvah 586 forbids us to withhold a security deposit from its owner if he needs it. For example, if the debtor were to give fancy pillows as collateral, we must return them to him at night in order for him to use them. The next day, the debtor gives them back to the lender. The debtor should not have to suffer even further while repaying his debt. Mitzvah 587 will discuss when the lender does not have to allow the debtor to use his items on a needs basis.

587. THE RELIGIOUS DUTY OF RETURNING A PLEDGED OBJECT TO ITS OWNER WHEN HE NEEDS IT

thou shalt surely restore to him the pledge when the sun goeth down, that he may sleep in his garment, and bless thee; and it shall be righteousness unto thee before the LORD thy God. (Deuteronomy 24:13)

Mitzvah 587 is the obligation to return the collateral to the debtor if we know that he needs it. If he puts up his work tools as collateral, we allow him to use them during the day. If it is a night time object such as a bed covering, we allow him to use it at night. The lender takes back the collateral when the debtor does not need them.

This Mitzvah allows us to show debtors acts of kindness.

This Mitzvah applies when we take the collateral not at the time of the loan. If we arrange the collateral at the time of the loan, then we are not obligated to return it on a needs basis. If we were obligated, that might reduce the debtor's incentive to repay the loan.

588. THE PRECEPT OF GIVING A HIRED MAN HIS DUE PAY ON HIS DAY–WHEN HE HAS EARNED IT

In the same day thou shalt give him his hire, neither shall the sun go down upon it; for he is poor, and setteth his heart upon it: lest he cry against thee unto the LORD and it be sin in thee. (Deuteronomy 24:15)

Mitzvah 588 requires bosses to pay their workers their wages on the days that they work. If hired for a day job, the employee must be paid at the end of the day. Withholding payment overnight is unacceptable. The employee may forego his right to immediate payment.

This Mitzvah extends to renting and leasing objects. If one pays rent, that person must pay at the time that the rent is due.

Consult my Mitzvah 230 write-up for additional reasons why this Mitzvah is in place.

589. THAT A NEAR RELATION OF A PERSON IN A COURT TRIAL SHOULD NOT GIVE TESTIMONY

The fathers shall not be put to death for the children, neither shall the children be put to death for the fathers; every man shall be put to death for his own sin. (Deuteronomy 24:16)

Mitzvah 589 prohibits relatives from testifying in court cases, whether capital or not.

There are instances when relatives are incapable of testifying impartially. Whether or not their clouded judgment stems from love or antipathy, dishonest testimony will become evidence. If his relatives live in close proximity, there is the possibility that this will lead to ongoing friction.

On the Torah level, this Mitzvah pertains to just paternal relatives. This applies to uncles, nephews, grandfathers, and grandsons. According to the author of Sefer HaHinnuch, maternal relatives, and relatives by marriage, are not included in the Biblical prohibition but the Sages added these relatives to this prohibition.

590. NOT TO PERVERT JUSTICE IN REGARD TO A PROSELYTE OR AN ORPHAN

Thou shalt not pervert the justice due to the stranger, or to the fatherless; nor take the widow's raiment to pledge. (Deuteronomy 24:17)

Mitzvah 590 forbids judges from intentionally ruling in favor of or against converts and orphans. The judge must rule objectively at all times and cannot allow personal sympathy or disdain to prevent that.

591. NOT TO TAKE ANYTHING IN PLEDGE FROM A WIDOW

Thou shalt not pervert the justice due to the stranger, or to the fatherless; nor take the widow's raiment to pledge. (Deuteronomy 24:17)

Mitzvah 591 forbids us from taking collateral from a widow. If she owes money, the lender cannot take collateral, while she is repaying the debt. If the widow intentionally refuses to pay her debt, the court can force her to honor her commitment. This Mitzvah is applicable, even if the widow is wealthy. Wealth does not eliminate the stress, the loss, the pain, and suffering caused by her husband's death. Seizing her collateral would add to her misery.

592. THE PRECEPT OF LEAVING FORGOTTEN SHEAVES

When thou reapest thy harvest in thy field, and hast forgot a sheaf in the field, thou shalt not go back to fetch it; it shall be for the stranger, for the fatherless, and for the widow;

that the LORD thy God may bless thee in all the work of thy hands. (Deuteronomy 24:19)

Mitzvah 592 commands us to leave sheaves that we forgot to collect, for the poor to claim.

In sum, a field of wheat has stalks that grow. As the wheat is cut it is placed into bundles, which are left on the ground until the owner (or his workers) comes by with a wagon to gather them. If any bundles are forgotten during collection, we must leave those for the poor to collect. However, if the bundle is larger than a certain size, the owner may return and gather it, as it is too large to be considered forgotten. This Mitzvah forces us to be charitable.

593. NOT TO TAKE A FORGOTTEN SHEAF OF GRAIN OR FORGOTTEN FRUIT OF TREES

When thou reapest thy harvest in thy field, and hast forgot a sheaf in the field, thou shalt not go back to fetch it; it shall be for the stranger, for the fatherless, and for the widow; that the LORD thy God may bless thee in all the work of thy hands. (Deuteronomy 24:19)

Mitzvah 593 prohibits us to return to our fields to retrieve sheaves and fruit that we forgot to gather. Those forgotten items become the property of the poor. Even if the original owner ground the wheat and baked it, he is still obligated to return it to the poor. If the owner reclaimed the sheaves and fruit he had forgotten, that person cannot place them back on the ground; instead, he must hand them directly to a poor person.

594. THE PRECEPT OF WHIPLASHES FOR THE WICKED

then it shall be, if the wicked man deserve to be beaten, that the judge shall cause him to lie down, and to be beaten before his face, according to the measure of his wickedness, by number. (Deuteronomy 25:2)

Mitzvah 594 commands the Bet Din (Jewish court) to give the wicked party lashes of the whip if his actions warrant it. Cases where violations require lashes include violating negative Mitzvot. However, if the consequence is capital punishment, then the guilty party does not receive lashes. If violating the negative Mitzvah does not involve a physical action, then the perpetrator is spared. For example, hating one's neighbor violates a negative Mitzvah, but no lashes are given because that does not involve a physical action. Lashes are also not administered where the Torah prescribes a rectification for a negative violation. For example, if one violates the Mitzvah of gathering sheaves for himself when they are designated for the poor, the guilty party does not get whipped because he can rectify the problem by handing over the sheaves to a poor person.

My Partner in Torah explained to me that the rationale for this Mitzvah is that Hashem cares for everyone. When the perpetrator dies, he should be able to receive Hashem's reward in the World to Come. Therefore, lashes are given if warranted so that would take care of the due, thus giving the guilty party a clean slate.

This Mitzvah is humane because, while the maximum is 39 lashes, each person who is to be whipped is evaluated to see how much his body can withstand. Even if one was assessed to receive six lashes but the Beit Din notices that he is suffering after the fifth, he is spared the sixth.

595. NOT TO ADD TO THE WHIPLASHES DUE SOMEONE WHO MERITS FLOGGING; SO LIKEWISE NOT TO STRIKE ANY JEW

Forty stripes he may give him, he shall not exceed; lest, if he should exceed, and beat him above these with many stripes, then thy brother should be dishonoured before thine eyes. (Deuteronomy 25:3)

Mitzvah 595 is the prohibition against excessively whipping someone who is supposed to be whipped. The Bet Din evaluates the violation and decides how many lashes that person is to get. Regardless of the severity of the punishment, no one is to receive more than 39 lashes. If the Bet Din orders 16 lashes, then that person is not to receive more than that number.

If the person can only withstand 20 lashes, then the court must reduce the amount to the next multiple of three. Instead of 20 lashes, the guilty party receives 18.

If the guilty party begins to relieve himself during his flogging, the whipping stops–even if that person did not receive the number that the Bet Din ordered. In such cases, the court must show compassion.

If the whip breaks before the flogger finishes administering the required number of lashes, the whipping stops, even if the guilty party had not yet received the number that the court ordered.

596. NOT TO MUZZLE A DOMESTIC ANIMAL DURING ITS WORK

Thou shalt not muzzle the ox when he treadeth out the corn. (Deuteronomy 25:4)

Mitzvah 596 is the prohibition against muzzling an animal while it is working. A muzzle prevents the animal from eating. If the animal is working in the fields, or with foods, muzzling the creature would be inappropriately cruel. This Mitzvah forces us to practice acts of kindness. In addition, a Jew cannot even ask a non-Jew to muzzle the animal for him.

597. THAT A YEVAMAH SHOULD NOT MARRY ANYONE BUT THE YAVAM

(Yevamah is a woman awaiting her levirate marriage and Yavam means brother-in-law.)

If brethren dwell together, and one of them die, and have no child, the wife of the dead shall not be married abroad unto one not of his kin; her husband's brother shall go in unto her, and take her to him to wife, and perform the duty of a husband's brother unto her. (Deuteronomy 25:5)

Mitzvah 597 forbids the Yevamah to marry anyone, except her brother-in-law. If a married woman's husband dies before they have children, she has to marry her husband's brother. However, the brother can refuse to marry her; if that happens, then she cannot marry anyone else until she performs "Halitzah," (the removal of the brother-in-law's shoe). Deuteronomy Chapter 25, Verses 7-10 explain the entire procedure:

And if the man like not to take his brother's wife, then his brother's wife shall go up to the gate unto the elders, and say: 'My husband's brother refuseth to raise up unto his brother a name in Israel; he will not perform the duty of a husband's brother unto me.' Then the elders of his city shall call him, and speak unto him; and if he stand, and say: 'I like not to take her'; then shall his brother's wife draw nigh unto him in the presence of the elders, and loose his shoe from off his foot, and spit in his face; and she shall answer and say: 'So shall it be done unto the man that doth not build up his brother's house.' And his name shall be called in Israel the house of him that had his shoe loosed.

598. THE PRECEPT OF LEVIRATE MARRIAGE

If brethren dwell together, and one of them die, and have no child, the wife of the dead shall not be married abroad unto one not of his kin; her husband's brother shall go in unto her, and take her to him to wife, and perform the duty of a husband's brother unto her. (Deuteronomy 25:5)

Mitzvah 598 commands the Yavam to marry the Yevamah if she is childless. According to Sefer HaHinnuch, a wife is like one of her husband's limbs and organs. The root of this argument is in Genesis chapter 2 verses 21 to 23:

And the LORD God caused a deep sleep to fall upon the man, and he slept; and He took one of his ribs, and closed up the place with flesh instead thereof. And the rib, which the LORD God had taken from the man, made He a woman, and brought her unto the man. And the man said: 'This is now bone of my bones, and flesh of my flesh; she shall be called Woman, because she was taken out of Man.'

The levirate marriage allows the brother's name to live on.

There are cases when the Yevamah is excused from fulfilling the levirate marriage and the Halitzah ceremony: The reasons include:

Her late husband was a born eunuch, the Yavam was mentally challenged or was a born after the husband's death. If the Yevamah is a forbidden relation to the Yavam (other than being his brother's wife), e.g. the Yavam is married to the Yevamah's sister, then the Mitzvah also does not apply.

599. THE PRECEPT OF HALITZAH, TO RELEASE A CHILDLESS WIDOW

then shall his brother's wife draw nigh unto him in the presence of the elders, and loose his shoe from off his foot, and spit in his face; and she shall answer and say: 'So shall it be done unto the man that doth not build up his brother's house.' (Deuteronomy 25:9)

Mitzvah 599 commands the "Yevamah" to do "Halitzah." As mentioned in my write-up of Mitzvah 598, the husband and wife are connected. If he dies before he impregnated her, he then left the world without fulfilling the Mitzvah of being fruitful and multiplying. His essence, his soul, is isolated. He becomes isolated in terms of serving Hashem. When the brother marries the widow and has children with her, they carry on his late brother's divine mission.

At another level, a person's complete service of Hashem is not only about himself; it is about having children so that they can serve Hashem. It perpetuates the continuity of servicing Hashem. If that Mitzvah remains unfulfilled, the deceased's soul becomes incomplete for not perpetuating the service of Hashem. Halitzah is performed when the brother-in-law refuses to marry the widow, or is Rabbinically prohibited from doing so.

I stated in my Mitzvah 597 write-up that Halitza entails the widow removing her brother-in-law's shoe. A slave does that service. She does it in the presence of the Bet Din so that they see that she was supposed to also service him. She also must spit on the ground in front of his face to show the Bet Din that she no longer has to honor him or tend to his needs. They are now strangers to one another. After Halitza, the widow has the status of a divorcee and is free to remarry.

600. THE RELIGIOUS DUTY TO SAVE A PERSON PURSUED BY A KILLER

then thou shalt cut off her hand, thine eye shall have no pity. (Deuteronomy 25:12)

Mitzvah 600 commands us to save a person whose life is in danger. If killing the pursuer is the only way to save the victim, then it is permissible as a last resort. If there is a way to avoid killing the aggressor, then we are not to take his life. Ways to stop the pursuer without killing him include shooting him in the legs instead of the head or heart.

This Mitzvah applies to abortion. If the fetus threatens the mother's life, then abortion is permitted because the fetus is endangering the mother and is considered a pursuer. (Tractate Ohalot, Chapter 7, Mishnah 6.)

This Mitzvah extends to protecting a woman from a man forbidden to touch her. If he tries to molest her and killing him is the only way to save her, then homicide becomes justifiable (forbidden women include those who are close relatives and those who are married to another man).

601. TO HAVE NO MERCY ON A PURSUER WITH INTENT TO KILL

then thou shalt cut off her hand, thine eye shall have no pity. (Deuteronomy 25:12)

Mitzvah 601 commands us not to have mercy for the aggressor who is trying to kill another person. The purpose of this Mitzvah is to show compassion to weak individuals unable to take care of themselves. Additional details are covered in Mitzvah 600.

602. THAT WE SHOULD NOT KEEP DEFICIENT SCALES OR WEIGHTS WITH US, EVEN IF WE WILL NOT USE THEM IN TRADING

Thou shalt not have in thy bag diverse weights, a great and a small. Thou shalt not have in thy house diverse measures, a great and a small. (Deuteronomy 25:13-14)

Mitzvah 602 is the prohibition against having short weights and measures in our possession. We use weights and measures in commerce to weigh items. If one has a block of metal that is supposed to weigh half a pound, that person cannot have it lighter than that. If he were to use such a weight during the sale of items, he would be shortchanging the buyers. Over time, the block's size reduces. Then that object becomes unusable. In addition, we cannot even possess it because of the possibility of either using it accidentally or having the desire to do so. Not possessing the shortened weight eliminates the possibility of that occurring. This Mitzvah emphasizes the requirement to be honest and scrupulous in all business dealings.

603. THE RELIGIOUS DUTY TO REMEMBER WHAT AMALEK DID TO THE ISRAELITES WHEN THEY CAME OUT OF EGYPT

Remember what Amalek did unto thee by the way as ye came forth out of Egypt; (Deuteronomy 25:17)

Mitzvah 603 commands us to remember that Amalek attacked the Israelites after they left Egypt. The whole world saw G-d free the Israelites from Pharaoh. The Amalekites were regarded as brazen and brutal to attack the Jewish nation, even seeing that G-d personally would intervene on their behalf.

Hashem commands us to remember six things:

1. Remember the revelation on Mount Sinai.
2. Remember that Hashem took us out of Egypt.
3. Remember that we angered G-d in the desert.
4. Remember the Sabbath Day.
5. Remember what Hashem did to Miriam (by punishing her for speaking Lashon HaRah).
6. Remember what Amalek did to us.

Active remembering according to the Sages refers to verbal recitation. Some people have the custom to recite those six verses each day, in order to ensure regular fulfillment of these Mitzvot. Performing these Mitzvot requires us just to remember these six things, which we can do by verbally reciting the relevant verses.

604. THE PRECEPT TO ERADICATE THE PROGENY OF AMALEK

Remember what Amalek did unto thee by the way as ye came forth out of Egypt; how he met thee by the way, and smote the hindmost of thee, all that were enfeebled in thy rear, when thou wast faint and weary; and he feared not God. Therefore it shall be, when the LORD thy God hath given thee rest from all thine enemies round about, in the land which the LORD thy God giveth thee for an inheritance to possess it, that thou shalt blot out the remembrance of Amalek from under heaven; thou shalt not forget. (Deuteronomy 25:17-19)

Mitzvah 604 commands us to eradicate all of Amalek's descendants–man, woman, and child. This Mitzvah was applicable when the Israelites entered Israel because Amalekites lived there. The Israelites had to destroy them. Although this Mitzvah is still applicable today, we cannot fulfill it because we do not know who his descendants are.

605. THAT WE SHOULD NOT FORGET THE DEED OF AMALEK WHICH HE WROUGHT UPON OUR FOREFATHERS WHEN THEY CAME OUT OF EGYPT

Remember what Amalek did unto thee by the way as ye came forth out of Egypt; how he met thee by the way, and smote the hindmost of thee, all that were enfeebled in thy rear, when thou wast faint and weary; and he feared not God. Therefore it shall be, when the LORD thy God hath given thee rest from all thine enemies round about, in the land which the LORD thy God giveth thee for an inheritance to possess it, that thou shalt blot out the remembrance of Amalek from under heaven; thou shalt not forget. (Deuteronomy 25:17-19)

Mitzvah 605 is the prohibition against forgetting what Amalek did to us. We are supposed to hate the Amalekites and never forget their heinous deeds, which include rape and castration. For further details, consult Sifrei, Paragraph 296, Tanchuma 10; Rashi – Deuteronomy 25:17. Visit the link: http://www.aish.com/atr/Wiping_Out_Amalek.html for further information.

606. THE PRECEPT OF THE RECITAL OVER FIRST-FRUITS

that thou shalt take of the first of all the fruit of the ground, which thou shalt bring in from thy land that the LORD thy

God giveth thee; and thou shalt put it in a basket and shalt go unto the place which the LORD thy God shall choose to cause His name to dwell there. And thou shalt come unto the priest that shall be in those days, and say unto him: 'I profess this day unto the LORD thy God, that I am come unto the land which the LORD swore unto our fathers to give us.' And the priest shall take the basket out of thy hand, and set it down before the altar of the LORD thy God. And thou shalt speak and say before the LORD thy God: 'A wandering Aramean was my father, and he went down into Egypt, and sojourned there, few in number; and he became there a nation, great, mighty, and populous. And the Egyptians dealt ill with us, and afflicted us, and laid upon us hard bondage. And we cried unto the LORD, the God of our fathers, and the LORD heard our voice, and saw our affliction, and our toil, and our oppression. And the LORD brought us forth out of Egypt with a mighty hand, and with an outstretched arm, and with great terribleness, and with signs, and with wonders. And He hath brought us into this place, and hath given us this land, a land flowing with milk and honey. And now, behold, I have brought the first of the fruit of the land, which Thou, O LORD, hast given me.' And thou shalt set it down before the LORD thy God, and worship before the LORD thy God. (Deuteronomy 26:2–10)

Mitzvah 606 commands us to recite specific verses from the Torah when we bring our first fruits. Because Hashem brought us to Israel, we show our gratitude by bringing Him the first fruits.

Feeling grateful does not suffice. By verbalizing our appreciation, it makes the display of gratitude complete.

If a woman or a messenger brings the fruit, they are not to recite the blessing because the verse pertains to ownership of the land; they do not own that land. By virtue of the specific law, we must be careful about what to say to Hashem. Because the verse is also about receiving the land, the messenger and woman cannot recite the prayer because the land was not given to them. On the other hand, a convert can recite the prayer. Even though his forefathers did not receive the portion of land, the converts are now the children of Abraham. They can recite the prayer not because they can now own land, but because now they are the children of Abraham due to converting (See Bartenura's commentary to Tractate Bikkurim, Chapter 1, Mishnah 4.)

When my Partner in Torah and I studied *Book of our Heritage* by Eliyahu Kitov, we covered Ruth and the significance of the number 606. According to Kitov, Ruth was originally just responsible for fulfilling the seven Noahide Mitzvot, but after she converted to Judaism, she was now responsible for the remaining 606. The numeric value of the Hebrew letters that spell Ruth is 606 (The Hebrew letters are Resh equals 200, Vav equals 6, and taf equals 400.)

607. THE PRECEPT OF THE AVOWAL OVER THE TITHES

then thou shalt say before the LORD thy God: 'I have put away the hallowed things out of my house, and also have given them unto the Levite, and unto the stranger, to the fatherless, and to the widow, according to all Thy commandment which Thou hast commanded me; I have not transgressed any of Thy commandments, neither have I forgotten them. (Deuteronomy 26:13)

Mitzvah 607 commands us to give a verbal accounting for all the tithes that we have to separate. When a male Israelite goes to the Holy Temple in Jerusalem, he has to say, "I properly separated the amounts that go to the Levites and Priests; two percent to the Priests, and ten percent of the rest to the Levites."

In certain years (3 and 6) of the Sh'mittah cycle, he is supposed to give a percentage to a poor person. He must say that all the crops have had the appropriate portions separated out and distributed to the specific persons. Saying this out loud makes one careful about fulfilling this Mitzvah correctly. Even though it is preferred to perform this Mitzvah at the Temple, he can perform it anywhere (if he is not in the Land of Israel, he is not obligated to bring the portions.). He can technically fulfill the Mitzvah outside of The Land of Israel. He recites these words on the last day of Passover during the fourth and the seventh years of the seven-year cycle.

608. NOT TO EAT OF THE SECOND TITHE WHILE IN GRIEF OVER THE DEATH OF A CLOSE KIN

I have not eaten thereof in my mourning, neither have I put away thereof, being unclean, nor given thereof for the dead; I have hearkened to the voice of the LORD my God, I have done according to all that Thou hast commanded me. (Deuteronomy 26:14)

Mitzvah 608 prohibits the eating of the Second Tithes on the day that one loses a close relative. This prohibition takes place in the first, second, fourth, and fifth years of the seven-year cycle. After a man gives the primary tithes to the Levite, he takes out the Second Tithes for himself. He has to bring those Second Tithes to Jerusalem in order to eat them. Jerusalem is a holy city and eating the tithes there is a holy act. One cannot eat anything that has a level of holiness while mourning; that includes sacrificed animals and the tithes. This is not a punishment. The mourner is filled with sorrow. He is not in a positive spiritual state of wellbeing. Prophecy does not occur when the prophet is unhappy. To reach a high spiritual state, a positive state of mind is required.

609. THE PROHIBITION AGAINST EASTING SECOND TITHE WHEN RITUALLY UNCLEAN

I have not eaten thereof in my mourning, neither have I put away thereof, being unclean, nor given thereof for the dead; I have hearkened to the voice of the LORD my God, I have done according to all that Thou hast commanded me. (Deuteronomy 26:14)

Mitzvah 609 is the prohibition against eating Second Tithes when the tithes become impure. In such a case, the tithes must be exchanged for money (redeemed) adding

20 %. With that money, one buys other foods and eats them in the manner of the original tithe. The tithe can become impure if it touches a corpse, a specific dead creature, a woman during her menstrual period, a leper, or a man or woman who see blood coming out of their bodies on days when that is not supposed to happen. These are sources of **Tumah** (impurity). On those occasions, should the tithe have had contact, then it also becomes impure. If the tithe is edible, then it cannot be redeemed in Jerusalem, but if it is impure, then it can be redeemed. In either case (whether the original tithe is pure or impure), the tithe is redeemable outside Jerusalem. If the owner of the tithe is impure, he cannot eat the Second Tithe. If the tithe is pure, but not the owner, he must wait until he becomes pure in order to eat it inside Jerusalem.

610. NOT TO SPEND THE EXCHANGE-MONEY OF SECOND TITHE ON ANYTHING BUT FOOD AND DRINK

I have not eaten thereof in my mourning, neither have I put away thereof, being unclean, nor given thereof for the dead; I have hearkened to the voice of the LORD my God, I have done according to all that Thou hast commanded me. (Deuteronomy 26:14)

Mitzvah 610 commands us to spend money from redeeming Second Tithes on just food and drink. The restriction stems from needing to thank Hashem for the food and crops that He provides. A man can share the tithe with whomever he wants; but the flipside, is that he cannot buy anything other than food or drink. However, he may not buy water or salt.

611. THE PRECEPT TO EMULATE THE GOOD AND RIGHT WAYS OF THE ETERNAL LORD

The LORD will establish thee for a holy people unto Himself, as He hath sworn unto thee; if thou shalt keep the commandments of the LORD thy God, and walk in His ways. (Deuteronomy 28:9)

Mitzvah 611 is the obligation to emulate Hashem. He bestows love and kindness upon us, so we must bestow that on our fellow man. Whatever we do, we must be thinking about Hashem. That is why we say blessings before and after we eat and drink. We are not supposed to perform (or refrain from) tasks in an extreme way. For example, talking Lashon HaRah, is undesirable, so we cannot go to the other extreme and choose not to talk at all.

If one like meat but believes that eating it constantly exudes animalistic behavior, the extreme would be to refrain from eating it altogether. The better option would be to limit meat eating to Shabbat and Festive Holidays.

612. THE PRECEPT TO ASSEMBLE THE ENTIRE PEOPLE TO HEAR THE TORAH READ, AFTER THE SEVENTH YEAR

Assemble the people, the men and the women and the little ones, and thy stranger that is within thy gates, that they may hear, and that they may learn, and fear the LORD your God, and observe to do all the words of this law; (Deuteronomy 31:12)

Mitzvah 612 is the obligation to gather the entire nation of Israel on the Second Day of Sukkot in the first year of the seven-year cycle to hear the Torah. The term used to describe this Mitzvah is Hakhel, which means to congregate, to gather. When we gather, we read publicly certain portions from the Book of Deuteronomy. This strengthens the Jewish nation's connection as a whole, and it also strengthens our connection to the Torah and to Hashem. This Mitzvah includes the women and children.

At the time of the Temple, trumpet blowers blasted their instruments on a huge stage. The king would come in and everybody would be there. The location was the courtyard of the Temple. They took out a Torah scroll, handed it to the High Priest who would then give it to the king and he would place it on the stand and recite the blessings. The king would read from the beginning of Deuteronomy to the portion that has the SH'MA (Deuteronomy 6:4-9). Then he would skip to the section that has blessings and curses.

613. THE RELIGIOUS DUTY FOR EVERY JEW TO WRITE A TORAH SCROLL FOR HIMSELF

Now therefore write ye this song for you, and teach thou it the children of Israel; put it in their mouths, that this song may be a witness for Me against the children of Israel. (Deuteronomy 31:19)

Mitzvah 613 commands all of us–every Jew–to write the Torah scroll, from Genesis to Deuteronomy. Each person should train himself in the proper way to write the Torah.

My Partner in Torah told me that probably 99+ percent of the Jews today are not qualified to do this. The Mitzvah can be performed if one hires a scribe. That is the second best thing to writing a Torah, which is hire the scribe to do it. This Mitzvah's objective is for every Jew to have access to the Torah Scroll in order to learn. Writing a Torah was more common before the days of the printing press. The Torah has the moral laws, and the proper path for serving Hashem. Every Jew needs one available, so he has to write it. Even if one has an inherited scroll, the obligation to write a Torah is still required. The reason for this Mitzvah is to increase the number of Torah scrolls in the world. A way to fulfill this Mitzvah today is to give our synagogues money for new Torah scrolls. It is not determined at the Biblical level, if this Mitzvah can be fulfilled by buying Torah scrolls. If one cannot afford to have the Torah written, then this is a suitable alternative.

Level 1 Write a Torah Scroll.
Level 2 Hire someone to write a Torah Scroll.
Level 3 Purchase a printed Torah book ("Chumash") instead of a Torah Scroll.

Most people cannot afford to have a Torah Scroll written.

Addendum

Rabbi Alpert told me about the seven additional Rabbinic Mitzvot. These are not part of the 613 Mitzvot. It is worth mentioning them.

1. Saying blessings before and after eating. (This does not include the Birkat HaMazon because that is a Torah commandment. See my write-up of Mitzvah 430 for more details about the Birkat HaMazon.)
2. Lighting Shabbat candles
3. Lighting Hanukkah candles.
4. Reciting "Hallel" (praise) on Rosh Chodesh and on Festivals.
5. Reading and/or listening to the Book of Esther on Purim.
6. Constructing an Eruv.
7. Washing our hands before eating.

These seven Rabbinic Mitzvot are applicable today.

Printed in Great Britain
by Amazon

47985888R00304